CRIMINAL PROCEDURE

TENTH EDITION

STEVEN L. EMANUEL

Founder and Editor-in-Chief, the *CrunchTime* series,
Emanuel Law Outlines, and *Emanuel Bar Review*

Harvard Law School, J.D. 1976
Member, NY, CT, MD and VA bars

The *Emanuel CrunchTime*® Series

ASPEN PUBLISHING

To contact Customer Service, e-mail customer.service@aspenpublishing.com, call 1-800-950-5259, or mail correspondence to:

> Aspen Publishing
> Attn: Order Department
> PO Box 990
> Frederick, MD 21705

Printed in the United States of America.

2 3 4 5 6 7 8 9 0

ISBN 978-1-5438-0575-8

This book is intended as a general review of a legal subject. It is not intended as a source for advice for the solution of legal matters or problems. For advice on legal matters, the reader should consult an attorney.

SUSTAINABLE
FORESTRY
INITIATIVE

Certified Chain of Custody
Promoting Sustainable Forestry

www.sfiprogram.org

About Aspen Publishing

Aspen Publishing is a leading provider of educational content and digital learning solutions to law schools in the U.S. and around the world. Aspen provides best-in-class solutions for legal education through authoritative textbooks, written by renowned authors, and breakthrough products such as Connected eBooks, Connected Quizzing, and PracticePerfect.

The Aspen Casebook Series (famously known among law faculty and students as the "red and black" casebooks) encompasses hundreds of highly regarded textbooks in more than eighty disciplines, from large enrollment courses, such as Torts and Contracts to emerging electives such as Sustainability and the Law of Policing. Study aids such as the *Examples & Explanations* and the *Emanuel Law Outlines* series, both highly popular collections, help law students master complex subject matter.

Major products, programs, and initiatives include:

- **Connected eBooks** are enhanced digital textbooks and study aids that come with a suite of online content and learning tools designed to maximize student success. Designed in collaboration with hundreds of faculty and students, the Connected eBook is a significant leap forward in the legal education learning tools available to students.

- **Connected Quizzing** is an easy-to-use formative assessment tool that tests law students' understanding and provides timely feedback to improve learning outcomes. Delivered through CasebookConnect.com, the learning platform already used by students to access their Aspen casebooks, Connected Quizzing is simple to implement and integrates seamlessly with law school course curricula.

- **PracticePerfect** is a visually engaging, interactive study aid to explain commonly encountered legal doctrines through easy-to-understand animated videos, illustrative examples, and numerous practice questions. Developed by a team of experts, PracticePerfect is the ideal study companion for today's law students.

- The **Aspen Learning Library** enables law schools to provide their students with access to the most popular study aids on the market across all of their courses. Available through an annual subscription, the online library consists of study aids in e-book, audio, and video formats with full text search, note-taking, and highlighting capabilities.

- Aspen's **Digital Bookshelf** is an institutional-level online education bookshelf, consolidating everything students and professors need to ensure success. This program ensures that every student has access to affordable course materials from day one.

- **Leading Edge** is a community centered on thinking differently about legal education and putting those thoughts into actionable strategies. At the core of the program is the Leading Edge Conference, an annual gathering of legal education thought leaders looking to pool ideas and identify promising directions of exploration.

TABLE OF CONTENTS

Preface

Thank you for buying this book.

This new edition includes full coverage of the Supreme Court's term that ended in June 2019, as well as one 2020 Supreme Court case. It features extensive coverage of several important recent cases, including:

- ❏ *Carpenter v. U.S.*, where the Court held that when government requests that a wireless carrier supply significant amounts of *"cell site location information" ("CSLI")* about a person: (1) government is *performing a search* for Fourth Amendment purposes; (2) the person *maintains a reasonable expectation of privacy* in that CSLI *even though the information is held by a third party;* and (3) government must therefore demonstrate to a judge or magistrate *probable cause* for a search warrant and must *obtain the search warrant. Carpenter* looks as though it will cause a search warrant to be required before the police may request access to many types of databases that are *maintained by private companies* and that contain detailed personal information.

- ❏ *Collins v. Virginia*, where the Court held that the automobile exception to the search warrant requirement does not apply to allow the warrantless search of a *vehicle* that is located within the *curtilage of a person's dwelling*, so the police must obtain a warrant issued on probable cause.

- ❏ *McCoy v. Louisiana*, where the Court held that the decision whether to *concede guilt* during the guilt phase of a capital murder trial falls into the category of decisions about what the objectives of the defense are, and therefore *belongs solely to the client.* Consequently, the lawyer's violation of the defendant's right to make that decision necessarily constitutes the denial of the Sixth Amendment right to *effective assistance of counsel*, triggering an automatic right to a *new trial* without the need to produce additional proof of prejudice.

The *CrunchTime*® Series is intended for people who want Emanuel quality, but don't have the time or money to buy and use the full-length *Emanuel*® *Law Outline* on a subject. We've designed the series to be used in the last few weeks (or even less) before your final exams.

This book includes the following features, most of which have been extracted from the corresponding *Emanuel® Law Outline*:

❏ *Flow Charts* — We've reduced many of the principles of *Criminal Procedure* to a series of six Flow Charts, created specially for this book and never published elsewhere. We think these will be especially useful on open-book exams. The Flow Charts begin on p. 1.

❏ *Capsule Summary* — This is a 108-page summary of the subject. We've carefully crafted it to cover the things you're most likely to be asked on an exam. The Capsule Summary starts on p. 49.

❏ *Exam Tips* — We've compiled these by reviewing dozens of actual essay and multiple-choice questions asked in past law-school and bar exams, and extracting the issues and fine distinctions that surface most often on exams. The Exam Tips start on p. 163.

❏ *Short-Answer* questions and answers — The questions are generally in a Yes/No format, with a "mini-essay" explaining each one. The questions start on p. 203. The answers begin on p. 243.

❏ *Essay* questions — These questions are actual ones asked on law school exams. They start on p. 275. A sample answer follows each question.

My deepest thanks go to two of my colleagues, Barbara Lasoff and Barbara Roth, who have helped greatly to assure the reliability and readability of this and my other books for many years.

Good luck in your Criminal Procedure course. If you'd like any other Aspen Publishing publication, you can find it at your bookstore or at **www.AspenPublishing.com.** If you'd like to contact me, you can email me at **semanuel@westnet.com.**

Steve Emanuel
Larchmont NY
June 1, 2020

FLOW CHARTS

TABLE OF CONTENTS
to
FLOW CHARTS

Figure

Figure 1A

Was There a 4th Amendment "Search" or "Seizure"?

Use this chart to determine whether a "search" or "seizure" (as those terms are used in Fourth Amendment law) occurred at all. **D** is the person who is claiming that a search/seizure occurred, and that it violated his Fourth Amendment rights. We refer to the person doing the search as "the **police**," but the same answers follow if the search is done by **any government agent** seeking to **find evidence** or otherwise **investigate** something. If the police have **not** made a search or seizure, you never need to reach the issue of whether the Fourth Amendment was violated (covered in Fig. 1B), since a search or seizure is a pre-requisite to a Fourth Amendment violation.

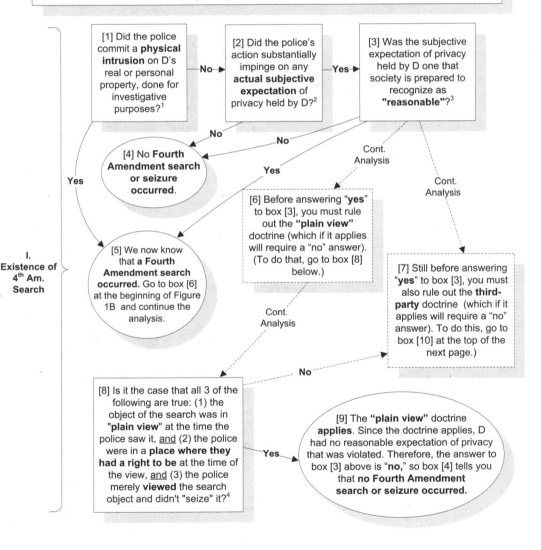

I. Existence of 4th Am. Search

[1] Did the police commit a **physical intrusion** on D's real or personal property, done for investigative purposes?[1]

[2] Did the police's action substantially impinge on any **actual subjective expectation** of privacy held by D?[2]

[3] Was the subjective expectation of privacy held by D one that society is prepared to recognize as **"reasonable"**?[3]

[4] No **Fourth Amendment search or seizure** occurred.

[5] We now know that **a Fourth Amendment search occurred**. Go to box [6] at the beginning of Figure 1B and continue the analysis.

[6] Before answering **"yes"** to box [3], you must rule out the **"plain view"** doctrine (which if it applies will require a "no" answer). (To do that, go to box [8] below.)

[7] Still before answering **"yes"** to box [3], you must also rule out the **third-party** doctrine (which if it applies will require a "no" answer). To do this, go to box [10] at the top of the next page.)

[8] Is it the case that all 3 of the following are true: (1) the object of the search was in **"plain view"** at the time the police saw it, <u>and</u> (2) the police were in a **place where they had a right to be** at the time of the view, <u>and</u> (3) the police merely **viewed** the search object and didn't "seize" it?[4]

[9] The **"plain view"** doctrine **applies**. Since the doctrine applies, D had no reasonable expectation of privacy that was violated. Therefore, the answer to box [3] above is "**no,**" so box [4] tells you that **no Fourth Amendment search or seizure occurred.**

See footnotes after page 2 of chart.

Figure 1A (cont.)

Was There a 4th Amendment "Search" or "Seizure"? (p. 2)

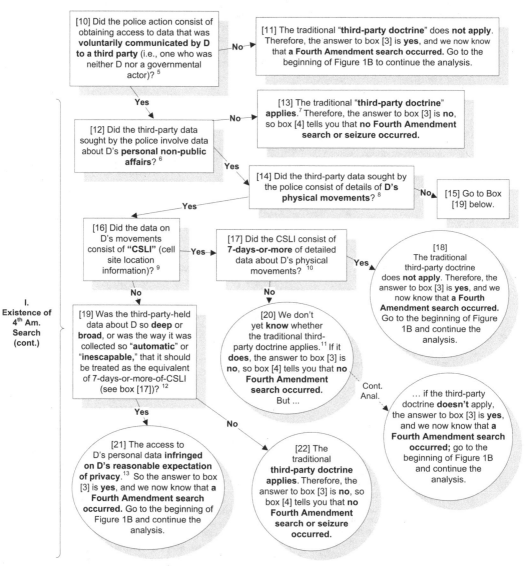

Footnotes begin on next page.

Notes (p. 1) to
Figure 1A (Was There a 4th Amendment "Search" or Seizure"?)

[1] Example: While D's car is in a public parking lot, police put a wireless GPS tracker on the car's underside. They use transmission from this device to learn where D drives on the public roads during the next 2 hours. Because the police, acting for investigative purposes, have committed a physical intrusion on D's property, they have automatically committed a search for Fourth Amendment purposes. That's true even though D probably did not have a reasonable expectation of privacy in his public movements (since any member of the public could have observed his movements by following him on the roads). So the presence of a physical intrusion means that the fact that the answers to boxes [2] and [3] below are probably "yes" won't prevent the police action from being a search. [*U.S. v. Jones*]

[2] Examples of situations where D will probably be found to have had no actual subjective expectation of privacy: (1) abandoned property, such as trash; (2) things a person says or does in public.

[3] Example: D puts dead marijuana leaves in a garbage bag at the edge of his lawn, so that sanitation workers will pick it up. The police, acting on a tip, ransack the bag before it's picked up, and seize the plants as evidence that D is cultivating marijuana in his house. Even if D subjectively believed that no one would open up the bag (i.e., he had a subjective expectation of privacy), this expectation of privacy was not a "reasonable" one. (See *Cal. v. Greenwood.*) Therefore, you'd answer "no" to the question in box [3]. Consequently, no Fourth Amendment search would be deemed to have taken place.

[4] These three requirements mean that the plain-view doctrine applies only to police actions that would otherwise be *searches*, not things that would otherwise be *seizures*.

Example 1: O, a police officer, responds to a call that a domestic disturbance is occurring at D's house. As D is standing in the open doorway, O looks over D's shoulder and sees a brightly lit table in D's living room, containing what appear to be marijuana plants. O cannot rely on the plain-view doctrine to permit him to go into the room and seize the plants, even though he saw them in plain view. (But see Example 2 below for how the plain-view doctrine *would* apply on these facts.)

Example 2: Same facts as prior example (marijuana plants in living room). O's *view* of the plants is covered by the plain-view doctrine (since O was standing in a place he had a right to be -- the open doorway, following the disturbance call -- and since O only saw, rather than seized, the plants). Now, what O saw can supply probable cause for O to obtain a search warrant, which when issued would permit O to seize the plants. Furthermore, O would be entitled to remove D from the premises while a warrant was being sought, so that D couldn't destroy the evidence.

[5] In a typical fact pattern, you will answer "yes" if the data has been collected by a private business with whom the suspect (D) interacted. Examples include: cell-service providers to D; banks who process checks written by or to D; credit card companies who handle transactions involving cards issued to D; Internet Service Providers who transmit emails or text messages to or from D.

[6] The types of data referred to in the prior footnote will typically yield a "yes" answer, since these sorts of transactions are ones that D would normally expect would remain private. But evidence of D's movements in the public sphere, where there are only a few datapoints, and where each datapoint refers to a location that could have been observed by a member of the public, would typically yield a "no" answer; in that case, the traditional third-party doctrine will apply. Where that doctrine applies, the fact that the data was voluntarily communicated by D to the third party means that D had no justifiable expectation of privacy in the data, so that no Fourth Amendment search will be deemed to have occurred when government acquires the data from the third party.

Example: D robs Store, a convenience store. A surveillance camera makes a video

Notes continue on next page.

Notes (p. 2) to
Figure 1A (Was There a 4th Amendment "Search" or Seizure"?)

recording of D doing the robbery. The police subpoena, and receive, a copy of the video from Store, and use it to identify D.

 Because the tape merely recorded a small amount of publicly-visible non-intimate material about D, and because the material was in effect voluntarily placed by D in the possession of a third party (the store), the police's acquisition of the material was not a search or seizure for Fourth Amendment purposes. Therefore, the police did not need either probable cause or a search warrant in order to subpoena the tape.

[7] Remember, the traditional third-party doctrine says that when D voluntarily gives possession of information to a third party, D is <u>deemed not to have a reasonable expectation of privacy in that information</u>. Consequently, government never commits a Fourth Amendment search or seizure when it demands and receives the information from the third party.

<u>Example</u>: D writes checks to various parties on an account she has with X Bank. Since D knew that X Bank would make and keep copies of the checks, D is deemed to have no reasonable expectation of privacy with respect to the copies. Therefore, government can subpoena the copies from X Bank without committing a Fourth Amendment search, and can do so without possessing either probable cause to suspect D, or a search warrant. [U.S. v. *Miller*]

[8] The main type of data requiring a "<u>yes</u>" answer is CSLI (discussed in the next footnote). Other types of data requiring a "yes" answer consist of: video from security cameras; logs of photo IDs scanned by machines installed in public places (workplaces, hospitals); and non-CSLI data from other ways of tracking D's physical movements outside of the home. Types of data requiring a "<u>no</u>" answer include methods of tracking personal data about D apart from D's physical movements, such as: (1) charges recorded by a bank made on a credit card issued to D; (2) records kept by a website of the email addresses D used to send emails, or at which D received emails; and (3) records kept by a search engine company of web

addresses visited by D, with or without information about the search D performed.

[9] "CSLI" means cell site location information. CSLI is information kept by a wireless carrier providing cell service to D, where the information shows the location of D's phone at a given time.

[10] If you answered "yes" to box [17], you've got a scenario covered by the landmark case of *Carpenter v. U.S* (2018). That case held that a police request for 7 days or more of D's CSLI so infringes on D's reasonable expectation of privacy that the traditional third-party doctrine will not apply -- the police are thus performing a Fourth Amendment search, for which they need probable cause and a search warrant.

<u>Example</u>: The police know from V, a since-released kidnap victim, that whoever kidnapped V on July 1 and held her captive at an unoccupied house at 100 Center St. until July 15 stayed with V at the house for the whole 15 days. The police suspect that the kidnapper may have been D. Therefore, acting without a search warrant, the police subpoena D's wireless carrier for all records showing the location of D's cell phone during the July 1-July 15 timespan. The carrier produces the records, which show that D's phone was, indeed, continuously at the 100 Center St. location during this time.

 Because the police have requested more than 6 days' worth of CSLI concerning D's phone's (and thus D's) movements, *Carpenter* says that the subpoena was a Fourth Amendment search and seizure, for which a warrant (issued upon probable cause) was required. In other words, even though the data was placed by D into the possession of a third party (the carrier), *Carpenter* says that the traditional third-party doctrine won't apply, because of the deeply intimate data involved, and because cell service is so indispensable in modern life that D's entrusting a third party with the data can't really be said to have been voluntary.

Notes continue on next page.

Notes (p. 3) to
Figure 1A (Was There a 4th Amendment "Search" or Seizure"?)

[11] Because the CSLI data delivered by the carrier to law enforcement in *Carpenter v. U.S.* covered seven days' worth of D's phone's movement, the Supreme Court didn't have to decide whether a demand for fewer than seven days' worth of CSLI data would still have constituted a Fourth Amendment search. Therefore, we simply don't know whether or when a demand for less-than-seven-days' worth of CSLI data may still be so invasive that the traditional third-party doctrine won't apply.

[12] Here's why a "yes" answer would get you to box [21]: *Carpenter* directly applies only to CSLI. But the majority's reasoning in that case suggests that the Court will eventually hold that many other privately-held databases of personal information are so deep, broad, and intimate, or so automatically and inescapably collected, that the third-party doctrine should not apply to these databases either. In that event, D would be deemed to have a reasonable expectation of privacy in the data despite having entrusted it to the third party, and law enforcement would need a search warrant issued upon probable cause before requesting the data.

Example: D is suspected of having poisoned his wife, V, to death by mixing antifreeze in her coffee. The police, acting without probable cause or a search warrant, issue two subpoenas: (1) to Google (the search engine used by D) for a list of all searches performed under D's login during the 60 days prior to V's death where any word on a list of various poison-related terms was part of the search request; and (2) to Bank, which issued a credit card to D, for a list of all charges that D put on the card in the 60 days before V's death.

Both of the databases requested by the police consist of deeply private and broad personal data, data that D had no choice but to allow Google and Bank to collect automatically and inescapably if D wanted the modern amenities of Internet searching and credit-card use. Therefore, the Supreme Court would probably hold that these types of data are analogous to large collections of CSLI. If the Court so held, then the traditional third-party doctrine wouldn't apply to either request,

and each request (if honored) would be found to be a Fourth Amendment search and seizure. That being so, the police would need to show probable cause, and to obtain a search warrant, before requesting the data from Google or Bank.

[13] You should arrive at box [22] (third-party doctrine will apply) only if all of the following are true:

(1) The police action substantially impinged on an actual subjective expectation of privacy held by D;

(2) The plain-view doctrine didn't apply to the police's conduct;

(3) The police obtained access to D's intimate personal information held by a third party, information that was not CSLI;

(4) The information was not so deep, broad, and/or automatically-or-inescapably-collected that it should be treated as the equivalent of a sizeable quantity (seven days' or more) of CSLI.

Here are two examples that would likely lead you to box [22]:

Example 1: D is suspected of robbing a 7/11 at about 1 pm on Sept.1. The police subpoena the 7/11's security-camera tapes for 12:30 to 1:30 pm on Sept. 1, to see if D is shown on the tapes.

Example 2: Same facts as the Example in note12, where D is suspected of poisoning his wife, V, with antifreeze. Now, assume that the police find a receipt in D's garage for antifreeze bought one week before V's death from the local Wal-Mart. (The receipt doesn't disclose who made the purchase or how they paid.) The police ask the Wal-Mart to check its records to see whether a credit card known to have been issued by Bank to D was used to make the antifreeze purchase, and to supply the record if found.

In both of these Examples, it's likely that a court applying the logic of *Carpenter* would conclude that the data sought by the police was so limited in scope, and disclosed so little intimate information, that *Carpenter* shouldn't apply, and that the traditional third-party doctrine should apply instead. If so, the police would not need probable cause or a warrant in order to obtain the date from the store.

Figure 1B
Was the Search or Seizure a Violation of the Fourth Amendment?

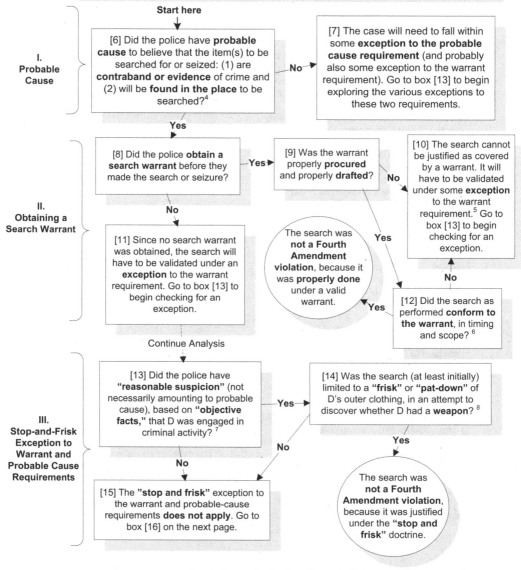

> You should be consulting this chart only if you concluded, based on Fig. 1A, that a **Fourth Amendment search and/or seizure occurred**. When that's so, the general rule is that a **search warrant** and **probable cause** are **both required**; the chart helps you figure out whether one or both of these requirements will be **dispensed with** in a particular situation.

Start here

I. Probable Cause

[6] Did the police have **probable cause** to believe that the item(s) to be searched for or seized: (1) are **contraband or evidence** of crime and (2) will be **found in the place** to be searched?[4]

No →

[7] The case will need to fall within some **exception to the probable cause requirement** (and probably also some exception to the warrant requirement). Go to box [13] to begin exploring the various exceptions to these two requirements.

Yes

II. Obtaining a Search Warrant

[8] Did the police **obtain a search warrant** before they made the search or seizure?

Yes →

[9] Was the warrant properly **procured** and properly **drafted**?

No →

[10] The search cannot be justified as covered by a warrant. It will have to be validated under some **exception** to the warrant requirement.[5] Go to box [13] to begin checking for an exception.

No

[11] Since no search warrant was obtained, the search will have to be validated under an **exception** to the warrant requirement. Go to box [13] to begin checking for an exception.

The search was **not a Fourth Amendment violation**, because it was **properly done** under a valid warrant.

Yes

No

[12] Did the search as performed **conform to the warrant**, in timing and scope?[6]

Yes

Continue Analysis

III. Stop-and-Frisk Exception to Warrant and Probable Cause Requirements

[13] Did the police have **"reasonable suspicion"** (not necessarily amounting to probable cause), based on **"objective facts,"** that D was engaged in criminal activity?[7]

Yes →

[14] Was the search (at least initially) limited to a **"frisk"** or **"pat-down"** of D's outer clothing, in an attempt to discover whether D had a **weapon**?[8]

No

Yes

[15] The **"stop and frisk"** exception to the warrant and probable-cause requirements **does not apply**. Go to box [16] on the next page.

The search was **not a Fourth Amendment violation**, because it was justified under the **"stop and frisk"** doctrine.

See footnotes beginning after p. 6 of chart.

Figure 1B (cont.)
Was the Search or Seizure a Violation
of the Fourth Amendment? (p. 2)

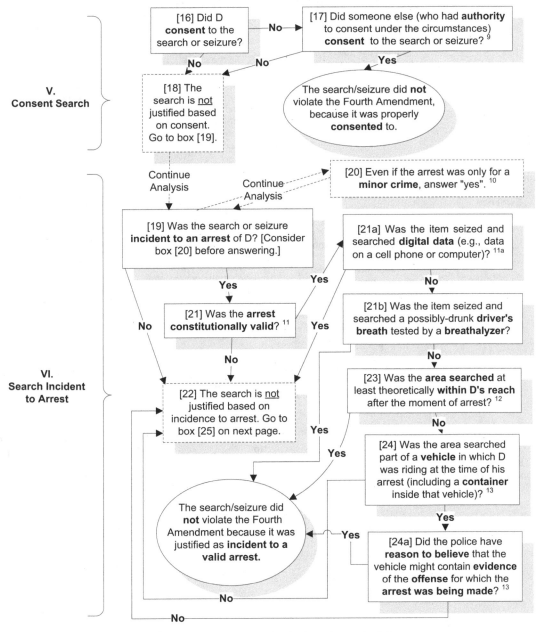

See footnotes beginning after p. 6 of chart.

Figure 1B (cont.)
Was the Search or Seizure a Violation
of the Fourth Amendment? (p. 3)

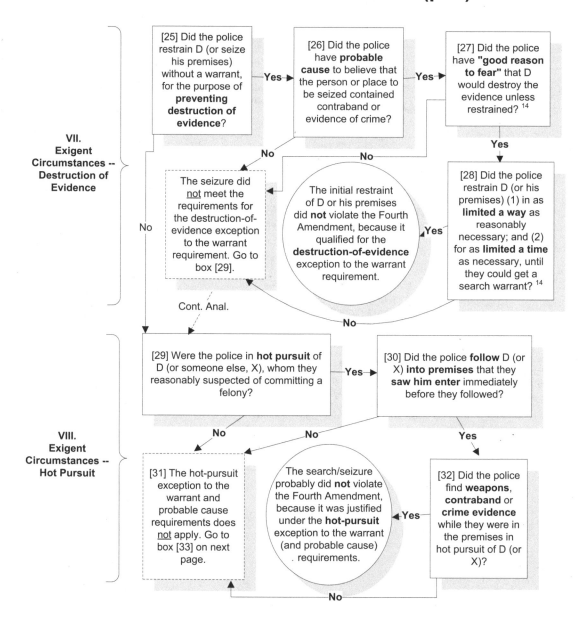

Figure 1B (cont.)
Was the Search or Seizure a Violation of the Fourth Amendment? (p. 4)

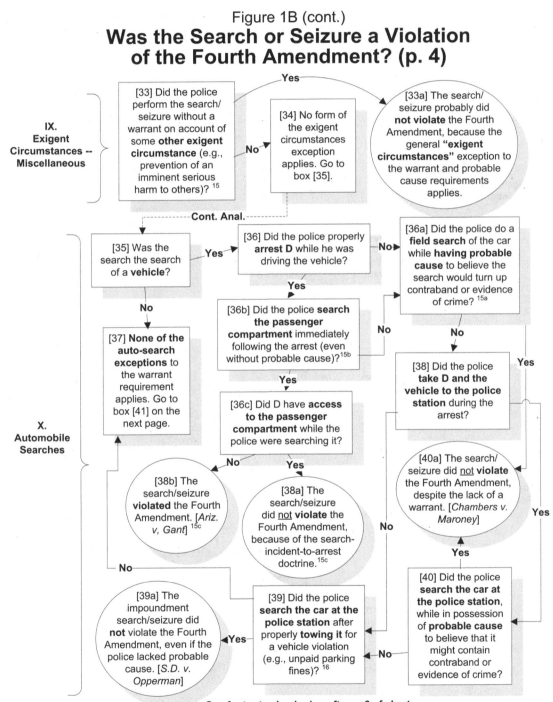

IX. Exigent Circumstances -- Miscellaneous

[33] Did the police perform the search/seizure without a warrant on account of some **other exigent circumstance** (e.g., prevention of an imminent serious harm to others)? [15]

Yes

[33a] The search/seizure probably did **not violate** the Fourth Amendment, because the general **"exigent circumstances"** exception to the warrant and probable cause requirements applies.

No

[34] No form of the exigent circumstances exception applies. Go to box [35].

---- Cont. Anal. ----

X. Automobile Searches

[35] Was the search the search of a **vehicle**?

Yes

[36] Did the police properly **arrest D** while he was driving the vehicle?

No

[36a] Did the police do a **field search** of the car while **having probable cause** to believe the search would turn up contraband or evidence of crime? [15a]

Yes (from [36])

[36b] Did the police **search the passenger compartment** immediately following the arrest (even without probable cause)? [15b]

No

[36c] Did D have **access to the passenger compartment** while the police were searching it?

No → [38b] The search/seizure **violated** the Fourth Amendment. [*Ariz. v, Gant*] [15c]

Yes → [38a] The search/seizure did **not violate** the Fourth Amendment, because of the search-incident-to-arrest doctrine. [15c]

No (from [36a])

[38] Did the police **take D and the vehicle to the police station** during the arrest?

Yes → [40a] The search/seizure did **not violate** the Fourth Amendment, despite the lack of a warrant. [*Chambers v. Maroney*]

No →

[37] **None of the auto-search exceptions** to the warrant requirement applies. Go to box [41] on the next page.

[40] Did the police **search the car at the police station**, while in possession of **probable cause** to believe that it might contain contraband or evidence of crime?

Yes (to [40a])

No →

[39] Did the police **search the car at the police station** after properly **towing it** for a vehicle violation (e.g., unpaid parking fines)? [16]

Yes → [39a] The impoundment search/seizure did **not** violate the Fourth Amendment, even if the police lacked probable cause. [*S.D. v. Opperman*]

No

See footnotes beginning after p. 6 of chart.

Figure 1B (cont.)
Was the Search or Seizure a Violation of the Fourth Amendment? (p. 5)

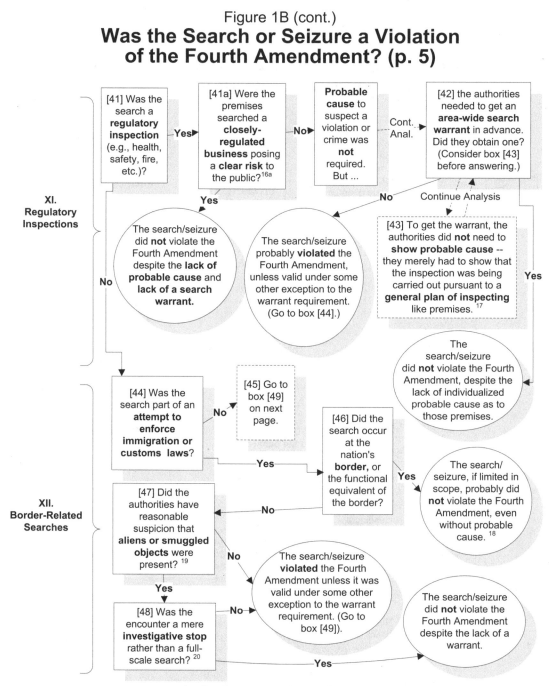

See footnotes beginning after p. 6 of chart.

Figure 1B (cont.)
Was the Search or Seizure a Violation of the Fourth Amendment? (p. 6)

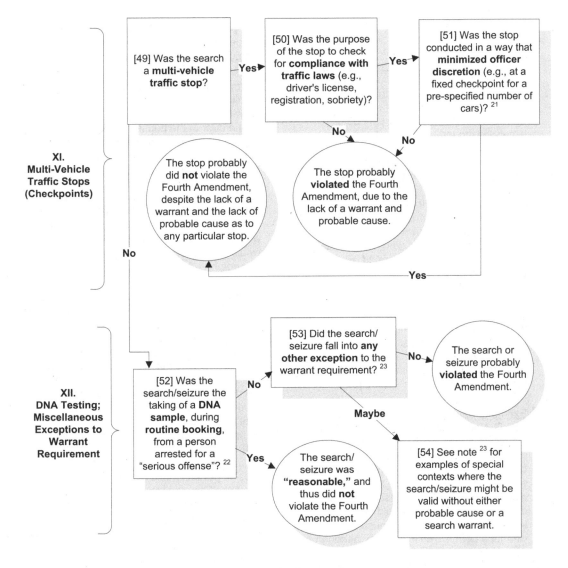

Footnotes begin on next page.

Notes (p. 1) to
Figure 1B (Search and Seizure)

[1-3] [Intentionally omitted]

[4] "Probable cause" seems to mean merely a "reasonable likelihood," not "more likely than not." Cf. *Maryland v. Pringle*. So to have probable cause to make the search or seizure, the police must be in possession of facts causing them to believe that it is reasonably likely that (1) the items to be searched for or seized are connected with criminal activities, and (2) those items will be found in the place to be searched.

[5] The remaining boxes cover various exceptions to the requirement of a search warrant (e.g., stop-and-frisk, consent, search-incident-to-arrest, exigent-circumstances, automobile searches, etc.).

[6] Example: Suppose that a properly-issued search warrant authorizes search of the "bedroom" of D's apartment. The police ransack D's living room, and find a hidden stash of cocaine. On these facts, you'd answer "no" to box [12], because the search exceeded the scope of the warrant.

[7] Example: V tells O, a police officer, that she was just mugged by a tall, thin, white male wearing a blue windbreaker. 2 blocks away and 10 minutes later, O sees D, a tall, thin, white male wearing a windbreaker. On these facts, you'd answer "yes" to box [13].

[8] Example: Same basic facts as Example in note 7. Now, assume that O stops D to ask him some questions. If, prior to the questions, O does a pat-down of D's outer clothing to see if D is carrying a weapon, you would answer "yes" to box [14]. Then, if O discovered a gun (not licensed as required) during the pat-down, O would be able to seize the gun and arrest D for carrying it without a permit. The initial stop, although a Fourth Amendment "search," would not be a Fourth Amendment violation, because even though it was done without either a search warrant or probable cause, it qualifies under the stop-and-frisk doctrine.

In the case of a vehicle stop, the police may pat down either the driver or a passenger, if they have reason to believe that the person may be armed or dangerous. They may do the pat-down even if they have no reason to suspect the driver or passenger of wrongdoing. [*Ariz. v. Johnson*]

[9] Example: H and W are husband and wife. O, a police officer, suspects that H has been growing marijuana in his garage. O knocks on the door of the house and W answers (H is not home). O explains that he's heard a tip that H may be growing pot. W is angry at H because he's been having an affair, so W gives permission to O to do the search. Assuming that the garage is an area used by both H and W, W has authority to consent to the search. [Cf. *U.S. v. Matlock*] (But if H was present and objected, W's consent wouldn't be effective as against H. [*Ga. v. Randolph*])

[10] In other words, a warrantless search can be performed incident to a proper arrest for even a minor violation. Example: P, while driving, is stopped by Officer for not signalling while changing lanes. Officer examines P's driver's license and finds that it has expired. Officer arrests P for this very minor violation. Officer will then be entitled to search P's person incident to this arrest (and will also be entitled to search the passenger compartment of P's car, as described in box [24]).

[11] Most importantly, this means that the arrest must itself be supported by probable cause to believe that D committed the offense in question. So if, at trial (or at a pre-trial suppression hearing) D can establish that the arresting officer did not have probable cause to make the arrest, the search incident to that arrest will be invalid, and its fruits will

Notes continue on next page.

Notes (p. 2) to
Figure 1B (Search and Seizure)

normally have to be suppressed.

By the way, the police can have probable cause to arrest for Offense *A* even if they tell the suspect, at the time of the arrest, that the arrest is for Offense *B*. So as long as the police at the time of arrest were in possession of facts making it reasonably likely that D committed Offense *A*, that will make the arrest valid even if they subjectively believed (and told D) that they were arresting for Offense B, for which they later turned out not to have had probable cause. Cf. *Devenpeck v. Alford.*

[11a] Even if the police properly make a custodial arrest of a person who happens to be carrying a cell phone, the incident-to-arrest doctrine does not allow the police to perform a warrantless search of the digital contents of the phone. Therefore, they must procure a search warrant based on probable cause (though they may seize the physical phone and impound it while they try to get the warrant). [*Riley v. Calif.* (2014)] The same rule almost certainly applies to any digital data found on any other type of electronic device that the arrestee is carrying at the time of the arrest (e.g., a laptop computer found in the arrestee's backpack).

Example: Officer (O) watches while D sells a small plastic baggie of white powder to X and receives cash in exchange. Assume that this gives O probable cause to arrest D for sale of narcotics. O makes the arrest, then demands that D empty his pockets. D pulls out a cell phone. O is entitled to *seize* the cell phone incident to this lawful arrest. But O is not permitted to open the phone and scroll through, say, the digital address book entries in it to see if any relate to narcotics sales. Instead, although O may keep possession of the cell phone, she must obtain a search warrant (based on probable cause to believe that the phone contains evidence of a crime or contraband) before she may examine the phone's digital contents. [*Riley, supra.*]

[12] Example: D is arrested in the front hall of his house. The police then search the entire house, even though they have no reason to believe that anyone else is present. In the bedroom, they look into a chest of drawers that is too small to hold a person, and in one drawer they find heroin. This search will not be justified by the search-incident-to-arrest doctrine, because it was not even theoretically within D's reach after the arrest.

Note that where an arrest occurs in the suspect's home, the police may make a "protective sweep" of all or part of the premises, if they have a "reasonable belief" based on "specific and articulable facts" that another person who might be dangerous to the officer may be present in the areas to be swept. [*Maryland v. Buie*] So on the facts of the above example, if the arresting officers knew that D's wife, W, was present, they would be entitled to do a sweep through the house to make sure that W was not present and dangerous. (But this would not justify the police in looking in places too small to contain W, such as the drawers above.)

Where the arrest is of a driver, it's now the case that the same "within the arrestee's reach" requirement applies, a big change from pre-2009 law. So if the driver has been, say, handcuffed and placed in the patrol car, the police can no longer automatically search the passenger compartment incident to the arrest. See note 13 for more about this.

[13] It's no longer the case (as it was before 2009) that the police can automatically search the passenger compartment, and any container in it, as long as the arrest of the driver was proper. (This was the rule of *N.Y. v. Belton*, which was overruled in 2009 by *Ariz. v. Gant.*) Therefore, even if the driver arrest was valid, the police can search the car incident to the arrest only if *either*:

[1] The police didn't take steps to prevent the driver, post-arrest, from gaining access to the passenger compartment (i.e., the

Notes (p. 3) to
Figure 1B (Search and Seizure)

situation is one that's covered by box [23] above, a situation that will never occur if standard police procedures are followed, by which the arrested driver is handcuffed and placed in the patrol car or otherwise immobilized); or

[2] The police had "reason to believe" that the vehicle "might" contain evidence of the offense for which the arrest was being made. Notice that this is an easier-to-satisfy standard than "probable cause."

Example: There is an outstanding arrest warrant for D, on a charge of selling meth out of his 2006 red Taurus. Police spot the red Taurus and stop D, who is alone in the car. They arrest D on the warrant, handcuff him, and then put him in the squad car. They then search D's car's interior. In the glove compartment, they find marijuana. Since the warrant gave the police "reason to believe" that meth (evidence of the crime for which D was being arrested) "might" still be in the Taurus, they were allowed to search anywhere in the interior in which meth might have plausibly been found, including the glove compartment. Therefore, the marijuana came into plain view during a legal search, and may be admitted against D. That's true even though: (1) the passenger compartment was no longer within D's theoretical access by the time of the search; and (2) the police did not necessarily have "probable cause" (merely the lesser "reason to believe") that evidence relating to the crime of arrest would be found. [*Ariz. v. Gant*]

Notice that in the typical case of an arrest for a traffic infraction observed by the arresting officer (e.g., running a red light), the officer won't have reason to believe that evidence of the crime of arrest will be found, so reason [2] above won't apply. In that situation, if the driver has been immobilized the passenger compartment may not be searched incident to the arrest. (But if the police develop full

probable cause to believe that contraband or evidence of crime will be found anywhere in the car, they may search for it even though the contraband or evidence doesn't relate to the crime of arrest – that's because there's a general exception to the search warrant requirement for field searches of vehicles where there's probable cause. See note 15a for more about this.)

[14] Example: Acting on a tip from D's wife, W, the police learn that D may have been growing marijuana in his living room. They ring his doorbell and ask him if this is so. He seems evasive and worried. They tell him that they want to procure a search warrant. They also give him a choice between: (1) staying outside the house until they can get the warrant; or (2) having an officer with him at all times until they get the warrant. (Assume that under the circumstances, a reasonable officer would have good reason to fear that D would destroy the marijuana before the police could return with the warrant.) They then return with the warrant in less than one hour (a reasonable time under the circumstances) and conduct the search. On these facts, you'd answer "yes" to both box [27] and [28].

Consequently, a court would hold that giving D a choice between staying out of his house or having an officer with him was not a violation of D's Fourth Amendment rights. [*Ill. v. McArthur*]

In evaluating box [27], keep in mind the "police-created-emergency" doctrine: If the police's own conduct "created" or "manufactured" the threat of evidence destruction, then the main evidence-destruction exception to the warrant requirement won't apply, and the police will need to get a warrant before searching. But the police-created-emergency doctrine applies only if the police gain entry by means of an actual or threatened Fourth Amendment violation. [*Kentucky v. King*]

Notes continue on next page.

Notes (p. 4) to
Figure 1 (Search and Seizure)

Example: Police, without a warrant, sneak onto D's premises and illegally look through his window, where they see what appears to be a pile of marijuana. They then knock on the front door, shout "Police. Open up," and hear running steps and flushing toilets. Any forced entry will not qualify for the destruction-of-evidence exception, because the police got themselves in a position to fear evidence destruction only because they violated D's Fourth Amendment rights at the outset.

[15] Example: The police get word from the FBI that a member of the Al Qaeda terrorist network is planning to kill himself and many others with a suicide bomb in New York's Times Square at about 6 pm that evening. At 5:58, Officer sees D, a man of Middle Eastern appearance, wearing a coat that seems too heavy and bulky for the balmy spring night. Officer believes that D may be the bomber, and that if he approaches D and just tries to pat him down, D will detonate the bomb immediately. Instead, Officer tackles D without warning, handcuffs him, and extensively searches him. Officer doesn't find a bomb, but does find cocaine. On these facts, you'd answer "yes" to box [33] -- Officer's reasonable belief in the need to prevent imminent and serious bodily harm to others and himself justified the warrantless seizure of D's body and the warrantless search of his person. Therefore, the drugs would be admissible against D in a criminal trial for drug possession. [Cf. *Brigham City v. Stuart* (police who look through screen door and see fight may enter without warrant under exigent-circumstances exception).]

[15a] Under a vehicle-specific version of the exigent-circumstances exception to the warrant requirement, the police may do an in-the-field search of any properly-stopped car if they have probable cause to believe that contraband or evidence of crime will be found. That's because vehicles can be rapidly driven away if the police take the time to get a search warrant. [*Carroll v. U.S.*]

Note that the requisite probable cause can develop during the course of the encounter, thus permitting the police to make a warrantless search when they would not have been allowed to do so immediately after the stop.

Example: The police stop a driver for having a broken tail light, a slight offense for which an arrest would not be allowed under state law. They hand the driver, D, a ticket while he is still in the car. They then walk around the car, and smell marijuana from a hole in the trunk.

Assuming that the smell of marijuana gives the police probable cause to believe that the trunk contains marijuana (which it probably does), the police may open the trunk and search it, without first getting a search warrant. They have this right pursuant to the general exception under *Carroll* for warrantless vehicle searches done with probable cause.

[15b] For more about the rules for searches incident to arrest in connection with vehicle stops, see boxes [23]-[24a] on p. 2 of the flow chart.

[15c] For more about the rule of *Arizona v. Gant*, see note 13 on previous page.

[16] Notice that if the police tow a car for a vehicle violation, they do not need either a search warrant or probable cause to make an impoundment search, provided that they search all similarly-towed cars in this way.

[16a] So far, the only types of businesses that the Supreme Court has recognized as falling within this "closely regulated / risky" category, for which no pre-inspection search warrant is required, are: (1) businesses that sell liquor on the premises; (2) firearms dealers; (3) mining businesses; and (4) auto

Notes continue on next page.

Notes (p. 5) to
Figure 1B (Search and Seizure)

junkyards. Conversely, hotels are not closely regulated for this purpose; therefore, inspectors without at least an administrative search warrant may not demand to make a regulatory inspection of a hotel's guest registry. [*City of Los Angeles v. Patel* (2015)]

[17] Example: The Fire Dept. gets a warrant to inspect all office buildings in a particular square block, in order to assess the buildings' compliance with fire codes. The magistrate can issue this warrant without probable cause as to any particular building. The point is that the generality of the plan -- all buildings in a particular neighborhood -- itself guarantees that the fire officials won't be using undue discretion in deciding which buildings to search. Therefore, any criminal violation that they uncover while executing the warrant will be admissible notwithstanding the lack of probable cause.

[18] However, the search must not be unduly intrusive if it is to avoid being a Fourth Amendment violation. If they are acting without particularized suspicion, the border officials may examine packages and perhaps a traveller's outer garments, but they may not, say, conduct an intrusive "body cavity" search. (For that they would need at least reasonable suspicion of smuggling).

[19] If the authorities stop a car to ask preliminary border-related questions, they do not need probable cause, but they do need to be able to point to "specific factors" that gave rise to reasonable suspicion that an immigration violation has occurred.

Example: Immigration officials who are patrolling a stretch 100 miles inside Texas' border with Mexico stop a particular car only because its inhabitants appear to be Hispanic. Since the police did not rely on appropriate specific factors causing them to suspect that the passengers were illegal aliens (or smugglers), the search will violate the Fourth Amendment.

Note that if the immigration stop in the above Example were at a "fixed checkpoint" (even though in the interior of the country) at which all cars were stopped, then the police would not need particularized suspicion as to any one car.

[20] In other words, such a stop is like a stop in a non-border "stop-and-frisk" situation, as covered in boxes [13]-[15].

[21] Example: The police decide to stop the first 100 cars that get to a particular intersection after 8 PM on a Friday night, to check that each driver is properly licensed and is sober. Since this arrangement strips the police of their discretion to pick a particular car (e.g., because of the race of the occupant), and since it's related to legitimate traffic-safety concerns, it's valid even though the police have no probable cause (or even reasonable suspicion) as to any particular driver, and no warrant.

[22] Example: D is properly arrested for a just-committed robbery. At the station, as part of routine booking procedures (along with taking D's fingerprints and a mug shot) the police swab D's cheek for a DNA sample. The sample, when run through a national database of unsolved crimes, matches a semen sample left in an unsolved five-year-old rape.

The taking of the DNA is a Fourth Amendment search, but it is a "reasonable" (and thus constitutional) one, since it helped the police be sure that their arrestee was who he said he was. Therefore, the sample can be introduced against D for the rape, even though it was taken without a search warrant and without probable cause to believe that D was guilty of any crime except the recent robbery. [Cf. *Maryland v. King*.]

[23] There are a number of special contexts in which warrantless (and probable-cause-less) searches are sometimes allowed: schools; parolees and probationers; and government

Notes continue on next page.

Notes (p. 6) to
Figure 1B (Search and Seizure)

employees, to name a few. Generally, the search must be related to the legitimate and special needs associated with that particular context.

Example: Officials at a Department of Motor Vehicles suspect that D, an employee, has been taking bribes to alter the records of drivers whose licenses have been suspended. The DMV may cause the police to examine the contents of D's desk for evidence of bribe-taking, because a government employer may search an employee's workspace without probable cause or a warrant, as long as the search is "reasonable under all the circumstances," which this would be.

Figure 2
Electronic Surveillance and Secret Agents

Use this chart to determine whether the government has acted properly when it has either conducted electronic surveillance or made use of a secret agent. This chart tries to alert you to possible violations of both the Fourth Amendment and the Sixth Amendment right to counsel, as well as violations of the federal "Title III" statute on electronic surveillance. "D" in the chart is the (or a) person suspected of wrongdoing.

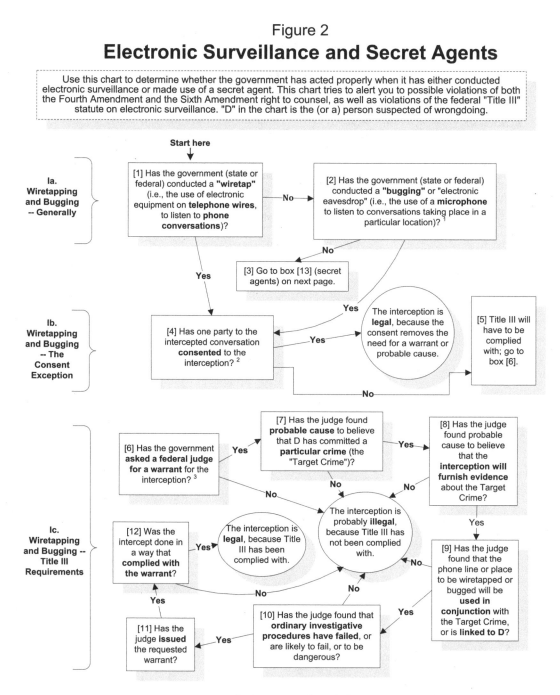

Footnotes start after p. 2 of chart.

Figure 2 (cont.)
Electronic Surveillance and Secret Agents (p. 2)

You should only be checking part II (boxes [13]-[19]) if D (1) had conversations with, or while in the presence of, another person (S), and (2) knew that S was present. (If S's presence was secret, analyze the case as involving an ordinary Fourth Amendment search -- if D had a reasonable expectation of privacy, S's presence on behalf of the government was probably an unreasonable Fourth Amendment search.[4])

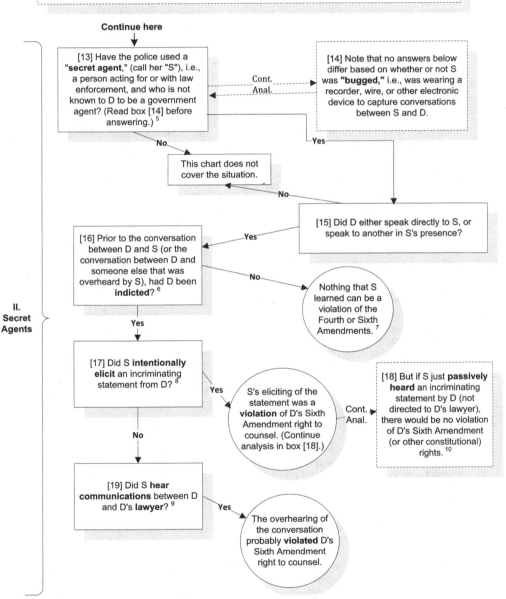

Notes to
Figure 2 (Electronic Surveillance & Secret Agents)

[1] Here's the distinction between wiretapping and bugging: wiretapping is the electronic interception of a conversation or other message that is being transmitted across phone lines. Bugging is the electronic interception of a conversation or other message that is not being transmitted on phone lines. Example 1 (wiretap): FBI agents put a tap in the phone-junction box outside D's premises, enabling them to listen to D's phone conversations. Example 2 (eavesdropping): FBI agents put a "bug" (a small microphone) in the lampshade in D's dining room, allowing them to listen to conversations that occur in that room.

Very little turns on the distinction between wiretapping and bugging. For instance, both types of police activity have to be approved by a federal judge, under Title III.

[2] Example: The police are investigating two men suspected of a particular crime, A and B. A learns of their suspicions (B does not), and agrees that in return for prosecutors' recommendation of leniency for himself, A will secretly plead guilty and then let the police listen in on phone conversations between A and B, in which police hope that B will implicate himself. When the police listen in and tape calls between A and B, they can do so without a warrant and without complying with Title III (covered in boxes [6]-[12]), because the consent of one party to a conversation renders the interception of the conversation legal without more.

[3] Both state and federal police or prosecutors must get permission from a federal judge, under Title III, before any electronic surveillance (wiretapping or bugging) may take place.

[4] Example: The police believe that D, a suspected criminal, may use a particular pay phone booth in a hotel lobby. The police make arrangements for O, an officer, to hide in a conference room on the other side of the booth, and to listen to conversations taking place in the booth. D does not realize that O is listening or even present when he uses the booth (that's the whole point). On these facts, O is not a "secret agent," and the case would not be covered by this chart. You should instead analyze the case as involving a classic Fourth Amendment search (which

would on these facts be illegal in the absence of a warrant and probable cause).

[5] As used here, a "secret agent" is a person who is known to the target (D) to be present, but whose affiliation with the police is unknown to D.

Perhaps the most important thing to realize about secret agents is that their secret link with the police never violates the constitution, or Title III, unless it interferes with D's right to counsel, as set out in boxes [16]-[18]. In other words, the fact that the agent is secretly cooperating with the police to the disadvantage of D will never by itself be a violation of D's Fourth Amendment rights or of Title III. A person who is victimized by "misplaced trust" has, essentially, no constitutional remedy (except in the oddball case of certain post-indictment breaches of trust that may be found to be violations of the right to counsel, as detailed in boxes [16]-[19].)

Example: D is a crime kingpin. X is (D believes) D's trusted right-hand man. Unbeknownst to D, X has been cooperating with the police for 4 years, and has been paid by them a full-time salary for being an informant. No criminal charges are pending against D. No matter what D discloses to X (and whether it's merely memorized by X or recorded or broadcast by a wire that X wears), X's re-disclosure of the material to the police won't violate D's Fourth Amendment or Title III rights.

[6] Answer "yes" only if D has not only been indicted but has retained counsel.

[7] In other words, no disclosure by D to S can violate D's Sixth Amendment rights.

Example: Same facts as the Example in note 5. Now, assume that D says to X, "If they charge me and try me on anything, I'll plead insanity. I've worked this out with L [D's lawyer]." X immediately passes this info on to the prosecution. Because D has not yet been indicted, D's "misplaced trust" in X will not constitute a violation of D's Sixth Amendment right to counsel, even though the disclosure relates to D's legal strategy.

Notes (cont.) to
Figure 2 (Electronic Surveillance & Secret Agents)

[8] Example: Same basic facts as in the Examples in notes 5 and 7. Now, however, assume that D has been indicted for ordering the murder of V, and has retained L as his lawyer. X knows this. X says to D, "Did you really order V wacked, the way the feds say you did?" D, still believing that X is loyal to him, says, "Yeah, I had Joey the Pistol take care of him ... Too big a chance he'd rat us out." X tapes this conversation and gives it to the federal prosecutors. This conduct will constitute a violation of D's Sixth Amendment right to counsel, under *Massiah v. U.S.*, because X has "deliberately elicited" the incriminating statement. (But if X just waited patiently while D happened to volunteer on his own that he had had V killed, the use of this confession -- even the taping of it -- by X and the police would not be a Sixth Amendment violation, because of the "deliberately elicit" requirement.)

[9] Example: Same basic facts as Example 8. Now, assume that D and X are both charged with the murder (though the authorities know that X had nothing to do with it -- they're just charging X to preserve his cover.) X and D and their lawyers have a 4-way meeting. Again, D (and his lawyer L) have no idea that X is cooperating with the police. X hears L describe the strategy that he and D will use in their half of the upcoming trial, and X passes this news on to the prosecution. This use of D's lawyer-client communications will be a violation of D's Sixth Amendment right to counsel.

[10] Example: Same facts as Example in note 6. The parenthetical remark at the end of that note illustrates how, if D spontaneously explains to X that D had V killed, X can pass this information on to the police (or record it) without violating D's Sixth Amendment rights.

Figure 3
Confessions and
Police Interrogation

Use this chart to analyze a police interrogation that results in a confession or other inculpatory statement by D. (We'll refer to both types of utterances simply as "D's statement.") The chart will help you determine whether D's statement is admissible in the prosecution's case in chief, and if not, whether it's admissible for some other use (e.g., impeachment of D's testimony).

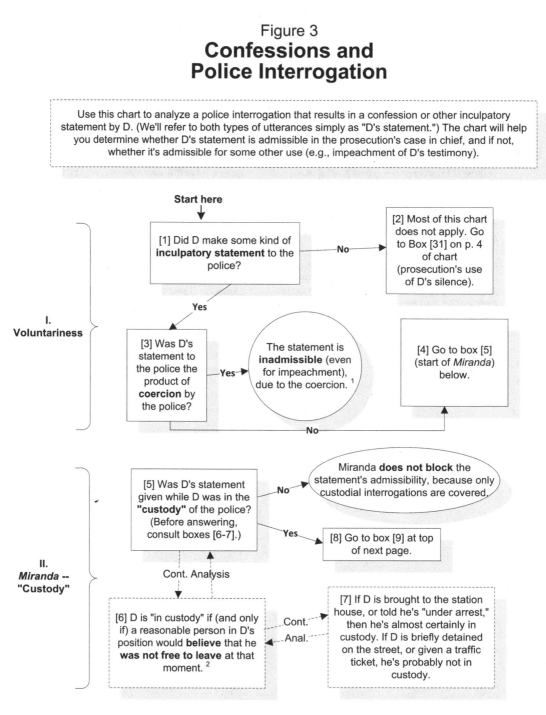

Start here

I. Voluntariness

[1] Did D make some kind of **inculpatory statement** to the police?

— No → [2] Most of this chart does not apply. Go to Box [31] on p. 4 of chart (prosecution's use of D's silence).

Yes

[3] Was D's statement to the police the product of **coercion** by the police? — Yes → The statement is **inadmissible** (even for impeachment), due to the coercion. [1]

[4] Go to box [5] (start of *Miranda*) below.

No

II. Miranda -- "Custody"

[5] Was D's statement given while D was in the **"custody"** of the police? (Before answering, consult boxes [6-7].) — No → Miranda **does not block** the statement's admissibility, because only custodial interrogations are covered.

Yes → [8] Go to box [9] at top of next page.

Cont. Analysis

[6] D is "in custody" if (and only if) a reasonable person in D's position would **believe** that he **was not free to leave** at that moment. [2]

Cont. Anal.

[7] If D is brought to the station house, or told he's "under arrest," then he's almost certainly in custody. If D is briefly detained on the street, or given a traffic ticket, he's probably not in custody.

See footnotes on p. 5 of chart.

Figure 3 (cont.)
Confessions and
Police Interrogation (p. 2)

You should be on this page only if you've concluded that D made a statement to the police while in their custody.

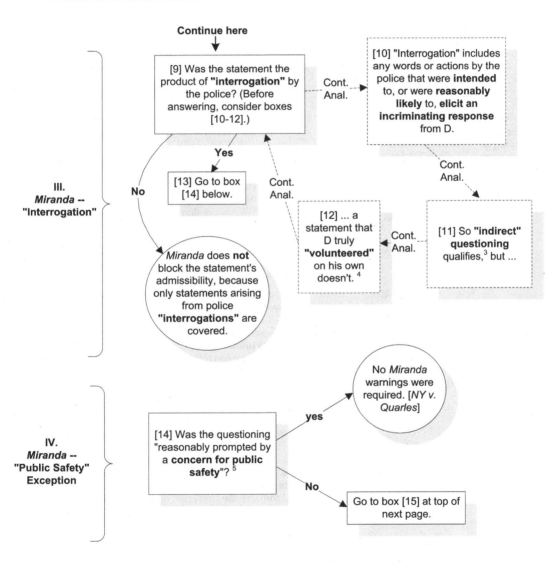

See footnotes on p. 5 of chart.

Figure 3 (cont.)
Confessions and Police Interrogation (p. 3)

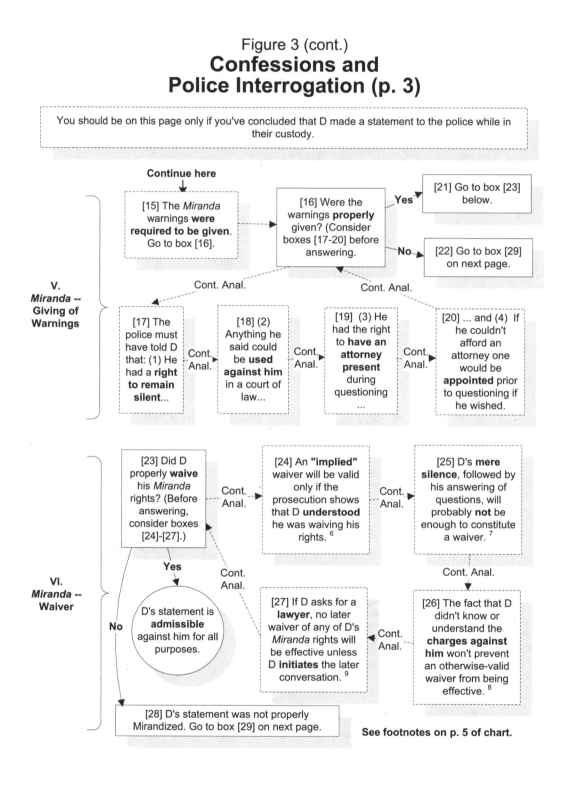

You should be on this page only if you've concluded that D made a statement to the police while in their custody.

Continue here

[15] The *Miranda* warnings **were required to be given**. Go to box [16].

[16] Were the warnings **properly** given? (Consider boxes [17-20] before answering.

Yes → **[21]** Go to box [23] below.

No → **[22]** Go to box [29] on next page.

V. *Miranda* -- Giving of Warnings

Cont. Anal.

[17] The police must have told D that: (1) He had a **right to remain silent**...

Cont. Anal.

[18] (2) Anything he said could be **used against him** in a court of law...

Cont. Anal.

[19] (3) He had the right to **have an attorney present** during questioning ...

Cont. Anal.

[20] ... and (4) If he couldn't afford an attorney one would be **appointed** prior to questioning if he wished.

[23] Did D properly **waive** his *Miranda* rights? (Before answering, consider boxes [24]-[27].)

Cont. Anal.

[24] An **"implied"** waiver will be valid only if the prosecution shows that D **understood** he was waiving his rights. [6]

Cont. Anal.

[25] D's **mere silence**, followed by his answering of questions, will probably **not** be enough to constitute a waiver. [7]

Yes

Cont. Anal.

D's statement is **admissible** against him for all purposes.

VI. *Miranda* -- Waiver

No

[27] If D asks for a **lawyer**, no later waiver of any of D's *Miranda* rights will be effective unless D **initiates** the later conversation. [9]

Cont. Anal.

Cont. Anal.

[26] The fact that D didn't know or understand the **charges against him** won't prevent an otherwise-valid waiver from being effective. [8]

[28] D's statement was not properly Mirandized. Go to box [29] on next page.

See footnotes on p. 5 of chart.

Figure 3 (cont.)
Confessions and
Police Interrogation (p. 4)

You should be at the top of this page (box [29]) only if either: (1) D didn't receive proper *Miranda* warnings; or (2) D received proper warnings, but didn't effectively waive his Miranda rights. You should be at the bottom (at box [31]) only if D remained silent during a police interrogation.

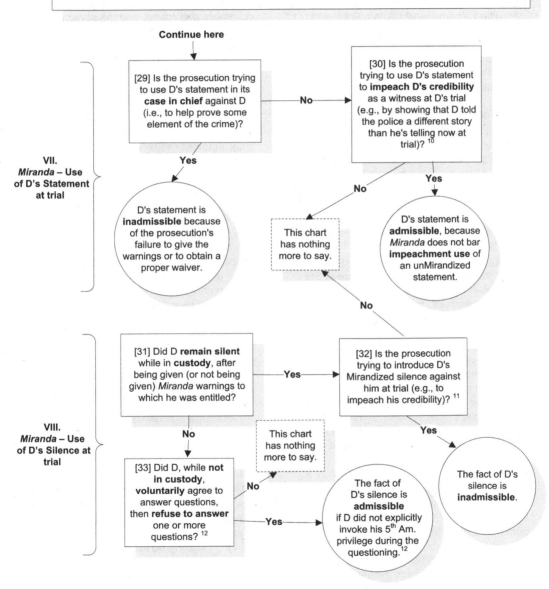

See footnotes beginning on next page.

Notes (p. 1) to
Figure 3 (Confessions and Police Interrogation)

[1] In other words, involuntary confessions are not admissible no matter how closely police adhere to *Miranda*. But that's true only where the involuntariness is due to coercion by the police, not coercion by some other source.

Example 1 (admissible): X finds out that D has committed a crime, and starts blackmailing D. To put an end to the blackmail, D walks in to the local police station and confesses. This confession, though in a sense "involuntary" (since it's the product of duress from X's blackmail) is still admissible, because the coercion wasn't done by the police or by one acting for/with the police.

Example 2 (inadmissible): The police arrest D for a crime, bring him to the station, and then beat him with a truncheon. They then read him his *Miranda* warnings, and he waives his *Miranda* rights (fearing that if he doesn't, he'll be beaten again). The confession is inadmissible, because it's the product of police coercion -- the fact that the *Miranda* warnings were given doesn't insulate it.

[2] Example: O, a police officer, is investigating a recent murder. He goes to the scene of the crime, where he spots D lurking in a suspicious manner. He asks D what D is doing there. At that moment, O has decided that he won't let D leave until D gives a convincing explanation, but D doesn't know this. D gives an incriminating answer. D was not "in custody" at the time of his answer, because a reasonable person in D's situation wouldn't have known that O intended not to let D go without a good answer. (Therefore, O was not required to give D Miranda warnings before D answered, and D's statement will be admissible against him.)

[3] Example: Officer 1 and Officer 2 have arrested D on suspicion of murdering D's wife, and have him in their patrol car. By a pre-staged maneuver, Off. 1 says to Off. 2, "I guess we'll have to hold D overnight unless he convinces us he had nothing to do with his wife's death." The officers hope that this will induce D to talk, and (let's assume) a reasonable person would regard this ploy as having a decent chance of succeeding. D is indeed induced to talk, and makes an incriminating remark.

Off. 1's remark would count as "indirect questioning," and would therefore satisfy the "interrogation" requirement for *Miranda*. Since the other requirement (custody) is also satisfied, D was entitled to be warned before his statement was made, and the statement would therefore not be admissible in the prosecution's case in chief against him.

[4] Example: D is held without bail after being arrested for murder. Officer approaches D in his cell, and before Officer can do anything but identify himself, D blurts out, "I didn't mean to kill her." Since D has volunteered the statement, the "interrogation" requirement is not satisfied. Therefore, the statement is admissible against D despite the absence of *Miranda* warnings. (But if Officer wants to ask follow-up questions, he must give D the warnings first.)

[5] Example: The police have received a tip that a terrorist, having a certain physical appearance, is planning to detonate a bomb at 5 PM at or near the George Washington Bridge. At 4:55, the police spot a man near the bridge matching the description and behaving in a suspicious way. They arrest him, pin his arms back, and say, "Where's the bomb?" D answers, "You'll never find it." This statement was "reasonably prompted by a concern for public safety," under *N.Y. v. Quarles*. Therefore, it's admissible in the prosecution's substantive attempt-to-bomb case against D, even though it met the "interrogation" and "custody" requirements and would therefore ordinarily have triggered the duty to give *Miranda* warnings.

[6] Example: The police give D his *Miranda* warnings, and ask him to sign a waiver form. He says, "I'm willing to talk to you, but I ain't signing no form." He then makes a confession. Assuming that D was of normal intelligence and ability to understand English, a court would probably find that D understood the warnings and therefore implicitly waived his rights by talking.

Notes (p. 2) to
Figure 3 (Confessions and Police Interrogation)

[7] But if the prosecution can prove that D <u>understood</u> the warnings, made no comment, and then answered questions, this typically <u>will</u> be enough to create an implied waiver of the right to remain silent. [*Berguis v. Thompkins*]

[8] Example: The police arrest D for a recent local burglary, which they in fact believe (correctly) that he committed. At the time of the arrest, the police also suspect D of having committed a murder two years in another state. The police read D his *Miranda* warnings, and say they want to question him about the burglary. He signs the standard waiver form (which does not mention what crime[s] the questioning will concern.) During the interrogation, the police change the subject from the burglary to the murder. D implicates himself.

The fact that the police switched the crime does not make the waiver un-knowing, and therefore does not nullify the waiver's effectiveness. [*Col. v. Spring.*] (But if the police affirmatively and intentionally misled D, e.g. by saying that they "only" wanted to question him about the burglary, probably D's waiver *would* be found involuntary or mis-informed, and thus invalid.)

[9] Example: The police arrest D on murder charges, and read him his *Miranda* rights. He says, "I'm not talking until you get me a lawyer." The police say, "OK, that's your right. We don't have any court-appointed lawyers on duty now." They leave D alone in his cell all day, and come back the next day. They then say, "Do you want to talk to us now?" D agrees, and incriminates himself. This statement will not be admissible against him, because his waiver will be found to have been invalid -- once D asked for a lawyer, the only way he could undo that request (i.e. waive his *Miranda* rights) was if he initiated the next conversation, which isn't what happened here. [*Edwards v. Arizona.*]

Note: But if D, after requesting counsel, is <u>released from custody for 14 days</u> or more, then the above rule does not apply, and the police may re-initiate questioning without having supplied the requested lawyer (as long as they give a new set of warnings and get a waiver). [*Maryland v. Shatzer*]

[10] Example: D is charged with murdering his ex-wife while she was at home in St. Louis on the night of August 14. At trial, D takes the stand and asserts an alibi defense, namely that on the evening in question he was on a business trip in Kansas City. During cross-examination, the prosecutor reads to D a statement that D made while in custody, in which he said that on the evening in question, he was at a movie in St. Louis. (The statement was not properly Mirandized, and was made under interrogation.) The prosecutor then says to D, "So the story you're telling now is different than the one you told the police the night you were arrested, right?"

The prosecutor's conduct has not violated D's *Miranda* rights -- *Miranda* only protects against the prosecution's use of a non-Mirandized statement to directly prove that D has committed the offense, not against the use of such a statement to impeach D's credibility as a witness. [*Harris v. N.Y.*]

[11] Example: Same basic facts as prior Example. Now, assume that when D was originally in custody, he remained silent after being given his *Miranda* warnings. At trial, D gives his "I was in Kansas City" alibi defense. The prosecution may not say to D on cross, "Well, if you had such a convincing alibi, why didn't you tell it to the police when you were in custody? Didn't you want to clear your name?" Even though this use is merely an impeaching use (rather than a substantive use), the Supreme Court has held that the fact of D's silence may not be used for impeachment in this way. [*Doyle v. Ohio.*]

Notes continue on next page.

Notes (p. 3) to
Figure 3 (Confessions and Police Interrogation)

[12] Example: O, a police officer, suspects D of robbing a Wal-Mart on the evening of Aug. 1. O asks D to come to the police station voluntarily; O falsely tells D that the purpose of the visit will be to ask D some questions about a different crime, a home burglary that occurred on Aug. 15. D agrees, and comes to the station. O tells D that he is free to cut off questioning, and leave, at any time. After a few questions about the Aug. 15 burglary (which D willingly answers), O suddenly changes the subject and asks, "Did you rob the Wal-Mart on Aug. 1?" D refuses to answer, and cuts off the questioning without giving a reason. At trial on the Wal-Mart robbery, D takes the stand, and gives an alibi defense (that on the evening of Aug. 1 he was 200 miles away).

The prosecution will be permitted to ask D on cross, "Why didn't you tell officer O this story when he questioned you in the police station?" Furthermore, O will be permitted to testify in the prosecution's direct case that when D was asked about the Wal-Mart robbery, he refused to answer and ended the questioning. Here's why both of these uses of D's silence under questioning will be allowed: since D wasn't being subjected to custodial questioning (i.e., he knew he was free to leave and was thus not in custody), the court will not infer that his silence was due to his invocation of the privilege against self-incrimination. Therefore, unlike the Mirandized / custodial-questioning scenario covered in the prior footnote, the court will not conclude that the prosecution's demonstration of D's silence – whether done as direct proof of his guilt or for impeachment of his testimony – would violate D's privilege against self-incrimination. (The result would probably be different if D expressly told O that he was declining to answer on self-incrimination grounds.) [*Salinas v. Texas*]

Figure 4
Lineups and Other
Pre-Trial Identification Procedures

Use this chart to analyze either of the following types of pre-trial identification procedures used by the police: (1) the taking of physical specimens from D (e.g., fingerprints, blood samples, voice samples, etc.); or (2) the soliciting of eyewitness identifications of D (e.g., lineups, photo showups).

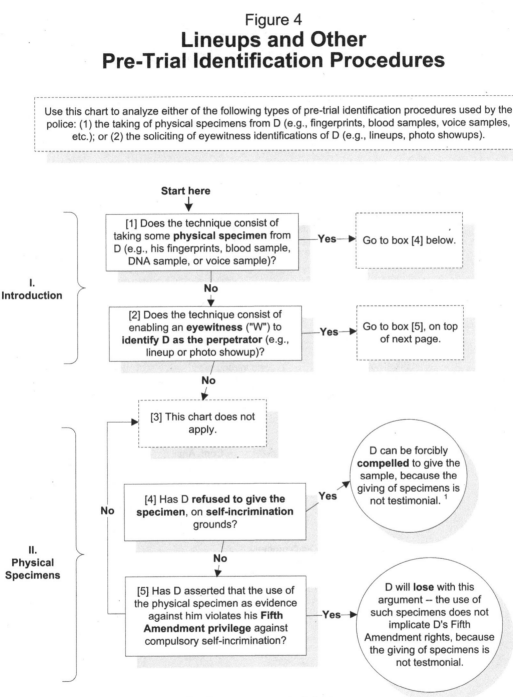

See footnotes on p. 4 of chart.

Figure 4 (cont.)
Lineups and Other
Pre-Trial Identification Procedures (p. 2)

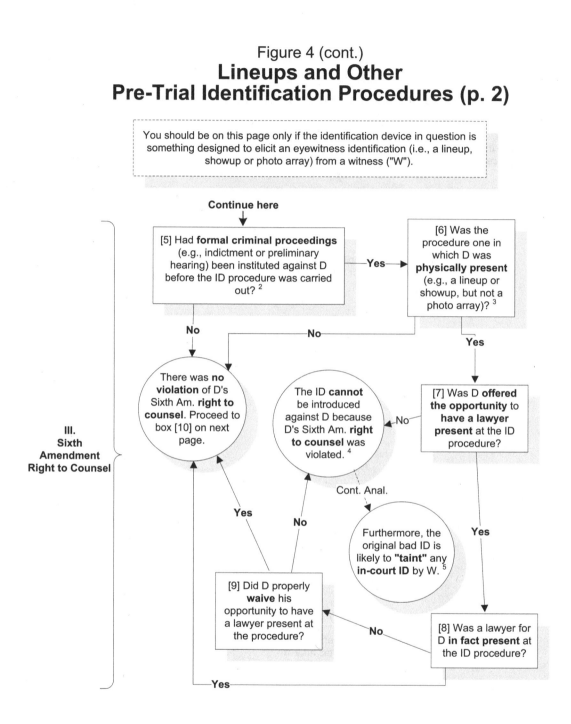

You should be on this page only if the identification device in question is something designed to elicit an eyewitness identification (i.e., a lineup, showup or photo array) from a witness ("W").

Continue here

[5] Had **formal criminal proceedings** (e.g., indictment or preliminary hearing) been instituted against D before the ID procedure was carried out? [2]

[6] Was the procedure one in which D was **physically present** (e.g., a lineup or showup, but not a photo array)? [3]

III. Sixth Amendment Right to Counsel

There was **no violation** of D's Sixth Am. **right to counsel**. Proceed to box [10] on next page.

The ID **cannot** be introduced against D because D's Sixth Am. **right to counsel** was violated. [4]

[7] Was D **offered the opportunity** to have a lawyer **present** at the ID procedure?

Cont. Anal.

Furthermore, the original bad ID is likely to **"taint"** any **in-court ID** by W. [5]

[9] Did D properly **waive** his opportunity to have a lawyer present at the procedure?

[8] Was a lawyer for D **in fact present** at the ID procedure?

See footnotes on p. 4 of chart.

Figure 4 (cont.)
Lineups and Other
Pre-Trial Identification Procedures (p. 3)

As with the prior page, you should be on this page only if the identification device in question is something designed to elicit an eyewitness identification (i.e., a lineup, showup or photo array). "W" is the witness, who has identified D as being the perpetrator.

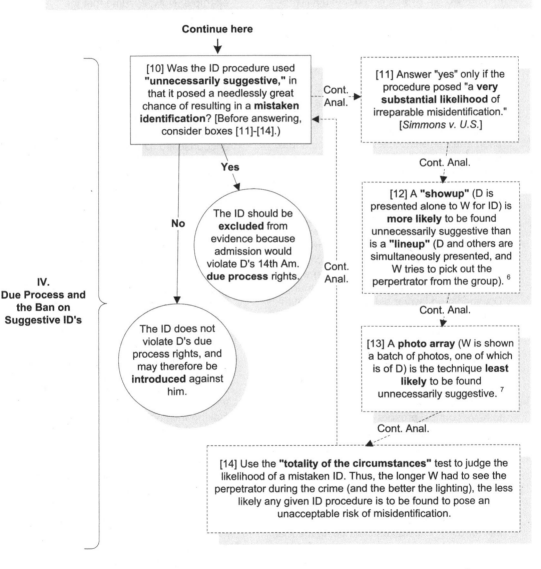

Continue here

[10] Was the ID procedure used **"unnecessarily suggestive,"** in that it posed a needlessly great chance of resulting in a **mistaken identification**? [Before answering, consider boxes [11]-[14].)

Cont. Anal.

[11] Answer "yes" only if the procedure posed "a **very substantial likelihood** of irreparable misidentification." [*Simmons v. U.S.*]

Cont. Anal.

Yes

The ID should be **excluded** from evidence because admission would violate D's 14th Am. **due process** rights.

No

[12] A **"showup"** (D is presented alone to W for ID) is **more likely** to be found unnecessarily suggestive than is a **"lineup"** (D and others are simultaneously presented, and W tries to pick out the perpertrator from the group). [6]

Cont. Anal.

IV.
Due Process and the Ban on Suggestive ID's

The ID does not violate D's due process rights, and may therefore be **introduced** against him.

Cont. Anal.

[13] A **photo array** (W is shown a batch of photos, one of which is of D) is the technique **least likely** to be found unnecessarily suggestive. [7]

Cont. Anal.

[14] Use the **"totality of the circumstances"** test to judge the likelihood of a mistaken ID. Thus, the longer W had to see the perpetrator during the crime (and the better the lighting), the less likely any given ID procedure is to be found to pose an unacceptable risk of misidentification.

See footnotes on p. 4 of chart.

Notes (p. 1) to
Figure 4 (Lineups and Other Pre-Trial ID Procedures)

[1] See *Schmerber v. Cal.* (compelling D to submit to blood test does not violate his Fifth Amendment right against self-incrimation, because the amendment protects only against compelled "testimonial" evidence.)

[2] In other words, even if D is a "suspect" (the police have focused on him as a possible or likely perpetrator), D has no right to have counsel present at ID procedures, unless formal criminal proceedings, such as an indictment or arraignment, have already been commenced against him.

If D has been arrested under an arrest warrant, answer "yes" (i.e., this counts as "formal criminal proceedings.") But if D has been arrested without a warrant, you should probably answer "no" (though the Supreme Court has never definitively decided that this is the correct answer.)

[3] In other words, there's no right to counsel if D was not present at the identification. Example: D is indicted for murdering V, and counsel is appointed for him. After this indictment, in an attempt to prepare for trial, the police visit a person, W, who claims to have seen a strange man near V's house the night of the murder. D's appointed lawyer asks to be present at this visit, but the police refuse. The police show W a book of 40 photos, one of which is a photo of D. W picks out D's photo as the person she saw that night.

This identification will be admissible against D at his murder trial, notwithstanding the absence of D's lawyer -- there is no right to have counsel present at a photo array.

[4] Example: D is arrested (for rape) under an arrest warrant, and is brought to the stationhouse. He is put into a lineup with 4 other men of similar complexion and build, and the victim, V, views the lineup from behind a one-way glass. D is not offered the chance to have a lawyer present (nor does he ask for one). V identifies D as being the man who raped her.

The fact that V made this identification will not be admissible against D at his trial, because: (1) D's arrest under a warrant constituted the commencement of formal criminal proceedings against him; and (2) that commencement triggered his Sixth Amendment right to have counsel present to supervise the identification procedures.

[5] Example: Same basic facts as prior example. Now, assume that the prosecution does not want to introduce into evidence the fact that V identified D at the police-station lineup. The prosecution does, however, want to call V to the stand, and ask V whether she now recognizes D as the person who raped her.

Unless the prosecution puts on "clear and convincing evidence" that the uncounselled ID procedure did not "taint" the later in-court ID, the in-court ID must also be excluded. (Anything that makes the court believe that the earlier ID was of questionable accuracy -- e.g., V's prior identification of someone else as the perpetrator -- will negate the admissibility of the in-court ID.)

[6] An important factor in determining how suggestive a lineup is is the degree of similarity between D and the other people in the lineup. Example: D is a black 6-footer. Everyone else in the lineup is white or Asian, and is less than 6 feet tall. The police know from previously speaking to V that the perp. is a 6-foot black male. The fact that D is the only person in the lineup who comes even close to matching V's description will go a long way towards making the lineup "unnecessarily suggestive."

On the other hand, if everyone in the lineup was black and about 6 feet tall, the lineup would probably be found not to have been unnecessarily suggestive (assuming that the police didn't "steer" V to D, as by saying, "Look closely at number 3.")

[7] Again, as in the prior note, if there are a number of other photos in the array that are somewhat similar to D's photo, this will cut in favor of a finding that the array was not unnecessarily suggestive.

Figure 5
The Exclusionary Rule

This chart will help you determine whether a particular piece of evidence may be admitted against D. D is the defendant in a criminal case (and is not necessarily the one whose constitutional rights were violated when the government obtained the evidence). The chart applies both to evidence that was itself directly obtained in violation of a constitutional guarantee, and to evidence that merely derives indirectly from a constitutional violation.

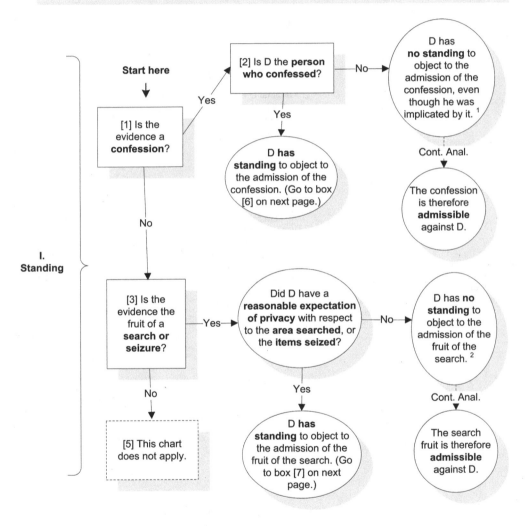

See footnotes after p. 5 of chart.

Figure 5 (cont.)
The Exclusionary Rule (p. 2)

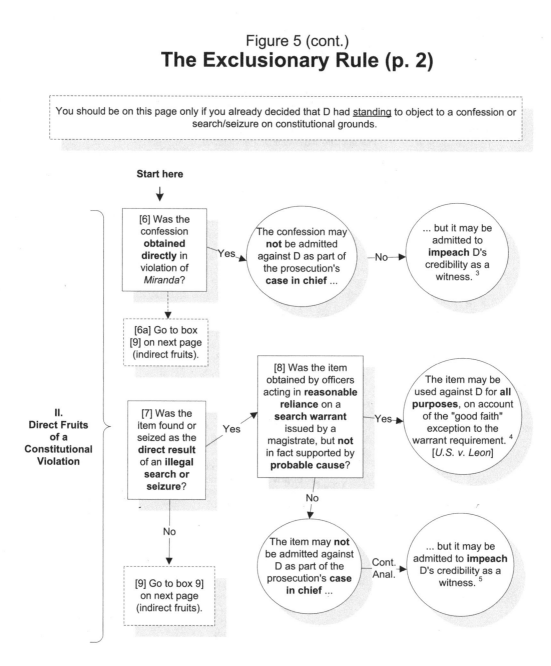

You should be on this page only if you already decided that D had <u>standing</u> to object to a confession or search/seizure on constitutional grounds.

Start here

[6] Was the confession **obtained directly** in violation of *Miranda*?

Yes → The confession may **not** be admitted against D as part of the prosecution's **case in chief** ...

—No→ ... but it may be admitted to **impeach** D's credibility as a witness. [3]

[6a] Go to box **[9]** on next page (indirect fruits).

II. Direct Fruits of a Constitutional Violation

[7] Was the item found or seized as the **direct result** of an **illegal search or seizure**?

Yes → **[8]** Was the item obtained by officers acting in **reasonable reliance** on a **search warrant** issued by a magistrate, but **not** in fact supported by **probable cause**?

Yes → The item may be used against D for **all purposes**, on account of the "good faith" exception to the warrant requirement. [4] [*U.S. v. Leon*]

No ↓

The item may **not** be admitted against D as part of the prosecution's **case in chief** ...

Cont. Anal. → ... but it may be admitted to **impeach** D's credibility as a witness. [5]

No ↓

[9] Go to box 9 on next page (indirect fruits).

See footnotes after p. 5 of chart.

Figure 5 (cont.)
The Exclusionary Rule (p. 3)

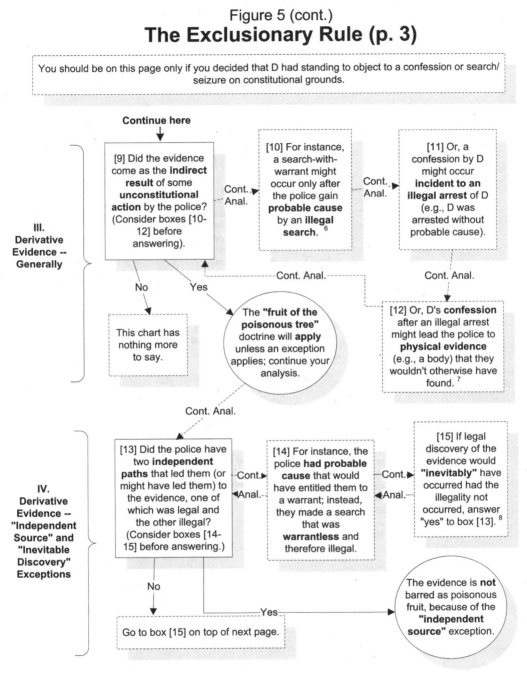

You should be on this page only if you decided that D had standing to object to a confession or search/seizure on constitutional grounds.

Continue here

III. Derivative Evidence -- Generally

[9] Did the evidence come as the **indirect result** of some **unconstitutional action** by the police? (Consider boxes [10-12] before answering).

Cont. Anal.

[10] For instance, a search-with-warrant might occur only after the police gain **probable cause** by an **illegal search**. [6]

Cont. Anal.

[11] Or, a confession by D might occur **incident to an illegal arrest** of D (e.g., D was arrested without probable cause).

No → This chart has nothing more to say.

Yes

Cont. Anal.

The **"fruit of the poisonous tree"** doctrine will **apply** unless an exception applies; continue your analysis.

Cont. Anal.

[12] Or, D's **confession** after an illegal arrest might lead the police to **physical evidence** (e.g., a body) that they wouldn't otherwise have found. [7]

Cont. Anal.

IV. Derivative Evidence -- "Independent Source" and "Inevitable Discovery" Exceptions

[13] Did the police have two **independent paths** that led them (or might have led them) to the evidence, one of which was legal and the other illegal? (Consider boxes [14-15] before answering.)

Cont. Anal.

[14] For instance, the police **had probable cause** that would have entitled them to a warrant; instead, they made a search that was **warrantless** and therefore illegal.

Cont. Anal.

[15] If legal discovery of the evidence would **"inevitably"** have occurred had the illegality not occurred, answer "yes" to box [13]. [8]

No → Go to box [15] on top of next page.

Yes → The evidence is **not** barred as poisonous fruit, because of the **"independent source"** exception.

See footnotes after p. 5 of chart.

Figure 5 (cont.)
The Exclusionary Rule (p. 4)

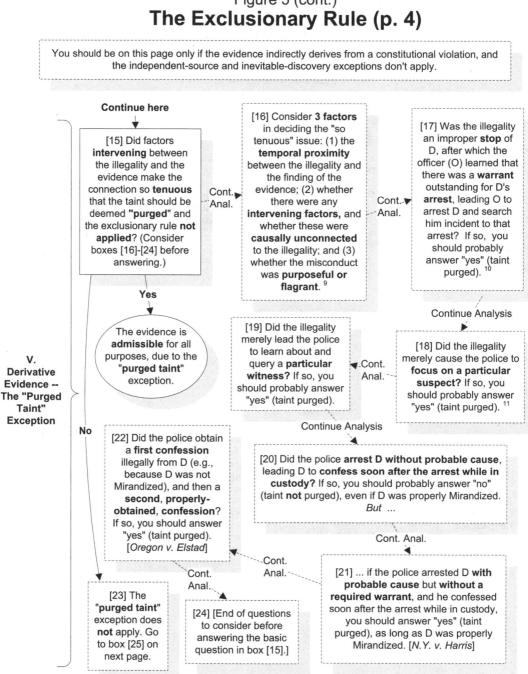

You should be on this page only if the evidence indirectly derives from a constitutional violation, and the independent-source and inevitable-discovery exceptions don't apply.

Continue here

[15] Did factors **intervening** between the illegality and the evidence make the connection so **tenuous** that the taint should be deemed **"purged"** and the exclusionary rule **not applied**? (Consider boxes [16]-[24] before answering.)

[16] Consider **3 factors** in deciding the "so tenuous" issue: (1) the **temporal proximity** between the illegality and the finding of the evidence; (2) whether there were any **intervening factors,** and whether these were **causally unconnected** to the illegality; and (3) whether the misconduct was **purposeful or flagrant**. [9]

[17] Was the illegality an improper **stop** of D, after which the officer (O) learned that there was a **warrant** outstanding for D's **arrest**, leading O to arrest D and search him incident to that arrest? If so, you should probably answer "yes" (taint purged). [10]

Cont. Anal.

Cont. Anal.

Yes

The evidence is **admissible** for all purposes, due to the **"purged taint"** exception.

[19] Did the illegality merely lead the police to learn about and query a **particular witness?** If so, you should probably answer "yes" (taint purged).

Continue Analysis

[18] Did the illegality merely cause the police to **focus on a particular suspect?** If so, you should probably answer "yes" (taint purged). [11]

Cont. Anal.

V. Derivative Evidence -- The "Purged Taint" Exception

No

[22] Did the police obtain a **first confession** illegally from D (e.g., because D was not Mirandized), and then a **second, properly-obtained, confession**? If so, you should answer "yes" (taint purged). [*Oregon v. Elstad*]

Continue Analysis

[20] Did the police **arrest D without probable cause**, leading D to **confess soon after the arrest while in custody?** If so, you should probably answer "no" (taint **not** purged), even if D was properly Mirandized. *But* ...

Cont. Anal.

Cont. Anal.

Cont. Anal.

[23] The **"purged taint"** exception does **not** apply. Go to box [25] on next page.

[24] [End of questions to consider before answering the basic question in box [15].]

[21] ... if the police arrested D with **probable cause** but **without a required warrant**, and he confessed soon after the arrest while in custody, you should answer "yes" (taint purged), as long as D was properly Mirandized. [*N.Y. v. Harris*]

See footnotes after p. 5 of chart.

Figure 5 (cont.)
The Exclusionary Rule (p. 5)

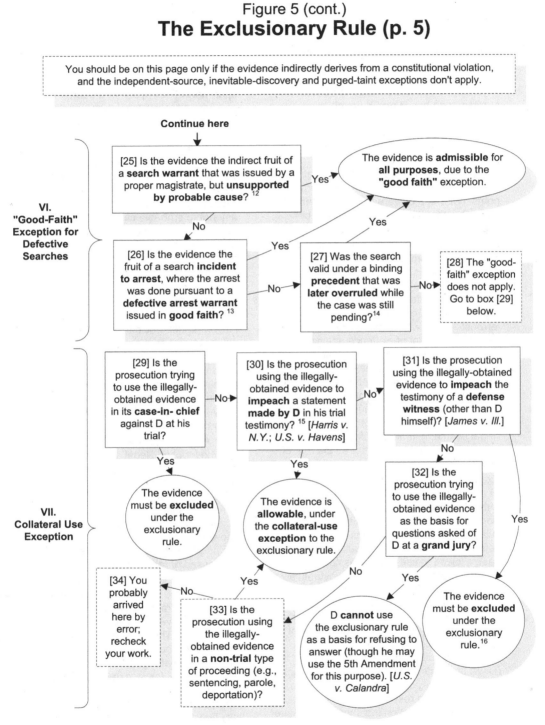

You should be on this page only if the evidence indirectly derives from a constitutional violation, and the independent-source, inevitable-discovery and purged-taint exceptions don't apply.

Continue here

VI. "Good-Faith" Exception for Defective Searches

[25] Is the evidence the indirect fruit of a **search warrant** that was issued by a proper magistrate, but **unsupported by probable cause**? [12]

— Yes → The evidence is **admissible** for **all purposes**, due to the **"good faith"** exception.

No

[26] Is the evidence the fruit of a search **incident to arrest**, where the arrest was done pursuant to a **defective arrest warrant** issued in **good faith**? [13]

— Yes →

No →

[27] Was the search valid under a binding **precedent** that was **later overruled** while the case was still pending? [14]

— Yes →

— No → [28] The "good-faith" exception does not apply. Go to box [29] below.

VII. Collateral Use Exception

[29] Is the prosecution trying to use the illegally-obtained evidence in its **case-in-chief** against D at his trial?

— No → [30] Is the prosecution using the illegally-obtained evidence to **impeach** a statement **made by D** in his trial testimony? [15] [*Harris v. N.Y.*; *U.S. v. Havens*]

— No → [31] Is the prosecution using the illegally-obtained evidence to **impeach** the testimony of a **defense witness** (other than D himself)? [*James v. Ill.*]

Yes → The evidence must be **excluded** under the exclusionary rule.

Yes → The evidence is **allowable**, under the **collateral-use exception** to the exclusionary rule.

No → [32] Is the prosecution trying to use the illegally-obtained evidence as the basis for questions asked of D at a **grand jury**?

Yes → The evidence must be **excluded** under the exclusionary rule. [16]

No → D **cannot** use the exclusionary rule as a basis for refusing to answer (though he may use the 5th Amendment for this purpose). [*U.S. v. Calandra*]

Yes →

[33] Is the prosecution using the illegally-obtained evidence in a **non-trial** type of proceeding (e.g., sentencing, parole, deportation)?

— No → [34] You probably arrived here by error; recheck your work.

Yes →

See footnotes starting on next page.

Notes (p. 1) to
Figure 5 (The Exclusionary Rule)

[1] Example: X is arrested by the policy on burglary charges. The police incorrectly fail to give X *Miranda* warnings. He confesses, and says that he and D conspired to perform the burglary together. D and X are charged together with burglary. The prosecution seeks to introduce X's confession to prove the substantive guilt of both X and D. D will not have standing to argue that the confession should be excluded as against him; that's because it's only X's *Miranda* rights, not D's, that were violated. So only X can argue that the confession should be suppressed as against him.

[2] Example: D writes a letter to his friend X, saying "Let's bomb the Empire State Building together." The police, acting without probable cause, break into X's apartment and search it. They find the letter, and arrest both D and X on charges of conspiracy to commit terrorist acts. D will not have standing to keep the letter out of evidence against him. That's because he had no reasonable expectation of privacy in the letter's contents, since once he sent the letter to X he ran the major risk that the letter's contents would be exposed to others. Consequently, D's Fourth Amendment rights were not violated by the illegal search, and he therefore has no standing to object to the letter as the fruit of that search.

[3] Example: D is arrested on murder charges. At the station house, he makes a confession without having first received *Miranda* warnings (which he was entitled to). At trial, D takes the stand and asserts an alibi defense. The prosecution would not have been allowed to use the confession as part of its case in chief (i.e., to prove, substantively, that D committed the murder). But now that D has taken the stand and given his alibi, the prosecution may read the confession to the jury, and ask D, "Isn't it true that instead of telling the police the alibi defense that you just told us, you instead told them you did it?" (D will be entitled to have the judge instruct the jury that they should consider this question and D's response only on the issue of D's credibility, not on the substantive issue of D's guilt.)

[4] Example: The police get an anonymous tip that D is selling illegal drugs out of his apartment. They apply for a search warrant, and correctly state what they know and how they know it. The magistrate issues a warrant. The police execute the warrant, and find drugs at the apartment. At a pre-trial hearing, D persuades the judge that the warrant should not have been issued, because the information held by the police when they applied for the warrant did not amount to probable cause. Nonetheless, the fruits of the search (the drugs) will be admissible against D, because the police acted in reasonable reliance on a warrant issued by one who had authority to do so. [*U.S. v. Leon.*]

[5] Example: The police, acting on an anonymous tip that D is dealing drugs out of his apartment, decide not to bother seeking a warrant because they don't like the paperwork. Instead, they break into D's apartment while he's at work. (Assume, as seems likely, that no exception to the general requirement of a search warrant applies.) They find drugs, and charge D with illegal possession.

At the trial, D takes the stand and says, "I've never used illegal drugs or ever had them in my possession." The prosecution will be permitted to put the searching officer on the stand to testify that he found the drugs during the search -- this testimony will be admitted not for the substantive purpose of showing that D committed the crime, but for the purpose of showing that D's "I never possessed drugs" testimony is a lie.

[6] Example: Same basic facts as prior Example (i.e., the police break into D's apartment without a warrant). Assume that the police also didn't have probable cause at the time of the break-in. They find drugs, and immediately leave the premises without disturbing anything. (D is at work at the time). They then ask for, and get, a warrant, based in part on their ability to describe that they have seen drugs in D's premises (they don't say how they got this view of the drugs).

Notes continue on next page.

Notes (p. 2) to
Figure 5 (The Exclusionary Rule)

They then conduct the "legal" search, and seize the drugs.

On these facts, you'd answer "yes" to box [9] -- the only reason the police got the probable cause was by the earlier illegality, so the evidence has been obtained as the indirect result of unconstitutional police action. (Therefore, if no exception to the exclusionary rules applies, the evidence will be inadmissible, because it's "fruit of the poisonous tree" [the initial warrantless search]).

[7] Example: Acting on a hunch (not probable cause), police arrest D for the murder of V, whose body has never been found. Immediately following the arrest, under questioning, D discloses that the body is buried under a particular tree under X's apple orchard. Police find the body as described. They charge D with the murder, and want to admit the body -- and the fact that D told them where the body was -- against him. On these facts, you'd answer "yes" to box [9] -- without the illegal arrest, police would probably never have gotten the confession, and the location of the body, so the body is the indirect result of the illegal arrest.

The same result would follow if the police had probable cause to arrest D, but failed to Mirandize him after the arrest -- again, the location of the body would stem from a constitutional violation (lack of *Miranda* warnings.)

[8] Example: Same basic facts as above example. Now, however, assume that the police have probable cause to believe that D murdered V, whose body hasn't been found. They break into D's house to arrest him without a warrant, even though an arrest warrant is required in such circumstances. They also fail to give him *Miranda* warnings. D confesses, and says that the body is buried beneath D's own basement. When police look in the basement, they see evidence of fresh cement in one portion. They excavate, and find the body. The prosecution then seeks to introduce the body -- and the fact that D told them where it was

-- against D in his murder trial.

The prosecution would probably be able to convince the judge that even without the illegal police behavior, the police would "inevitably" have discovered the body eventually. They can point out that they already had probable cause to arrest D. After they had legally arrested him, then even if they hadn't gotten a confession they would "inevitably" had searched the basement, and would have seen the fresh cement. Therefore, they can persuasively argue, they would inevitably have found the body.

[9] The 3 factors originated in *Brown v. Illinois*, and were then applied in *Utah v. Strieff* (2016). Here's how they work:

(1) For "temporal proximity," the longer the time between the illegal act and the gathering of the evidence (which is the possibly "tainted fruit"), the more likely the court is to find that the taint was purged. The elapsing of "substantial time" will cut in favor of purging, but a delay of "only minutes" will not. (Example: Officer (O) makes a stop of D that is illegal because O does not have reasonable objective grounds to believe D may be engaged in wrongdoing (though O has a good-faith but incorrect belief that he *does* have such grounds). O demands to see D's ID, radios D's name back to a dispatcher, and is told that there is an old arrest warrant outstanding for D. O arrests D on the warrant, searches him incident to that arrest, and finds narcotics on D's person. Because only a few minutes passed between the illegal stop and the arrest-and-search, the "temporal proximity" factor cuts against a finding that the taint of the illegal stop was purged.)

(2) For "intervening circumstances," if there are no significant events that intervene between the illegality and the finding of the evidence, this factor cuts against a finding that the taint was purged. But if there *are* significant intervening events -- and especially if these events are causally independent of the illegality -- that cuts in favor of the taint's being purged. (Example:

Notes (p. 3) to
Figure 5 (The Exclusionary Rule)

Same facts as above Example. O's discovery of the outstanding warrant for D's arrest was a significant intervening event; also, that event was completely independent of the illegal stop -- the arrest warrant would have existed even if D had not been stopped -- so this factor cuts strongly in favor of a finding that the taint of the illegal stop was purged.)

(3) For "purposefulness or flagrancy" of the "official misconduct," if the purpose of the police illegality was to find evidence of wrongdoing, this factor cuts against a finding that the taint was purged. Similarly, if the police *knew* their conduct was illegal -- and especially if the illegality was part of a pattern of "systemic or recurrent" police misconduct (as opposed to an "isolated instance of negligence" that occurred in connection with an otherwise-proper investigation) -- this makes the misconduct "flagrant," cutting against a finding that the taint was purged. (Example: Same facts as above 2 Examples. Since O honestly believed that he had grounds for a valid stop, and since there's no evidence that D made the stop as part of a systemic pattern of carrying out knowingly-wrongful stops in the hopes that there would turn out to be an outstanding arrest warrant that would purge the taint, this factor cuts strongly in favor of a finding that the taint of the illegal stop was purged).

See *Utah v. Strieff*, on which the above 3 Examples are based, and in which the Court held that since 2 of the 3 factors supported a finding of taint-purging (especially the all-important "purposefulness or flagrancy" factor), the discovery of the outstanding arrest warrant *was* sufficient to purge the taint from the illegal stop, causing the evidence found in the search incident to D's arrest to be admissible against him.

[10] See the facts of the 3 Examples in the prior footnote, based on *Utah v. Strieff*, for an illustration of the Court's handling of a scenario like the one in this box: the officer makes an illegal stop, discovers an outstanding arrest warrant, and makes the arrest (and then makes a search incident to it, which turns up evidence). The *Strieff* Court found that the discovery of the arrest warrant purged the taint of the illegal stop; so on similar facts you should answer "yes" (taint purged) to the question in box [15].

[11] Example: In seeking to solve the murder of V, the police regard D as one among several plausible suspects. There is evidence that D and V knew each other, but no evidence that they were ever together alone. Acting without probable cause and without a warrant, the police break into D's apartment. There, they find a ring that they recognize as having belonged to V. Realizing that this ring makes D a better suspect than before, they close up D's apartment without disturbing anything. They then question D intensively (while not violating his rights in any way). D eventually confesses.

The police's exclusive focus on D came about because of the illegal search. But given the fact that the police were suspicious of D anyway, the causal link between the illegal search and the confession would probably be found to be so tenuous that the exclusionary rule wouldn't apply. That is, the interrogation and the confession would be found to be intervening events that sufficed to "purge the taint" of the illegal search.

[12] To qualify for the "good faith" exception, it must be the case that the law enforcement officer who applied for the warrant acted in good faith when she did so – if the applicant furnished information that she knew to be false, or recklessly disregarded the truth or falsity of the information she supplied, the good-faith exception won't apply. [*U.S. v. Leon*]

[13] As long as the arresting officer reasonably believed that there was a valid arrest warrant for the defendant, it doesn't matter that the warrant wasn't really outstanding. And that's true whether the error was by the judiciary or by the police department. However, this variant of the "good faith" exception to the warrant requirement applies only where any police misconduct consisted of "nonrecurring and attenuated" negligence. [*Herring v. U.S.*]

Figure 6
The Right to Counsel

This chart will help you identify: (1) whether D has a right to counsel (appointed or private) at a particular stage of the proceedings; (2) whether D validly waived that right; and (3) what that right entitled D to under the circumstances. We focus on the **Sixth Amendment** right, but occasionally mention the Fifth Amendment privilege against self-incrimination when it intersects with a right to have counsel present. The focus of this chart is on indigents' right to **appointed** counsel, but most of the chart applies the same way to the rights of one who hires **private** counsel.

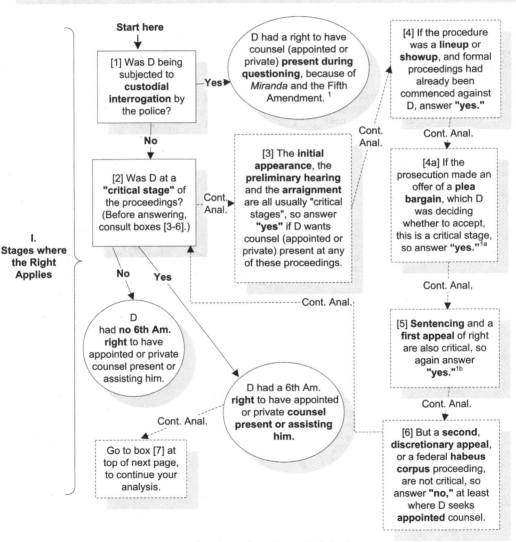

I. Stages where the Right Applies

Start here

[1] Was D being subjected to **custodial interrogation** by the police? —**Yes**▶ D had a right to have counsel (appointed or private) **present during questioning**, because of *Miranda* and the Fifth Amendment. [1]

No

[2] Was D at a **"critical stage"** of the proceedings? (Before answering, consult boxes [3-6].)

[3] The **initial appearance**, the **preliminary hearing** and the **arrangment** are all usually "critical stages", so answer **"yes"** if D wants counsel (appointed or private) present at any of these proceedings.

No   **Yes**

D had **no 6th Am. right** to have appointed or private counsel present or assisting him.

D had a 6th Am. **right** to have appointed or private **counsel present or assisting him.**

Cont. Anal.

Go to box [7] at top of next page, to continue your analysis.

[4] If the procedure was a **lineup** or **showup**, and formal proceedings had already been commenced against D, answer **"yes."**

Cont. Anal.

[4a] If the prosecution made an offer of a **plea bargain**, which D was deciding whether to accept, this is a critical stage, so answer **"yes."**[1a]

Cont. Anal.

[5] **Sentencing** and a **first appeal** of right are also critical, so again answer **"yes."**[1b]

Cont. Anal.

[6] But a **second, discretionary appeal**, or a federal **habeus corpus** proceeding, are not critical, so answer **"no,"** at least where D seeks **appointed** counsel.

See footnotes after p. 3 of chart.

Figure 6 (cont.)
The Right to Counsel (p. 2)

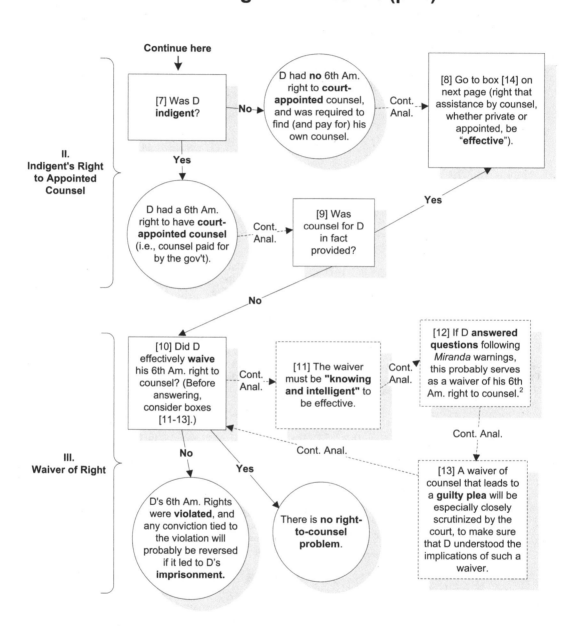

See footnotes after p. 3 of chart.

Figure 6 (cont.)
The Right to Counsel (p. 3)

You should be on this page only if you concluded that: (1) D was **entitled** to counsel (appointed or private); (2) D did **not waive** his right to that counsel and (3) D actually **received some representation** (i.e., assistance) by counsel. This page will help you determine whether the assistance given to D was "**effective**," as the Sixth Amendment requires. Generally, the same standards for "effectiveness" apply whether counsel is appointed or private; but see box [21] for an exception.

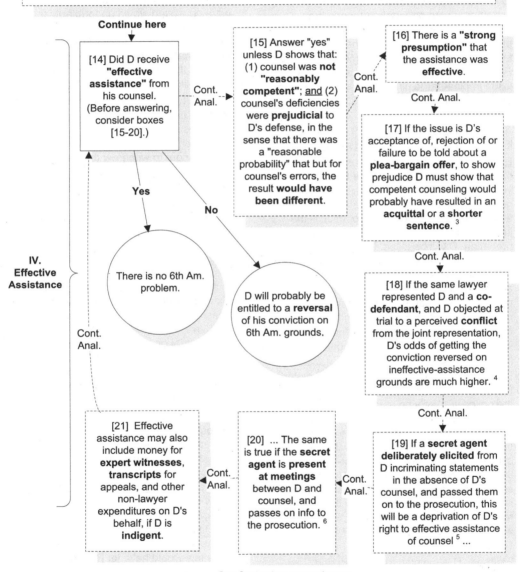

Continue here

[14] Did D receive **"effective assistance"** from his counsel. (Before answering, consider boxes [15-20].)

Cont. Anal.

[15] Answer "yes" unless D shows that: (1) counsel was **not "reasonably competent"**; <u>and</u> (2) counsel's deficiencies were **prejudicial** to D's defense, in the sense that there was a "reasonable probability" that but for counsel's errors, the result **would have been different**.

[16] There is a **"strong presumption"** that the assistance was **effective**.

Cont. Anal.

Cont. Anal.

[17] If the issue is D's acceptance of, rejection of or failure to be told about a **plea-bargain offer**, to show prejudice D must show that competent counseling would probably have resulted in an **acquittal** or a **shorter sentence**. [3]

Cont. Anal.

Yes

No

There is no 6th Am. problem.

D will probably be entitled to a **reversal** of his conviction on 6th Am. grounds.

IV. Effective Assistance

Cont. Anal.

[18] If the same lawyer represented D and a **co-defendant**, and D objected at trial to a perceived **conflict** from the joint representation, D's odds of getting the conviction reversed on ineffective-assistance grounds are much higher. [4]

Cont. Anal.

[21] Effective assistance may also include money for **expert witnesses**, **transcripts** for appeals, and other non-lawyer expenditures on D's behalf, if D is **indigent**.

Cont. Anal.

[20] ... The same is true if the **secret agent** is **present at meetings** between D and counsel, and passes on info to the prosecution. [6]

Cont. Anal.

[19] If a **secret agent deliberately elicited** from D incriminating statements in the absence of D's counsel, and passed them on to the prosecution, this will be a deprivation of D's right to effective assistance of counsel [5] ...

See footnotes on next page.

Notes (p. 1) to
Figure 6 (The Right to Appointed Counsel)

[1] The *Miranda* rights are essentially based on the Fifth Amendment (the privilege against compulsory self-incrimination) rather than the Sixth Amendment (the right to counsel).

[1a] D is entitled to the assistance of counsel (whether private or appointed) once the prosecution makes an offer to enter into a plea bargain. That's true whether D ends up taking the offer or rejecting it. [*Missouri v. Frye*; *Cooper v. Lafler*.] The more serious issue in plea-bargaining cases is whether the assistance has been "effective"; see note 3 below.

[1b] There's a right to assistance of counsel even if the judge gives a suspended sentence.

Example: D, an indigent, is charged with misdemeanor theft, punishable by up to one year in prison. To save money, the state does not supply counsel. D is convicted, and given a suspended sentence and probation – the judge says that if D violates the terms of the probation, D will be jailed. Later, the state claims that D has violated his probation. The state can't remedy its original refusal to appoint counsel for D's trial/sentencing by now appointing counsel for D's probation-revocation hearing. So D can't in fact be jailed for violating his probation, even though the judge originally told him that he could be. [*Alabama v. Shelton*]

[2] Even if D has already had counsel appointed for him, D's willingness to be interrogated by the police will likely be a valid waiver of his Fifth Am. right to counsel if he's been given *Miranda* warnings. And that's true even though D has not yet consulted with the counsel. That is, there's no bright-line rule (as there is in the Fifth Amendment *Miranda* context) that once a suspect asks for counsel, interrogation must be initiated by the suspect rather than by the police in order for the waiver of rights to be effective. [*Montejo v. Louisiana*]

Example: D is indicted for murder, and counsel is appointed for him. D is released on bail. The police show up at his house, give him *Miranda* warnings, ask him questions about the murder, but make it clear that D is free to ask them to leave at any time. D voluntarily answers, even though (as the police know) D hasn't yet consulted with his appointed counsel, who if she were consulted would undoubtedly tell D not to talk to the police. D's decision to talk will be a valid waiver of his 6th Am. right to have counsel present (assuming D made the decision to talk "knowingly and intelligently").

[3] This will typically be a hard showing for D to make in the plea-bargaining scenario. That's especially true where under state law either the prosecution would have had the right to withdraw the plea bargain once made (e.g., because of changed circumstances) or the judge would have had the right to reject the bargain. [*Missouri v. Frye*]

Example: D drives drunk, and is charged with a felony punishable by up to three years in prison. P, the prosecutor, tells L, D's lawyer, that P will reduce the charge to a misdemeanor (punishable at most six months in jail) if D pleads guilty. L doesn't promptly tell D about this offer. D gets arrested again for drunk driving. D goes to trial on the original felony charge, is sentenced to three years, and argues that his right to effective assistance was violated when L didn't promptly tell him about P's offer.

L's failure to tell D about the offer is almost certainly a denial of the right to counsel. But D isn't entitled to any relief (e.g., the right to receive just the originally-offered 6-month jail term) unless D can show prejudice. This requires D to show that: (1) D would have promptly accepted the offer if he had known about it; (2) the new arrest wouldn't have caused P to withdraw the offer (assuming state law would have let P do so); and (3) the judge wouldn't have rejected the plea bargain. Cf. *Missouri v. Frye*, *supra*.

Notes continue on next page.

Notes (p. 2) to
Figure 6 (The Right to Appointed Counsel)

[4] Example: D1 and D2 are charged with conspiring to murder, and in fact murdering, V, by shooting V to death with a single bullet. A single lawyer, L, is appointed by the court to represent both. At trial, D1 tells the judge that he thinks that the same lawyer cannot fairly represent both him and D2, but the judge refuses to appoint separate lawyers. At trial, D2 takes the stand and says, "I didn't plan to murder V or try to murder him or shoot him. However, I saw D1 shoot him." D1 never takes the stand, on L's advice. Both D1 and D2 are convicted.

On these facts, the conflict between D1's defense needs and D2's is so clear that D1 will be entitled to a new trial due to the lack of effective assistance of counsel.

[5] See the example in note 8 to Figure 2, *supra*.

[6] See the example in note 9 to Figure 2, *supra*.

CAPSULE SUMMARY

TABLE OF CONTENTS
OF CAPSULE SUMMARY

CAPSULE SUMMARY

CHAPTER 1

CONSTITUTIONAL CRIMINAL PROCEDURE GENERALLY

I. STATE PROCEDURES AND THE FEDERAL CONSTITUTION

A. Meaning of "criminal procedure": The term "criminal procedure" refers to the methods by which the criminal justice system functions. Here are some of the topics that are usually included within criminal procedure:

1. The *arresting* of suspects.

2. The *searching* of premises and persons.

3. The use of *electronic surveillance* and *secret agents*.

4. The *interrogation* of suspects, and the obtaining of *confessions*.

5. The use of *line-ups* and other pre-trial identification procedures.

6. The *Exclusionary Rule*, and how it affects the admissibility of evidence obtained through methods that violate the Constitution.

7. The right to *counsel*.

8. *Grand jury* proceedings.

9. *Bail* and preventive detention.

10. *Plea bargaining*.

11. The right to a *speedy trial*.

12. Pre-trial *discovery*.

13. The *Double Jeopardy* clause.

B. Focus on U.S. Constitution: Many aspects of criminal procedure are regulated by the U.S. Constitution, particularly the Bill of Rights (the first ten amendments). As discussed below, most federal constitutional provisions concerning criminal procedure are binding on state proceedings as well as federal ones.

1. **Non-constitutional issues:** The states are free to develop their own procedures for dealing with criminal prosecutions, as long as these do not violate the federal constitution.

C. Applicability of Bill of Rights to states: In deciding how the federal constitution applies to state criminal prosecutions, the Supreme Court follows the *"selective incor-*

poration" approach. Under this approach, not all rights enumerated in the Bill of Rights are applicable to the state, but if *any aspect of a right* is found to be so necessary to fundamental fairness that it applies to the states, then *all aspects* of that right apply. Thus if a right is applicable in state courts, its *scope* is the same as in federal courts.

1. **All but two rights applicable to states:** All Bill of Rights guarantees have been held applicable to the states, except for two. The two Bill of Rights guarantees that have *not* been found applicable to the states are:

   a. **Bail:** The Eighth Amendment's guarantee against *excessive bail* (so that apparently, a state may choose to offer bail, but may then set it in an "excessive" amount); and

   b. **Grand jury indictment:** The Fifth Amendment's right to a *grand jury* indictment (so that a state may decide to begin a prosecution by using an "information" prepared by the prosecutor rather than a grand jury indictment).

D. **Raising constitutional claims in federal court:** A defendant in a state criminal proceeding can of course raise in the proceeding itself the claim that his federal constitutional rights have been violated (e.g., by the use against him of a coerced confession or the fruits of an illegal search and seizure).

   1. **Federal habeas corpus:** But the state criminal defendant has in some situations a *second chance* to argue that the state trial has violated his federal constitutional rights: He may bring a *federal* action for a writ of *habeas corpus*. The defendant may bring a habeas corpus proceeding only after he has been convicted and has exhausted his state appellate remedies. The petition for habeas corpus is heard by a *federal district court judge*. If the judge finds that the conviction was obtained through a violation of the defendant's constitutional rights, he can order the defendant released (usually subject to a new trial).

      a. **Limits:** There are significant limits on the kinds of arguments a defendant can make in a federal habeas corpus proceeding. Here are two:

         i. **Search and seizure cases:** Iin search and seizure cases, if the state has given D the opportunity for a *"full and fair litigation"* for his Fourth Amendment claim (that is, the defendant got a fair chance to argue that evidence should not be introduced against him because it was the fruit of an illegal search or seizure), D may not make this argument in his *habeas corpus* petition, even if the federal court is convinced that the state court reached the wrong constitutional conclusion. [*Stone v. Powell*]

         ii. **Mistakes of law:** Under a 1996 federal statute, a federal court can't give *habeas* relief for a state-court mistake of law unless the state decision was either *"contrary to"* or an *"unreasonable application of"* some *"clearly established"* principle of federal law *as determined by the Supreme Court*.

         Example: Suppose the Supreme Court has never decided a particular issue of federal constitutional law. The state court decides that issue of law against D. A federal district court cannot give habeas relief even if the court believes (based on, say, federal Courts of Appeals decisions) that the state court erred on that issue of constitutional law.

II. STEPS IN A CRIMINAL PROCEEDING

1. Here is a brief summary of the steps in a criminal proceeding:

2. **Arrest:** When a police officer has probable cause to believe that a suspect has committed a crime, the officer makes an ***arrest***. An arrest may occur either with or without a warrant (most are made without a warrant). Arrest usually involves taking the suspect into custody and transporting him to the police station.

3. **Booking:** At the police station, the suspect undergoes ***"booking,"*** which includes entering information about him into a police blotter, and photographing and fingerprinting him.

4. **Filing complaint:** A prosecutor now decides whether there is enough evidence to file charges; if so, the prosecutor prepares a ***"complaint."***

5. **First appearance:** After the complaint has been filed, the suspect is brought before a ***magistrate***. In most states, this is called the ***"first appearance."*** Here, the magistrate informs D of the charges, notifies him that he has the right to counsel, and sets bail or releases D without bail.

6. **Preliminary hearing:** If the case is a felony case, a ***"preliminary hearing"*** is held. Again, this is in front of a magistrate, and usually involves live witnesses so the magistrate can determine whether there is probable cause to believe that D committed the crime charged.

7. **Filing of indictment or information:** In the federal system, or in a "grand jury" state, the next step is for a grand jury to hear the prosecutor's evidence and to issue an ***indictment***. In a non-grand-jury state, the prosecutor now prepares an ***"information,"*** reciting the charges.

8. **Arraignment:** After the indictment or information has been filed, D is ***"arraigned"***; that is, he is brought before the trial court and asked to plead innocent or guilty.

9. **Pre-trial motions:** Defense counsel now makes any pre-trial motions.

10. **Trial:** Next comes the ***trial***. If the charge is a felony, or a misdemeanor punishable by more than six months in prison, all states (and the federal system) give D the right to have the case tried before a ***jury***.

11. **Sentencing:** If D pleads guilty or is found guilty during the trial, he is then ***sentenced*** (usually by the judge, not the jury).

12. **Appeals:** A convicted defendant is then entitled to ***appeal*** (e.g., on the grounds that the evidence admitted against him at trial was the result of an unconstitutional search).

13. **Post-conviction remedies:** Both state and federal prisoners, even after direct appeal, may challenge their convictions through federal-court ***habeas corpus*** procedures.

CHAPTER 2

ARREST; PROBABLE CAUSE; SEARCH WARRANTS

I. GENERAL PRINCIPLES

A. Fourth Amendment: The Fourth Amendment to the U.S. Constitution provides, "The right of the people to be secure in their persons, houses, papers, and effects, *against unreasonable searches and seizures*, shall not be violated, and *no Warrants shall issue, but upon probable cause*, supported by Oath or affirmation, and *particularly describing* the place to be searched, and the persons or things to be seized."

B. Applies to both searches and arrests: The Fourth Amendment thus applies both to *searches and seizures* of *property*, and to *arrests* of persons.

   1. Invalid arrest no defense: Generally, the fact that D was *arrested in an unconstitutional manner* makes *no difference*: a defendant may generally be tried and convicted regardless of the fact that his arrest was made in violation of the Fourth Amendment. However, when evidence is seized as part of a *warrantless search* conducted *incident to an arrest*, the evidence will be excluded as inadmissible if the arrest was a violation of the Constitution (e.g., the arresting officer did not have probable cause to believe that D had committed a crime).

   2. Probable cause for issuance of warrant: Where a search or arrest warrant is issued, the Fourth Amendment requires that the warrant be issued only based on *"probable cause."* This requirement is quite strictly enforced.

   3. Where warrant required: A warrant is usually *required* before a *search or seizure* takes place, unless there are "exigent circumstances." An *arrest* warrant, by contrast, is usually *not* constitutionally required.

   4. Search must always be "reasonable":   Whether or not there is a search warrant or arrest warrant, the arrest or search *must not be "unreasonable."*

   5. Probable cause for warrantless search or arrest: But there is *no* requirement in the Fourth Amendment that a warrantless search or seizure take place only upon *probable cause*. This is why police may conduct a brief "stop and frisk" even without probable cause: They are making a Fourth Amendment "seizure," but merely need some reasonable suspicion, not probable cause. (See *Terry v. Ohio*, discussed below.)

II. THE "REASONABLE EXPECTATION OF PRIVACY"; THE INTERESTS THAT ARE PROTECTED BY THE FOURTH AMENDMENT

A. Two different ways to "search": There are *two different ways* in which government may be deemed to have carried out a Fourth Amendment search:

   [1] Physical intrusion: First, government will be deemed to have done a "search" of a defendant if government *physically intrudes* on the defendant's personal or real *property* (in an attempt to find something or to obtain information). This is a concept of searches as being a form of *trespass* on the defendant's property. [*U.S. v. Jones*]

[2] **Reasonable expectation of privacy:** Second, a search will be deemed to occur if the government infringes on the defendant's *"reasonable expectation of privacy"* (again, in an attempt to find something or to obtain information). [*Katz v. U.S.*]

We'll consider the second of these types first.

B. *Katz* **"expectation of privacy" doctrine:** Aside from the physical-intrusion scenario, a Fourth Amendment search or seizure only takes place when a person's *"reasonable expectation of privacy"* has been violated. [*Katz v. U.S.*]

1. Waiver of privacy right: Thus a person's conduct may mean that he has *no* reasonable expectation of privacy in a particular situation. If so, no Fourth Amendment search or seizure will result, even if the police are doing something that a non-lawyer would think of as being a "search" or "seizure."

> **Example:** D puts some papers into a public trash bin, unaware that the police are watching his conduct through binoculars. Because a person who disposes of trash normally does not have a "reasonable expectation of privacy" as to the trash, the police do not commit a Fourth Amendment search or seizure when they go through the trash bin's contents and remove the papers belonging to D (and use these in a subsequent prosecution of D).

More precisely, a person will be found to have had a "reasonable expectation of privacy" in some matter only if *two tests* are satisfied:

[1] The person exhibited an *"actual (subjective) expectation of privacy"* in the matter; and

[2] That expectation is *"one that society is prepared to recognize as 'reasonable.'"*

[*Katz v. U.S.*, concurrence by Harlan]

a. Contexts: Some types of evidence that are likely to be found *not protected* by any "reasonable expectation of privacy" are:

[1] *abandoned property*, such as *trash*;

[2] things that can be seen from the perspective of a person *stationed on public property* (e.g., a police officer stands on a sidewalk and looks through binoculars into a window at the front of D's house);

[3] things a person says or does while *in public* (e.g., D1 talks to D2 in a restaurant, while a police officer is eavesdropping nearby); and

[4] information the police learn by use of *other senses* while the police are in a place they have a right to be (e.g., the police use dogs to *smell* odors coming from luggage in a public place and, thus, detect drugs).

C. Digital databases of personal information: Vast amounts of sensitive personal data about each American are compiled into huge *electronic databases* maintained by private companies. An individual who wishes to make use of modern technology – by talking on a cell phone, making online purchases, sending emails, etc. – has essentially no choice but to allow service providers to amass this sensitive information. If government then demands or requests this information from the service provider that has collected it, ***does the individual have a reasonable expectation of privacy as to the compiled data?***

1. **Tentative answer:** As of this writing (early 2020), we don't have a full understanding of how the Supreme Court would answer this question. But we *do* know that there is one type of personal data as to which a person definitely *does* have a reasonable expectation of privacy:

    Seven days' or more worth of ***"CSLI,"*** or ***"cell site location information."***

2. **What CSLI is:** CSLI specifies, for any particular cell phone at a particular time, ***the precise location of the phone, and thus of the person carrying the phone.*** CSLI is maintained by the wireless carrier from whom the person receives cell phone service. [*Carpenter v. U.S.* (2018), discussed *infra*, 64.]

    a. **Significance:** The significance of the fact that a person has a reasonable expectation of privacy with respect to seven days or more of her CSLI is that if government demands that the cell carrier turn over the person's CSLI, government is ***performing a search*** for Fourth Amendment purposes.

    b. **Rationale:** Here's the reasoning by which the Court in *Carpenter*, *supra*, concluded that a person has a reasonable expectation of privacy in seven days' or more worth of her own CSLI:

        [1] Before the rise of high-tech location-tracking methods (i.e., before about 1990), a person (call her X) did not have a reasonable expectation of privacy with respect to her ***physical movements in public over a short time period***, since any member of the public (or the police) could follow X by car or on foot.

        [2] But high-tech location-tracking methods such as CSLI are ***far more intrusive*** than traditional location-tracking by a human. Cell phone tracking via CLSI is vastly ***easier, cheaper, and more efficient*** than the traditional tracking method. CSLI lets the police track a person's movements with great precision, over long periods of time, with much less effort than traditional tracking. Also, the technology can track a person's movements ***inside a home*** or other structure, which traditional tracking cannot do.

        [3] The ***"time-stamped" data*** furnished by CSLI is ***highly revealing***; it "provides an ***intimate window into a person***'s life, revealing not only his particular movements, but through them his '***familial, political, professional, religious, and sexual associations***.'" [*Carpenter*]

        [4] Furthermore, CSLI gives government access to ***historical information, unlike traditional tracking.*** With CSLI, the government "can now ***travel back in time*** to retrace a person's whereabouts, subject only to the retention polices of the wireless carriers[.]"

        [5] In sum, while an individual might not have a reasonable expectation that her public movements over a short period of time won't be tracked by tra-

ditional human-based methods, the individual *does* have a reasonable expectation that government will not do the sort of longer-term tracking — of *her every movement, both prospectively and retrospectively, over long periods of time* — that CSLI permits.

[6] Therefore, when government demands seven or more days' worth of CSLI data about a person from a carrier, government has *conducted a Fourth Amendment search* of that person's information.

[*Carpenter*]

D. The property-based "trespass" approach to searches: Apart from government intrusions that infringe on a person's reasonable expectation of privacy, a Fourth Amendment search can occur if government *physically intrudes* on a person's property, and does so for the purpose of finding evidence or other information. This is an *alternative* path by which a defendant can show that a Fourth Amendment search occurred — if there is a *physical intrusion by government on a person's property* coupled with an investigative purpose, a search has occurred *even if the individual had no reasonable expectation of privacy* as to the type of information the police end up learning.

> **Example 1:** The police have reason to suspect that D is engaged in cocaine trafficking. Without a valid warrant, they secretly put a GPS tracking device on the underside of a Jeep belonging to D, while the Jeep is in a public parking lot. For 28 days, the tracker sends the government constant wireless signals showing the vehicle's movements over public roads. When D is tried for narcotics trafficking, the government uses the locational evidence from the tracker to show that D visited the "stash house" where large amounts of cocaine were found. D claims that the placement and use of the tracker was a Fourth Amendment search.
>
> *Held* (by the Supreme Court) for D. The *mere conducting of a physical intrusion* by the government — the placing the GPS tracker underneath D's vehicle — was itself *enough* to constitute a Fourth Amendment search, *regardless* of whether D's reasonable expectation of privacy was ever violated. [These facts are a slight modification of the facts of *U.S. v. Jones*.]

> **Example 2:** Local police get an unverified tip (not constituting probable cause for a search or arrest) that marijuana is being grown in D's house. A "trained canine handler" who works for the police brings his trained drug-sniffing dog, Franky, onto D's front porch. Franky sniffs the base of the front door, and then indicates that narcotics are being stored inside the house. The police use this information to procure a search warrant for the inside of the house, do the search, and find marijuana. D argues that the dog-sniffing on the porch was an illegal Fourth Amendment search, making the ensuing search warrant invalid.
>
> *Held* (by the Supreme Court), for D. When the government obtains information by physically intruding into a person's "house," a Fourth Amendment search has occurred. A person's "house" for Fourth Amendment purposes includes the area immediately surrounding the physical structure (an area called the "curtilage"; see Par. (D) below), which in this case included the porch. When D hung a front-door knocker, he implicitly gave consent to anyone (including the police) to come on the porch, knock, and wait briefly for a response. But bringing a trained

dog onto the porch to try to find incriminating evidence went beyond the scope of this implied consent. Therefore, the dog's sniffing was a physical intrusion into the curtilage portion of D's "house," making the sniffing a Fourth Amendment search whether or not the entry and sniffing violated any *legitimate expectation of privacy* on D's part. [*Florida v. Jardines*]

E. Curtilage: For purposes of the "physical intrusion" test (as well as apparently for the "reasonable expectation of privacy" test), the police normally commit a search if they enter or investigate a person's "house." But a person's "house" does *not include* all of a person's residential real estate, merely the actual house and what the Supreme Court calls the house's *"curtilage."* The curtilage is *"the area 'immediately surrounding and associated with the home'."* [*Florida v. Jardines*]

    1. Four factors: Four factors should be looked to in determining whether a structure or area is or isn't within the "curtilage":

        [1] the *proximity* of the home to the area claimed to be curtilage (closer = curtilage);

        [2] whether the area is included within an *enclosure* that surrounds the home (enclosed = curtilage);

        [3] the nature of the *uses* (domestic vs. non-domestic) to which the area is put (domestic = curtilage); and

        [4] the *steps taken* by the resident to *protect* the area from *observation* by people passing it (more protective steps = curtilage).

    [*U.S. v. Dunn*]

        Example: D owns a 190-acre ranch, enclosed by an outer fence. D's farmhouse is surrounded by an interior fence that does not include any other structures. The issue is whether a barn, located about 60 yards from the farmhouse (and outside the interior fence surrounding the farmhouse), is within the farmhouse's curtilage.

        Held (by applying the above four factors), the barn was not within the curtilage. For instance, as to factor (3), the barn was not (as the police knew prior to the start of the episode) being used for any activities related to the home — the police had evidence that drugs were being manufactured in the barn. *U.S. v. Dunn, supra.*

      a. Open fields: *Open fields* on a farm or ranch (i.e., fields that are not close to the house, and/or are not within the same tight fencing that includes the house) are not part of the "curtilage," and are therefore *not protected by the Fourth Amendment*. [*Oliver v. U.S.*]

      b. Front porches and garages: By contrast, *Jardines* (*supra*, pp. 59-60) shows that the *front porch* of a house *is* within the curtilage. Similarly, a residential homeowner's *garage*, and her front and back yards (at least if they're enclosed by a fence), will normally be held to be within the curtilage.

      c. Driveway: A recent case, *Collins v. Virginia* (2018), holds that in the case of a *driveway* to a house, the portion of the driveway that *immediately abuts the house is* usually part of the curtilage.

Example: A police officer, Rhodes, suspects that a particular orange-and-black motorcycle has been stolen and is now in the possession of D at D's girlfriend's house. Rhodes drives to the street in front of the house to investigate. From there, Rhodes can see that at the top of the driveway, next to the house and partly visible from under a tarpaulin, there is a parked motorcycle. Now, having probable cause to believe that the partially-visible motorcycle is probably the stolen one, Rhodes walks up the driveway, lifts the tarp, and sees that the motorcycle resembles the stolen orange-and-black one. He uses his hands to examine the cycle, uncovers the vehicle's license plate and VIN, verifies by cell phone that these match the details of the stolen motorcycle, and replaces the tarp. Rhodes then goes to the front door of the house, where he eventually arrests D for receiving stolen property.

Held, when Rhodes went up to the motorcycle and touched it, he was standing in a portion of the driveway that was curtilage. That part was curtilage because it was an enclosure (walls on three sides), it was adjacent to the house, and it was next to an entrance to the house. Therefore, Rhodes was conducting a Fourth Amendment search of D's home, for which a search warrant was required. [*Collins v. Virginia*]

2. **Significance of curtilage:** In sum, the curtilage of a house is ***protected*** against warrantless searches by the police, even if the area is one as to which the homeowner might ***not otherwise have a reasonable expectation of privacy.***

   a. **Visibility to public is irrelevant:** If an area is curtilage, it receives this protection against warrantless searches even though a person standing in a public place (e.g., the street) can ***see into the curtilage.***

      Example: In *Collins*, *supra*, the portion of the driveway in which the motorcycle was parked was curtilage, even though Officer Rhodes (or any member of the public) could see part of the motorcycle from the street.

F. **Trash and other abandoned property:** ***Trash*** or other ***abandoned*** property will normally ***not*** be material as to which the owner has a reasonable expectation of privacy. Therefore, when a person puts trash out on the curb to be picked up by the garbage collector, the police may ***search that trash without a warrant***. [*California v. Greenwood*]

   1. **Trash on one's own property:** But if the owner puts his trash out for collection not on the public street or sidewalk but instead on a portion of his ***own property*** (and the trash collector comes onto the property to retrieve it), the police probably may not enter D's property to inspect the trash. (But they could wait until the collector collects the trash, and search it at the street.)

G. **Some special contexts:**

   1. **Jail cell:** A prisoner has no legitimate expectation of privacy in his ***prison cell***. Thus even if an inmate shows that a guard has without justification searched the inmate's personal possessions that are highly unlikely to relate to security issues, the inmate has not made out a Fourth Amendment claim. [*Hudson v. Palmer*]

2. **Guests:** *Guests* in a person's house may or may not have a legitimate expectation of privacy in the premises being visited.

    a. **Overnight social guest:** An ***overnight social guest*** normally ***has*** a legitimate expectation of privacy in the home where he is staying. Therefore, the police may normally not make a warrantless arrest or warrantless search of the premises where D is staying as an overnight guest. (But if the owner of the premises consents to a search, the guest is out of luck.) [*Minnesota v. Olson*]

    b. **Social guest not staying overnight:** A social guest who is ***not staying overnight*** probably ***also has*** a legitimate expectation of privacy in the premises, although the Supreme Court has not definitively decided this question yet.

    c. **Business guest:** A guest who is at the premises on ***business*** is ***less likely*** than a social guest to be found to have a legitimate expectation of privacy in the premises. Where the business visit is a relatively ***brief*** one, the court is especially likely to find that there is no legitimate privacy expectation.

    Example: D visits X's apartment for a couple of hours, for the purpose of bagging cocaine that D and X will later sell. The police snoop while the visit is going on. *Held*, the shortness of the visit and the business-rather-than-personal nature of what D did at the apartment meant that D had no legitimate expectation of privacy in the apartment. Therefore, D's Fourth Amendment rights couldn't have been violated, even if *X*'s rights were violated. [*Minnesota v. Carter*]

3. **Searches of passengers in, or non-owner drivers of, a vehicle:** Just as a social guest in another person's home may well have a legitimate expectation of privacy in that home (see *Minn. v. Olson, supra*), so a ***passenger*** in a ***vehicle***, or a ***driver who does not own the vehicle,*** will ordinarily have a reasonable expectation of privacy in the vehicle (and thus have standing to assert a Fourth Amendment violation) if the police stop the vehicle or search it.

    a. **Passengers:** A *passenger* in a vehicle that's stopped ("seized") and/or searched will generally have a reasonable expectation of privacy in the contents of the vehicle. That's true even if the passenger has ***no ownership or possessory interest*** in the vehicle — her mere ***presence*** in the vehicle at the time of the stop or search will generally be sufficient to give her a reasonable expectation of privacy in the vehicle. Consequently, if the stop or search occurs without probable cause (and no exception to the requirement of probable cause applies), the passenger will be able to assert that her Fourth Amendment rights have been violated.

    b. **Driver who is not owner:** Now, consider a person who is ***not the owner of a vehicle*** (call her D), but who is ***driving the vehicle*** at the time it is stopped by the police. Does D's lack of an ownership interest in the vehicle prevent her from having a reasonable expectation of privacy in the vehicle, so as to deprive her of standing to assert that the stop violated her Fourth Amendment rights?

        i. **Authorized use of vehicle:** If the driver D was ***authorized*** by the owner to drive the vehicle, the clear answer is ***"no."*** Just as a social guest in a home normally has a reasonable expectation of privacy with respect to the portion of the home where the owner has authorized the guest to be present (see, e.g., *Minnesota v. Olson, supra*, p. 62), so the authorized-driver D normally has such an expectation with respect to the car, and therefore has standing to raise the Fourth Amendment argument.

    ii.   **Unauthorized use – the rental car scenario:**   Now, let's assume the non-owner driver D is driving the vehicle *without authorization* by the owner. This scenario is most likely to arise when the vehicle is a *rental car*, and the rental agreement lists someone other than D as the sole person authorized to drive the vehicle. In this scenario, D's standing to assert the Fourth Amendment if the vehicle is improperly stopped is a closer question than in the authorized-use case above. But here, too, the Supreme Court has held that the fact that the rental agreement prohibits D from driving the vehicle will *not* normally deprive D from asserting that the stop violated his Fourth Amendment rights. [*Byrd v. U.S.* (2018)]

III. THE "THIRD-PARTY" DOCTRINE: VOLUNTARY DISCLOSURE TO OTHERS AS VOIDING THE EXPECTATION OF PRIVACY

A. Transfer to third person, generally: Under the so-called *"third-party doctrine,"* when an individual *voluntarily transfers information to a third party*, the transferor *enjoys no further Fourth Amendment protection* as to that information. Where the doctrine applies, government may *demand that the third party turn the information over,* even if government not only *lacks probable cause or a warrant,* but doesn't even have reasonable grounds for suspecting that the information may be relevant to a criminal investigation.

    Example: D, in his dealings with Bank (his own bank), gives Bank access to his checks, deposits, and financial statements. The federal government, acting without a warrant, subpoenas Bank's microfilm copies of these records, and uses the copies to prosecute D. D claims that the government's seizure of these records was a Fourth Amendment search, requiring probable cause and a search warrant.

    Held, for the government. D had no reasonable expectation of privacy with respect to these documents. "The depositor takes the risk, in revealing his affairs to another, that the information will be conveyed by that person to the government." [*U.S. v. Miller* (1976)]

B. Modern digital databases and the third-party doctrine (*Carpenter v. U.S.*): The key cases applying the third-party doctrine (including *Miller*, above) were decided in the 1970s, *before* the *rise of smart phones, the Internet,* and other technological advances that allow *non-governmental third-parties to amass huge amounts of potentially-intimate data about a person.*

    1.   **Consequence:** During the decades since the 1970s, it became clear that if the third-party doctrine was applied broadly so as to encompass all privately-operated databases fed by these emerging communications technologies, the Fourth

Amendment would be no barrier to a vast enlargement of government's surveillance powers.

2. ***Carpenter* changes the rules:**   The Supreme Court responded to this danger by dramatically weakening the scope of the third-party doctrine in a major case, ***Carpenter v. U.S.*** (2080). In *Carpenter*, a 5-4 decision, the Court decided that when private cell phone companies compile a digital database of *"cell-site location information" ("CSLI"),* the third-party doctrine should ***not*** apply.

   a. **Nature of CSLI:** CSLI refers to information — typically held by phone companies — showing the ***location of a person's cell phone*** from moment to moment.

   b. **Holding in *Carpenter*:** *Carpenter* held that because CSLI exposes far more private information than, say, the limited bank records in *Miller*, a person ***maintains a reasonable expectation of privacy*** in her own CSLI ***even though the information is held by a third party.*** (See *supra*, pp. 58-59.)

   c. **Consequence:** *Carpenter* means that when police officers request at least seven days' worth of a person's CSLI from a wireless carrier, the officers are ***conducting a Fourth Amendment search.*** This means that before the police may even request — let alone demand — this amount of CSLI from the carrier, the police must:

      [1] ***demonstrate*** to a judge or magistrate ***probable cause*** to believe that the information sought will reveal evidence of crime or contraband (i.e., the police must have probable cause for a search warrant); and

      [2] ***obtain the search warrant.***

   d. **Prior third-party case law not overruled:** *Carpenter* does not officially overturn the third-party doctrine as it existed prior to that case. However, it looks as though the doctrine will be confined to a ***small number*** of situations, those in which the third-party database does not consist of very revealing personal information.

      Example: Suppose the police want to demand, from the bank at which X has an account, images of all checks X wrote during a particular time period. The third-party doctrine will probably still apply (exactly as it did in the 1970s-era case of *Miller, supra*), because this type of data does not contain hugely intimate details. Therefore, the police will not need a search warrant (or probable cause to believe that the checks will contain evidence of wrongdoing).

C. ***Carpenter*'s application to non-CSLI databases:**   Beyond the ***direct*** consequences of *Carpenter* we've just discussed – which are limited to the treatment of government requests to phone carriers for CSLI data – the case probably also changes the constitutional analysis of government attempts to access *any* digital database containing large amounts of individuals' intimate data.

   1. **The *Carpenter* multi-factor test:** *Carpenter* indicates that the following are the most important factors in determining whether a particular database of an individual's personal information is one as to which the individual has a reasonable expectation of privacy:

[1] whether the information is *"deeply revealing"*;

[2] whether the information's *"reach"* is *"deep,"* *"broad,"* and *"comprehensive"*; and

[3] whether the *process* by which the information is collected is *"inescapable and automatic."*

2. **Electronic databases of non-location information:** The logic of *Carpenter* will probably require courts to change how they analyze collections of even third-party-maintained electronic business records that do *not* consist primarily of location information.

    a. **Credit card charges, movie rentals, and other intimate details:** Here are a few examples of non-location data that the police might want to request:

        [1] *credit card charges* by a particular card holder;

        [2] records of *numbers called from, or calls received by*, a given phone number;

        [3] information identifying each person with whom a given *email account* or *instant messaging app* communicated;

        [4] records of *search queries* made via a particular user ID, or from a particular computer or cell phone.

    b. **Analysis:** These collections of electronic records seem to share most of the same relevant traits as CSLI information. Thus the data is typically *"deeply revealing"* – it gives (to quote *Carpenter*) "an *intimate window into a person's life* … [including] his *familial, political, professional, religious, and sexual associations."* Similarly, the data is usually *"deep,"* in the sense of containing a lot of "detail and precision." The data will often have considerable *"breadth"*: it's generally collected at frequent intervals, and over a long period of time. Finally, it tends to be collected in an *"inescapable and automatic" way* – anyone who wants to buy something with a credit card, communicate by phone or email, or query an online database has no practical alternative but to use these tools, and to leave behind a detailed record of the transaction.

    c. **Conclusion:** Therefore, most modern-era digital databases that capture the details of individuals' electronically-recorded communications or transactions probably *should* be considered to be Fourth Amendment searches, for the same reasons that *Carpenter* articulated in connection with CSLI. Consequently, government will need both probable cause and a search warrant before requesting or subpoenaing the records from the third party that collected them.

3. **Does not apply to the contents of emails:** There's one final category of electronic data as to which the rationale of *Carpenter* might conceivably (but probably *doesn't*) apply. That data consists of the actual *contents* of a person's *emails or instant messages*, when maintained on a third party's computer (say, the server of an ISP who handled the message).

    a. **Analogy to a mailed letter:** Even before *Carpenter*, most of the federal cases to consider the issue held that a user who sends an email – even if she knows a copy is going to reside on some third-party computer system – should not be viewed as having thereby surrendered any expectation of privacy in the email's contents. That's because the Supreme Court has long held that the Fourth Amendment protects mailed *letters*, as well as sealed packages sent with postage, from being warrantlessly inspected by postal authorities. Since an email is analogous to a letter, the lower courts have held that government can't compel a third party (e.g., an ISP) to turn over the contents of an email either.

    b. *Carpenter* **doesn't change this:** Nothing in *Carpenter* should change this result. Emails are, if anything, more likely to be deeply revealing of intimate thoughts than is the CSLI data at issue in *Carpenter*. So the Supreme Court would likely hold that the rationale of *Carpenter* dictates that the third-party doctrine not be applied to the contents of emails, text messages, or other electronic communications.

IV. THE "PLAIN VIEW" DOCTRINE

A. The plain view doctrine, generally: In general, the police do not commit a Fourth Amendment search where they see an object that is in the *plain view* of an officer who has a *right to be in the position to have that view*. This is the "plain view doctrine."

    Example: While Officer is walking down the street, he happens to glance through the picture window of D's house. He spots D strangling V to death with a stocking. Because D's conduct took place in "plain view" of Officer — that is, Officer perceived the conduct while being in a place where he was entitled to be — Officer can give testimony at D's trial about what he saw, with no Fourth Amendment problem. By contrast, if Officer had without a warrant secreted himself in D's house, then observed the murder, Officer would not be permitted to testify about what he saw, because the view would not have occurred from a place from where Officer had a right to be.

    1. Distinguish from seizure: The fact that the police may have a plain view of an item does not mean that they may necessarily *seize* that item as evidence. Unless the officer is already legally in a place where he can touch the item, the fact that he sees it will not dispense with the need for a warrant to seize the item.

    Example: On the facts of the above example, the fact that Officer has seen D strangle V with a stocking does not automatically entitle Officer to enter D's house without a warrant and to seize the stocking.

B. Use of mechanical devices, generally: The "plain view" doctrine will often apply where the police stand on public property, and use *mechanical devices* to obtain the view of D or his property.

    1. Flashlights: Thus if a police officer, standing on public property, uses a *flashlight* to obtain a view of D or his property, this will nonetheless be a "plain view" and will, therefore, not be a Fourth Amendment search. [*Texas v. Brown*]

2. **Electronic "beeper":** Similarly, the Court held in 1983 that police may attach a simple electronic *"beeper"* on a vehicle, and use the beeper to follow the vehicle along public roads — because any member of the public could see the driver's public movements, the tracking by beeper does not violate the driver's reasonable expectation of privacy, and thus does not constitute a Fourth Amendment search. [*U.S. v. Knotts*]

   a. **More modern tracking technology:** But suppose the police in a post-*Carpenter* era — say in 2020 or later — use a modern-era *location-tracking device* such as a *"cell site simulator"*[1] that enables them to track, cheaply and easily, the movements of a cell phone over long periods of time. Such a device enables far *deeper and longer surveillance* than a police officer could perform by visual observation.

      i. **Consequence:** Therefore, it's likely that police use of the simulator device *will* be a Fourth Amendment search for which probable cause and a warrant are required. Thus the situation will need to be analyzed not by the easy-to-satisfy standard used to analyze the old-fashioned beeper in *Knotts* (no expectation of privacy because the person's movements are visible to any public observer), but by the "high-tech devices not in civilian use" standard applied in the "thermal imager" case of *Kyllo v. U.S.*, immediately *infra*, or even by use of the multi-factor test applied to CSLI in *Carpenter v. U.S.*, *supra*, p. 64.

C. **High-tech devices not in general public use:** If government obtains special *high-tech devices, not in general civilian use*, and employs them from public places to gain "views" that could *not* be had by the naked eye, the use of such devices will be *considered a search*. [*Kyllo v. U.S.*]

   Example: Drug agents think D is growing marijuana inside his house with the use of high-intensity heat lamps. They therefore obtain a "thermal imager" and point it at the outside of D's house from across the street. The device detects heat escaping from D's house, and shows the relative amounts of heat as black and white images. The images show that D's garage is much hotter than the rest of his house. The agents use this information to get a warrant to search D's house, and find marijuana being grown, as suspected, under lamps in his garage.

   Held, the use of the imager here was a Fourth Amendment search, which was presumptively unreasonable without a warrant. Since the device was not in general civilian use, and enabled the agents to learn information about what was going on inside the house, its use does not fall within the plain view exception. [*Kyllo v. U.S.*]

D. **Aerial observation:** When the police use an *aircraft* to view D's property from the air, *anything the police can see with the naked eye* falls within the "plain view" doc-

---

1. Such a simulator poses as a cell tower, and causes each cell phone in an area to transmit the phone's number and location to the simulator, where government can store and track the information.

trine (as long as the aircraft is in ***public, navigable*** airspace). [*California v. Ciraolo*; *Florida v. Riley*]

E. Use of other senses: Probably the same "plain view" rule applies to ***senses other than sight*** (e.g., touch, hearing, or smell).

1. Smell: For instance, if a police officer (or a dog being used by an officer) ***smells contraband*** while standing in a place where he has a right to be, no Fourth Amendment search has taken place.

> **Example:** While D's car is properly stopped for a routine traffic violation, a police officer escorts a trained dog to sniff around the exterior of the car to find narcotics. *Held*, the dog-sniffing was not a Fourth Amendment search or seizure, since the sniffing did not reveal (and could not have revealed) anything as to which the car's owner had a legitimate expectation of privacy. The sniff could only have revealed the presence of contraband, which no one has the right to possess, and as to which there is therefore no reasonable expectation of privacy. [*Illinois v. Caballes*]

2. Touch: Similarly, if an officer is conducting a legal pat-down of a suspect under the "stop and frisk" doctrine (see below), and touches something that feels like contraband, the officer may seize it under a ***"plain touch"*** analog to the plain view doctrine.

> **a. Police must have a right to touch:** But this "plain touch" doctrine applies only if the police have the ***right to do the touching in the first place*** (just as the "plain view" doctrine applies only where the police have the right in the first place to be in the position from which they get the view).
>
> **Example:** A U.S. Border Guard gets on a bus (as he has a statutory right to do), then squeezes the luggage of every passenger that's located on the overhead storage rack. When he squeezes a soft suitcase owned by D, he feels a brick-like substance. That causes him to suspect illegal drugs, so he opens the suitcase and indeed finds narcotics. *Held*, for D: because the agent didn't have the right to squeeze D's luggage in the first place (the squeezing violated D's reasonable expectation of privacy), the agent wasn't entitled to act on the suspicions that he developed from the squeezing, and therefore didn't have probable cause to open the suitcase. [*Bond v. U.S.*]

F. Police on defendant's property: The plain view doctrine applies not only where the police obtain a view from public property, but also where they are ***lawfully on the owner's property***.

> **Example:** The police come to D's house to make a lawful arrest of him. Any observation they make while in the ordinary process of arresting him does not constitute a Fourth Amendment search. (But this does not allow the police to open closed containers or packages while they are making the arrest, or even move items to get a better view — this would not fall within the plain view doctrine, and would be a Fourth Amendment search.)

V. PROBABLE CAUSE GENERALLY

A. Where requirement of probable cause applies: The requirement of "probable cause" applies to two different situations: (1) before a judge or magistrate may issue a *warrant* for a search or arrest, she must be satisfied that probable cause to do so exists; and (2) before the police may make a *warrantless* search or arrest (permissible only in special circumstances described below), the officer must have probable cause for that search or arrest.

1. **Source of requirement:** Only case (1) above — the requirement of probable cause prior to issuance of a warrant — is expressly covered in the Fourth Amendment. But the Supreme Court has, as a matter of constitutional interpretation, held that probable cause must exist before a warrantless search or arrest as well, to avoid giving the police an incentive to avoid seeking a warrant.

B. Requirement for probable cause: The meaning of the term "probable cause" is not exactly the same in the search context as in the arrest context.

1. **Probable cause to arrest:** For there to be probable cause to *arrest* a person it must be *reasonably likely* that:

   a. a *violation of the law* has been committed; and

   b. the *person* to be arrested *committed* the violation.

2. **Probable cause to search:** For there to be probable cause to *search* particular premises, it must be *reasonably likely* that:

   a. the specific items to be searched for are *connected* with *criminal* activities; and

   b. these items will be *found in the place to be searched*.

3. **Less than 50-50 chance:** It appears that as long as the police have "particularized suspicion" regarding the existence of fact X, they need *not* reasonably believe that fact X exists *more likely than not* in order to have "probable cause" to believe it. For instance, a *1/3 chance* of fact X apparently *can* constitute probable cause.

   Example: The police properly stop a car containing three occupants, and during a legal search find cocaine in the backseat. When none of the three make any explanation, the officer arrests all three. One of the three, D (who was the front-seat passenger) confesses at the stationhouse to owning the cocaine; he then tries to have this admission suppressed as the fruit of an arrest made without probable cause. *Held*, even though D was only one of three occupants of the car, and he was no more likely than the other two to be the cocaine's owner, the police had probable cause to believe that he was the owner, and thus probable cause to arrest him. [*Maryland v. Pringle*]

C. No admissibility limitation: Any trustworthy information may be considered in determining whether probable cause to search or arrest exists, *even if the information would not be admissible at trial*.

D. Only evidence heard by magistrate used: Probable cause for the issuance of a warrant must be judged only by reference to the *facts presented to the magistrate* who is to issue the warrant. (Usually, information for a warrant will be in the form of a police officer's affidavit, not oral testimony.)

> **Example:** Officer asks for a warrant to search Dwight's apartment for the fruits of a recent specified burglary. Officer's supporting affidavit does not mention to Magistrate the basis for Officer's belief that such fruits will be found there. Magistrate grants the warrant, the search takes place, fruits of the burglary are found, and Dwight is tried for the burglary. At Dwight's trial, Dwight probably can successfully move to have the fruits of the search excluded, because the Magistrate was not presented with specific facts that would have given Magistrate probable cause to believe that the fruits would be found at Dwight's premises.

1. Perjured affidavit: If D can show, by a preponderance of the evidence, that affidavits used to obtain the warrant contained *perjury* by the affiant, or a *"reckless disregard for the truth"* by the affiant, the warrant will be *invalidated* (assuming that the rest of the affidavit does not contain materials sufficient to constitute probable cause). [*Franks v. Delaware*] But D can't knock out the warrant merely because it contains *inaccurate* material; he must show actual perjury or reckless disregard of the truth by the affiant himself (not merely by the affiant's sources, such as informers).

    a. Honest police error: So if the police make an *honest error* — they honestly and reasonably, but erroneously, believe certain information and use it in affidavits to get a warrant — the warrant will not be rendered invalid when the error later comes to light. [*Maryland v. Garrison*]

VI. PARTICULAR INFORMATION ESTABLISHING PROBABLE CAUSE

A. Information from informants: When the information on which probable cause is based comes from *informants* who are themselves engaged in criminal activity, courts closely scrutinize the information. Whether the informant's information creates probable cause for a search or arrest is to be determined by the *"totality of the circumstances."* [*Illinois v. Gates*]

1. Two factors: The magistrate should consider two factors in evaluating the informant's information: (1) whether the informant is a generally *reliable witness*; and (2) whether facts are set forth showing the informant's *"basis of knowledge,"* that is, the particular means by which the informant came upon the information that he supplied to the police.

    a. Strong factor can buttress weak factor: But a strong showing on one of these factors can make up for a weak showing on the other one.

    Example: If a particular informant is known for being unusually reliable, his failure to set forth the basis of his knowledge in a particular case will not be a bar to a finding of probable cause based on his tip.

b. Prediction of future events: Also, if later events help *corroborate* the informant's story, these events can be combined with the informant's story to establish probable cause, even though neither by itself would suffice.

B. Non-criminal sources: Where the police procure information from *non-criminal sources* (e.g., ordinary citizens, victims of crime, etc.), the courts are more *lenient* concerning the information than where it comes from, say, informants who are themselves criminals.

1. Other police officers: But where an officer making an affidavit for a warrant (or making a warrantless search or arrest) acts in response to statements made by *other police officers*, probably the arrest or search is valid only if the *maker* of the original statement acted with probable cause.

> **Example:** The County Sheriff broadcasts a bulletin stating that D1 and D2 are wanted for breaking and entering. Officer, a city police officer, hears the bulletin, and without knowing anything else, arrests D1 and D2, who happen to live on his beat. Probably, probable cause for the arrest will be found only if the County Sheriff himself had probable cause to make the arrest.

2. Trained sniffer dog as reliable informant: A *dog* that is trained to *sniff the odor* of drugs or other contraband, and to alert his handlers to the contraband, can be the source of probable cause. The *reliability* of the dog as an "informant" is to be determined by the same *"totality of the circumstances"* rule that applies to humans under *Gates, supra*. This standard means that if the dog has satisfactorily performed in an odor-detection *training course*, that fact alone will typically allow the dog's "I smell drugs here" alert to constitute probable cause. [*Florida v. Harris*]

VII. SEARCH WARRANTS — ISSUANCE AND EXECUTION

A. Who may issue: A search warrant must be issued by some sort of *judicial officer*, usually either a judge or a magistrate. (We'll use the term "magistrate" here.)

1. Neutrality: The magistrate must be a *neutral party*, detached from the law-enforcement side of government.

B. Affidavit: Normally, the police officer seeking a search warrant must put the facts establishing probable cause into a *written, signed affidavit*.

C. *Ex parte* nature of warrant: The proceeding for issuing a warrant is *ex parte*. That is, the suspect whose premises are to be searched *does not have the opportunity to contest the issuance of the warrant*; only the police officer's side of the story is heard by the magistrate. (However, the suspect, if he becomes a criminal defendant, will eventually have a chance to show, at a suppression hearing, that the warrant was issued without probable cause.)

D. Requirement of particular description: The Fourth Amendment requires that a warrant contain a *particular description of the premises to be searched, and the things to be seized*. This means that the warrant must be specific enough that a police officer executing it, even if she had no initial connection with the case, would know where to search and what items to seize.

1. **Description of place:** The description of the *place* to be searched must be precise enough that the officer executing the warrant can figure out where to search. For instance, if the search is to be in an apartment building, the warrant must probably contain the name of the occupant, or the number of the particular apartment, not merely the address of the entire building.

2. **Things to be seized:** The *things to be seized* must also be specifically identified in the warrant.

   a. **Not such a strict requirement:** However, this requirement is not very strictly interpreted today.

   Example: The warrant refers to a particular alleged crime of selling real estate by false pretenses. The warrant then authorizes a search for various types of documents, "together with other fruits, instrumentalities and evidence of [this particular] crime" but does not specify anything about these other fruits or instrumentalities. *Held*, the warrant is not fatally vague. [*Andresen v. Maryland*]

   b. **Contraband:** *Contraband* (property the possession of which is a crime, such as illegal drugs or outlawed firearms) does not have to be described as particularly as material that is innocuous on its face — the officer executing the search is presumed to be able to identify contraband by its very nature.

E. **What may be seized:** Any item that is the subject of a valid search warrant may be *seized* by the police executing the warrant.

   1. **Incriminating evidence:** In particular, this rule means that even items whose only interest to the police is that they *incriminate* the defendant may be seized. [*Warden v. Hayden*]

   2. **No Fifth Amendment interest:** Even items, such as documents, that contain *incriminating statements* made by the defendant may be seized — this does not violate the defendant's Fifth Amendment privilege against self-incrimination.

   Example: Police, executing a valid warrant, seize business records from D's office. These records contain incriminating statements made by D. *Held*, seizure of these records did not violate the Fifth Amendment, even though it might have been a violation of D's Fifth Amendment rights to have required him to produce these records under a subpoena. [*Andresen v. Maryland*]

F. **Warrants against non-suspects:** The Fourth Amendment permits searches to be made of the premises of persons who are *not criminal suspects*, if there is probable cause to believe that the search will produce evidence of someone else's crime.

   1. **Subpoena not necessary:** Such a search of a non-suspect's premises may be made *even if a subpoena would be equally effective*. [*Zurcher v. The Stanford Daily*]

G. **Execution of warrants:** The Fourth Amendment requires that the *procedures* which the police use in carrying out a search not be *"unreasonable."* Thus in general, the police may not behave in an unduly intrusive manner.

1. **Entry without notice:** As a general rule, the officer executing the warrant must knock on the door and ***announce*** that he is a law enforcement officer, that he possesses a warrant, and that he is there to execute it. Thus usually, the police may not forcibly break into the premises to be searched unless they have first announced their presence and waited a reasonable time for a response. This is known as the ***"knock and announce"*** requirement.

   a. **Preventing the destruction of evidence:** However, the Supreme Court has recognized at least one exception: Officers may constitutionally enter without first identifying themselves if the circumstances pose a threat of ***immediate destruction of evidence***.

      Example: D is a narcotics suspect, believed to be carrying a small amount of narcotics. He eludes police shortly before they come to arrest him at his house. *Held*, the officers' suspicion that D would probably destroy the narcotics by, for instance, flushing them down the toilet, justified the police in breaking into the house without first identifying themselves or ringing the doorbell. [*Ker v. California*]

   b. **Physical danger to police:** Similarly, lower courts have held that the possibility of ***physical danger to the police*** sometimes justifies unannounced entry.

      Example: The police have reason to think that D has a gun, and won't be "taken alive." They can probably break in without first knocking or announcing themselves.

2. **Where no response or entry refused:** If the officer identifies himself, and is then refused entry (or gets no response), he may use ***force*** to break into the premises.

   a. **Need not wait for answer:** Similarly, if the officer identifies himself but there's a risk of ***immediate destruction of evidence,*** the officer may break in ***without giving the occupant enough time to get to the door.***

      Example: Police have a warrant to search D's house for cocaine. They knock, then break down the door within 15-20 seconds after knocking (not enough time for D to get to the door). *Held*, the break-in was not unreasonable — on these facts, waiting any longer would have given D time to destroy the cocaine. [*U.S. v. Banks*]

3. **Search of persons on premises:** Assuming that the police have only a search warrant, and not an arrest warrant (or probable cause to arrest anyone), the police may ***not*** automatically search everyone found on the premises.

   a. **Named items on person:** If the police have probable cause to believe that an individual has ***on his person*** items that are named in the search warrant, they may search him.

   b. **Person attempting to leave:** Similarly, if a person attempts to ***leave*** during a premises search, and the items being sought are of a type which might be easily carried away, the police may probably temporarily detain the person to make sure he is not carrying the items away.

c. Persons unrelated to search: But where a person simply happens to be on the premises to be searched, and appears not to have any connection with the criminal activity giving rise to the search warrant or with items mentioned in the warrant, that person may not be searched or detained. [*Ybarra v. Illinois*]

4. Restricted area of search: In executing a search pursuant to a warrant, the police must confine their search to the **area specified** in the warrant, and they must look only in those places where the items sought might possibly be concealed.

Example: If the police are looking for a full-size rifle, they may not look into drawers that are too small to contain such a rifle.

5. Seizure of unnamed items in "plain view": If the police are properly conducting a search, and come across items that are **not listed in the warrant** (but that appear relevant to a crime), the police may generally **seize** the unlisted items. This right is an aspect of the **"plain view"** doctrine.

a. Incriminating evidence: The evidence must be sufficiently connected with criminal activity that a warrant could have been procured for it.

i. Unrelated items: The items discovered in plain view don't have to relate to the same criminal activity that gave rise to the warrant, as long as there is probable cause for the seizure of these new items.

Example: If the police are executing a warrant naming stolen property and they come upon illegal narcotics, they may seize the narcotics even though they have nothing to do with the stolen property charge.

b. Inadvertence not required: It is **not** required, for application of the plain view doctrine, that the police's discovery of an item in plain view be **"inadvertent."** [*Horton v. California*]

Example: When police apply for a warrant to search D's home in connection with a robbery, they have a description of the weapons used. But they get a warrant authorizing the search only for robbery proceeds. While executing the warrant, they come across the weapons. *Held*, the police could constitutionally seize the weapons under the plain view doctrine, even though the discovery of the weapons was not "inadvertent." [*Horton, supra.*]

6. Bodily intrusions: A search warrant can be issued for search of a **person**, rather than a place. Such a bodily search (whether done pursuant to a search warrant or not) must of course be "reasonable." In general, courts measure reasonableness by weighing the individual's interest in privacy against society's interest in conducting the search.

a. Allowable procedures: Thus the forcible **taking of blood** from a drunk-driving suspect, and the use of x-rays to obtain evidence that D is concealing drugs in his stomach, have been held to be "reasonable" and therefore allowable.

b. Surgery: On the other hand, it is *not* reasonable to place D under a general anesthetic and to remove a bullet lodged deep in his chest, in order to show that D was involved in a particular robbery. [*Winston v. Lee*]

H. "Good faith" exception: Normally, if a search warrant is *invalid* (e.g., it is not supported by probable cause), any search done pursuant to it will be unconstitutional, and the evidence will be excluded at trial. However, if the police *reasonably (but erroneously) believe* that the warrant which they have been issued is valid, the exclusionary rule will *not apply*. (See *U.S. v. Leon*, discussed in the treatment of the exclusionary rule below.)

CHAPTER 3
WARRANTLESS ARRESTS AND SEARCHES

I. INTRODUCTION

A. Warrant not always required: The Fourth Amendment mentions warrants specifically, but does not actually *require* warrants — the amendment merely says that "no warrants shall issue, but upon probable cause, supported by Oath or affirmation, and particularly describing the place to be searched, and the persons or things to be seized." So going by the literal text of this amendment, a warrant might *never* be constitutionally required.

1. Judicial interpretations sometimes requires: But the Supreme Court has *interpreted* the Fourth Amendment to sometimes require a warrant. In very general terms, the rules for when a warrant is required may be summarized as follows:

a. Arrest warrants: An *arrest* warrant will *rarely* be required. Only when the police need to *enter a private home* to make the arrest, and there are *no exigent circumstances*, does the Fourth Amendment require the police to procure an arrest warrant before they make the arrest.

b. Search warrant: But just the converse is true in the case of a *search*: the *general rule* is that a warrant is *required*. Only if some special exception applies will the requirement of a search warrant be dispensed with. Some of the more common exceptions are:

i. A search *incident to a valid arrest*;

ii. A search motivated by *exigent circumstances* (e.g., to avoid destruction of evidence);

iii. Certain types of *automobile* searches (e.g., a search of a car when the driver is arrested and both driver and car are taken to the police station);

iv. Searches done after the person to be searched or the owner of the property to be searched *consents*;

v. Partial searches done pursuant to the *"stop and frisk"* doctrine; and

vi. Certain *inspections* and *regulatory searches* (e.g., immigration searches at U.S. borders, sobriety checkpoints on highways, etc.).

Note: The fact that in a particular situation no search warrant is required does *not* necessarily mean that *probable cause* is not required. In some but not all of the above listed situations (e.g., exigent circumstances), the police must have probable cause to believe that a search will furnish evidence of crime, even though they are not required to get a warrant. In others of the above situations, something less than probable cause, and perhaps no real suspicion at all, will be needed. (*Example*: Less than probable cause, but some suspicion, is required for "stop and frisk," whereas no suspicion is required for a consent search.)

II. WARRANTLESS ARRESTS

A. Not generally required: An *arrest* warrant is *not* generally required by the Constitution. This is true even where the police have sufficient advance notice that procurement of a warrant would not jeopardize the arrest. [*U.S. v. Watson*]

B. Entry of dwelling: The only situation in which an arrest warrant *is* likely to be constitutionally required is where the police wish to enter *private premises* to arrest a suspect. In that instance, the requirement for a warrant will depend on whether exigent circumstances exist.

1. **No exigent circumstances:** If there are no exigent circumstances, the police *may not enter a private home* to make a warrantless arrest. [*Payton v. New York*]

    a. **Result of invalid arrest:** A warrantless arrest made in violation of *Payton* will not prevent D from being brought to trial (since he can always be re-arrested after a warrant has been issued). However, if the police make an in-house arrest that required a warrant because there were no exigent circumstances, then any evidence seized as a result of a *search* incident to the arrest will be excluded.

2. **Exigent circumstances:** If there *are* exigent circumstances, so that it is impractical for the police to delay the entry and arrest until they can obtain an arrest warrant, no warrant is necessary (at least if the crime is a serious one, such as a felony — as to minor crimes, see *Atwater*, below).

    a. **Destruction of evidence:** For instance, if the police reasonably believe that the suspect will *destroy evidence* if they delay their entry until they can get a warrant, the requisite exigent circumstances exist.

    b. **Hot pursuit:** Similarly, if the police are pursuing a felony suspect, and he runs into his own or another's dwelling, a warrantless entry and arrest may be permitted under the "hot pursuit" doctrine.

C. No exception for fine-only or other minor crimes: A warrantless arrest for a crime committed in an officer's presence is permissible even where the crime is *so minor* that the only potential punishment is a *fine* rather than imprisonment. (This assumes that the arrest is not made inside a private dwelling, the situation discussed above.)

Example: Officer stops D, a driver, for not wearing a seat belt. This offense is punishable under state law only by a $25 fine, not imprisonment. Officer decides to arrest D, handcuffs her in front of her young children (who are in the car with her), books her in the station house, and causes her to be held in a cell until she can post bail.

Held, Officer's arrest of D without a warrant was not "unreasonable," and thus not a violation of the Fourth Amendment. As long as an officer has reasonable cause to believe that an offense has been committed in his presence, he may make an arrest no matter how minor the offense is, and regardless of the fact that only a fine rather than imprisonment is the maximum punishment for it. [*Atwater v. Lago Vista*]

D. Probable cause need not be for offense stated at time of arrest: Suppose that at the time of the warrantless arrest the officer specifies to the suspect that the arrest is being made for *Offense A*; if it finally turns out that there was not probable cause for Offense A, but that there *was* probable cause for *Offense B* (never mentioned by the arresting officer), there is no problem for the police: even if Offense B is *not closely related* to Offense A, the arrest is still *valid*. [*Devenpeck v. Alford*]

   1. **Significance:** This rule is of special significance when the police conduct a *search incident to the warrantless arrest* (see *infra*, p. 77). Even if there's no probable cause for the offense on which the police purport to make the arrest, as long as it turns out that there was *some* offense as to which the police knew facts amounting to probable cause, the search incident to the arrest will be valid even though the police never mention (or even think about) that offense at the time of the arrest.

E. Statutory requirements: In addition to the constitutional requirements regarding arrest warrants described above, many states impose some *statutory* requirements regarding such warrants.

   Example: Many states allow an officer to make a warrantless misdemeanor arrest only if the misdemeanor was committed in the officer's presence.

F. Use of deadly force to make arrest: The Fourth Amendment also places limits on *how* an arrest may be made. The main rule is that the police may *not* use *deadly force* to make an arrest, if the suspect poses *no immediate threat* to the officer and no threat to others. [*Tennessee v. Garner*]

   1. **No need to abandon chase:** On the other hand, if the suspect *does* pose a serious threat to the police or to others, the police may use deadly force to stop or arrest him. And they may do so instead of reducing the threat by abandoning the chase. [Scott v. Harris]

III. SEARCH INCIDENT TO ARREST

A. Search incident to arrest generally allowed: In general, when the police are making a lawful arrest, they may *search* the area within the arrestee's *control*. This is known as a *"search incident to arrest."* The search-incident-to-arrest doctrine is the most important exception to the general rule that a search warrant is required before a search takes place.

   Example: Officer watches D run out of a coin shop at night, while the shop's alarm is ringing. Assuming that these facts give Officer probable cause to arrest D (which they almost certainly do), Officer may conduct a fairly full search of D's person after the arrest. For instance, Officer can require D to empty his pockets to show that there are no weapons, contraband, or stolen property from the coin shop on his person. If on these facts Officer had arrested D while D was driving a car, Officer would also be permitted, under the search-incident-to-arrest doctrine, to search the passenger compartment of the car for weapons, contraband, etc.

1. Limited area around defendant: Only the area that is at least theoretically within D's ***immediate control*** may be searched incident to arrest. (The basic idea is that only the area that D might get to in order to destroy evidence or gain possession of a weapon may be searched.)

> **Example:** Officers come to arrest D at his house for a recent robbery. They have an arrest warrant but no search warrant. After arresting D, the police conduct a full-scale search of D's three-bedroom house. They discover some of the stolen property in one of the bedrooms, not the room in which they arrested D. *Held*, the property may not be admitted against D because it was found pursuant to a search that was unnecessarily widespread. Only the area within D's immediate control could be searched incident to the arrest. [*Chimel v. California*]

B. Protective sweep: The Supreme Court also upholds ***"protective sweeps"*** under the search-incident-to-arrest doctrine. That is, where the arrest takes place in the suspect's ***home***, the officers may conduct a protective sweep of ***all or part of the premises***, if they have a "reasonable belief" based on "specific and articulable facts" that ***another person*** who might be dangerous to the officer may be present in the areas to be swept. [*Maryland v. Buie*]

1. Adjoining spaces: But "specific and articulable facts" are ***not*** needed for the officers to search in ***closets*** and other spaces ***immediately adjoining*** the place of an arrest, to make sure that no possible attacker lurks there.

C. Automobile searches incident to arrest: The basic rule that a warrantless search incident to arrest must be limited to areas within the arrestee's "immediate control" applies to ***searches of vehicles*** after the arrest of the driver. So in most driver arrests for ***traffic violations***, the police will ***not*** be entitled to ***search the passenger compartment*** incident to the arrest. [*Arizona v. Gant*]

1. Two-part rule: More precisely, the search-incident-to-arrest rationale allows a warrantless search of the passenger compartment ***only*** if ***one of two things*** is true:

[1] the arrestee has ***access to the passenger compartment*** at the moment of the search (which will virtually never be the case if the standard police practice of placing the driver ***securely in a patrol car*** is followed prior to the search); or

[2] the police reasonably believe that the passenger compartment might contain ***evidence of the offense for which the arrest is being made.***

[*Gant, supra*]

2. Traffic arrest where driver is handcuffed: In the most common driver-arrest scenario — the police make an arrest for a ***traffic violation***, handcuff the driver and put him in the patrol car, and then find evidence of some other crime when they search the passenger compartment — *Gant* means that the search *cannot be justified by the incident-to-arrest doctrine.*

> **Example:** The police reasonably (and correctly, as it turns out) believe that D's driver's license has been suspended and that there is an outstanding warrant for his arrest for driving with a suspended license. They wait for D at his residence and, when he drives into the driveway, arrest him on the warrant. They then handcuff him, lock him in the back seat of the patrol car, and search the passenger compartment of his car. There, they find cocaine in the pocket of a jacket on the back seat.
>
> *Held*, for D: the search of the passenger compartment was not a proper search incident to arrest because by the time of the search, the compartment was not even theoretically within D's immediate control, as is required for a search incident to arrest. [*Gant, supra*]

a. **Search for evidence of offense that led to arrest:** But even if the driver has been secured so that he has no possible access to the passenger compartment, rationale [2] of *Gant* (see immediately *supra*) may apply: if the police "reasonably believe" that the passenger compartment might contain *evidence of the offense for which the arrest is being made, they may search that compartment.* This rationale will almost never apply to a traffic arrest, but will often apply to arrests on outstanding warrants for, say, *drug offenses*.

> **Example:** The police learn that a warrant has been issued for the arrest of D on charges of smuggling heroin from Mexico into Arizona in his black Ford Explorer with license plate "XYZ123." Officer Brown, while patrolling in Arizona near the Mexican border, spots a black Explorer with that plate. He pulls the vehicle over, sees that D is the driver, arrests D on the warrant, and handcuffs him to the inside of the patrol car. Brown then conducts a search of the passenger compartment, and finds heroin in the glove compartment.
>
> The search will likely be *valid* under the "search for evidence of the offense for which the arrest is being made" rationale. Even if Brown didn't have "probable cause" to believe that the vehicle was currently being used to smuggle drugs, the fact that D was driving that vehicle in Arizona near the Mexican border probably gave Brown "reason to believe" that the vehicle "might" contain evidence relevant to the drug-smuggling charges. ("Reason to believe" that evidence "might" be found is clearly a much-easier-to-satisfy standard than "probable cause" to believe such evidence "will" be found, the usual standard for a proper search.) If the court agrees that Brown had such "reason to believe," then the search of the vehicle for evidence relating to the "offense of arrest" (the drug smuggling) will be valid as a special form of search incident to arrest. [Cf. *Gant*]

3. **Other opportunities for vehicle search:** Keep in mind that in passenger-compartment search cases, *Gant only* wipes out the search-incident-to-arrest doctrine, not *other long-established doctrines* that may independently permit a warrantless search of the compartment.

a. **Driver possibly dangerous:** For instance, suppose the police have stopped the car, asked the driver to exit, and are interrogating him, but have *not* *arrested* him. If the police reasonably conclude that the driver may be ***dangerous and might gain access to a weapon*** inside the car once he's permitted to return to the car post-interrogation, under a form of the ***stop-and-frisk*** doctrine, the police may conduct a ***brief protective search of the passenger compartment*** for weapons. Then, if they find some contraband item (e.g., drugs), they can seize the item. This scenario does not rely on the search-incident-to-arrest doctrine, and is therefore not affected by the new rule of *Arizona v. Gant*. [See *Michigan v. Long, infra*, p. 97.]

    b. Probable cause to search: Similarly, when the police properly stop a car, then whether they make an arrest of the driver or not, if they have ***probable cause*** to believe that the vehicle contains ***contraband or evidence of crime***, they may search ***any part*** of the vehicle where the evidence ***might plausibly be found.*** [*U.S. v. Ross, infra*, p. 88.] Again, this exception to the warrant requirement does not depend on the search-incident-to-arrest doctrine, and is therefore unaffected by *Gant*. And this exception applies even though the stop (and/or the arrest) is ***not for the same crime*** to which the probable-cause-for-search relates.

D. Contemporaneity of search: For the search to be incident to arrest, it need ***not*** be exactly ***contemporaneous*** with the arrest — a search that takes place some time before, or sometime after, the arrest, will still be held "incident" to that arrest as long as it is closely connected to it logically speaking.

    1. Search prior to arrest: Thus the police may make a search before they arrest D, as long as they already have probable cause to make the arrest and are doing the search in order to protect themselves. Generally, the arrest must follow quite quickly on the heels of the protective search. [*Rawlings v. Kentucky*]

    2. Search long after arrest: Similarly, the search-incident-to-arrest exception is applicable even to searches that do not occur until sometime ***after*** the arrest, at least where the search is made of objects in the suspect's possession at the time of arrest.

        a. Search of person: Most commonly, the police may arrest D, take control of the objects in D's possession at the time of the arrest, and examine those objects at a later time.

E. Legality of arrest: The search-incident-to-arrest exception to the search warrant requirement applies only where the arrest is ***legal***. Thus if the arrest turns out to have been made without probable cause, the search incident to it cannot be justified on the search-incident-to-arrest rationale, and the arrest must be suppressed unless some other exception to the warrant requirement (e.g., prevention of destruction of evidence) justifies it.

F. Applicable even to minor crimes: The search-incident-to-arrest exception seems to apply to arrests even for ***minor*** crimes. For instance, if D is arrested for a ***traffic violation***, he may be searched incident to the arrest even though the crime is not an especially "serious" one. [*U.S. v. Robinson*]

1. **Must be custodial arrest:** However, for the search-incident-to-arrest doctrine to apply, the arrest must be a *"custodial"* one. That is, the officer must be planning to take D to the station-house for booking.

> **Example:** Suppose that Officer stops D, a driver, for driving with an expired registration sticker. Suppose further that this is a misdemeanor, and that under local police department procedures, a driver stopped for such an offense is virtually never arrested, but is instead given a summons to be answered at a later date. On these facts, D is not really being "arrested," and his body, or his car, may not be searched incident to arrest.

   a. **D may be required to step out of car:** However, even in the case of such a non-custodial stop, D may be required to *step out of the car*. Once he has stepped out of the car, presumably he may be subjected to at least a cursory frisk under the stop-and-frisk doctrine, discussed below.

G. **Search of items carried on person of arrestee:** When a search is properly made incident to a lawful arrest, the police may examine *items of personal property found on the person of the arrestee.*

1. **Items that are not suspected of being weapons or evidence:** Furthermore, this right to examine items found on the arrestee's person is *not limited* to items that the officer reasonably fears may be *weapons* or may constitute *evidence of crime* — putting aside the issue of digital devices (discussed below), the Supreme Court's incident-to-arrest cases indicate that *any* physical item found on the arrestee's person (or within his immediate control) can be searched.

> **Example:** A police officer properly makes a traffic-related arrest of D. The officer pats D down, feels a soft package in his pocket, removes the package, and discovers that it is a crumpled cigarette package containing what turns out to be heroin. The officer concedes that when he patted D down, he had no reason to fear that the crumpled package he was feeling might be a weapon or might constitute evidence of crime.
>
> *Held* (by the Supreme Court), the package containing the heroin was properly searched and seized incident to D's lawful arrest. It's true that the need to protect arresting officers from weapons, and helping them prevent destruction of evidence being carried by the arrestee, were the reasons for which the incident-to-arrest doctrine was originally adopted. The arresting officer's right to search for and examine items on the arrestee's person does not depend on what a court may later decide was the probability that in the particular arrest situation at issue now, *weapons or evidence would in fact be found* on the arrestee's person or within his control. [*U.S. v. Robinson*]

   a. **Purses, contents of pockets:** Lower courts interpreting *Robinson* have reasoned that the right of search incident to arrest covers *any items found on or in the control of the arrested person,* such as *purses, billfolds, address books,* and anything *found in the arrestee's pockets.*

2. **Cell phones and their digital contents:** But the Court has held (unanimously) that when the police properly make a custodial arrest of a person who happens to be carrying a *cell phone*, the incident-to-arrest doctrine does *not* permit the police

to perform a ***warrantless search of the digital contents of the phone.*** [***Riley v. California*** (2014)]

a. Rationale: The Court in *Riley* reasoned that "modern cell phones, as a category, ***implicate privacy concerns far beyond*** those implicated by the search of a cigarette pack, a wallet, or a purse." For instance, the Court said, "the ***sum of an individual's private life can be reconstructed*** through a ***thousand photographs*** labeled with dates, locations, and descriptions [on a cell phone]; the same cannot be said of a photograph or two of loved ones tucked into a wallet."

b. Warrant now required before search: Here's the rule set out in *Riley* that now governs searches of data on cell phones found incident to arrest: "Our answer to the question of ***what police must do before searching a cell phone seized incident to an arrest*** is . . . *simple — get a warrant.*"

    i. Illustration from *Riley*: *Riley* was based on two separate cases that were consolidated before the Supreme Court. The following Example shows the facts of one of those cases, and illustrates how the Court's rule disallowing cell phone data searches incident to arrest limits the way the police may proceed.

        Example: Police see D make a drug sale from a car, arrest him, and seize a "flip phone" (a phone with fewer features than a smart phone) from his person. At the station house, the police notice that the phone is ringing with calls from a source listed on the phone's display as "my house." The police access the call log to find the phone number associated with "my house." They then use an online phone directory to trace that phone number to an address at an apartment building. At that building, the police see D's name on a mailbox, obtain a search warrant for the apartment, and while executing the warrant find narcotics that become the basis for prosecuting D.

        Held, the police violated D's Fourth Amendment rights when, without first getting a search warrant, they retrieved data from the phone, including accessing the call log. Therefore, D's conviction is reversed as deriving from unconstitutionally-obtained evidence. [*Riley v. California*]

c. Broad reading likely: It seems fair to read *Riley* as holding that whenever ***any*** modern device containing ***significant amounts of digital data*** is found on or near an arrestee, the police may not search (i.e., read or examine) the digital data without first getting a search warrant. Presumably this logic applies not only to small handheld digital devices, but even to somewhat ***larger*** ones — ***tablets and laptops,*** for instance — found on or near the arrestee.

H. Breath and blood tests incident to arrest: Suppose the police arrest a ***driver*** based on probable cause to suspect ***drunk driving***; can the police then rely on the search-incident-to-arrest doctrine to perform a warrantless test of the driver's ***breath*** or ***blood*** in order to confirm the driver's blood alcohol content (***"BAC"***)? As the result of a trio of 2016 cases decided under the name ***Birchfield v. North Dakota***, a warrantless test of the driver's ***breath*** is ***permissible***, but such a test of the driver's ***blood*** is ***not***.

1. **Breath test:** *Birchfield* establishes that when the police make a *legal* drunk-driving arrest (i.e., when they have probable cause to believe that D was driving while drunk), they may ***conduct a breath test ("Breathalyzer") without first getting a search warrant***. Furthermore, the states may make it a ***crime*** for the driver to ***refuse to consent to a breath test*** after his legal arrest for drunk driving.

2. **No warrantless blood tests:** But even if the driver refuses to consent to the warrantless breath test (making him vulnerable to a criminal conviction for doing so), that does ***not entitle*** the police to take him to the hospital and forcibly subject him to a ***blood test*** — the police ***must get a search warrant*** before doing this (assuming there are no exigent circumstances at play, such as the need to test for non-alcohol substances that are suspected, and that if they are present would likely be rapidly disappearing from the bloodstream). [*Birchfield, supra*]

IV. EXIGENT CIRCUMSTANCES

A. **Exigent circumstances generally:** Even where the search-incident-to-arrest exception to the search warrant requirement does not apply, there may be ***exigent circumstances*** that justify dispensing with the warrant requirement. The most common exigent circumstances are: (1) preventing the imminent ***destruction of evidence***; (2) preventing ***harm to persons***; and (3) searching in ***"hot pursuit"*** for a suspect.

B. **Destruction of evidence:** The police may conduct a search or seizure without a warrant, provided that they have probable cause, and provided that the search or seizure is necessary to prevent the possible ***imminent destruction of evidence***.

1. **Blood alcohol concentration (BAC) test:** One scenario that often calls for use of the "exigent circumstances" rationale for a warrantless search is where the police have probable cause to believe that a person (call him D) has been driving drunk, but there is a risk that D's ***blood-alcohol concentration (BAC)*** (see *supra*, pp. 82-83, Par. (H)) ***will drop*** significantly before the police can get a warrant authorizing them to seize a blood sample. If it's indeed the case that getting a warrant will delay the BAC breath test to the point where the results will likely be unusable, the police may proceed without a warrant. [*Schmerber v. California*]

   a. **Not a categorical rule:** But the Supreme Court has ***refused*** government requests to establish a ***categorical*** (automatic) rule that the risk of destruction of BAC evidence necessarily allows the police to take a driver's blood sample without a warrant if they have probable cause to suspect him of drunk driving. (The Court's main rationale is that BAC dissipates over time in a ***predictable way***, so the passage of a certain amount of time while a warrant is obtained will not prevent prosecutors from using even the results of a delayed test to establish the suspect's BAC as of an earlier pre-test moment.) [*Missouri v. McNeely*]

      i. **Result:** So in drunk-driving cases and any other case where a suspect's BAC is at issue, the police may not use the destruction-of-evidence rationale to avoid getting a warrant unless they can show that taking the time to get a warrant would likely have significantly *undermined the value* of the eventual BAC test.

    ii. Breath test distinguished: But keep in mind that the police *never need* a warrant to require a driver whom they properly arrest for drunk-driving to take a roadside *breath* test. Therefore, the presence or absence of exigent circumstances won't even matter if that's the only sort of test the arresting officer wants to perform; see *Birchfield v. No. Dakota, supra*, pp. 82-83.

2. Easily-destroyed contraband: Another common "destruction of evidence" scenario occurs when the police have probable cause to believe that particular *premises contain contraband or evidence of crime*, but fear that if they leave the premises unguarded while obtaining a search warrant, an occupant will destroy the evidence before the warrant can be obtained. Most commonly, the police have reasonable cause to believe that there are *narcotics* in the premises, and wish to search for and seize the drugs before they can be destroyed (e.g., *flushed down the toilet*) or moved to another location.

    a. Sealing off premises: Often, the police can and should deal with this disposal-of-evidence problem by *sealing off the premises* (a "seizure" under the Fourth Amendment) until a search warrant can be obtained. That is, the police can *require the occupants to leave the premises* (or remain under police observation); police officers are then *posted outside the premises* to make sure that no one else enters for the purpose of destroying the evidence. Once a search warrant for the premises has been obtained, the police conduct the search.

        i. Generally successful: This warrantless and searchless "seizure to preserve evidence" will generally *comply* with the Fourth Amendment, as long as the police have a reasonable belief that without a seizure of the premises, the occupants will learn of the danger and destroy the evidence before the police can get a search warrant. [*Illinois v. McArthur*]

3. The "police-created-exigency" exception: Courts recognize an "exception to the exception" in this destruction-of-evidence scenario: the *"police-created-exigency"* doctrine. Under this doctrine, if the police's own conduct *"created"* or *"manufactured"* the exigency (the threat of evidence-destruction), then the main evidence-destruction exception to the warrant requirement will not apply, and the police will need to get a warrant before they conduct a search.

    a. Narrowly interpreted: But the police-created-exigency doctrine is narrowly interpreted; it will nullify the police's right to enter warrantlessly only when the police "gain entry to premises by means of an *actual or threatened violation of the Fourth Amendment*." [*Kentucky v. King*]

    Example: The police are chasing X, a drug suspect. They know he went into an apartment seconds ago, but don't know whether it was the left-hand one or the right-hand one. They smell marijuana coming from the one on the left. They knock, hear sounds suggesting that the occupants are destroying narcotics, break down the door, and find D and others smoking marijuana. They arrest D and search incident to that arrest, finding additional contraband. It turns out that X went into the right-hand apartment, and D had nothing to do with X. At trial, D claims that the police "manufactured" the emergency (when they picked the wrong apartment, and then without a warrant broke down the door), so that the police-created-exigency doctrine makes the entry unlawful.

Held, for the prosecution. It's true that the police-created-exigency exception to the right to enter warrantlessly to stop the threatened destruction of evidence will sometimes invalidate the search. But that will happen only if the police committed or threatened to commit a Fourth Amendment violation in order to gain entry. That didn't happen here (they made a reasonable and honest mistake), so the entry and search were lawful. [*Kentucky v. King*]

C. Danger to life: A warrantless search may be allowed where ***danger to life*** is likely if the police cannot act fast.

> **Example:** At 3 a.m., police respond to a call that a loud party is taking place at a house. When they arrive, they hear shouting and see, through a screen door, a fight taking place in the kitchen. They open the screen door, enter, announce themselves, and arrest several people for fighting.
>
> *Held*, the police entry, though warrantless, did not violate the Fourth Amendment, because the entry was justified by the exigent circumstances. The police may make a warrantless entry into a home to assist an injured occupant or prevent imminent injury. [*Brigham City v. Stuart*]

D. Hot pursuit: If the police are pursuing a felony suspect, and have reason to believe that he has entered particular premises, they may enter those premises to search for him. While they are searching for him, they may also search for weapons which, since he is still at large, he might seize. This is called the ***"hot pursuit"*** exception to the search warrant requirement.

1. **Other items:** The "hot pursuit" exception is often combined with the "plain view" exception (discussed in detail below). That is, while the police are engaged in a hot pursuit of a suspect and any weapons he might have, they may seize any other evidence of criminal behavior that they stumble upon in plain view.

E. Entry to arrest non-resident: One commonly occurring situation does ***not*** automatically constitute "exigent circumstances": Where the police are not in hot pursuit, and there are no specific exigent circumstances, the police ***may not enter one person's private dwelling to arrest another***, even if they are acting pursuant to an arrest warrant. [*Steagald v. U.S.*]

> **Note:** But this rule does not apply where the suspect is to be arrested at his *own* premises. That is, a warrant for D's arrest, even without a search warrant, will be enough to allow the police to enter D's house to make the arrest; while there, they may make a search incident to an arrest, and also seize any evidence they find in plain view. It is only where the police have a warrant for *A's* arrest, and use it to enter *B's* residence, that the special *Steagald* rule summarized above applies to prevent a warrantless search of *B's* premises.

V.   THE "PLAIN VIEW" DOCTRINE AND SEIZURE OF EVIDENCE

A. The doctrine generally: The *"plain view"* doctrine is often applied to allow police who are on premises for lawful purposes to make a warrantless seizure of evidence that they come across.

B. Requirements for doctrine: For the plain view doctrine to be applied so that a warrantless seizure of evidence is allowable, three requirements must be met:

❑   The officers must *not have violated the Fourth Amendment in arriving at the place* from which the items are plainly viewed;

❑   The incriminating nature of the iterms must be *immediately apparent*;

❑   The officers must have a *lawful right of access* to the *object itself*.

Let's look at these three requirements in more detail.

1. Legally on premises: First, the officers must *not have violated the Fourth Amendment* in arriving at the place from which the items were plainly viewed.

> **Example:** Officer trespasses on D's front lawn to look into D's front window, where Officer gets the plain view. The doctrine does not apply, because Officer has violated the Fourth Amendment by getting into the position from which he has the view.

2. Incriminating nature must be apparent: Second, the incriminating nature of the items seized must be *"immediately apparent."* To put it another way, the police must, at the time they first see the item in plain view, have *probable cause* to believe that the object is incriminating.

> **Example:** Officer is legally in D's apartment. Officer notices an expensive stereo. He picks the stereo up, reads the serial number on the bottom, and learns by phone that a unit with that number has recently been stolen. *Held*, the plain view doctrine does not apply, because at the moment Officer picked up the stereo, he did not have probable cause for the search he performed by moving it. [*Arizona v. Hicks*]

3. Lawful right of access: Finally, the officer must have a lawful *right of access* to the *object itself.*

> **Example:** Officer, standing on the public sidewalk, can see through the window of D's house and can view marijuana growing in D's living room. Officer may not make a warrantless entry into D's house to seize the marijuana, because she doesn't have lawful access to the inside of the house.

C. No requirement of inadvertence: The plain view doctrine applies even where the police discovery of a piece of evidence that they want to seize is *not inadvertent*.

VI. THE "AUTOMOBILE EXCEPTION" TO THE REQUIREMENT OF A SEARCH WARRANT

A. Relation of car searches to other kinds of searches: All of the exceptions to the requirement of a search warrant that we've discussed above may apply to the search of an automobile as well as to the search of persons and premises.

   1. **Exigent circumstances:** For instance, *exigent circumstances* will often cause the warrant requirement to be suspended when a car search is involved. Thus the police may search a vehicle without a warrant if such a search is necessary to *preserve evidence*, as will be the case where the car can be quickly *driven out of the jurisdiction*.

   2. **Incident to arrest:** Similarly, if the police arrest the driver, and have "reason to believe" that the vehicle may contain evidence of the crime for which they made the arrest, they may search the car under a form of search incident to arrest.

B. The "automobile exception" to the warrant requirement – generally: Even apart from the above situations in which the *general* exceptions to the requirement of a search warrant apply to the automobile context, the Supreme Court has long recognized a specific auto-related exception, which is usually called the *"automobile exception"* to the warrant requirement.

   1. **Main statement of rule:** Here's a general statement of the automobile exception: A police officer may *search a motor vehicle without first getting a search warrant, as long as she has probable cause to believe that evidence or contraband is located in the vehicle.* [*California v. Carney*]

   2. **Rationales for the exception:** There are two distinct rationales for the automobile exception:

      [1] **"Ready mobility":** The first rationale is based on the *inherent mobility* of motor vehicles. Even though a person has a constitutionally-protected privacy interest in her vehicle, the *"ready mobility"* of vehicles justifies giving the vehicle a lesser degree of protection than in the case of a fixed structure. Why? Because when the police arrive at probable cause to believe that evidence or contraband is located in the vehicle, it is usually *not practicable for them* to obtain and execute a search warrant before the vehicle is moved.

      [2] **Lesser expectation of privacy:** The second rationale is that a person should be *deemed to have a lesser expectation of privacy* with respect to a vehicle she owns than with respect to, say, her home or workplace, because of the *"pervasive regulation"* of vehicles.

      [*California v. Carney*]

C. The "automobile exception" – special contexts: Here are some contexts in which the "automobile exception" to the search-warrant requirement has (or hasn't) been applied.

   1. **Search at station house after arrest:** Where the police arrest the driver, take him and his car *to the station*, and search the car there, no search warrant is generally required.

Example: The police, hearing a description of the getaway car used in a robbery, stop a car meeting that description, driven by D. They arrest D, and take D and the car to the station house. There, they search the car without a warrant, and find incriminating evidence. *Held*, the search was valid, despite the fact that once the car was at the station house the police could easily have gotten a search warrant. [*Chambers v. Maroney*]

2. **Search at place where vehicle is stopped:** If the police properly stop a vehicle and have probable cause to believe that the vehicle contains contraband or evidence of crime, they may use the automobile exception to conduct an immediate warrantless search at the *scene of the stop.* (That is, they don't need to drive the car to the police station and search it there, as in Chambers, supra.) [*California v. Carney*]

3. **Search of vehicle parked in the driveway of a home:** The automobile exception may also apply to dispense with the need for a warrant where the vehicle to be searched is located not on a public street, but on *private residential property*, such as on the *driveway* of a home.

   a. **Vehicle not in curtilage:** If vehicle is on a portion of a homeowner's property that is *not* part of the property's "curtilage," then the automobile exception will *apply*, assuming the police have probable cause to believe the vehicle contains contraband or evidence of crime.

   b. **Vehicle in curtilage:** But where the vehicle *is* located within the curtilage of a person's dwelling, the automobile exception will *not apply* to allow the warrantless search of the vehicle, even if the police have probable cause for a search. That's because the automobile exception *does not "override"* the special Fourth Amendment protections given to the "home" (and a home's curtilage is deemed part of the home, just as, say, any room inside the home would be). [*Collins v. Virginia* (2018)]

4. **Extends to search of closed containers in the vehicle:** When the automobile exception applies to allow a warrantless search of a vehicle, the exception also allows the police to *search any closed container inside the vehicle.* (This assumes that the container might plausibly hold evidence or contraband relating to whatever it was that gave the police probable cause to stop and search the vehicle.) [*U.S. v. Ross*]

   a. **Passenger's belongings:** Once the police have probable cause to believe that the car contains contraband or evidence of crime, they may search closed containers inside it that could hold that type of contraband or evidence, even if those containers belong to a *passenger*, and even if there is no probable cause to believe that the passenger has been involved in carrying the contraband or any other illegality. [*Wyoming v. Houghton*]

5. **Traffic stop followed by ticket:** Where the police make a routine stop to issue a *traffic ticket*, and don't make an "arrest," they *don't thereby get the right to search the car.* [*Knowles v. Iowa*]

D. **Actions directed at passengers:** If the driver's conduct leads the police to make a proper stop and/or arrest, this does *not* mean that the officer has the right to search the person of any *passenger* who happens to be in the car. No matter what the driver has done, the officer may search a passenger only if the officer has has either: (1) probable cause to believe that the passenger possesses evidence of a crime, or (2) probable cause to arrest the passenger (in which case the search is justified as being incident to arrest).

However, the officer *does* have several other rights regarding passengers:

❑ As a method of protecting officer safety, the officer may demand that the passenger *step out of the vehicle*.

❑ Also as a matter of protection, if the officer has a reasonable fear that the passenger may be armed or dangerous, he may *frisk and pat down* the passenger, to make sure that the passenger is not carrying a weapon.

❑ Finally, if the officer has the right to search the vehicle, he may as noted above also *search any container* in the car that might contain the thing being looked for, even if the officer knows that the container *belongs to a passenger*, and even if the officer has no probable cause to believe that the container contains that thing.

E. **Lack of probable cause:** Of the various automobile scenarios that present an exception to the requirement of a search warrant, in most of them *probable cause* to make the search is required but in a few it is not:

1. **Needed if searched on scene:** Where the driver is stopped and the police want to search the car *on the scene*, they will normally need probable cause to conduct that search: belief that they will find either incriminating evidence or contraband. (Remember that they may sometimes perform a search incident to the arrest of the driver, in which case no probable cause is needed; but this right applies only if either the driver hasn't been restrained, or the police have reason to believe they'll find evidence relating to the offense for which the driver has been arrested.)

2. **Plain view:** If the police find evidence in *plain view* in a vehicle as they are impounding it, they may seize the evidence even though they did not previously have probable cause to search or seize.

3. **Impoundment:** If the car has been *impounded* by the police pursuant to standardized procedures, the police may usually conduct a search at the station house even though they do *not* have probable cause. For instance, where a police department routinely tows cars for *illegal parking*, the police may unlock and search each such towed car in the impoundment lot. [*South Dakota v. Opperman*]

   a. **Containers in car:** Similarly, once the impounded vehicle is searched, even *closed containers* inside it may be subjected to a warrantless and probable-cause-less inventory search.

   b. **Standardized procedures and good faith:** But such warrantless inventory searches must satisfy two conditions: (1) the police must follow *standardized procedures*, so that the person searching does not have unbridled discretion to determine the scope of the search; and (2) the police must not have acted in *bad faith* or for the *sole purpose of investigation*.

Example: If the arrest or impoundment took place just to furnish an excuse for a warrantless search, the inventory-search exception will not apply. [*Colorado v. Bertine*]

VII. CONSENT SEARCHES GENERALLY

A. Consent generally: The police may make a warrantless search if they receive the *consent* of the individual whose premises, effects, or person are to be searched.

B. D need not know he can refuse consent: A person's consent will be *effective* even if the person *did not know she had a right to refuse to consent* to the search. [*Schneckloth v. Bustamonte*]

   1. Must be voluntary: The consent, to be effective, must be *"voluntary,"* rather than the product of duress or coercion. But the Court measures voluntariness by a *"totality of the circumstances"* test, and the fact that the consenter did or did not know she had a right to refuse consent is merely *one factor* in measuring voluntariness.

   2. Consent given in custody: Even where the consent is given while the person is in *custody*, the fact that the person is not told that he may refuse consent appears not to render the consent involuntary. [*U.S. v. Watson*] In other words, nothing like the *Miranda* rule — where the suspect *must* be warned that he has the right to remain silent — applies to a custodial suspect's consent to search his person or premises.

C. Claims of authority to search: Suppose the consent to search is procured after the officer states that she has, or will get, *authority to search* if the person does not give consent. Courts generally distinguish between *false claims of present authority*, and *threats of future action* — a false claim of present authority is much more likely to negate the voluntariness of the consent than is a threat of future action.

   1. False claim of present authority: Where an officer *falsely asserts that he has a search warrant*, and then procures "consent," the consent is *invalid*. [*Bumper v. North Carolina*]

   2. Consent induced by reference to invalid warrant: Similarly, if the police *truthfully* state that they have a search warrant, but the warrant is in fact *invalid* (e.g., because rendered with a lack of probable cause), the consent of the person whose premises are to be searched is *invalid*.

   3. Threat to obtain warrant: But where the police merely *threaten to obtain a warrant* if consent is not given (and the consent is given), the result depends on whether the police *in fact have grounds* to get a warrant. If they do, the consent is usually found valid; if they don't, the consent is likely to be nullified. (However, the Supreme Court has not yet decided this issue explicitly.)

D. Misrepresentation of identity: Where the police *misrepresent their identity* by acting *undercover*, this deception does *not* vitiate any "consent."

   Example: Officer, wearing plain clothes, comes to D's house pretending to be the meter reader for the local electric company. D, believing Officer's cover story, lets

Officer into D's basement. While purporting to read the meter, Officer spots incriminating evidence in the basement in plain view. D will almost certainly be found to have consented to Officer's entry, notwithstanding the deception.

E. Physical scope of search: Where D's consent is reasonably interpreted to apply only to a *particular physical area*, a search that extends *beyond* that area will not be covered by the consent, and will be invalid unless it falls within some other exception to the warrant requirement.

> **Example:** Officer asks D for permission to search D's living room for certain evidence. D responds, "O.K." Officer then goes into the kitchen and basement, and finds incriminating evidence. Since Officer went beyond the scope of the consented-to search, the evidence will be suppressed if no other exception to the search warrant requirement applies.

1. Plain view exception: But always keep in mind the *"plain view"* exception to the warrant requirement — if while the searching officer is standing within part of the consented-to area, she spots evidence in another part of the premises, she can seize that evidence under the plain view doctrine.

VIII. CONSENT BY THIRD PERSONS

A. The problem generally: Be careful of consent issues raised when the police seek the consent of *one person* for the search of the *property of another*, or for the search of an area as to which another has an expectation of privacy — the mere fact that the first person has voluntarily consented does not mean that the police may conduct the search and introduce evidence against the second person. In general, *A* may not consent to a search that would invade *B's* expectation of privacy — only if special circumstances exist (e.g., both *A* and *B* have authority over the premises) will *A's* consent be in effect binding on *B*.

B. Joint authority: In cases in which the defendant and a *third person* have *joint authority* over the premises, that third party's consent will often be binding on the defendant. We will consider two separate scenarios: (1) where D is *absent* at the time the third person consents; and (2) where D is *present*, and *refuses to consent*, while the third person consents.

By "joint authority," we mean a situation in which D and the third party have some sort of *joint access to*, and some sort of *joint expectation of privacy in*, the place to be searched. Common examples of joint authority are:

- ❑ *roommates*, as to the common areas of the dwelling or any shared bedroom;
- ❑ *husband and wife*, as to the marital dwelling;
- ❑ a homeowner (or tenant) and his *social guest*, where the homeowner gives the consent and the evidence is then used against the guest.

All of these scenarios are evaluated according to the same basic set of rules.

1. D is absent when third person consents: Where D is *absent*, and the police ask for and receive consent of the third person to search the jointly-controlled premises, the basic rule is that the third party's consent is *effective*, if that third party either (a) *actually* has or (b) is *reasonably believed* by the police to have, joint authority over the premises.

> **Example:** G cohabits in a house together with D. The police show up at this house one day, arrest D in the front yard, and put him in a squad car nearby. They then knock on the front door, and G answers. They explain that they are looking for money and a gun from a recent bank robbery, and ask if they can search the house. G gives consent to the police to search the house, including her and D's bedroom. In the bedroom, the police find money and the gun from the robbery.
>
> *Held*, G's consent was valid as against D. G had joint authority over the bedroom. In such a joint-authority scenario, "it is reasonable to recognize that *any of the co-inhabitants* has the right to permit the inspection in his own right and that the others have *assumed the risk* that one of their number might permit the common area to be searched." [*U.S. v. Matlock*]

    a. **Reasonable mistake:** The third-party consent will be binding on the absent defendant even if the police were *mistaken* about whether the consenter in fact had joint authority over the premises, as long as the *mistake was a reasonable one.* For instance, if the consenting third person falsely tells the police that she lives in the premises to be searched, and the police reasonably believe her, the lie will not invalidate the consent. [*Illinois v. Rodriguez*]

2. **D is present and objecting when third person consents:** Now, let's consider the second scenario: D is *present* when the third party consents to a search of the premises over which the two have joint authority, and D makes it clear that he, D, is *not consenting.* Here, the third party's consent is *not binding on D*, at least where it appears to the police that the third person and D have equal claim to the premises.

> **Example:** W, who is estranged from her husband D, returns to the former marital residence. There, she calls the police. They arrive without a warrant and meet W. D then arrives back at the house. W tells the police that there are items showing D's drug use in the house. The police ask D for his consent to a search of the house, and he refuses. The police then ask W for consent and she gives it. In D's bedroom, the police find cocaine.
>
> *Held*, W's consent was not effective as against D. Where as here the two parties are not living within some "recognized hierarchy" (like a household with parent and child), the co-tenant who wishes to open the door to a third person "has no recognized authority in law or social practice to prevail over a present and objecting co-tenant." Consequently, even though W may have had joint authority with D over the house, the police's warrantless entry in the face of D's express refusal to consent made this an unreasonable search. [*Georgia v. Randolph*]

C. Other theories: Even where the person doing the consenting does not have joint authority over the premises, some other theory may apply to justify a search that would otherwise violate D's rights:

1. **Agency:** First, it may be the case, as a factual matter, that D has *authorized* a third person to consent, even though the third person does not have direct ownership or control.

   Example: D gives X, his trusted valet, complete run of the premises, and the authority to decide who will be admitted. If X consents to a police search, this will be binding on D under the doctrine of agency.

2. **Property of consenter:** If the person doing the consenting is the *owner of the particular item* to be searched or seized, this will be binding even if the search or seizure violates D's property interests.

   Example: X owns a rifle, and consents to have the police seize it and test it. The rifle turns out, as the police suspect, to have been used by D, X's grandson, in a crime. This evidence can be used against D, because X as the owner of the item seized had the right to consent to the seizure.

3. **Assumption of risk:** Finally, the relationship between the third party and D may be such that D will be found to have *"assumed the risk"* that the third party might see or scrutinize D's property, in which case the third party may also consent to a search.

   Example: D shares a duffle bag with X, his cousin. X consents to a police search of the bag. *Held*, this consent was binding on D, because D assumed the risk that X or others would look in the bag, and thus D had no expectation of privacy in the bag's contents. [*Frazier v. Cupp*]

D. **Relatives:** Consent issues often arise where one person consents to a search that implicates the privacy interests of the consenter's *relative*.

   1. **Husbands, wives, and lovers:** Where one *spouse* consents to the search of the property of the absent other, the search will usually be *upheld*. (See, e.g., *Matlock, supra*, p. 92.)

      a. **Personal effects:** One of the rare exceptions is that if one spouse permits the search of the other's *personal effects* stored in a separate drawer or closet used only by the other, the consent may be invalid.

   2. **Parent/child:** Most courts have held that when a *child* is living at home with his parents, the parents may consent to a search of the *child's room*.

      a. **Consent by child:** The child, on the other hand, may *not* normally consent to a full-scale search of the parents' house. (But if the child merely lets the police into the front area of the house and the child is generally allowed to admit strangers to that front area, the limited consent will probably be valid and anything the police can see from there will fall under the plain view doctrine.)

E. **Other situations:** Here are some other situations that frequently arise regarding third-party consent:

   1. **Landlords:** Generally, a *landlord* may not consent to a search of his tenants' rooms, even though the landlord has the right to enter them for cleaning. But the

landlord may consent to a search of the areas of "common usage," such as hallways and common dining areas.

2. **Employer:** An *employer* probably may consent to a search of his employee's work area if the search is for items *related to the job*. But probably the employer cannot consent to a search of areas where the employee is, by the terms of the job, permitted to store personal effects (e.g., a locker given to the employee to store his street clothes at a factory).

F. Ignorance of consenter: It is irrelevant that the consenter does not know the purpose of the search, or mistakenly believes that the person for whom she is consenting is innocent and has nothing to hide.

IX. STOP-AND-FRISK AND OTHER BRIEF DETENTION

A. Problem generally: Sometimes the police, when they encounter a suspect, do not want to make a full arrest, but merely want to *briefly detain* the person. This happens most typically when the police are not investigating any particular crime, and are simply performing routine patrolling functions. The two questions which the "stop-and-frisk" doctrine deals with are: (1) When may the police *briefly detain* a person even though they *do not have probable cause* to arrest him or to search him, and (2) to what extent may the police conduct a protective, limited *search* for weapons on the suspect's person?

B. General rule: In general, the stop-and-frisk doctrine lets the police do both of the above things in appropriate circumstances:

1. **Right to stop:** Where a police officer *observes unusual conduct* which leads him reasonably to conclude that criminal activity is afoot, he may briefly detain the suspect in order to make inquiries. Probable cause is not required — *reasonable suspicion*, based on *objective facts*, that the individual is involved in criminal activity, will suffice. (The stop is a seizure under the Fourth Amendment, but it does not require probable cause, merely reasonable suspicion.)

2. **Protective frisk:** Once the officer conducts a stop as described above, then assuming nothing in the initial encounter dispels his reasonable fear for his or others' safety, the officer may conduct a *carefully limited search* of the *outer clothing* of the suspect in an attempt to discover *weapons*. This limited *"frisk"* or *"patdown"* is a Fourth Amendment search, but is deemed "reasonable." Consequently, any weapons seized may be introduced against the suspect. [*Terry v. Ohio*; *Brown v. Texas*]

C. Stop of vehicle: The "stop and frisk" doctrine also may apply to allow an officer to order the stop of a *vehicle*.

Example: Officer, while in his patrol car, is approached by an informant he knows, who says that D, in a parked car nearby, possesses a gun and narcotics. Officer detains the car and driver, waits for D to roll down his window, then puts his head in, discovers a weapon in D's waistband, and removes it. *Held*, the informant's tip had sufficient indicia of reliability to allow Officer to forcibly stop D's car; given that the stop was reasonable, the pat-down of D's waistband and removal of the gun were justified to protect Officer. [*Adams v. Williams*]

1. **Suspect and passengers required to leave car:** Once the officer conducts a justified "stop" of a vehicle, the officer may also require the stopped motorist and even the passengers in the vehicle to *leave the car*, as a legitimate safety measure. [*Pennsylvania v. Mimms*; *Maryland v. Wilson*]

   a. **Pat-down of non-suspect passenger:** Similarly, if the car has been properly stopped and the occupants temporarily detained, the police are entitled to do a *pat-down* of any *passenger — even if the police have no reason to suspect the passenger of wrongdoing* — as long as the police have a reasonable suspicion that the passenger may be *armed and dangerous*. [*Arizona v. Johnson*]

D. Degree of probability required: Something *less than probable cause* to arrest or search is required in order for the officer to make a "stop."

1. **Vague suspicion not enough:** *Vague suspicion* is not enough. The officer may "stop" the suspect only if he has a "*reasonable suspicion*, based on *objective facts*, that the individual is involved in criminal activity."

   Example: D is stopped because: (1) he is walking in an area having a high incidence of drug traffic; (2) he "looks suspicious" to Officer; and (3) he has not been seen in that area previously by Officer. *Held*, these facts don't meet the "reasonable suspicion based on objective facts" test. Therefore, the stop was an unreasonable seizure in violation of the Fourth Amendment. [*Brown v. Texas*]

2. **"Modest suspicion" enough:** But a fairly modest amount of suspicion *will* be enough for a brief stop.

   a. **Innocent acts taken together:** For instance, suppose D engages in a number of acts in sequence, each of which is *innocent in itself*; if, viewed under a *"totality of circumstances"* approach, the acts together would create reasonable suspicion that D is engaged in wrongdoing, that will suffice for a *Terry* stop.

3. **Flight as a cause for suspicion:** The fact that an individual has *attempted to flee* when seen by the police will normally raise the police's suspicion, and may even without more justify the police in making a *Terry*-style stop.

   Example: D flees when he sees police officers patrolling the high-crime area where he is walking. They therefore stop him and pat him down. *Held*, the officers were justified in stopping D, because the combination of his fleeing from the police and his presence in a high-crime area created a reasonable suspicion that D was engaged in some sort of wrongdoing. [*Illinois v. Wardlow*]

4. **Informant's tip:** A *Terry*-like "stop" may be justified not only based on the officer's own observations, but also based on an *informant's tip*. Again, all that is required is "reasonable suspicion," and in the case of an informant's tip this is to be determined by the "totality of the circumstances."

    a. Prediction of future events: A key factor is whether the informant has *predicted future events* that someone without inside information would have been unlikely to know.

    b. Knowledge of hidden criminality: Also, where the informant is *anonymous*, the police must have reason to believe that the *informant's knowledge about the suspect's criminal conduct* is *reliable*. It's not enough that the informant merely knows something non-criminal about the suspect that anyone could know (e.g., the suspect's physical appearance and present location).

        Example: The police get an anonymous phone tip that a black male wearing a plaid shirt is standing on a particular street corner and carrying a concealed illegal weapon. The police stop D (who meets that description), pat him down, and find an illegal weapon on him.

        Held, the police didn't have enough suspicion from the tip to make the stop. That's because the anonymous informant didn't give the police any reason to believe that his information about D's *criminal conduct* (hidden weapon) was reliable — the mere fact that the informant knew something non-criminal and publicly-visible about D (what D was wearing and where he was standing) was not an indicator of the informant's reliability as to the criminal conduct. [*Florida v. J.L.*]

E. What constitutes a "stop": Not every brief encounter between a police officer and a person on the street or in a car constitutes a *"stop"* within the meaning of the Fourth Amendment (i.e., a detention of such severity that it rises to the level of a Fourth Amendment seizure and must therefore be "reasonable").

    1. The "reasonable person" test: Here is the test for determining whether an encounter constitutes a Fourth Amendment "seizure": "A person has been 'seized' within the meaning of the Fourth Amendment only if, in view of all of the circumstances surrounding the incident, a *reasonable person* would have believed that he was *not free to leave*." [*U.S. v. Mendenhall*])

        a. Illustrations showing lack of freedom to leave: Here are examples (cited by the Court in *Mendenhall, supra*) of circumstances that might indicate to a reasonable person that he is not free to leave: (1) the *threatening presence* of several officers; (2) the *display of a weapon* by an officer; (3) some *physical touching* of the person; or (4) the use of *language* or *tone of voice* indicating that compliance with the officer's request might be compelled.

        Example: Suppose Officer, upon passing D in the street, says, "Could I ask you a question, sir?" At this point, probably no Fourth Amendment seizure has occurred, because a reasonable person in D's situation would probably think he was free to refuse to answer the question and continue walking. If so, Officer would not need any "reasonable suspicion, based on objective facts…," and even in the absence of such suspicion any incriminating statement made by D would be admissible against him. (That is, D could not have his statement excluded as the fruit of the poisonous tree, because no illegal Fourth Amendment seizure would have occurred.)

2. Chase by police: If the police are *chasing* a suspect, the chase itself does *not* constitute a "seizure" — until the suspect *submits* to the chase (by stopping), there is no seizure.

F. "Stop" vs. arrest: At some point, the stop is sufficiently long and intrusive that it turns into a *full-scale arrest*. Remember the significance of the distinction between stop and arrest: for a stop, only "reasonable suspicion" is required, whereas for an arrest, probable cause is required. Here are the factors the Court looks to in determining whether a detention has remained a "stop":

1. No longer than reasonably necessary: The detention must not be *longer* than the circumstances justifying it require. Typically, this will not be more than a few minutes, but in unique situations (e.g., waiting for a suspected "alimentary canal" drug smuggler to void), longer may be allowed.

2. No more intrusive than reasonably necessary: The stop must also be *no more intrusive than needed* to verify or dispel the officer's suspicions.

a. May demand identification: The police may demand that D orally *identify himself*. [*Hiibel v. Sixth Judicial Dist. Ct.*] But we don't yet know whether the police may demand to see an identification document like a *driver's license*.

3. Transporting D to somewhere else: Finally, if the police *transport* the suspect to another place, especially the *station house*, this is likely to turn the stop into an arrest. Thus even if *no formal arrest* is made, the police cannot transport a suspect to the police station without probable cause. [*Dunaway v. New York*]

G. Scope of permissible frisk: When the police perform a *frisk* after making a stop, the frisk must be limited to a search for *weapons*, or other sources of *danger*. That is, the purpose of the frisk may not be to search for *contraband* or *incriminating evidence*.

Example: Officer temporarily stops D, a patron in a bar, and frisks him. Officer feels, through D's clothing, what appears to be a cigarette pack with some objects in it. Officer then removes the pack, and discovers heroin packets inside it. *Held*, the search went beyond the permissible scope of a frisk pursuant to a stop-and-frisk: Officer had no reasonable belief that D was armed or dangerous, so Officer was not entitled to even start the frisk. [*Ybarra v. Illinois*]

1. Armed or dangerous: The frisk may take place only if the officer has a reasonable belief that D may be *armed or dangerous*. Thus if D's hands are empty, he gives no indication of possessing a weapon, he makes no gestures indicating an intent to commit assault, and he acts generally in a non-threatening manner, the officer probably may not conduct even the basic outside-the-clothes pat-down. See *Ybarra v. Illinois, supra*]

H. Search of automobile: When the police make a "stop" of a person in a car, the police may then search for weapons in the car's *passenger compartment*, even though the suspect is no longer inside the car. [*Michigan v. Long*] Just as the police may frisk the body of a suspect who has merely been stopped rather than arrested if the officers reasonably believe the suspect may be armed, so the police may search the passenger compartment if: (1) the officers reasonably believe that the driver is dangerous and may gain control of weapons that may be in the car; and (2) they look only in those parts of the passenger compartment where weapons might be placed or hidden.

1. **Limited application:** In the typical situation of a stop for a **traffic violation**, there probably will be no right to search the passenger compartment for weapons, because the police would not have a "reasonable belief based on specific and articulable facts" that weapons may be found in the car. But if the police find weapons on the suspect's **person**, or they see a weapon in plain view in the car, then presumably they become entitled to conduct a weapons search throughout the passenger compartment.

I. Detention during house search: When the police are **searching a residence** for contraband, pursuant to a **search warrant**, they may **detain the occupants** while the search continues. [*Michigan v. Summers*]

1. **Use of force, including handcuffs:** When the police exercise this right to detain the occupants while executing a search warrant, they may use **reasonable force** to carry out the detention. If they're searching for **weapons**, reasonable force includes the **handcuffing** of all occupants of the house. [*Muehler v. Mena*]

2. **Applies only to immediate vicinity of arrest:** The holding of *Michigan v. Summers, supra* — that while police are executing a search warrant, they may temporarily detain any persons present on the searched premises — applies only to persons who are detained while they are either **on** the premises or **in the immediate vicinity of** those premises. Once a person is permitted to **leave** the immediate vicinity of the premises being searched, the automatic "police may detain" rule of *Summers* no longer applies, **no matter how "reasonable" it may be** for the police to then detain that person. Instead, the usual Fourth Amendment procedures (including the rules on "stop and frisk") apply. [*Bailey v. U.S.*]

> **Example:** The police have a valid search warrant for 103 Lake Drive, to search for a .380 caliber handgun. While they are outside the building and about to start their search, they see someone (D) drive away from number 103. They follow him for a mile, then stop and detain him. When they question him about his connection to number 103, he tells inconsistent stories, which lead the police to disbelieve him and search him (which results in incriminating evidence). D claims that the police had no right to detain him merely because he had just left the place they had a warrant to search.
>
> *Held*, for D. The fact that the police were about to execute a search warrant at number 103 did not give them the right to detain anyone who was no longer in the "immediate vicinity of the premises to be searched." Since D was not stopped until he was nearly 1 mile away from number 103, the right of the police to detain him under *Summers* had passed, no matter how reasonable the police behavior was. Therefore, the stop of D will have to be justified on some other principle (e.g., stop-and-frisk). [*Bailey v. U.S., supra.*]

X. REGULATORY AND OTHER "SPECIAL NEEDS" SEARCHES

A. **Summary:** So far, we've looked at the Fourth Amendment only in the context of the investigation of specific crimes. In that context, as we've seen, probable cause to search is usually necessary, and a search warrant is necessary unless there is a specific exception to the warrant requirement.

Now, we turn to certain kinds of law enforcement activities that may invade areas protected by the Fourth Amendment, but whose *special nature* may justify dispensing with either *probable cause*, or a *search warrant*, or both. These activities are commonly said to be ones presenting *"special needs."* Most of these activities have a *"regulatory"* rather than "investigation of crime" flavor.

The "special needs" activities that we'll examine here are:

[1] *health, fire* and other *safety-related inspections* of *physical premises* by government inspectors who are *not investigating suspected crimes*;

[2] *border* and other *immigration-related* searches;

[3] routine *traffic stops* (including *sobriety checkpoints*);

[4] capturing the *DNA* of arrestees;

[5] searches of *parolees and probationers*; and

[6] *school searches*.

B. **Health and safety inspections of physical premises:** The Supreme Court has laid down special rules governing how the Fourth Amendment restricts the circumstances under which government *inspectors* may perform inspections of physical premises to ensure that *health, fire and other safety regulations* are being complied with. We'll refer to this sort of premises inspection as a *"building search."*[2]

1. **Summary of rules:** Here is a summary of these special rules governing building searches:

[1] Most importantly, the inspector *does not need to have any suspicion at all* that there are health or safety violations at the particular premises to be inspected. Thus *"area-wide building inspections"* are possible.

[2] On the other hand, the inspector is *not* free to demand an inspection of premises *without some sort of warrant.* As shown in rule [3] below, the warrant can be of a special and easy-to-obtain sort, but the inspector cannot simply demand to inspect a particular building "empty handed," assuming there is no emergency.

[3] The required warrant is quite different from a standard "search warrant" as described in the warrant clause of the Fourth Amendment for use in criminal

---

2. The inspector is always free to arrive at premises without any warrant or grounds for suspicion and to ask the owner or occupant to *consent* to a building search; if the latter agrees, then the search is lawful regardless of whether the inspector had any grounds for suspicion, and regardless of whether she had any kind of search warrant. Our discussion here focuses on the rules that apply if the owner/occupant *refuses consent*.

investigations. In the building-search context, the warrant requirement (essentially a *judge-made rule* created by the Supreme Court in interpreting the Fourth Amendment's general "no unreasonable searches" clause, *not* the warrant clause) works this way:

[a] The official seeking the warrant does *not* have to show *probable cause* that the particular building to be inspected *violates* any health or safety regulation.

[b] Instead, the official merely has to show that government is proposing to conduct an *"area inspection"* that is *reasonably tailored to making sure that the relevant health or safety codes are being observed.*

[c] The main function of the warrant requirement in this building-inspection context is to make sure that government inspectors are *not given undue discretion* that they can use to harass particular owners or occupants for non-safety-related purposes.

Example: The need for an area-wide warrant would help prevent a corrupt building inspector from "shaking down" a particular restaurant owner — if the inspector wasn't required to have such a warrant, the inspector could threaten to conduct a bogus "for harassment only" health inspection of the restaurant premises twice a day for months if the owner didn't pay her a bribe.

[4] The inspector doesn't necessarily have to be in possession of the warrant at the time she *first seeks to enter the premises.* Instead, the inspector can ask the owner to consent to the search, and if he refuses, hand him an administrative subpoena. The owner can then delay the search while seeking to having the subpoena quashed by a judge.

[Cf. *Camara v. Municipal Court of San Francisco*]

2. **Houses and businesses, generally:** The above rules, requiring an administrative "area-wide" warrant, apply to both *housing inspections* and to *safety-related inspections of businesses generally*.

Example: A federal occupational-safety statute, OSHA, purports to let federal inspectors search any workplace covered by OSHA during regular working hours, in order to inspect for violation of federal job-safety standards. The statute says that the inspector does not need any sort of search warrant before demanding the inspection. P, an owner of an ordinary, non-closely-regulated business, contends that such warrantless inspections violate his Fourth Amendment rights.

Held, for P. Warrantless inspections of certain types of *closely-regulated* businesses (discussed below) may be permissible. But the Fourth Amendment requires some sort of a warrant before a compulsory regulatory inspection of an ordinary, non-closely-regulated, business, such as the one here. [*Marshall v. Barlow's, Inc.*]

3. **Special rule for closely-regulated businesses:** But the Supreme Court has *allowed* governments to make warrantless regulatory inspections of certain types

of *closely-regulated businesses.* The Court has not given a consistent explanation of when this "closely-regulated business" exception applies. But a 2015 case says that the exception applies only to businesses that "pose[] a clear and significant *risk to the public welfare.*" [*Los Angeles v. Patel, infra*]

a. **What businesses are deemed "closely-regulated":** The Supreme Court has, over many decades, identified only *four types* of businesses as falling within this "closely-regulated" category for which no prior inspection warrant is required:

[1] businesses that *sell liquor* on the premises (e.g., liquor stores and catering halls);

[2] *firearms dealers*;

[3] *mining* businesses; and

[4] *automobile junkyards*.

4. **Hotels are not closely-regulated:** One category of business that the Court has held *not* to be "closely regulated" is *hotels*. Therefore, inspectors who are not equipped with at least an administrative search warrant may not demand to make a regulatory inspection of a hotel's registry of guests. [*City of Los Angeles v. Patel* (2015)]

> **Example:** D (the City of Los Angeles) enacts an ordinance requiring every hotel operator to keep a registry of information about each guest including name, address, license plate number, etc. The ordinance also requires every operator to make this registry available for inspection by any L.A. police officer on demand. The Ps, a group of motel operators, claim that by requiring them to furnish such information to the police without a warrant and without any provision for pre-compliance judicial review, the ordinance violates their Fourth Amendment rights.
>
> *Held* (by a 5-4 vote), for the Ps. Even administrative search schemes — allowing searches whose primary purpose is regulatory, not crime control — must normally give the person whose property is being searched the opportunity to have a neutral decision maker (not the officer seeking to do the search) review the reasonableness of the search before the property owner is required to comply.
>
> It's true that owners of businesses in a few types of "closely-regulated" industries, ones posing a "clear and significant risk to the public welfare." may be subjected to warrantless searches. But hotels as a category do not pose such a risk. Therefore, the Ps have the right to insist on not being searched unless and until a magistrate first reviews the propriety of the inspector's administrative subpoena. [*City of Los Angeles v. Patel, supra*]

C. **Immigration searches:** Certain types of *immigration*-related searches may be carried out without a warrant and without probable cause.

1. **Border searches:** At the *border*, immigration and customs officials may search baggage and vehicles (and to a limited extent, the traveler's own person) *without*

probable cause to believe that there is an immigration violation or smuggling, and *without a warrant*. [*Almeida-Sanchez v. U.S.*]

2. **Interior patrols and checkpoints:** Where a search does not occur at the border or its "functional equivalent," however, a stronger showing of reasonable suspicion is required. A vehicle inside the border and *not known to have recently crossed the border* may be stopped and searched only if there is probable cause to believe that aliens or smuggled objects are present. [*Almeida-Sanchez, supra.*] But there are two exceptions to this tougher rule:

    a. **Roving patrol:** Where immigration officials, as part of a *"roving patrol,"* stop a car in the interior not to make a search, but to briefly question the occupants, probable cause is not required. The officials must, however, point to *specific factors* giving rise to some *significant suspicion* that a violation has occurred.

    Example: The Mexican appearance of the car's inhabitants is not by itself sufficient to allow even a brief stop for questioning, even in, say, southern Texas.

    b. **Fixed check-point:** Where a *fixed checkpoint* is set up in the interior, *all* cars may be stopped for brief immigration-related questioning. Then, if the questioning gives rise to additional suspicion, motorists may be referred to a second place where they can be questioned and if necessary searched. [*U.S. v. Martinez-Fuerte*]

D. Routine traffic stops: Apart from the border-search and immigration issues, the police may wish to stop cars for regulatory purposes (e.g., to make sure that the driver is *licensed* and the car is *registered*).

1. **Random stops:** If the police *randomly* stop cars to do this checking, they may not make a particular stop unless they have a *suspicion* of wrongdoing based upon an "objective standard." That is, a practice of making *totally random* stops, where a stop is made even though the officer has no objective grounds for suspicion, violates the Fourth Amendment. [*Delaware v. Prouse*]

2. **Checkpoint:** However, the police may set up a *fixed checkpoint* on the highway to test for compliance related to driver safety. Thus they can stop to check for drunkenness [*Mich. Dept. of State Police v. Sitz*], and can probably check to see that the driver is licensed and the vehicle is registered. [Dictum in *Delaware v. Prouse*]

    a. **Seeking of eyewitnesses to crime:** Similarly, the police may set up a fixed roadblock or checkpoint to *find witnesses* to a recent crime, if that's a reasonable method of finding such witnesses.

    Example: V is killed in a hit-and-run accident on a highway late on a Saturday night. One week later, at the same place and time, the police stop each car and hand the driver a flier seeking witnesses to the crime. D, who is stopped but has nothing to do with the hit-and-run, is arrested when the police smell alcohol on his breath. *Held*, the stop here was reasonable, because it searched for witnesses, not suspects, and did so in a minimally-intrusive way. [*Illinois v. Lidster*]

3. **No general crime-fighting:** But police may *not* set up a fixed checkpoint to pursue *general crime-fighting objectives*, such as *narcotics detection*.

   Example: Police set up a fixed checkpoint and stop a pre-determined number of cars. When each car is stopped, police walk around it to see if they can spot (in plain view) any evidence that the car contains narcotics. They also use a drug dog to sniff for narcotics. *Held*, these warrantless stops are unreasonable and thus a violation of the Fourth Amendment, because they are being done for general crime-fighting purposes, not administrative concerns relating to road safety. [*Indianapolis v. Edmond*]

E. **Capturing the DNA of arrested persons:** The police may, without a search warrant, *take a DNA sample* from *anyone arrested for a serious crime*. Consequently, federal, state and local police may all *build databases of the DNA of anyone they arrest* for a "serious offense," and use that data to match suspects with prior or future unsolved crimes. [*Maryland v. King* (2013)]

   Example: D is arrested in Maryland in 2009 on assault charges. A Maryland statute permits police to collect DNA samples from any individual who has been *charged* with an actual or attempted *crime of violence*, even if the person hasn't yet been convicted. Since the assault charge against D involves a crime of violence, the police — as part of their *routine booking procedures* — collect D's DNA sample by swabbing the inside of his cheek. D's sample, when checked against an FBI database, matches the DNA taken from a victim in an unsolved 2003 rape case. D is charged with the 2003 rape and convicted. D argues that the Maryland statute, by authorizing the taking of a DNA sample from him based on *mere arrest* — not yet followed by conviction — gave rise to an "unreasonable" search, and thus violated his Fourth Amendment rights.

   Held, for the prosecution: D's conviction is valid, and the Maryland statute does not violate an arrestee's Fourth Amendment rights. It's true that the taking of a DNA swab from an arrestee without consent constitutes a Fourth Amendment search. But such searches serve the government's legitimate interest in identifying the person taken into custody. Therefore, the taking of a DNA swab is, *"like fingerprinting and photographing*, a legitimate police *booking procedure* that is *reasonable under the Fourth Amendment."* [*Maryland v. King, supra*]

F. **Other contexts:** Here are some other contexts in which government's right to make inspections and regulatory searches has arisen:

1. **Supervision of parolees and probationers:** *Parolees* and *probationers* may be subjected to warrantless searches by officials responsible for them, even if probable cause is lacking. [*Griffin v. Wisconsin*] Instead of probable cause and a warrant, all that is required for the search of a probationer or a parolee is that it be conducted pursuant to a *valid regulation*.

   a. **Search on street:** In fact, the police may subject parolees to a warrantless stop and search at any time *even if the officer has no grounds to suspect* *wrongdoing at all,* so long as this condition is disclosed to the prisoner prior to his release on parole. That's because parolees have "severely diminished expectations of privacy by virtue of their status alone." [*Samson v. California*] (It's not clear whether this "no suspicion required" rule also applies to *probationers,* who seem to have greater constitutional rights than parolees.)

b. Pre-trial detainee: Similarly, *pre-trial detainees* may be subjected to cell searches and in some cases searches of body cavities, without probable cause or a warrant. Such a detainee, even though he has not been convicted of any crime, has a *"diminished"* reasonable expectation of privacy. [*Bell v. Wolfish*]

2. Searches in schools: The rules regarding when searches of *students* and their possessions may take place without a warrant and without probable cause are still uncertain. We do know that the schools have substantial power to take these actions if they don't act in connection with the police.

a. Warrantless search for violation of school rules: Thus a *school official* acting alone (not acting in concert with law enforcement authorities) may search the person and premises of a student *without a warrant.* All that is required is that the official have "*reasonable grounds* for *suspecting* that the search will turn up evidence that the student has violated or is violating either the law or the *rules of the school.*" [*New Jersey v. T.L.O.*]

Note: It's not clear whether the same "suspicion of violating school rules" standard applies where the search of the student is actually carried out by law enforcement officials as opposed to school officials. Probably the Supreme Court would say that the Fourth Amendment applies once the police get involved.

b. Drug tests for competitive extracurricular activities: Similarly, a school district may require that all students who want to participate in *"competitive extracurricular activities"* (e.g., interscholastic sports) submit to a *drug test* (urinalysis), at least where the results are not shared with the police, and the testing is conducted in a relatively unintrusive manner. This is true even if the school district does not yet have a significant drug problem. [*Bd. of Ed. v. Earls*]

CHAPTER 4
ELECTRONIC SURVEILLANCE AND SECRET AGENTS

I. ELECTRONIC SURVEILLANCE

A. Wiretapping and bugging generally: There are two main techniques of "electronic surveillance" often used by law enforcement officials, on which the Fourth Amendment places strict limits. These two techniques are *"wiretapping"* and *"bugging."*

1. Wiretap: In a wiretap, the listener (in our context, the government) places electronic equipment on the *telephone wires,* and uses this equipment to listen to conversations that take place on the telephone.

2. **Bugging:** In "bugging" (also known as "electronic eavesdropping"), the listener puts a microphone in or near the place where a conversation is to occur, and uses this equipment to listen directly to the conversation. (An example of bugging would be the placement of a microphone inside a lamp inside the suspect's bedroom, where the microphone is used to pick up and transmit conversations taking place in that room.)

B. **Requires warrant and probable cause:** Both wiretapping and bugging normally constitute *Fourth Amendment searches*, and must therefore satisfy the requirements of *probable cause* and a *warrant*. That is, so long as the conversation that is intercepted is one as to which both participants had a *reasonable expectation of privacy*, the fact that the microphone or wiretapping equipment is located outside the suspect's premises makes no difference. The famous case of *Katz v. U.S.*, in which the Supreme Court first articulated its "justifiable expectation of privacy" test for determining when the Fourth Amendment applies, was in fact a bugging case.

1. **Participant monitoring:** But where the wire-tapping or eavesdropping occurs with the *consent* of one of the parties to the conversation, then there is *no Fourth Amendment problem*.

   Example: The FBI learns that D and X will be having a conversation in which D is likely to implicate himself in a crime. They ask X for permission to place a wiretap on X's phone; X agrees. The conversation takes place, and the agents record it. This wiretapping is not a violation of the Fourth Amendment, because it occurred with the permission of one of the participants. Therefore, the recording can be introduced against D at his criminal trial.

C. **Federal statutory regulation:** The use of wiretapping and electronic eavesdropping by government is now tightly regulated by a federal statute, Title III of the Omnibus Crime Control and Safe Streets Act of 1968.

1. **Regulates state and federal law enforcement:** No *federal or state* law enforcement official may conduct electronic surveillance except by following the strict procedural requirements of Title III. (Also, a state official may not do so unless her state has passed enabling legislation, which fewer than half the states have done.)

2. **Requirements:** Under Title III, electronic surveillance may not take place except under a special *judicial order* authorizing the surveillance *in advance*. The judge may authorize an intercept only if he finds that (*inter alia*): (1) there is *probable cause* to believe that a *specific individual* has committed one of certain crimes listed in the statute; (2) there is probable cause to believe that the intercept will *furnish evidence* about the crime; (3) normal investigative procedures have been tried and have failed, or reasonably appear likely to fail or be dangerous; and (4) there is probable cause to believe that the facilities where the intercept is to be made are being used in conjunction with the offense or are linked to the suspected individual.

3. Covert entry allowed: Once officials get a Title III judicial order authorizing bugging, they may make a *covert entry* even into private premises to install the bug. [*Dalia v. U.S.*]

4. Consenting party exception: Title III does not apply where an interception takes place with the *consent* of one of the parties to a communication; in this situation, no warrant is needed (because, as noted above, the Fourth Amendment itself is never triggered).

II. SECRET AGENTS

A. Secret agents generally: Fourth Amendment questions can also arise where the police make use of *"secret agents."* A secret agent is, in essence, a person who has *direct contact* with a suspect, under circumstances in which the suspect *does not realize* that he is dealing with someone who is helping the government. A secret agent can either be "bugged" (i.e., equipped with an electronic device that records and/or transmits conversations) or "unbugged."

1. Summary of law: In brief, *neither "bugged" nor "unbugged" secret agents pose Fourth Amendment problems* — so long as the target is aware that a person (the agent) is present, the fact that the target is unaware that the agent is indeed a secret agent or informer (as opposed to being the suspect's friend, for instance) does not turn the mission into a "search" or "seizure" under the Fourth Amendment.

B. Bugged agents: Thus the Supreme Court has held several times that "bugged agents" — secret agents equipped with electronic surveillance equipment — are not eavesdropping and thus cannot possibly violate the Fourth Amendment. [*On Lee v. U.S.*; *U.S. v. White*]

> **Example:** Informer is wired to transmit to narcotics agents conversations that he hears or is a part of. Informer then has conversations with D in a restaurant, in D's home, and in Informer's car. Tapes of these transmitted conversations are introduced at D's criminal trial. *Held*, no Fourth Amendment right has been triggered. When a person misplaces his trust and makes incriminating statements to an informer, he does not have any justifiable expectation of privacy which has been violated — there is no Fourth Amendment protection given to "a wrongdoer's misplaced belief that a person to whom he voluntarily confides his wrongdoing will not reveal it." This is true whether the informer is bugged or not. [*U.S. v. White, supra.*]

C. Unbugged agents: Since the use of bugged agents does not implicate the Fourth Amendment, it is not surprising that the use of *unbugged* agents does not violate that amendment either.

> **Example:** A Teamster-turned-informant visits Jimmy Hoffa's hotel room and overhears conversations concerning Hoffa's plan to bribe jurors. The informant testifies about these conversations in Hoffa's later jury-tampering trial.
>
> *Held*, Hoffa's Fourth Amendment rights were not even implicated, let alone violated, by introduction of these statements. Hoffa's "misplaced trust"

was his own fault, and did not vitiate his consent to the informant's entry into the hotel suite. [*Hoffa v. U.S.*]

Note on the right to counsel: But the use of a bugged or unbugged informer against a suspect who has already been *indicted* may violate the suspect's *Sixth Amendment right to counsel*, discussed below. Once a suspect has been indicted and has counsel, it is a violation of that right to counsel for the secret agent to "deliberately elicit" incriminating statements from the suspect in the absence of counsel, and to pass these on to the prosecution for use in the case involving the indictment. For instance, in *Hoffa, supra*, if Hoffa had already been indicted by the time the informant came to Hoffa's hotel room — which he had not — the statements could not have been used against Hoffa in the trial on that indictment.

D. Entrapment: Very occasionally, a secret agent may be so active that his role constitutes *"entrapment"* of the defendant. In most jurisdictions, entrapment occurs if a law enforcement official, or someone cooperating with him, has *induced* D to commit a crime which D was not otherwise *predisposed* to commit.

> **Example:** X, a secret government agent, repeatedly says to D over many months, "Why don't we rob the local 7-11?" D resists each time. Finally, D agrees to drive a car and wait while X does the robbery. As they arrive at the 7-11, police arrest D and charge him with attempted robbery. D may be able to establish that he was not predisposed to commit robbery and did so only because X induced him; if so, D may succeed with an entrapment defense.

1. Not a constitutional defense: The Supreme Court has never recognized any *constitutional basis* for the entrapment defense. Thus it is up to each state legislature (and, in the federal system, up to the Supreme Court in the exercise of its supervisory powers over the administration of justice in the federal court system) to decide under what facts the entrapment defense should be allowed. So in an exam question that is focusing on constitutional criminal procedure, you can probably ignore the possibility that the secret agent's conduct amounted to entrapment.

CHAPTER 5

CONFESSIONS AND POLICE INTERROGATION

I. INTRODUCTION

A. Two requirements for confessions: In both state and federal courts, a *confession* may be introduced against the person who made it only if the confession satisfies *each* of the following two requirements:

1. Voluntary: The confession must have been *voluntary*, i.e., not the product of *coercion* by the police; and

2. *Miranda* **warnings:** The confession must have been obtained in *conformity* with the *Miranda* decision — in brief, if the confession was given by the suspect while he was in custody and under interrogation by the authorities, the suspect must have been warned that he had the right to remain silent, that anything he said could be used against him, and that he had the right to have an attorney present.

II. VOLUNTARINESS

A. Voluntariness generally: Regardless of whether *Miranda* warnings are given to the suspect, his confession will only be admissible against him if it was given *voluntarily*.

   1. Must be police coercion: But the test for determining the "voluntariness" of a confession is one that is fairly easy to satisfy. Apparently the only thing that can now prevent a confession from being found to be "voluntary" is *police coercion*. Thus neither coercion by non-government personnel, nor serious *mental illness* on the suspect's part, is relevant to this question.

   > **Example 1:** Victim says to Suspect, "Because you shot me, I will take revenge on you by shooting your sister unless you turn yourself into the police and confess." Suspect goes to the police and confesses. It appears that this confession would be treated as "voluntary," and admitted against Suspect at his criminal trial, even though it was in a sense the product of coercion by Victim — so long as there was no police coercion, nothing else matters in deciding the question of voluntariness.

   > **Example 2:** Suspect is in a psychotic schizophrenic state. He confesses to a crime because the "voice of God" tells him he should do so. *Held*, this confession is admissible against Suspect, because there was no police or other governmental wrongdoing. [*Colorado v. Connelly*]

   2. Collateral use: If a confession *is* obtained by police coercion (and is thus "involuntary"), it must be excluded not only from the prosecution's case in chief, but also from use to *impeach* D's testimony. (This makes involuntary confessions quite different from confessions given in violation of *Miranda*, which may be admitted to impeach D's testimony on the stand.)

III. *MIRANDA* GENERALLY

A. *Miranda:* The main set of rules governing confessions in both state and federal courts derive from *Miranda v. Arizona*. In general, *Miranda* holds that when a suspect is questioned in custody by the police, his confession will be admissible against him only if he has received the "*Miranda* warnings."

B. Three requirements for application: Before *Miranda* will be found to apply, *three requirements* must be satisfied:

   1. Custody: First, *Miranda* warnings are necessary only where the suspect is taken into *custody*. (Thus if the police ask a question to someone they meet on the street, without formally detaining him, *Miranda* is not triggered.)

   2. Questioning: Second, the *Miranda* rule applies only where the confession comes as the result of *questioning*. (Thus statements that are truly *"volunteered"* by the suspect are not covered.)

3. **Authorities:** Finally, *Miranda* applies only where both the questioning and the custody are by the ***police*** or other ***law enforcement authorities***. (Thus if a private citizen, acting independently of law enforcement officials, detains a suspect and questions him, any resulting confession is not covered.)

C. **Warnings required:** There are ***four warnings*** that are required once *Miranda* applies at all. The suspect must be warned that:

1. He has the right to ***remain silent***;

2. Anything he says can be ***used against him*** in a court of law;

3. He has the right to the ***presence*** of an ***attorney***; and

4. If he cannot ***afford*** an attorney, one will be ***appointed for him*** prior to any questioning if he desires.

D. **Inadmissibility:** Any statement obtained in violation of the *Miranda* rules will be ***inadmissible*** as prosecution evidence, even if the statement is in a sense "voluntary."

1. **Impeachment use:** But a confession given in violation of *Miranda*, although not admissible as part of the prosecution's case in chief, may generally be introduced for purposes of ***impeaching*** testimony that the defendant has given. This "impeachment exception" to *Miranda* is discussed further below.

E. **Rights may be exercised at any time:** The suspect may exercise his right to remain silent, or to have a lawyer present, at ***any time*** during the questioning. Thus even if the suspect at first indicates that he waives his right to silence and to a lawyer, if he ***changes his mind*** the interrogation must ***cease***.

F. **Waiver:** The suspect may ***waive*** his right to remain silent and to have a lawyer. However, this waiver is effective only if it is ***knowingly and intelligently made***. The suspect's ***silence*** may not be taken as a waiver.

1. **Suspect already aware of rights:** The police must give the *Miranda* warnings even if they have reason to believe that the suspect is already ***aware*** of his rights.

G. **Right to counsel:** Here's what's key about the right to counsel under *Miranda*:

1. **Right to appoint counsel applies only where questioning occurs:** If the suspect says that he wants his own lawyer present, or that he cannot afford a lawyer and wants one appointed for him, the police do ***not*** have an absolute duty to provide the previously-retained lawyer or a new appointed one — the rule is merely that the police ***must not question the suspect*** until they get him a lawyer. So the police can avoid the need for procuring counsel by simply not conducting the interrogation.

2. **Right to have lawyer present during questioning:** The right to counsel imposed by *Miranda* is not merely the right to ***consult*** a lawyer prior to the questioning, but the right to ***have the lawyer present*** while the questioning occurs.

H. **Fifth Amendment basis for:** The basis for *Miranda* is the ***Fifth Amendment's*** privilege against ***self-incrimination***, ***not*** the Sixth Amendment's right to counsel. The basic idea is that when a suspect is questioned while in custody, this questioning is likely to induce confessions made in violation of the Fifth Amendment.

1. **Congress or state legislature can't override:** Because *Miranda* was based on the Court's interpretation of the constitution, Congress and state legislatures ***can't impose different rules*** that make non-*Mirandized* confessions substantively admissible.

> **Example:** Shortly after the *Miranda* decision, Congress passes a statute saying that in federal prosecutions, any confession that was voluntary under all the circumstances must be admissible against the defendant, even if the *Miranda* warnings were not given. *Held*, this provision is unconstitutional, because *Miranda* is a "constitutional rule," and Congress can't change the scope of constitutional guarantees. [*Dickerson v. U.S.*]

IV. WHAT IS A "CUSTODIAL" INTERROGATION

A. **"Custody" required:** *Miranda* warnings must be given only when police questioning occurs while the suspect is in ***"custody."***

1. **"Focus of investigation" irrelevant:** In deciding whether the suspect is in "custody," the fact that the police investigation has (or has not) ***"focused"*** on that suspect is ***irrelevant***.

2. **Objective "reasonable suspect" test:** Whether a suspect is or is not in "custody" as of a particular moment is to be determined by an objective ***"reasonable suspect"*** test: the issue is ***whether a reasonable person in the suspect's position would believe that he was (or was not) in custody at that moment.***

   a. **Officer's unexpressed intent irrelevant:** This "reasonable suspect" standard means that the ***unexpressed intent of the interrogating officer*** to hold (or not hold) the suspect is ***irrelevant***.

   > **Example:** D, a motorist, is stopped by Officer and required to get out of his car. Officer asks D a question, to which D gives an incriminating response. At the moment Officer asked the question, Officer had decided to arrest D, but had not yet told D of this fact.
   >
   > *Held*, D was not necessarily in custody from the moment he was required to get out of the car — the issue is "how a reasonable person in the suspect's position would have understood his situation," and a reasonable person on these facts might have believed he was free to go. [*Berkemer v. McCarty*]

   b. **Suspect is minor:** Suppose that the suspect is a ***child***. When the objective "reasonable suspect" test is being applied, the child's ***age will be taken into account*** in determining whether a reasonable person in the suspect's position would believe he was in custody. So the younger the child, the quicker the court will be to conclude that a reasonable person of that child's age would have believed that he was in custody and not free to leave. [*J.D.B. v. North Carolina*]

3. **Undercover agent:** One consequence of the "reasonable suspect" rule is that if D talks to an ***undercover agent*** or to a government ***informant***, and D does not know he is talking to a law enforcement officer, no "custodial interrogation" has taken place. This is true even if D is ***in jail***. [*Illinois v. Perkins*]

Note: However, the use of undercover agents, although it will never cause a *Miranda* violation, may lead to a violation of the suspect's ***Sixth Amendment*** right to ***counsel*** — once a suspect has been indicted or otherwise charged, it violates his right to counsel for a secret agent to deliberately obtain incriminating statements from him in the absence of counsel.

B. Place of interrogation: The ***place*** in which the interrogation takes place will often have an important bearing on whether "custody" exists. The test is always whether a reasonable person in D's position would believe he was free to leave, and this will depend in part on the locale.

1. **Station-house:** Thus interrogations that take place in a ***station house*** are more likely to be found "custodial" than those in, say, the defendant's home.

    a. **Arrest:** If D has been told that he is ***"under arrest"*** and is escorted to the police station, that's virtually dispositive — D is clearly in custody, because a person under arrest is not free to leave (at least until further steps, such as arraignment, have taken place).

    b. **Placed in patrol car:** Similarly, if D has been placed in a ***patrol car*** under circumstances suggesting that D has been arrested, he is clearly in "custody."

    c. **Voluntary station house questioning:** A suspect who ***"voluntarily"*** comes to the police station in response to a police request is normally ***not*** in custody, and is therefore not entitled to *Miranda* warnings. [*Oregon v. Mathiason*]

        i. **Lack of formal arrest not dispositive:** However, the mere fact that there has been ***no formal arrest*** will ***not*** by itself suffice to prevent station house questioning from being custodial. If the surrounding circumstances would indicate to a reasonable person in D's situation that he was not free to leave the station house, then the questioning is "custodial" however voluntary D's initial decision to come to the station may have been.

            Example: During the course of "voluntary" questioning, the police let D know that they now consider him the key suspect in the crime. This is likely to be enough to convince a reasonable person in D's position that the police are about to arrest him; if so, D is already in custody.

2. **Street encounters:** The issue of whether D is in custody often arises where the encounter takes place on the ***street***.

    a. **Scene-of-the-crime questioning:** The police may engage in a general questioning of persons ***near the scene of a crime*** without giving *Miranda* warnings.

        i. **Focus on suspect:** But if the police seize one particular suspect fleeing the scene of the crime, the warnings presumably have to be given.

    b. **D acts suspiciously:** The police may sometimes detain a person not as part of a general "scene of the crime" investigation for a specific known crime, but because the person is ***acting suspiciously***. (*Example:* A brief "stop and frisk" detention.) Such encounters are usually not custodial, even where the suspect is frisked for the policeman's safety.

3. **Traffic stops:** Stops of *motorists* for *minor traffic violations* will normally *not* be "custodial." Here, as in other contexts, the test is whether one in the motorist's position would believe that he was or was not free to leave. Usually a driver in this position would reasonably believe that he was free to leave after a ticket had been issued to him.

   a. **Arrest:** Of course, if the police notify the motorist that he is *under arrest*, he is immediately deemed to be in custody.

4. **Interview at home:** If the encounter takes place at D's *home*, while he has not been placed under arrest, D is probably *not* in custody.

V. MINOR CRIMES

A. No "minor crimes" exception: There is *no "minor crimes" exception* to the *Miranda* requirement. That is, if an interrogation meets all of the standard require-ments for *Miranda* warnings (especially the requirement that the suspect be "in cus-tody"), these warnings must be given *no matter how minor the crime*, and regardless of the fact that *no jail sentence* may be imposed for it. [*Berkemer v. McCarty, supra.*]

1. **Traffic stops:** This means that if the suspect is charged with a *minor traffic vio-lation*, but is then taken into custody, he is entitled to *Miranda* warnings.

VI. WHAT CONSTITUTES INTERROGATION

A. Volunteered statements: A *"volunteered statement"* is not covered by *Miranda*. That is, if a suspect, without being questioned, *spontaneously* makes an incriminating statement, that statement may be introduced against him, despite the absence of *Miranda* warnings.

1. **Voluntary custodial statements:** This is true even if the statement comes from a suspect who is *in custody*. So long as the statement is not induced by police questioning, the fact that the suspect is in custody is not enough to trigger *Miranda*.

B. Indirect questioning: But "interrogation" for *Miranda* purposes includes more than just direct questioning by the police. Interrogation will be deemed to occur whenever a person in custody is subjected to either express questioning, or to words or actions on the part of the police that the police "should know are *reasonably likely* to *elicit* an *incriminating response* from the suspect." [*Rhode Island v. Innis*]

1. **No interrogation found:** Application of this "should know are reasonably likely to elicit an incriminating response" test will often mean that even though the police make comments that lead directly to an incriminating result, no "interroga-tion" is found.

   Example: D is arrested for a murder committed by use of a sawed-off shot-gun, which has not been found. While D is being transported near the crime scene, Officer comments to his colleagues in front of D that there is a school for handicapped children nearby, and that "God forbid one of the children might find a weapon with shells and they might hurt themselves." D then directs the officers to the place where the gun can be found. *Held*, Officer's comment did not constitute interrogation of D, so D was not entitled to *Miranda* warnings. [*Rhode Island v. Innis, supra.*]

C. Police allow situation to develop: The requirement of "interrogation" means that even if the police allow a situation to develop that is likely to induce the suspect to volunteer an incriminating remark, no *Miranda* warnings will be given if the police do not directly interact with the suspect. For instance, where the police allow a meeting between D and his spouse in which D is likely to incriminate himself while under covert observation, probably no "interrogation" occurs. [*Arizona v. Mauro*]

    1. Police set up situation: But if the police intentionally set up a compromising situation for the ***purpose*** of inducing D to incriminate himself, interrogation is much more likely to be found.

D. Identification questions: Routine questions asked to a suspect for ***identification only*** probably do not require *Miranda* warnings.

    Example: Routine questions asked during the booking of a suspect, such as questions about D's name, address, height, weight, etc., do not require *Miranda* warnings.

E. Questions by non-police: Where questions are asked by people other than the police, these will invoke *Miranda* only if asked by other ***law enforcement*** officials.

    1. Investigator or victims: Thus questions asked of a suspect by a ***private investigator***, or by a victim of the crime, will not be covered by *Miranda*.

    2. Government officials: But questions by ***probation officers***, ***IRS agents*** conducting tax investigations, or a court-ordered psychiatrist evaluating D's sanity for purposes of penalties, are all likely to be found to trigger a requirement of *Miranda* warnings.

VII. THE "PUBLIC SAFETY" EXCEPTION TO *MIRANDA*

A. The public safety exception generally: *Miranda* warnings are ***unnecessary*** where the questioning is "reasonably prompted by a concern for the ***public safety***." [*New York v. Quarles*]

    Example: Officer and three colleagues accost D, a suspected rapist, in a grocery store. When he sees the officers, D runs towards the back of the store, where he is caught and handcuffed. Officer, without giving D *Miranda* warnings, asks him whether he has a gun and where it is. D answers, "Over there." The gun is found, and D's statement — plus the gun — are introduced against him at his trial.

    Held, even though D was in custody and was under interrogation at the time of his statement, he was not entitled to *Miranda* warnings because the police questioning was motivated by a need to protect the public safety. [*Quarles, supra.*]

    1. Objective standard: The existence of a threat to the public safety is to be determined by an ***objective***, not subjective, standard. That is, the questioning officer's subjective belief that there is or is not a significant threat to the public safety is *irrelevant*, and the test is whether a *reasonable officer* in that position would conclude that there was such a threat.

2. **May still show compulsion:** Despite the "public safety" exception to *Miranda*, the defendant is always allowed to show that his answers were *actually coerced*. If he can make this showing, he will still be entitled to have those answers excluded — this exclusion will be based on lack of voluntariness, not on the police failure to give *Miranda* warnings.

VIII. WAIVERS AND INVOCATIONS OF *MIRANDA* RIGHTS

A. Waivers and invocations generally: After being read the *Miranda* warnings, a suspect may *waive* his right to a lawyer and his right to remain silent. Conversely, the suspect may *invoke* his *Miranda* rights.

1. **Two different rights:** Keep in mind that there are *two distinct Miranda rights* that may be the subject of a waiver or invocation: the right to have *questioning cease* until the suspect can *consult a lawyer*, and the right to *remain silent*. The rules on waiver and invocation are similar, but not identical, as between the two contexts.

B. Determining whether a waiver occurred: Here are the rules for determining *whether a suspect has waived* one or both of his *Miranda* rights.

1. **"Knowing and voluntary":** For the suspect to be deemed to have waived either *Miranda* right (silence or counsel), the prosecution will have to show that the waiver was *"knowing and voluntary."*

   a. **Fact of confession not enough:** The mere fact that the suspect *answered questions* after being given his *Miranda* warnings will not, without more, constitute the required proof of knowing and voluntary waiver. There must in addition be affirmative evidence of both the voluntary element (i.e., lack of coercion) and the knowing element (understanding of at least some of the consequences of waiving).

      Example: At a hearing on whether D in fact waived his *Miranda* rights before speaking to the police, the arresting officer O testifies that he read D his *Miranda* warnings from a printed card, and that D then confessed when asked whether he was involved in the crime in question. O testifies that he cannot remember whether he asked D if he understood the rights, or whether O made an effort to determine if D was capable of understanding these warnings.

      Held, this testimony is not enough to demonstrate waiver, because it does not satisfy the "knowing" element. The mere fact that warnings were read to the suspect, and that the suspect thereafter immediately confessed, does not establish that he understood the nature of the rights he was waiving. [*Tague v. Louisiana*]

2. **Express waivers:** Waivers can, of course, be *"express."* For instance, if a suspect signs a standard waiver form, that's an express waiver. Express waivers can

be oral, too; if the suspect says to the police, "I understand these rights but I'm willing to talk to you," that's an express waiver. Express waivers will be *valid* as long as there is no indication of *coercion* or of basic *lack of understanding* by the suspect.

3. **Implied waivers:** But *"implied"* waivers are also possible, and, indeed, common. That is, in some cases waiver can be clearly *"inferred* from the *actions and words* of the person interrogated." [*North Carolina v. Butler*]

   a. **Answering of questions:** The most common form of implied waiver comes after the suspect is read his warnings, indicates that he understands them, never expressly says that he is waving his rights, and then *answers one or more questions*. This will certainly be a waiver of the right to silence, and will probably be a waiver of the right to counsel.

   b. **Additional factors:** Here are two additional factors that will make it more likely that an implied waiver will be found to have occurred:

   ❏ D was *familiar with the criminal justice system* by virtue of his having been arrested and interrogated on multiple recent occasions. This familiarity makes it more likely that D understood his rights and understood the consequences of waiving them.

   ❏ D answers *some* questions but refuses to answer others. This selective response makes it more likely that D understood his rights and intended to waive them.

4. **Information about scope of questioning:** For a waiver to be valid, the suspect does not need to be told much if anything about the *scope* of the proposed questioning, as long as the police do not intentionally mislead the subject on this point.

   Example: Suppose the suspect believes that the upcoming interrogation will focus only upon the *minor crime* for which he has been arrested, and waives his *Miranda* rights so as to permit the interrogation. If the police suddenly change the questioning to cover a different, much more major crime (e.g., a murder committed years ago), this does not make the waiver invalid. [*Colorado v. Spring*]

5. **Knowledge that D's lawyer is trying to contact him:** Suppose the suspect is *represented by an attorney who is trying to see him,* and this fact is known to the police but not to the suspect. (For instance, perhaps the lawyer has been retained *on the suspect's behalf* not by the suspect himself but by a *friend or family member*). The suspect's waiver of his *Miranda* rights will be *effective* even though the police: (1) *decline to tell* the suspect that a lawyer has been retained for him or is trying to see him; and (2) *prevent*, or by use of trickery discourage, the lawyer from seeing his client. [*Moran v. Burbine*]

6. **Mentally ill defendant:** Suppose that a suspect who waives his *Miranda* rights is *mentally ill*, and his illness in some sense causes him to waive his *Miranda* rights and confess. Assuming that there is no police coercion, does the fact that the suspect's decision to waive his rights is not fully rational make the waiver invalid? The answer is "no" — *no matter how irrational the suspect's decision to waive*

his Miranda rights, the waiver will stand so long as there was no police coercion. [*Colorado v. Connelly*]

> **Example:** D is a chronic schizophrenic, and is in a psychotic state when he walks up to Officer, waives his *Miranda* rights, and confesses. D, in confessing, thinks he is following the "voice of God." There is no evidence that Officer knew of D's mental state, or used any coercion.
>
> *Held,* the confession is admissible. "*Miranda* protects defendants against **government coercion** leading them to surrender rights protected by the Fifth Amendment; it goes **no further** than that." [*Colorado v. Connelly*]

a. Significance: As *Connelly* and other cases show, the Court refuses to **consider anything but police coercion** in determining whether a waiver of *Miranda* rights is "voluntary."

C. Invocation must be "clear and unequivocal": Just as a *waiver* of either *Miranda* right must be **"clear and unequivocal,"** so an **invocation** of either right must be clear and unequivocal.

1. Police can keep trying: Consequently, until a clear and unequivocal invocation of either right has occurred, the police may **continue to question the suspect** and/or to **repeatedly request a waiver.**

> **Example:** D is interrogated by Detective Helgert and another detective in connection with a fatal shooting one year earlier. They read D *Miranda* warnings from a document, and then ask him to sign the waiver clause at the bottom. D makes an ambiguous indication about whether he understands the rights listed on the document, and refuses to sign the form. The police interrogate him for two and three-quarter hours, during which he mostly remains silent but occasionally gives a one-word non-incriminating answer. Then, Helgert asks D, "Do you pray to God?", to which D answers yes. Helgert next asks, "Do you pray to God to forgive you for shooting that boy down?" D answers yes, and looks away. D later tries to have this last remark suppressed from his trial, arguing that when he gave an ambiguous statement about whether he understood his right to remain silent and intended to invoke it, the police were required to clarify his intent before they resumed questioning.
>
> *Held,* the incriminating remark is admissible. An invocation of the *Miranda* right to remain silent must be unambiguous. D's conduct was ambiguous as to whether he was asserting his right of silence, so he will be deemed not to have asserted that right. Since there is no evidence that he was coerced, the police were entitled to continue questioning him up until the incriminating remark. [*Berguis v. Thompkins*]

2. Mere answering of questions: So the prosecution must demonstrate only three things in order to establish an implied waiver of the right to silence:

[1] that the police gave the suspect *Miranda* warnings;

[2] that the suspect **understood** the warnings; and

[3] that the suspect **answered** one or more questions following the warnings.

If they can show these three things, then the fact that the police **continued to** *interrogate* the suspect at length after he made an ambiguous indication about whether he was invoking his right to silence will not matter.

D. Waiver after successful invocation of the right: Let's turn now to the rules governing what happens when the suspect *does* invoke with sufficient clarity either his right to remain silent or his right to counsel. The suspect's later words or conduct can sometimes be deemed to be an *undoing* of that invocation. The rules for undoing an invocation of the right to counsel are somewhat stricter than those for undoing an invocation of the right to remain silent.

1. Right to counsel: Where the defendant asserts in the first session that he *wants a lawyer*, the Supreme Court has made it *very hard* for the prosecution to establish that this demand has subsequently been waived. The bright-line rule is that once the suspect says he wants to deal with the police only through counsel, he "is *not subject to further interrogation* by the authorities *until counsel has been made available to him*, unless the *accused himself initiates* further communication, exchanges or conversations with the police." [*Edwards v. Arizona*]

    a. Response to questioning: Waiver will not be established by the mere fact that the suspect *responded* to later *police-initiated* interrogation (even if that interrogation was preceded by a new reading of the *Miranda* warnings). [*Edwards*]

    b. "Initiating the conversation" test: So once a suspect indicates a desire to have a lawyer, any subsequent *waiver* of that right will not be measured by the usual tests for waiver (the "knowing and voluntary" standard; see *supra*, p. 114). Instead, the only way the suspect may waive a previously-asserted desire to have a lawyer present at interrogation is by *initiating the conversation* with the police.

    c. Questioning after a suspect has consulted lawyer: Suppose the suspect asks for a lawyer, *consults* with this lawyer, and is subsequently interrogated by the police outside the lawyer's presence. In this situation, the rule that a suspect who asks for a lawyer may not then be subject to police-initiated interrogation will be deemed to be *violated*. In other words, the lawyer must be present *during the subsequent questioning*, and a mere consultation before the questioning will be no substitute for this. [*Minnick v. Mississippi*]

    d. Break in custody: The "no police-initiated questioning after invocation of the right to counsel" rule *ceases to apply* once there has been a substantial *break in custody*. Once the suspect has been *out of custody for at least 14 days*, the police may initiate questioning even though they never furnished counsel in response to the suspect's initial request for it. [*Maryland v. Shatzer*]

    Example: In August 2003, while D is already in prison on an unrelated crime, a detective tries to question him about allegations that he sexually assaulted his son. D invokes his right to counsel; questioning ceases, and D is returned to the general prison population, without being given counsel. Then, in March, 2006, a different detective learns new information about the assault incident, and decides to question D again. D, who is still in prison, signs a written waiver of his *Miranda* rights, and then undergoes several questioning sessions during which he incriminates himself. He argues that the 2006 questioning was invalid because it was initiated by the police, after D had previously requested counsel and not been given it.

Held, for the prosecution. The break in custody (2 1/2 years) was sufficiently long that the ***coercive effect*** of the initial interrogation, which had led D to invoke his right to counsel, should be deemed to have ***dissipated***. In fact, any break in custody longer than ***14 days*** would have sufficed to dissipate this coercive effect. And even though D remained in prison for the 2 1/2 years, this doesn't count as "custody," because D was part of the general prison population and was not subjected to coercion of the sort that *Miranda* was designed to prevent. [*Maryland v. Shatzer*]

2. **Right to silence:** When may the police initiate a new interrogation after the suspect has invoked his ***right to silence***? In the right-to-silence scenario there is no equivalent of the bright-line "police may not initiate questioning" rule that applies after the suspect requests counsel.

   a. **"Scrupulously honored" standard:** Instead, the Court applies a much-weaker standard: *"scrupulously honored."* That is, "the admissibility of statements obtained after the person in custody has decided to remain silent depends [on] whether his 'right to cut off questioning' was 'scrupulously honored.'" [*Michigan v. Mosley*]

   Example: D is interrogated about two robberies after receiving his *Miranda* warnings. He says he does not want to answer police questions. Questioning is then immediately terminated. Several hours later, D is taken to a different floor of the building where he is being held, and, after again being given his *Miranda* warnings, is questioned by a different officer about a fatal shooting which had occurred in a third robbery. Williams implicated himself. At trial, he moves to strike his statements on the ground that they were procured in violation of his right not to be questioned after he initially exercised his *Miranda* rights.

   Held, for the prosecution. D's right not to be questioned was ***not violated*** by the resumption of questioning. The issue is whether D's right was "scrupulously honored." The police here "***immediately ceased*** the interrogation, resumed questioning only after the passage of a ***significant period of time*** and the provision of a ***fresh set of warnings***." That was enough to constitute a scrupulous honoring of D's right of silence. [*Michigan v. Mosley*]

   i. **Significance:** According to post-*Mosley* lower-court cases, the police must satisfy ***three requirements*** in order to be deemed to have "scrupulously honored" the suspect's invocation of his right to remain silent:

   ❑ The police must have ***immediately ceased the interrogation*** once the suspect invoked his right;

   ❑ The ***gap*** between the cessation of questioning and the initiation of the new session must represent a ***significant passage of time*** (a ***"cooling off"*** period); and

   ❑ Prior to the second interrogation, the police must give a ***second set*** of

Miranda warnings.

(1) No ban on re-initiating questioning: Unlike the situation in which the suspect invokes the right to *counsel*, the police are permitted to *re-initiate* questioning in the right-to-silence scenario. In other words, the bright-line rule for right-to-counsel cases (that when a suspect has invoked the right to counsel, any new questioning session must be initiated by the suspect, not the police) does *not apply* where the right being invoked is the right to silence.

b. Ambiguous invocation of right: If the police give the *Miranda* warnings and the suspect gives an ***ambiguous*** response as to whether he means to assert his right to silence, two things happen:

❑ The ambiguous response does *not* constitute an invocation of the right (because only unambiguous invocations count; see *supra*, p. 116); and

❑ The police may ***continue asking questions*** to the suspect, rather than either stopping the interrogation or even trying to clarify the suspect's intent.

Taken together, these two facts mean that until the police receive an unambiguous indication that the suspect wants to remain silent and not be further questioned, the police have an ***incentive to continue asking questions***.

IX. OTHER *MIRANDA* ISSUES

A. Grand jury witnesses: A witness who is subpoenaed to appear before a ***grand jury*** probably does *not* have to be given *Miranda* warnings.

B. Impeachment: A confession obtained in violation of *Miranda* may not be introduced as part of the prosecution's case-in-chief. But the prosecution *may* use such statements to *impeach* D's testimony at trial. [*Harris v. New York*]

Example: D is charged with selling heroin on two occasions. At his trial, he takes the stand and denies making one of these sales. The prosecution then reads a statement, obtained in violation of *Miranda*, in which D admits making both sales. *Held*, even though the statement was made without benefit of *Miranda* warnings, it may be used to impeach D's trial testimony. [*Harris, supra.*]

1. Coercion: Although a statement obtained in violation of *Miranda* may be admissible for impeachment purposes, it may *not* be used even for this limited purpose if it was the product of *coercion*, or was *involuntary* for some other reason. [*Mincey v. Arizona*]

C. Use of D's silence: A key issue is whether and when the prosecution may call to the jury's attention at trial the fact that the defendant has ***remained silent at some prior point,*** thus raising a reasonable ***inference of guilt.*** The answer depends heavily on the situation in which the silence occurred.

1. Comment on D's failure to take the stand: Where D exercises his Fifth Amendment right ***not to take the stand at his trial***, the Fifth Amendment itself ***prevents the prosecution from pointing out to the jury*** that D ***could have taken the stand***

to "tell his story" and elected not to do so. [*Griffin v. California*] Similarly, the trial judge ***may not instruct the jury*** that D's silence (his failure to take the stand) constitutes evidence of guilt. [*Id.*]

2. **Impeachment by showing D's silence in custodial interrogation:** Suppose D raises a particular defense at trial (e.g., an alibi defense), and the prosecution would like to disprove that defense and/or impeach D's credibility as a witness, by showing that while D was ***being subjected to custodial interrogation***, he ***remained silent***, in a way that is inconsistent with his story at trial.

   a. **D does not take the stand:** Where D does ***not even take the stand***, the prosecution ***may not comment*** on the fact that D invoked his right to remain silent during questioning. And that's true even if D is asserting at trial (through third-party witnesses) an ***alibi*** that an innocent suspect would be likely to have explained to police during the interrogation.

   b. **Impeachment of D's credibility:** Now, let's suppose that D *does* elect to take the stand, and recites his present version of the facts (e.g., an ***alibi***). On cross-examination, may the prosecution attempt to impeach D's credibility by saying, in effect, "If your story is true, ***why didn't you tell that story to the police*** when they had you in custody and gave you your *Miranda* warnings"? Here, too, the prosecution ***may not refer, directly or indirectly, to D's silence under custodial questioning,*** even if that silence is inconsistent with D's present trial testimony. [*Doyle v. Ohio*]

3. **Silence under non-custodial questioning:** Now, suppose that at a time when the police have ***begun to suspect D*** of a particular crime, but ***before*** they have ***arrested*** him, they ask him to ***undergo voluntary questioning*** and he agrees. If D then refuses to answer a particular question or to discuss a particular topic, may the prosecution comment on that refusal at trial? The answer seems to depend on whether D is found to have ***formally invoked*** his ***Fifth Amendment*** rights during the questioning:

   [1] If D *has* formally invoked those rights, it's not yet clear as of this writing whether the prosecution may comment on his silence (though the odds are good that the Court will ultimately decide that the prosecution may not comment). But ...

   [2] If D has ***not*** explained why he is remaining silent (so that he is ***not found to have invoked*** his Fifth Amendment rights), it's clear that the prosecution ***may comment*** on that silence. [*Salinas v. Texas* (2013)]

   Example of [2]: In a double-shotgun-murder case, the police have come to suspect D, so they visit him at his home. During the home visit, D agrees to hand over his shotgun for ballistic testing. The police then ask D if he will voluntarily accompany them to police headquarters for questioning; D agrees. At the station, the officers do not arrest or charge D, and do not read him his *Miranda* warnings. D initially answers the officers' questions. But when the police ask him whether his shotgun will match the shells recovered at the scene of the murder, D declines to answer (without giving a reason), and behaves with evasive body language. At trial, D does not take the stand. The prosecution introduces testimony by the officers about D's silence (and physical reactions) during the questioning about shell-matching. D claims that this testimony violates his Fifth Amendment privilege against self-incrimination.

Held, for the prosecution. Five Justices believe either that (1) where a suspect is engaged in a *"voluntary"* rather than custodial interrogation, the suspect must *explicitly* tell the police that his silence is due to his reliance on his Fifth Amendment privilege, or else the prosecution may comment on his silence (three votes) or (2) it doesn't *matter* whether a suspect undergoing voluntary (non-custodial) interrogation expressly invokes his Fifth Amendment rights, because prosecutors may comment on a defendant's pre-custody silence even if he *did* make such an invocation (two votes). So a majority holds that here, the prosecution may comment, since D volunteered for the questioning, and then merely cut off his answers without citing his privilege against self-incrimination. [*Salinas v. Texas, supra*]

4. **D's silence without interrogation:** Finally, suppose D was never subjected to questioning (voluntary or custodial), but simply *failed to come forward* to tell the police his "story," under circumstances in which an innocent and truthful person would likely have done so. In this situation, like the "voluntary questioning" situation addressed in *Salinas, supra*, the prosecution *may comment* on the defendant's initial silence. [*Jenkins v. Anderson*]

> **Example:** D raises a self-defense claim at his murder trial. The prosecution impeaches this claim by pointing out that for two weeks after the murder, D failed to go to the authorities to surrender himself or explain the self-defense incident. *Held*, D's pre-arrest silence *may* be used to impeach his trial testimony, because D was not in custody at the time of his silence, *and* no governmental action induced him to remain silent before his arrest. [*Jenkins v. Anderson*]

CHAPTER 6

LINEUPS AND OTHER PRE-TRIAL IDENTIFICATION PROCEDURES

I. I.D. PROCEDURES GENERALLY

A. Various procedures: There are a number of methods by which the police may get an *identification* of a suspect to link him with a crime: *lineups*, *fingerprints*, *blood samples*, *voice prints*, the use of *photographs*, etc.

B. Possible constitutional problems: There are four plausible constitutional objections that D may be able to make to the use of one of these procedures against him: (1) that it violates D's privilege against *self-incrimination*; (2) that it constituted an *unreasonable search or seizure* in violation of the Fourth Amendment; (3) that if D did not have a lawyer present, the use of the procedure violated his *Sixth Amendment right to counsel*; and (4) that the procedure was so suggestive that it violated D's Fifth/Fourteenth Amendment right to *due process*.

C. Right to counsel as main weapon: The objection that is most likely to succeed is that use of one of these procedures (especially a lineup or show-up) without D's lawyer present violated his right to counsel; the next most-likely to succeed is the argument that the procedure was so suggestive that it violated due process (most likely to work where the procedure was a lineup, show-up, or photo I.D.). The self-incrimination argument will almost never work, and the search and seizure argument has a chance of working only if the police lacked a warrant and/or probable cause.

II.   THE PRIVILEGE AGAINST SELF-INCRIMINATION

A. General rule: *Physical identification procedures* — fingerprints, blood samples, voice prints, etc. — will generally *not* trigger the Fifth Amendment privilege against *self-incrimination*. That privilege protects only against compulsion to give *"testimony or communicative* evidence," and these physical procedures have been found not to be "testimony or communicative." [*Schmerber v. California*]

> **Example:** D is arrested for drunk driving. A blood sample is forcibly taken from him over his objection, by a physician acting under the direction of the police. *Held*, D's privilege against self-incrimination was not violated by the forcible test, because the privilege protects only against being compelled to give testimony or communicative evidence, not being forced to give real or physical evidence. [*Schmerber, supra.*]

1. Other procedures: This principle has been broadly applied, so that D has no self-incrimination privilege against being forced to: (1) appear in a *lineup*; (2) *speak* for identification; (3) give *fingerprints*; (4) be *photographed*; (5) be *measured*; (6) be required to make *physical movements*; (7) give a *handwriting* sample; or (8) be examined by ultraviolet light.

2. Non-cooperation: If the suspect refuses to cooperate with a request to provide one of these sources of physical identification, the court may order him to do so. If he still refuses, the court may hold him in contempt and jail him.

> **a. Prosecution's right to comment:**   Furthermore, if D refuses to cooperate with such a request, the prosecution may *comment* on that fact at D's later trial.

III.   THE RIGHT TO COUNSEL AT PRE-TRIAL CONFRONTATIONS

A. Rule generally: A suspect against whom formal criminal proceedings have been commenced has an *absolute right* to have *counsel present* at any pre-trial *confrontation* procedure. Such confrontations include both *lineups* (in which a witness picks the suspect out of a group of persons) and *show-ups* (in which the witness is shown only the suspect and asked whether the suspect is the perpetrator). [*U.S. v. Wade*; *Gilbert v. California*]

> **Example:** D is indicted for robbery, arrested, and brought to the police station. He is placed in a lineup with other men of similar appearance. V, the robbery victim, is asked to identify the perpetrator. V picks D out of the lineup. Unless the police

offered D the chance to have counsel present at the lineup, the results of the lineup will not be admissible against D at his criminal trial.

1. **Effect on in-court I.D.:** Furthermore, if the confrontation is conducted in violation of the right of counsel, the prosecution will not only be barred from introducing at trial the fact that D was picked out of the lineup, but may even be barred from having the witness who made the identification (V in the above example) *testify in court* that the person sitting in the dock is the person observed by the witness at the scene of the crime. Once the lineup is shown to have been improper, the prosecution will have to come up with *"clear and convincing evidence"* that the in-court identification is not the "fruit of the poisonous tree" (i.e., the product of the improper lineup identification).

B. **Waiver:** The right to have counsel at the pre-trial confrontation proceeding may be *waived*. But the waiver must be an "intelligent" one; probably, the police must inform D of his right to counsel, and D must be capable of understanding that right and must voluntarily choose to give it up.

C. **Exceptions to the right:**

1. **Before formal proceedings against D:** The right to have counsel at the pre-trial confrontation probably applies only to confrontations occurring after the institution of *formal proceedings* against the suspect. [*Kirby v. Illinois*] The right will be triggered by the fact that D has been formally charged, given a preliminary hearing, indicted, arraigned, or otherwise subjected to formal judiciary proceedings. Probably the right is triggered if an *arrest warrant* is issued; but the right is probably *not* triggered if D has merely been *arrested without a warrant* and then put in the lineup or show-up. Certainly the right seems not to be triggered where the police have not even arrested D yet, but have asked him to voluntarily appear in a lineup, and D agrees.

2. **Photo I.D.:** The right to counsel does *not* apply where a witness views *still or moving pictures* of the suspect for identification purposes.

   Example: D is not present when the police bring photos of D, together with photos of innocent people, to V, and ask V to pull the photo of the perpetrator from the group. The fact that D has not been given a chance to have a lawyer present during this procedure makes no difference, because D has no Sixth Amendment right to counsel in this non-face-to-face situation. [*U.S. v. Ash*]

   Note: But the due process right not to be subjected to "unduly suggestive" procedures may be triggered in this photo I.D. situation, as discussed below.

3. **Scientific I.D. procedures:** No Sixth Amendment right to counsel attaches where *scientific methods*, as opposed to eye witness identification procedures, are used to identify D as the perpetrator. Thus if the police extract or analyze D's fingerprints, blood samples, clothing, hair, voice, handwriting samples, etc., D does not have a right to have counsel present during these extractions or examinations.

IV. DUE PROCESS LIMITS ON I.D. PROCEDURES

A. Suggestive procedures: Even where the right to counsel is never triggered by an identification procedure (or has been triggered but complied with), D may be able to exclude the resulting identification on the grounds that it violated his *due process* rights. To do this, D will have to show that, viewed by the "totality of the circumstances," the identification procedure was so *"unnecessarily suggestive"* and so conducive to mistaken identification, as to be deeply unfair to D.

> **Example:** D is suspected of robbery. D is lined up with men several inches shorter than he. Only D wears a jacket similar to that known to have been used by the robber. After V is unable to positively identify anyone, the police then use a one-man show-up of D. When V is still uncertain, the police put on, several days later, a second lineup, in which D is the only repeater from the previous lineup.
>
> *Held*, the procedures used here were so suggestive that an identification of D as the perpetrator was "all but inevitable." Therefore, the fact that V picked D out of the second lineup must be excluded from D's trial, as a violation of his due process rights. (This is true regardless of whether D had, or used, any right to have counsel present.) [*Foster v. California*]

B. Suggestive procedures allowed if reliable: But an identification procedure is not violative of due process if the court finds that it is *reliable* (i.e., not likely to cause error), even if it is somewhat suggestive.

> **Example:** If V has a long time to view the perpetrator during the crime, under adequate light, up close, these facts will make it more likely that the resulting identification procedures are fair to D, even if there is some suggestiveness during the procedures themselves. Similarly, the fact that V is very certain of the identification, or that V has given an extremely thorough description of the perpetrator before the identification procedure, will make the court more likely to uphold it. [*Neil v. Biggers*]

C. Photo I.D.s: Where a witness identifies the suspect through the use of *photographs*, the "totality of the circumstances" test is used to determine whether D's due process rights have been violated, just as this test is used in the lineup or show-up situation. [*Simmons v. U.S.*; *Manson v. Brathwaite*]

> **Example:** The photo I.D. is more likely to be upheld if the police show V photographs of numerous people — without hinting to V which photo they believe to be of the prime suspect — than if the police show one photo to V, and say, "Is this the guy?"

1. Must be very likely to be mistaken: As with the lineup and show-up situation, a due process violation will be found only if the photo I.D. session is *very likely* to have produced a misidentification. The fact that the procedure is somewhat "suggestive" will not be enough. Thus if the victim had an usually good opportunity to view the perpetrator, or was unusually experienced at identifying perpetrators, this will probably overcome some suggestiveness in the procedure (e.g., the use of only a single photo). [See *Manson, supra.*]

THE EXCLUSIONARY RULE

I. THE RULE GENERALLY

A. Statement of rule: The "exclusionary rule" provides that evidence obtained by violating D's constitutional rights *may not be introduced by the prosecution* at D's criminal trial, at least for purposes of providing direct proof of D's guilt.

> **Example:** A car driven by D is randomly stopped by Officer, who has no reasonable grounds for suspecting D of any wrongdoing. Officer requires D to leave the car, and then searches the car. In the car's trunk, Officer finds heroin. At D's trial for possession of heroin, the prosecution will not be permitted to introduce the heroin itself (or the fact that the heroin was found in D's car) against D. The reason is that the discovery and seizure of the heroin was a direct result of the illegal stop and search, and any evidence directly derived from violation of D's constitutional rights is prevented by the exclusionary rule from being introduced against D as part of the prosecution's case in chief.

B. Judge-made rule: The exclusionary rule is a *judge-made*, not statutory, rule. Over the years, the rule has been shaped by a long series of Supreme Court decisions. The rule is binding on both *state* and *federal* courts.

   1. Not constitutionally required: The Supreme Court has held that the exclusionary rule is *not required by the Constitution*. [*U.S. v. Leon*] Instead, the rule has been created by the Supreme Court as a means of *deterring* the police from violating the Fourth, Fifth, and other Amendments.

C. Dwindling application: In general, the scope of the exclusionary rule has been steadily *cut back* during the last few decades.

II. STANDING TO ASSERT THE EXCLUSIONARY RULE

A. Standing rule generally: In general, D may assert the exclusionary rule only to bar evidence obtained through violation of *his own* constitutional rights. That is, D may not keep out evidence obtained through police action that was a violation of X's rights but not a violation of D's own rights.

> **Example:** The police illegally wire-tap a conversation between D1 and X (without the knowledge of either). Statements made in this conversation are used at a trial of D2. D2 argues that since the evidence was obtained by a violation of constitutional rights (the rights of D1), the evidence should not be usable against anyone, including D2. *Held*, for the prosecution. Evidence obtained by violation of the Fourth Amendment or any other constitutional provision may only be excluded by a person whose own rights were violated. [*Alderman v. U.S.*]

B. Confession cases: The standing requirement means that in the case of an illegally-obtained confession, only the person who *makes* the confession may have it barred by the exclusionary rule.

Example: Suspect A confesses without being given the required *Miranda* warnings. In his confession, A implicates B. The confession may still be introduced in evidence against B (though not against A), because B's constitutional rights were not violated by the obtaining of the confession.

C. Search and seizure cases: In search and seizure cases, the standing requirement means that D may seek to exclude evidence derived from a search and seizure only if his *own* "legitimate expectation of privacy" was violated by the search. [*Rakas v. Illinois*]

1. **Possessory interest in items seized:** This means that the mere fact that D has a *possessory interest* in the *items seized* is *not* by itself automatically enough to allow D to challenge the constitutionality of the seizure. Only if D had a legitimate expectation of privacy with respect to the items seized, may D exclude those items.

   Example: D and his friend Cox are both searched by the police. In Cox's handbag, the police find 1,800 tablets of LSD and other drugs. D claims ownership of these drugs, and can prove that he owns them. The search and seizure occurred without probable cause. D tries to have the drugs suppressed from his drug possession trial.

   Held, for the prosecution. Even though D owned the drugs, D's own rights were not violated by the search of Cox's handbag, because once D placed the drugs in Cox's handbag, he had no further legitimate expectation of privacy with respect to those drugs. [*Rawlings v. Kentucky*]

2. **Presence at scene of search:** Similarly, the fact that D is *legitimately on the premises* where a search takes place does *not* automatically mean that D can exclude the fruits of the search if the search was illegal. Again, only if D had a legitimate expectation of privacy with respect to the *areas* where the incriminating materials were found, may D benefit from the exclusionary rule.

   Example: D is riding as a passenger in a car that is illegally searched by the police. The police find a sawed-off rifle under the passenger seat occupied by D. *Held,* the mere fact that D was on the scene during the search did not give him standing to assert the exclusionary rule. Since D did not have a legitimate expectation of privacy as to the area under his seat, he could not assert the exclusionary rule and the rifle could be admitted against him. [*Rakas v. Illinois*]

3. **Vehicle searches:** When the police stop a *vehicle*, both the *driver* and *all passengers* will normally *have standing* to challenge the constitutionality of the vehicle stop.

   a. **Passengers:** Any *passengers* will have standing: "When a police officer makes a traffic stop, the driver of the car is seized within the meaning of the Fourth Amendment [and any] *passenger* is *seized as well* and so may challenge the constitutionality of the stop." [*Brendlin v. California*]

   b. **Driver:** The *driver*, too, will almost always have standing to challenge the constitutionality of the vehicle stop.

    i. **Where D is driver but not owner, and owner is absent:** The driver will normally have standing to challenge the stop even if the *owner* of the vehicle is *absent*. At least where the driver is *driving with the consent* of the absentee owner, the driver will normally be found to have *a reasonable expectation of privacy* with respect to the vehicle, and consequently will have standing to assert a Fourth Amendment claim. (We discuss the topic further *supra*, p. 62.)

4. **Co-conspirators:** Where one member of a *conspiracy* is stopped or searched, the *other members* of the conspiracy do *not* automatically get standing to object to the stop or search merely by virtue of their membership. [*U.S. v. Padilla*]

    Example: Suppose D1 is driving a car as part of a drug-dealing conspiracy of which D2 is a part, and the car is stopped by police and searched. D2 does not get standing to object to the search merely because he and D1 are part of a single conspiracy and the car is being used in that conspiracy — D2 must show that he has a privacy interest in the car or its contents, just as if there was no conspiracy.

III. DERIVATIVE EVIDENCE GENERALLY, AND THE "INDEPENDENT SOURCE" AND "INEVITABLE DISCOVERY" EXCEPTIONS

A. Derivative evidence generally: The exclusionary rule clearly applies to evidence that is the *direct* result of a violation of D's rights (e.g., evidence is seized from D's premises during an illegal search). But the exclusionary rule also applies to some *"derivative evidence,"* that is, evidence that is only *indirectly* obtained via a violation of D's rights. In general, if police wrongdoing leads in a relatively short, unbroken, chain to evidence, that evidence will be barred by the exclusionary rule, even though the evidence was not the direct and immediate fruit of the illegality.

1. **"Poisonous-tree" doctrine:** The idea that evidence deriving indirectly from a violation of D's constitutional rights should normally be excluded from use against D is often referred to as the *"poisonous-tree doctrine."* That is, once the original evidence (the *"tree"*) is shown to have been unlawfully obtained, *all evidence stemming from that illegality (the "fruit" of the poisonous tree) is equally unusable*.

    Example: Federal agents, acting without probable cause, break into Toy's apartment and handcuff him. Toy makes a statement accusing Yee of selling narcotics. The agents go to Yee, from whom they seize heroin.

    Held, the drugs seized from Yee are "fruits of the poisonous tree," since they were seized as the direct result of the agents' illegal entry into Toy's apartment. Therefore, the drugs from Yee cannot be introduced against Toy, under the exclusionary rule. [*Wong Sun v. U.S.*]

B. The independent source exception: The "fruits of the poisonous tree" doctrine has a couple of major *exceptions*, one of which is known as the *"independent source"* exception. When the police have *two paths* leading to information, and only one of these paths begins with illegality, the evidence is not deemed fruit of the poisonous tree, and is not barred by the exclusionary rule.

1. **Use for warrantless arrests or seizures:** The main utility of the "independent source" exception arises where the police have probable cause to obtain a search warrant, which would have led them to certain evidence; instead, the police make an illegal search, discover evidence, then go back and get a warrant. The law now seems to be that since the police *could have* lawfully obtained a warrant, they are deemed to have had an "independent source" for the evidence, so the evidence will not be barred by the exclusionary rule even though it was illegally obtained.

    a. **Scope:** More precisely, evidence will be admissible under this branch of the "independent source" exception when three requirements are satisfied:

        i.   **Illegally on premises:** First, the method by which the police discovered or seized the evidence or contraband in question must have been a violation of the Fourth Amendment (e.g., a warrantless search of the premises when a warrant was required).

        ii. **Probable cause for search warrant:** Second, although the police did not have a search warrant, at the moment of entry they must have had knowledge that would have *entitled* them to *procure* a search warrant. That is, they must have had *probable cause* to believe that contraband, or evidence of crime, would be found on the premises. (This theoretical availability of a warrant is the "independent source" that justifies the admission of the evidence even though the police were acting illegally at the moment they seized the evidence.)

        iii. **Would have gotten warrant anyway:** Third, the police must show that they would probably have *eventually applied for a search warrant* even had they not engaged in the illegality.

             Example: The police have probable cause to arrest D for narcotics violations, and probable cause to search his apartment for evidence. The police arrest D outside his apartment. They do not get a search warrant, even though warrantless entry is not allowed without one. They then enter the apartment, where they see narcotics paraphernalia. They post agents to prevent destruction of evidence, and 20 hours later get a warrant; they then conduct a search which turns up narcotics that they had not previously observed.

             Held, the seized narcotics are not the fruit of the poisonous tree, and thus not excludable in D's trial, because the police had an independent source for discovery those narcotics — since the police were already, prior to the illegal entry, entitled to get a search warrant, they could have staked out the apartment from the outside, gotten the warrant and seized the very same evidence. [*Segura v. U.S.*]

C. **Inevitable discovery:** There is a second exception related to the "independent source" exception, called the *"inevitable discovery"* exception. Evidence may be admitted if it would *"inevitably"* have been discovered by *other police techniques* had it not first been obtained through the illegal discovery.

1. **Discovery of weapon or body:** The "inevitable discovery" rule is most often applied where the evidence illegally obtained is a *weapon* or *body*, which the police would eventually have discovered anyway, even without the illegality.

> **Example:** The police, in violation of *Miranda*, induce D to reveal the location of the body of his murder victim. The police are then able to find the body, and evidence near the body that relates to the manner of death. D seeks to suppress this evidence at trial, on the theory that it was procured by violation of his *Miranda* rights.
>
> *Held,* because the facts were such that the police would inevitably have discovered the location of the body eventually anyway, even without D's statement, the evidence need not be excluded. This is true even though the police may have used bad faith in tricking D into revealing the location — there is no "good faith" requirement for application of the inevitable discovery exception. [*Nix v. Williams*]

IV. "PURGING THE TAINT" OF POLICE ILLEGALITY — THE SIGNIFICANCE OF SUBSEQUENT INTERVENING EVENTS

A. The "purged taint" exception in general: Suppose that the police obtain a piece of evidence indirectly through a constitutional violation, and that neither the independent source nor the inevitable discovery exceptions seem to apply. In such a situation, it may nonetheless be the case that the exclusionary rule does not apply, due to a long-recognized judicial exception known as the *"purged taint"* doctrine.

1. **Doctrine defined:** The principle of the purged taint doctrine is that if enough *additional factors intervene* between the original illegality and the final discovery of evidence, the link between the two is so tenuous that the exclusionary rule should not be applied. In this situation, the intervening factors are said to be enough to have *"purged the taint" of the original illegal police conduct.*

> **Example:** Wong Sun is arrested without probable cause, arraigned, and released on his own recognizance. Several days later, he voluntarily comes to the police station, where he receives *Miranda* warnings and makes an incriminating statement.
>
> *Held,* the statement may be introduced against Wong Sun, despite the exclusionary rule. It is true that Wong Sun's statement in some sense "derived" from his original illegal arrest. But the fact that Wong Sun had been released for several days between arrest and statement, and the voluntariness of his return to make the statement, so attenuated the connection between arrest and statement as to purge the taint of the illegality. [*Wong Sun v. U.S.*]

B. Standards for determining if intervening events "have purged the taint": The Supreme Court considers *three factors* in deciding whether an event (or even the passage of time) occurring between the illegal conduct and the police's acquisition of the possibly-tainted fruit is sufficient to *"purge the taint"* of the illegality. [*Brown v. Illinois* (1975)]

1. **Types of "fruit" covered:** In *Brown*, the illegality was an arrest that violated the Fourth Amendment, and the possibly-tainted "fruit" was a *confession* by the arrestee. But the Court has since indicated that these factors are to be applied in other types of derivative-evidence scenarios as well.

2. **Three factors listed:** According to *Brown*, here are the three factors the Court will take into account in deciding whether the taint from the illegality has been "purged":

    [1] The *"temporal proximity"* of the illegality to the fruit (in *Brown*, the proximity of the illegal arrest to the confession by the arrestee);

    [2] The "presence of *intervening circumstances*" between the illegality and the fruit; and

    [3] Of "particular" importance, "the *purpose and flagrancy* of the *official misconduct.*"

3. **Illegal stop is followed by discovery of outstanding arrest warrant:**   The main case in which the Court has applied the *Brown* three-factor test is a 2016 case posing the issue of whether the taint of an illegal stop will be purged by the officer's discovery that there is an *outstanding arrest warrant* for the suspect. The case holds that discovery of the warrant will normally be such an important intervening event that it will *purge the taint* of the stop, thereby permitting the police to *make an arrest* on account of the warrant and then a *search incident to that arrest.* [*Utah v. Strieff* (2016)]

    a. **Facts:** In *Strieff*, a police detective, Fackrell, stopped D, a pedestrian, in what was later stipulated to be an unlawful stop due to Fackrell's lack of reasonable grounds to suspect D of wrongdoing. Fackrell demanded D's ID, then called in D's name to a police dispatcher. The dispatcher reported that D had an outstanding arrest warrant for a traffic violation. Fackrell then arrested D on the warrant, searched him incident to the arrest, and discovered narcotics on D's person.

    b. **Holding:** The Supreme Court *agreed with the prosecution* that discovery of the outstanding warrant was *enough to purge the taint* of the illegal stop, based on the three-factor test of *Brown*, *supra*. The Court applied the three *Brown* factors this way:

        [1] **Temporal proximity:** *"Temporal proximity"* between the stop and the search cut in favor of suppression. The proximity factor will favor suppression unless "substantial time" elapses, and here, the search took place *"only minutes"* after the illegal stop, which was *not* a substantial amount of time.

        [2] **Intervening circumstances:** On the other hand, "the presence of *intervening circumstances"* factor cut strongly against suppression. The outstanding warrant predated Fackrell's investigation and was "entirely *unconnected with the stop."*

        [3] **"Purpose and flagrancy of misconduct":** Finally, the *"purpose and flagrancy* of the official misconduct" also cut strongly against suppression. Fackrell was *"at most negligent,"* and his main error — making the stop without having adequate grounds to suspect D of any wrongdoing — was a *"good-faith mistake."* Furthermore, there was no indication that this unlawful stop was part of any *"systemic or recurrent police misconduct."*

Since two of the three *Brown* factors cut strongly in favor of a finding that the taint from the unlawful stop was "sufficiently attenuated" by the preexisting arrest warrant, the fruits of the search incident to the arrest on the warrant were *not required to be excluded.*

    c. **Significance:** Here's what *Strieff* seems to allow the police to do: After every stop (even an illegal one, so long as the illegality is a good-faith mistake), the police can detain the person for long enough to determine whether he or she has an outstanding arrest warrant. And once the existence of the outstanding warrant is confirmed (no matter how old or minor the offense or the warrant), the officer is free to arrest the suspect. At that point, the officer can do a search incident to the arrest, and any contraband or evidence of criminality she finds can serve as admissible evidence in a prosecution predicated on that evidence. The prosecution can treat the original stop, and the reasons for it, as irrelevant to the crime being charged.

C. Illegality leads police to focus on particular suspect: If the illegality (an illegal search, arrest, lineup, etc.) leads the police to *focus on a particular suspect* they were not previously focusing on, usually the final arrest of the suspect will *not* be found to be tainted by the original illegality: the full-scale investigation that the police conduct between the time they first focus on the suspect and the time they arrest him is usually enough to purge this taint.

D. Lead to different crime: Now suppose the police are investigating one crime, and an illegal action they commit leads them to evidence of a *completely different crime*. Here, too, probably the evidence of the new crime may be introduced despite the earlier illegality.

    Example: D is illegally arrested for burglarizing an empty house, and is immediately photographed. Weeks later, the police show the photo to a witness, who identifies the person in the photo as having been one of three men who robbed a bank recently during the daytime. Probably this later-robbery I.D. would not be deemed tainted by the original illegal arrest and photograph.

E. Lead to witness: One of the fruits of police illegality may be the discovery of the *existence of witnesses* who can give testimony against D. In general, D is rarely successful in arguing that the testimony of the live witness should be suppressed because the witness would not have been found but for the illegality — it is far easier to suppress an "inanimate" fruit of illegality (e.g., contraband, or evidence of crime) than it is to suppress "animate" fruits such as witnesses who testify. [See *U.S. v. Ceccolini*]

    Example: The police, acting without probable cause, arrest D on suspicion of being one of two men who burglarized a particular premises. They interrogate D without giving him his *Miranda* warnings. D implicates X, who he says was the other person who took part in the burglary. The police, who had no previous reason to suspect X, accost X, and convince him to turn state's evidence against D. X's evidence will probably be admissible against D, even though it is in a sense the fruit of the original illegal arrest and interrogation of D — the courts hesitate to apply the "fruits of the poisonous tree" doctrine to a fruit consisting of a witness' live testimony.

F. Confession as tainted fruit: A *confession* may also be found to be tainted fruit. This is especially likely to be the case where the confession stems directly from the *illegal arrest* of the suspect who gives the confession. In general, where the confession comes in the period of *custody immediately following* the arrest, the court is likely to find that the confession is tainted fruit, and must therefore be excluded from the trial of the confessor.

> **Example:** Acting without probable cause, the police arrest D on suspicion of robbery. While D is in custody, the police give him his *Miranda* warnings, and he waives his rights, then confesses. A court would almost certainly hold that D's confession must be excluded as a fruit of the illegal arrest.

1. ***Mirandizing* of D not sufficient:** It is clear that the mere fact that D was given his *Miranda warnings* before confessing is *not* sufficient to purge the taint of the earlier illegality. [*Brown v. Illinois*]

2. Other factors: But the fact that the police gave *Miranda* warnings is a *factor* that the court will consider, in addition to other factors, in determining whether the confession was sufficiently distinct from the earlier illegality that it should be deemed untainted. Other factors that the courts consider are:

    a. Time delay: How long a *time* elapsed between the illegality and the confession (the longer the time, the more likely the taint is to have been purged);

    b. Police intent: The police *intent* in carrying out the illegal arrest or other illegal act (so that if the police knowingly arrest D illegally, for the purpose of being able to interrogate him, the taint will almost certainly not be purged); and

    c. Intervening factors: Whether *intervening events* have occurred that weaken the causal link between the illegality and the confession.

>   **Example:** If D is illegally arrested, then released from custody for several days, during which he consults with friends and relatives, a voluntary confession by D thereafter is much less likely to be found to be tainted than if D confessed without ever having left custody and without consulting with anyone.

3. Second confession as fruit of prior confession: Suppose D makes an *inadmissible confession*, and shortly thereafter makes a *second, otherwise-admissible, confession*. Does the illegality surrounding the first confession taint the second confession? Here are the general rules governing this two-confession scenario:

    ❑ The second confession will not be deemed tainted as long as it was *"voluntarily made,"* and the Court will ordinarily *presume* that the second confession is indeed voluntary if made after warnings, even though that confession followed an earlier unwarned confession. (That is, the voluntariness of the second confession normally ***won't*** be impaired by the fact that the suspect feels that since he has already ***"let the cat out of the bag,"*** there is little to be gained by remaining silent the second time.) [*Oregon v. Elstad*]

❑ The second confession is ***more likely*** to be deemed to be ***voluntarily*** made if the underlying circumstances do not make that second confession a ***mere continuation*** of the first. (So, for instance, the second is more likely to be found voluntary if the two were meaningfully ***separated*** by ***time, place, or interrogator***, or if it was made clear to the suspect that the first, unwarned, confession would not be admissible.) [*Elstad*]

❑ The second confession is less likely to be deemed tainted if the failure to warn prior to the first confession was the result of an ***inadvertent mistake*** by the police. [*Elstad*]

    ❑ By contrast, where the police follow an ***intentional "two-step" practice*** of eliciting an unwarned confession, then immediately giving a warning under circumstances that lead the suspect to believe that ***even the already-made confession can be used against him*** (so that the suspect sees no reason not to repeat the confession after the warning), the second confession ***will*** probably be deemed involuntary and thus ***tainted.*** [*Missouri v. Seibert*]

4. **Confession as "poisonous tree":** Suppose the police illegally obtain a confession, and this confession furnishes them with ***leads*** to other evidence (e.g., ***inanimate objects*** or ***witnesses*** who can testify). May this ***confession*** itself be a ***"poisonous tree"*** that taints the leads to other evidence? The answer is ***"no,"*** at least where the confession is illegally obtained only because of a lack of *Miranda* warnings, rather than because it is made following a no-probable-cause arrest.

    Example: D is arrested for domestic violence. He's questioned without *Miranda* warnings, and reveals that he's in possession of an unregistered pistol, whose location he shows the police. The gun will be admissible against D — the fact that the police would never have found the gun had D not confessed to its location during unwarned custodial questioning is irrelevant, because an unwarned confession won't ever be a "poisonous tree" with respect to physical fruits derived from that confession. [*U.S. v. Patane*]

    a. **Leads to witnesses:** The same result is almost certainly true of ***leads to third-party witnesses.***

    Example: The police, as the result of questioning D in a way that doesn't comply with *Miranda*, learn that W was a witness to a crime committed by D. Although the Supreme Court hasn't yet directly discussed the matter, it seems almost certain that *Patane, supra,* will be interpreted so that W's testimony can be used against D — the fact that the police would probably never have learned of W's existence had it not been for the non-Mirandized questioning of D will be irrelevant.

V.   COLLATERAL USE EXCEPTIONS

A. Collateral use generally: The exclusionary rule basically applies only to evidence presented by the prosecution as part of its *case in chief* at D's trial. In other contexts, the rule is much less likely to apply, as described below.

B. Impeachment at trial: Thus illegally-obtained evidence may be used to *impeach the defendant's trial testimony*, even though it cannot be used in the prosecution's direct case. [*Harris v. N.Y.*]

1.   **Statements made in direct testimony:**   Most obviously, illegally-obtained evidence may be used to impeach statements made by D *during his direct testimony*.

> **Example:** D is arrested on suspicion of burglarizing a particular premises. The police do not give him the required *Miranda* warnings. They ask him where he was on a particular evening, and he replies that he was at his girl-friend's house. At trial, during D's direct testimony after taking the stand, D says that at the time in question, he was at home. The prosecutor may bring out on cross-examination the fact that D told a different story in his non-*Mirandized* confession.

2.   **Statements made during cross-examination:**   Furthermore, illegally-obtained evidence may be used by the prosecution to impeach even statements that are made by D on *cross-examination*. So the prosecution can *elicit* one story from D during cross-examination, then impeach D by showing he told a different story while making his otherwise-inadmissible confession.

3.   **Impeachment of defense witnesses:**   But illegally-obtained evidence may *not* be used to impeach the testimony of *defense witnesses* other than the defendant himself. [*James v. Illinois*]

> **Example:** While D is under arrest for burglary, and without receiving *Miranda* warnings, D states that he was at home at the time of a burglary under investigation. At trial, D presents as a witness W, D's girlfriend, who says that at the time in question, D was with W at W's house. The prosecution may not impeach W's testimony by introducing D's contrary statment made during the un-*Mirandized* confession.

C. Impeachment in grand jury proceedings: A *grand jury witness* cannot prevent illegally-obtained evidence from being introduced against him during the grand jury proceeding. [*U.S. v. Calandra*]

VI.   THE "GOOD FAITH WARRANT" AND "KNOCK-AND-ANNOUNCE VIOLATION" EXCEPTIONS

A. The "good faith warrant" exception: The exclusionary rule does *not* bar evidence that was obtained by officers acting in *reasonable reliance* on a *search warrant* issued by a proper magistrate but ultimately found to be *unsupported by probable cause*. [*U.S. v. Leon*]

> **Example:** The police, relying on information from an informant as well as their own investigations, obtain a search warrant that is valid on its face. They search

several premises under the warrant, obtaining evidence of narcotics violations. Later, a judge holds that the information presented to the magistrate did not establish probable cause for the search. Now, the issue is whether the illegally-seized evidence may be admitted against D.

Held, the evidence may be admitted against D, because the exclusionary rule should not be applied where officers have a good-faith, objectively reasonable belief that they have probable cause, and the warrant is issued according to proper procedures. [*Leon, supra.*]

1. **Reliance on non-existent arrest warrant:** The "good faith" exception has been extended to one additional situation: If the police reasonably (but mistakenly) believe that there is an *arrest warrant outstanding* for a particular suspect and arrest him, evidence found during a *search incident to this wrongful arrest* will be *admissible*, at least where any police misconduct consists of *"nonrecurring and attenuated negligence."* [*Herring v. U.S.*]

   a. **Source of error irrelevant:** This is true whether the mistake is due to police error, or to error by some other part of government (e.g., the *judicial* system).

      Example: D drives to the Sheriff's Department to retrieve something from his impounded truck. A Sheriff's officer checks with his own county and a nearby one to see whether there are any outstanding warrants for D's arrest. A clerk in neighboring Dale County reports to the officer that her database shows that there is an active arrest warrant out for D. The officer therefore stops D as he drives out of the impound lot, arrests him on that warrant, searches his body, and finds contraband on him. But it turns out that there is no outstanding warrant — the warrant was recalled five months earlier, but this fact was never entered by the Dale County Sherriff's Department into its database.

      Held, the search is still valid as one properly made incident to arrest. The officer acted in good-faith reliance on the existence of the apparent warrant. When an arrest and incident search arises from "nonrecurring and attenuated negligence" by the police department, rather than from "systemic error or reckless disregard of constitutional requirements," the error will not invalidate the search incident to the (invalid) arrest. [*Herring v. U.S.*]

2. **Reliance on later-overruled legal principle:** The prosecution may also make use of the *Leon* good-faith-error exception in the case of a reasonable error about *what the appropriate legal rule is.* More precisely, when the police conduct a search that is legal under a binding legal precedent that is later *overruled*, the police and prosecution get the benefit of *Leon*, so that the exclusionary rule will not be applied to keep out the results of the search. [*Davis v. U.S.*]

   a. **Broader significance:** In fact, *Leon* will be applied (preventing application of the exclusionary rule) whenever the police obtain evidence "as a result of *non-culpable, innocent police conduct.*" [*Davis v. U.S.*]

      Example: The police make a routine traffic stop of a car in which D is a passenger and X is the driver. Both are handcuffed and placed in the back of separate patrol cars. The police then search the passenger compartment of the vehicle, and find a revolver inside the pocket of a jacket belonging to D. The incident happens in Alabama, which is part of the Eleventh Circuit. At the time of the search, the Eleventh Circuit (like most federal courts) interprets the prior Supreme Court case of *New York v. Belton* as holding that such a passenger-compartment search is legal regardless of whether the arrestee was within reaching distance of the vehicle.

Then, after D is convicted but while his appeal is still pending in front of the Eleventh Circuit, the Supreme Court in *Arizona v. Gant* overrules this reading of *Belton*, by validating searches incident to the arrest of a vehicle's occupants *only* if the arrestee was within reaching distance of the vehicle during the arrest (which D wasn't). D argues that since his case is not yet final, he should get the benefit of the new decision (*Gant*), and that the search should be ruled illegal.

Held, for the prosecution. The police and prosecution ***get the benefit of the precedent on which they reasonably relied***, even though the precedent turned out while the case was still pending to be bad law. Police reliance on what turns out to be an erroneous — but at the time, binding — appellate decision falls within the general rule that the good-faith exception applies to all ***"nonculpable, innocent police conduct."*** [*Davis v. U.S.*]

3. **Fourth Amendment only:** So far, the "good faith exception" summarized above applies only to evidence obtained in violation of the ***Fourth*** Amendment (search/ seizure and arrest), not evidence obtained in violation of other amendments (e.g., the Fifth or Sixth Amendments, each of which can be violated by, say, interrogation without benefit of *Miranda* warnings).

4. **Police must behave with objective reasonableness:** The exception applies only where the police behave in ***good faith*** and in an ***objectively reasonable*** manner. So, for instance, in cases where a search warrant is based on an incorrect affidavit, the exception does not apply if the police officer who prepares the affidavit for the warrant ***knows*** that the information in it is false, or recklessly disregards its truth or falsity. Also, the affidavit must on its face seem to be valid, and to be based on probable cause.

B. **Exception for "knock and announce" violations:** Under most circumstances, when the police wish to enter a private dwelling — for instance, to execute a search warrant — they are required by the Fourth Amendment to ***"knock and announce."*** That is, they are required to knock first, announce that they are the police, and give the occupant a chance to answer the door — only if the occupant does not answer may the police enter forcefully. (See *supra*, p. 73.) But even if the police violate this knock-and-announce rule, ***the exclusionary rule will not apply.*** [*Hudson v. Michigan.*]

1. **Consequence:** Therefore, even if D can show that certain evidence would not have been acquired by the police but for their failure to wait for the door to be answered (e.g., that if they had waited a reasonable time before entering with their warrant, D might have had time to destroy the evidence), the evidence will still be admissible against him.

CHAPTER 8

THE RIGHT TO COUNSEL

I.   THE INDIGENT'S RIGHT TO COUNSEL

A. Introduction: The Sixth Amendment says that "In all criminal prosecutions, the accused shall enjoy the right . . . to have the Assistance of Counsel for his defense."

1.   **Right to appointed counsel where jail is at stake:**   The Sixth Amendment right means that an ***indigent*** defendant has the right to have counsel ***appointed for him by the government*** in any prosecution where the accused can be sent to jail. Thus in any felony prosecution, and in any misdemeanor prosecution for which the sentence will be a jail term, the indigent has the right to appointed counsel.

2.   **Right to retained counsel:**   The Sixth Amendment also means that the government cannot materially interfere with a non-indigent defendant's right to ***retain*** (i.e., pay for) his own private lawyer.

B. Right to retained counsel, generally: The Sixth Amendment guarantees the right of a criminal defendant who does not need appointed counsel to ***hire private counsel of her own choosing*** to represent her. [*Caplin & Dysdale v. U.S.*]

1.   ***Per se*** **right:** If the private counsel chosen by defendant is qualified, the court's denial of permission for the lawyer to conduct the defense is ***automatically reversible error*** — the defendant does not even need to demonstrate on appeal that denial of counsel of choice is likely to have ***affected the outcome***. [*U.S. v. Gonzalez-Lopez*]

2.   **Federal or state:** This right to a counsel of one's own choosing, imposed by the Sixth Amendment, applies to ***both state and federal*** trials.

3.   **Limitations:** But the theoretically "unqualified" right to be represented by one's own retained attorney is ***not absolute***.

   a.   **Ability to pay may be blocked:** For instance, the government may place limits on the mechanism by which the defendant ***pays*** his retained lawyer. For example, federal "civil ***forfeiture***" statutes allow the government to seize and keep any property used in, or money earned from, violations of drug or other laws. Such forfeiture statutes may be enforced even where the forfeited property is the only property with which the defendant could pay his retained lawyer, and even if the effect of enforcement is that the lawyer refuses to represent the defendant because of the difficulty in obtaining payment. [*Caplin & Drysdale v. U.S.*].

   b.   **Conflict:**   Similarly, a defendant's right to a lawyer of his own choosing does not give him the right to choose a lawyer where this would result in a ***conflict*** between the lawyer's representation of the defendant and his representation of some other co-defendant. This is true even where all defendants are willing to "waive" the conflict.

C. The right to appointed counsel, generally: The most important aspect of the Sixth Amendment is that it guarantees ***indigent*** defendants the right to have counsel ***appointed for them*** by the government in felonies and in some misdemeanors.

   1. Applicable to states: The Sixth Amendment right to counsel applies to the ***states***, not just the federal government. [*Gideon v. Wainwright*]

   2. Various stages: The right to appointed counsel does not mean merely that the accused has the right to have a lawyer *at trial*; other parts of the prosecution that are found to represent a "critical stage" in the proceedings (e.g., the arraignment) also trigger the right to appointed counsel. This is discussed more extensively below.

   3. Right to effective assistance: The right to counsel includes the right to ***effective*** assistance — thus if the appointed counsel does not meet a certain minimal standard of competence, the Sixth Amendment has been violated. This aspect, too, is discussed below.

D. Proceedings where the right applies:

   1. Felonies: The right to appointed counsel clearly applies where the defendant is charged with a ***felony*** (i.e., a crime for which a prison sentence of more than a year is authorized).

   2. Misdemeanors with potential jail sentence: Additionally, the right applies in a ***misdemeanor*** prosecution, if the defendant is going to be sentenced to even a ***brief*** jail term. [*Argersinger v. Hamlin*]

   a. Jail sentence possible but not imposed: But if an indigent D is not ***sentenced*** to incarceration, the state is not required to appoint counsel for him, even if the offense is one which is ***punishable*** by imprisonment. [*Scott v. Illinois*]

   b. Conviction used to increase sentence for later crime: Also, a misdemeanor conviction ***may*** be used to increase the permissible prison sentence for a ***subsequent*** conviction, even though D was not offered appointed counsel during the first proceeding. [*Nichols v. U.S.*]

   3. Juvenile deliquency proceedings: The right to appointed counsel applies in a ***juvenile delinquency*** proceeding, if the youthful defendant may be committed to an ***institution*** (even a "youth facility" or "reform school" rather than a prison) upon conviction. [*In re Gault*]

E. Stages at which the right to counsel applies: In addition to the trial itself, the right to counsel applies at various other stages of the proceedings:

   1. Police investigation: A suspect will frequently have the right to counsel during the period in which the police are conducting their ***investigation***. But this right generally does not derive from the Sixth Amendment; instead, it stems from the Fifth Amendment's right against self-incrimination.

   Example: Although a defendant in custody has the right to an appointed lawyer before being questioned by the police, under *Miranda*, this right derives from the Fifth Amendment, not the Sixth.

2. **The "critical stage" doctrine:** The Sixth Amendment is triggered wherever there is a *"critical stage"* of the proceedings. In brief, a stage will be "critical" if D is compelled to make a decision which may later be formally *used against him*.

   a. **Initial appearance:** Thus the *initial appearance*, the *preliminary hearing*, and the *arraignment* are all likely to be found, in a particular case, to be critical stages. (But if local procedures make it clear that nothing done by D at a particular stage binds him, then presumably counsel does not have to be appointed.)

   b. **Post-trial stages:** Stages occurring *after* the trial may also be found "critical," thus triggering the right to counsel.

      i. **Sentencing:** For instance, a post-trial *sentencing* will normally be a "critical stage," requiring that D be furnished with an attorney. [*Mempa v. Rhay*]

         (1) Suspended sentence: Suppose D is convicted of a crime, and is given a *suspended sentence*, under which he is *placed on probation* and will be imprisoned if and only if he later violates the terms of the probation. Here, too, D has the right to appointed counsel *before* trial and imposition of the suspended sentence.

         Example: The state charges D, an indigent, with a minor misdemeanor. The state intends that if D is convicted, the state will recommend, in return for a plea bargain, that the judge give D a suspended sentence plus probation. If the state wants to preserve the ability to have D sent to jail for one year should he violate the probation, the state will have to supply counsel during trial and sentencing. (In other words, the state can't meet its appointed-counsel obligation by saying, "We won't supply counsel unless/until there's a probation-revocation proceeding.") [*Alabama v. Shelton*]

      ii. **Psychiatric exam:** Similarly, where the court orders a *psychiatric examination* to determine whether a murder convict deserves the death penalty, the convict is entitled to consult a lawyer before submitting to the exam. [*Estelle v. Smith*]

      iii. **Probation revocation not covered:** But there is *no* right of counsel in a proceeding to *revoke* the defendant's *probation*. [*Gagnon v. Scarpelli*]

   c. **Appeals:** A convicted defendant's right to appointed counsel during his *appeals* depends on the nature of the appeal. A defendant has the right to appointed counsel for his *first appeal as of right*, i.e., the appeal made available to all convicted defendants. [*Douglas v. California*]

      i. **Discretionary review:** But D has *no* right to appointed counsel to assist with his applications for *discretionary review*. That is, once D's conviction has been affirmed by the first appellate court, and the government provides a second discretionary review (e.g., discretionary review by the state supreme court, or petition for certiorari to the U.S. Supreme Court), D is on his own. [*Ross v. Moffitt*]

d. Habeas corpus: A defendant does ***not*** have a right to appointed counsel for pursuing ***federal habeas corpus*** relief after he has exhausted state remedies. But he does have a limited Sixth Amendment right to legal assistance: prison authorities are required to ***assist the inmate*** in filing *habeas corpus* papers. The prison must give at least one of the following forms of assistance: (1) an adequate law library; (2) the training of some inmates as paralegal assistants; (3) the use of non-prisoner paralegals and law students; or (4) the use of lawyers, perhaps on a part-time volunteer basis. [*Bounds v. Smith*]

II. ENTITLEMENTS OF THE RIGHT TO COUNSEL

A. Effectiveness of counsel: The Sixth Amendment entitles D not only to have a lawyer, but to have the *"effective assistance"* of counsel.

   1. Standard: Where a lawyer has actually participated in D's trial, D has a hard burden to show that he did not receive "effective assistance." D must show ***both*** that:

   [1] counsel's performance was *"deficient,"* in the sense that counsel was not a *"reasonably competent attorney"*; *and*

   [2] the deficiencies were ***prejudicial*** to the defense, in the sense that there is a "reasonable probability that, but for counsel's errors, the ***result*** of the proceeding ***would have been different."***

   [*Strickland v. Washington*] (These two requirements are frequently called the *"two prongs"* of *Strickland*.)

B. Advice as to plea-bargaining: The right to effective assistance of counsel applies during the ***plea-bargaining*** process. There are two distinct scenarios, in either of which counsel might be found to have failed to furnish effective assistance:

   [1] Due to poor advice from counsel, the defendant ***agrees to accept a plea bargain***, when going to trial would likely have led to a better outcome;

   [2] Due to poor (or no) advice from counsel, the defendant ***fails to accept a plea bargain*** offered by the prosecution, ***goes to trial***, gets convicted, and receives a ***longer sentence*** than the one offered under the plea bargain.

   In each scenario, the two-pronged test of *Strickland, supra,* applies.

   1. D accepts a bad plea-bargain offer: Suppose that due to bad legal advice, D unwisely ***takes*** the ***"bad" plea bargain***. If D can show that (1) his lawyer's "take the plea" advice was deficient, and (2) this advice caused him "prejudice," D can succeed on his effective-assistance claim.

   Example: D is a non-citizen who has resided lawfully in the U.S. for 40 years. He is charged with marijuana smuggling. His lawyer fails to tell him that if he pleads guilty to the charge, he will be automatically *deported* under federal immigration law. D pleads guilty, and then discovers that he is automatically and immediately deportable. D, claiming ineffective assistance, tries to withdraw the plea and get a trial.

Held, by the Supreme Court, for D (at least in part). The automatic-deportation consequences of a guilty plea here were so great that the lawyer's failure to mention those consequences caused his performance to fall below the level of competence (the first *Strickland* prong). However, to fully succeed with his ineffective assistance claim (i.e., to be entitled to withdraw his plea and go to trial), D will have to show on remand that he has suffered "prejudice." (Case remanded to the state courts to determine whether D can make this showing of prejudice.) [*Padilla v. Kentucky*]

a. **"Prejudice" standard for bad-plea-bargain cases:** Whenever a defendant makes an ineffective-assistance claim, as we noted he has to show that the poor representation caused him "prejudice." Where D's claim is that he was not accurately advised about the potential *negative consequences* of a plea bargain, the requirement to show prejudice means that D has to show "a reasonable probability that, but for counsel's unprofessional errors, *the result of the proceeding would have been different*" (the second prong of the *Strickland* formulation, *supra*, p. 140). But in the case where D takes a bad plea bargain, what does it *mean* to say that but for counsel's poor advice, "the result of the proceeding would have been different"? "Different" how?

   i. **The "I would have insisted on going to trial" standard:** Here's the Supreme Court's answer: The defendant does *not* have to make the difficult showing that had he not taken the bad plea-bargain, he would probably have been *acquitted* at trial. Instead, he *merely* has to make a much easier showing: a *"reasonable probability that,* but for counsel's errors, he *would not have pleaded guilty and would have insisted on going to trial."* [*Hill v. Lockhart*]

Example: D is a non-U.S. citizen who pleads guilty to a narcotics crime in order to get a somewhat shorter sentence (the difference between an 18-year sentence and one of 16 or 17 years) than he would get if convicted at trial. Before D takes the plea, his lawyer erroneously assures him that he will not be deported if he pleads guilty. (In reality, deportation is not just possible but *mandatory*, whether he pleads guilty or is found guilty at trial.) After taking the plea, D discovers the error and unsuccessfully tries to withdraw his plea. He claims that the lawyer's advice deprived him of effective assistance of counsel.

Held, for D. The issue is whether D can show a "reasonable probability that, but for counsel's errors, he would not have pleaded guilty and would have insisted on going to trial." Even though D would have had no "viable defense" at trial, he can still meet this "reasonable probability" test if there is substantial evidence that because of his circumstances he would have found it attractive to pursue "even the smallest chance of success at trial." Here, before he took the plea, D made it clear that his main objective was to ensure that he would not be deported; therefore, it was not irrational for him to prefer taking a small chance at acquittal rather bargaining for a slightly shorter prison sentence. Therefore, he has shown the required "prejudice" — that without the incorrect advice he would probably have gone to trial. Consequently, D is entitled to a new trial. [*Lee v. U.S.*]

2. D rejects a good plea-bargain offer: Now, let's look at the opposite situation: the prosecution offers the defendant a particular plea bargain, and due to counsel's bad advice (or total lack of advice), the defendant ***doesn't take the offer***, goes to trial, gets convicted, and gets a longer prison term than the one originally offered under the plea-bargain. There can be a violation of the Sixth Amendment right to effective assistance in this situation, too. Here are the main rules:

[1] Defense counsel has the ***duty to communicate*** to D ***any formal plea offer*** from the prosecution, if these may be favorable to D (so that failure to pass along the offer can be deficient assistance under the first prong of *Strickland*).

[2] Whether D does or doesn't learn about the offered plea bargain, if D fails to ***accept*** the bargain due to incompetent advice, D must still show all of the following to win any practical relief on ineffective-assistance grounds:

[a] a *"**reasonable probability**"* that D ***would have accepted*** the earlier plea offer had he been given competent legal advice;

[b] a "reasonable probability" that the plea would have been ***entered without the prosecution canceling it*** (if the prosecution had the power under state law to make such a cancellation); and

[c] a "reasonable probability" that the plea would have been entered ***without the trial court refusing to accept it*** (again assuming the judge had the power under state law to refuse to accept the plea).

[*Missouri v. Frye*; *Lafler v. Cooper*]

3. Other causes of ineffectiveness: Apart from actual blunders made by the lawyer at trial or in plea bargaining, some other events may be found to amount to a denial of effective assistance. These include a showing that:

[1] the court refused to grant a ***postponement*** to allow a newly-appointed lawyer ***adequate time to prepare*** for trial;

[2] the lawyer was not given a ***reasonable right of access*** to his client before or during the trial; or

[3] the lawyer represented ***multiple defendants***, and the interests of those defendants conflicted to the detriment of D.

C. Other aspects of the Sixth Amendment:

1. Expert assistance: The defendant may have a Sixth Amendment right to have the state pay for an ***expert*** to be retained on his behalf.

Example: If D raises the insanity defense, he is entitled to have the state pay for a psychiatrist to examine him, and to have that psychiatrist give testimony as to D's sanity.

2. Fees and transcripts: The defendant is entitled to have the state pay for any ***transcripts and records*** necessary to present an effective appeal, and any related ***fees***.

D. Secret agents: Once a suspect has been ***indicted*** and has counsel, it is a violation of the right of counsel for a ***secret agent*** to deliberately obtain incriminating statements from D in the absence of counsel, and to pass these on to the prosecution. [*Massiah v. U.S.*]

    1. Must be "deliberately elicited": But this ban on secret agents applies only where the agent ***"deliberately elicits"*** the incriminating testimony, not where the agent merely "keeps his ears open." [*Kuhlmann v. Wilson*]

        a. Does not cover pre-indictment situations: Even the ban on the deliberate eliciting of confidences by secret agents applies only ***after formal proceedings*** (e.g., an indictment) have begun against D. So during the pre-indictment investigation stage, the police may use a secret agent to entrap D even if the police or agent know that D has a regular lawyer, and even though the agent passes the confidences on to the police or prosecutors.

    2. Presence at attorney-client conference: The presence of an undercover agent at a ***conference*** between a suspect and his ***lawyer*** will also be a violation of the suspect's right to counsel, if materials from this conference are used by the prosecution, at least if the agent goes to the meeting for the purpose of spying (as opposed to going there for the purpose of maintaining his own cover).

    3. May be used for impeachment of D's testimony: Even where the police or prosecution violate D's Sixth Amendment rights by deliberately having an undercover informant elicit incriminating statements from D outside the presence of D's counsel, the prosecution may ***use*** these statements to ***impeach D's trial testimony.*** [*Kansas v. Ventris*] In other words, just as statements elicited in violation of D's Fifth Amendment *Miranda* rights may be used to impeach the defendant's trial testimony (see *Harris v. N.Y., supra*, p. 134), so statements elicited by informants in violation of D's Sixth Amendment rights may be used for this same purpose.

III. THE CLIENT'S RIGHT TO CONTROL THE DEFENSE

A. The right generally: There are some decisions about the defense that are the province of the lawyer, and others that are ***reserved to the defendant.***

        Note on self-representation: A defendant's right to ***represent himself*** does not really fall into either of the two categories. We consider this right separately *infra*, 147.

B. Rights reserved to lawyer: Assuming the defendant chooses to have a lawyer manage and present her case, then many of the decisions about how the case should be defended – typically decisions that can be described as matters of ***"trial strategy"*** – are ***reserved to the lawyer,*** not the client.

    1. Consequence: If a decision falls within this "trial strategy" category, two important Sixth Amendment consequences follow:

        [1] the ***lawyer*** is entitled to ***make the decision on her own***, and need not follow the wishes of the client; and

        [2] the fact that the lawyer has made her own decision rather than following the

client's wishes *will **not** constitute ineffective assistance of counsel.*[3]

2. **Decisions falling into the "lawyer's prerogative" category:** Decisions will be found to fall within this "province of the lawyer" category if the decision is primarily about the *tactics and strategy to be used by the defense,* rather than about what the *objectives* of the defense should be. As the Court has said, *"**Trial management** is the **lawyer's province."** [McCoy v. Louisiana* (2018)]

   a. **Examples:** Therefore, counsel – not the client – is empowered to make decisions about the following issues, all of which are deemed to be matters of "trial management":

   [1] whether to move to *suppress prosecution evidence* obtained by a constitutional violation (e.g., evidence from searches that violated D's Fourth Amendment rights);

   [2] whether to have D *wear civilian clothing* rather than prison garb during the trial;

   [3] whether to *object* to an improper *jury instruction*;

   [4] whether to *forgo cross-examination* of a witness;

   [5] whether to *call a witness* (other than D himself) at trial.

   b. **No obligation to argue all issues on appeal:** Here is another situation in which the lawyer, not the client, gets to make the decision: An *appellate* lawyer is *not required* by the Sixth Amendment to *raise all issues which his client would like him to argue.* Rather, the lawyer is permitted to *use his own professional judgment* about what issues have the best probability of success on appeal. Consequently, even if one or more appellate arguments urged by the client and rejected by the lawyer are non-frivolous, the client has not been deprived the effective assistance of counsel. [*Jones v. Barnes*]

C. **Decisions that belong solely to the client:** In contrast to the above category of "trial management" decisions, as to which the lawyer has control, there is a category of decisions that are so *"fundamental"* that the Supreme Court confers the decision-making power on the *client*, not the lawyer. [*McCoy v. Louisiana* (2018)] According to *McCoy*:

   [1] if the decision consists of *"strategic choices* about *how best to achieve a client's objective,"* the decision belongs to the *lawyer*; *but* …

   [2] if the decision concerns *"what the client's objectives in fact **are**"* (emphasis in original), then it's the *client*, not the lawyer, who holds the right to make the decision.

---

3. Of course, the lawyer's decision may be *so ill-advised* that it constitutes ineffective assistance. But when a reviewing court is later trying to decide whether the decision amounted to ineffective assistance, that court will essentially ignore the fact that the client objected to the decision.

1. **Examples where client has the decision-making power:** *McCoy, supra,* gives this list of choices that are sufficiently "*fundamental*" that they belong to the client:

   [1] whether to "*self-represent*";

   [2] whether to *plead guilty*;

   [3] whether to *waive a jury*;

   [4] whether to *testify in one's own behalf*;

   [5] whether to *take an appeal*; and ...

   [6] whether to *concede guilt* in the context of a capital-murder proceeding (the issue posed by *McCoy* itself).

   > **Example of [6]:** D is charged with the capital murder of three members of his estranged wife's family. He hires English to be his trial lawyer. English wants to concede D's guilt in the guilt phase (he thinks the evidence that D did the killings is overwhelming), so that D will be less likely to be sentenced to death. But D demands that English not concede guilt, and instead assert an alibi-plus-"corrupt cops did the killings" defense. English disobeys, telling the jury during the guilt phase that D did the killings. The jury convicts. In the penalty phase, English begs the jury to sentence D to life on account of his serious mental-and-emotional issues. However, the jury sentences D to death. On appeal, represented by new lawyers, D claims that English's refusal to follow D's instructions not to concede guilt deprived him of effective assistance of counsel.
   >
   > *Held* (by the U.S. Supreme Court), for D. Certain decisions are "reserved for the client." This category consists *not* of "strategic choices about how best to *achieve* a client's objectives" but rather, "choices about *what the client's objectives in fact are*." Whether to concede guilt is one of these reserved-to-the-client choices, since one in D's position might well "wish to avoid, above all else, the *opprobrium* that comes with *admitting he killed family members*."
   >
   > Furthermore, the error here, since it "block[ed] the defendant's right to make the fundamental choices about his own defense," was "*structural*" in nature. When an error is structural, it is *not subject to "harmless-error" review.* Thus D is automatically entitled to a new trial, with no need to show how the error caused him prejudice. [*McCoy v. Louisiana*]

IV. WAIVER OF THE RIGHT TO COUNSEL

A. **Appointed vs. retained:** In both the appointed-counsel and retained-counsel situations, the defendant may be found to have *waived* his Sixth Amendment right to counsel. Essentially the same standards apply for both situations.

B. **The "knowingly and intelligently" standard:** D will be found to have waived his right to counsel only if he acted "*knowingly and intelligently*." However, the government must prove merely by a "preponderance of the evidence" that D acted knowingly and intelligently, a relatively easy-to-satisfy standard.

1. ***Miranda* warnings suffice:** If D is given his ***Miranda*** warnings, and does not ask for counsel, this will normally be found to be a valid waiver of his Sixth Amendment right to counsel.

C. **Waiver after pre-trial appointment of counsel:** Suppose a suspect has been formally charged, and is represented by counsel (retained or appointed); trial has not yet begun, and the police want to ***question the suspect outside of the presence of his counsel.*** In this scenario, as a matter of Sixth Amendment law the police ***may*** ask the suspect whether he is willing to answer their questions, and treat his willingness to answer as constituting a waiver of his right to have his counsel present at any questioning. This principle is set forth in *Montejo v. Louisiana.*

1. **Non-custodial interrogations:** If the police interrogation takes place *in custody*, the police's freedom from Sixth Amendment problems won't help them very much. That's because the police still have to worry about *Edwards v. Arizona* (*supra*, 117), under which once a suspect has asked for counsel after being given *Miranda* warnings, any later custodial confession outside the presence of counsel will automatically be deemed a *Miranda* (Fifth Amendment) violation unless the conversation was ***initiated by the suspect.***

   But in the case of a ***non-custodial police-initiated interrogation*** (to which *Edwards* doesn't apply because *Miranda* doesn't apply to non-custodial questioning), *Montejo* means that the police ***don't have to worry about the suspect's Sixth Amendment right to counsel.*** (The court has to find that the suspect's willingness to speak to them outside the presence of his lawyer constituted a "knowing and intelligent" waiver of those Sixth Amendment rights; but there's no bright-line rule, as there is in the *Edwards/Miranda* context, that there can be no waiver if the police initiate the conversation.)

   > **Example:** D is charged with murder, and is arraigned before a magistrate. At D's request, the magistrate appoints counsel for him. D is then released on bail. The next day, the police visit D at his house and, without referring to the fact that D has had counsel appointed for him, ask him if he is willing to talk to them about the crime. D (having never consulted with his newly-appointed counsel) agrees to talk, and confesses. At trial, D tries to get the confession suppressed on the grounds that the court should impose a bright-line rule that any waiver of the right to counsel induced by police-initiated questioning outside the presence of counsel should be deemed invalid.
   >
   > D will lose with this argument. As long as the court finds that D's willingness to speak to the police constituted a "knowing and intelligent" waiver of the right to have counsel present (which the court will probably find), the confession will come in. In cases involving suspects in *custody*, the bright-line rule of *Edwards v. Arizona* (*supra*, p. 117) says that once a suspect has asked for counsel after being given *Miranda* warnings, any later custodial confession outside the presence of counsel must automatically be deemed invalid unless the conversation was initiated by the suspect. But no such rule applies in the case of the Sixth Amendment and non-custodial police-initiated conversations: the suspect's willingness to speak without having consulted his lawyer will be deemed to be an implied waiver of his Sixth Amendment rights, as

long as the facts indicate that the waiver was "knowing and intelligent." [Cf. *Montejo v. Louisiana, supra*]

D. Entry of guilty plea: If a purported waiver of the right to counsel is followed by entry of a *guilty plea,* courts are especially skeptical of whether the waiver was "knowingly and intelligently" made, which it is required to be.

   1. Minimum requirements: Thus courts generally hold that at the least, the defendant must be *aware of the charges against him* and must *understand the full significance of his decision* to waive counsel.

E. Right to defend oneself: The Sixth Amendment guarantees the right of a defendant to proceed *pro se*, i.e., to *represent himself without counsel*. [*Faretta v. California*] (By choosing to represent himself, D waives any later claim that he was denied the effective assistance of counsel.)

   1. Mentally incompetent defendant: But if the defendant has a *severe mental illness* that prevents her from being competent to conduct her own defense, the state may *insist on appointing counsel*.

CHAPTER 9

FORMAL PROCEEDINGS

Introductory note: In this last chapter, we cover aspects of the criminal procedure system once formal proceedings have begun against the defendant (as opposed to the investigative phase, covered above).

I. GRAND JURY PROCEEDINGS

A. Grand jury indictment generally: Defendants accused of federal felonies, and some state-court defendants, are "entitled" to a grand jury indictment.

   1. Federal practice: The Fifth Amendment provides that "no person shall be held to answer for a capital, or otherwise infamous crime, unless on a presentment or indictment of a Grand Jury." This provision means that anyone charged with a *federal felony* (i.e., a federal crime punishable by more than one year of imprisonment) may only be tried following issuance of a grand jury indictment.

   2. State courts: The Fifth Amendment's right to a grand jury indictment is one of the two Bill of Rights guarantees that is *not* binding on the states by means of the Fourteenth Amendment. So each individual state decides whether to require a grand jury indictment. Today, about 19 states require indictment for all felonies, with the remaining states dispensing with the requirement in at least some kinds of felonies.

B. Self-incrimination and immunity: The Fifth Amendment privilege against *self-incrimination* will frequently entitle a witness who is subpoenaed by a grand jury to refuse to testify. However, this refusal may be overcome by a grant of immunity.

   1. The privilege: The privilege against self-incrimination applies in grand jury proceedings — if the witness believes that the testimony she is being asked to give might incriminate her in a subsequent criminal case (whether in the jurisdiction that is conducting the grand jury investigation, or a different one), she may decline to testify on Fifth Amendment grounds. [*Counselman v. Hitchcock*] (The Fifth Amendment does *not* allow the witness to refuse to appear at all — the witness must appear in response to the subpoena, and must then state for the record the Fifth Amendment claim.)

2. Grant of immunity: The grand jury, acting under the prosecutor's direction, may combat Fifth Amendment claims by granting *immunity* to the witness. There are two types of immunity: *transactional* immunity (which protects the witness against any prosecution for the entire transactions about which the witness has testified), and *use* immunity (a much narrower protection, which protects only against the direct or indirect use of the testimony in a subsequent prosecution).

    a. Use immunity sufficient: *Use immunity is sufficient* to nullify the witness' Fifth Amendment privilege. [*Kastigar v. U.S.*] But use immunity is interpreted in a way that is favorable to the defendant — usually, use immunity requires that any eventual prosecution of the witness be conducted by someone who did not witness or read the transcript of the grand jury testimony.

II. BAIL AND PREVENTIVE DETENTION

A. Bail: The system of *bail* is the way courts have traditionally dealt with the problem of making sure that D shows up for trial. D is required to post an amount of money known as a "bail bond"; if he does not show up for trial, he forfeits this amount.

1. Right to non-excessive bail: The Eighth Amendment (applicable in both state and federal proceedings) provides that *"excessive bail shall not be required."* However, the Bail Clause does *not* give D a right to affordable bail in all situations — it merely means that when the court does set bail, it must not do so in an *unduly high* amount, judged on factors such as the seriousness of the offense, the weight of the evidence against D, D's financial abilities and his character.

    Example: If a judge were to set bail of $1 million for an indigent D accused of the non-violent crime of marijuana possession, this might be found to be "excessive" bail, in violation of the Eighth Amendment.

    a. Individualized consideration: The guarantee against excessive bail means that the judge must consider D's *individual circumstances* in fixing bail. The court may not consider the seriousness of the offense as the *sole* criterion (so that ability to pay, weight of the evidence, character of D, etc. must all be considered).

    b. Defendant's ability to pay: The fact that the defendant *cannot afford* the bail set in the particular case does *not* automatically make the bail "excessive" — D's financial resources are merely one factor to be considered.

B. Preventive detention: A jurisdiction may decide that bail will simply *not be allowed* at all for certain types of offenses. That is, the state or federal government may set up a *"preventive detention"* scheme, whereby certain types of defendants are automatically held without bail until trial. But a preventive detention scheme will violate the Eighth Amendment if its procedures do not ensure that only those defendants who are genuinely dangerous or likely to flee are denied release.

1. **Factors to be considered:** The jurisdiction may, of course, consider D's likelihood of *flight* before trial as a factor in whether to deny bail entirely. But the jurisdiction may consider other factors as well, most notably the likelihood that D will, if released before trial, commit *additional crimes*.

2. **Individualized circumstances of defendant:** A preventive detention scheme probably must give D the opportunity for a *hearing*, at which D's *individual circumstances* (e.g., his dangerous past tendencies, his community ties, his past convictions, etc.) may be considered.

   > **Example:** If a state were to provide that bail should automatically be denied without a hearing, and preventive detention ordered, for any defendant charged with any act of murder, this mandatory scheme would almost certainly violate the Bail Clause.

III. PLEA BARGAINING

A. Plea bargaining generally: Most criminal cases are resolved by *plea bargain* rather than by trial. To give D an incentive to "settle" the case rather than insist on a trial, the prosecutor normally gives D an inducement of a *lighter sentence* than what he would get if he were convicted at trial. The three common types of plea bargains are: (1) the plea to a *less serious charge* (*Example:* D is allowed to plead guilty to second-degree sexual assault rather than to the rape charge that is supported by the evidence); (2) D pleads guilty to the crime charged, but the prosecutor agrees to recommend a *lighter sentence* to the judge (but the judge will not necessarily follow the recommendation, though she usually does so); and (3) D pleads to one charge in return for the prosecution's promise to *drop other charges* that might also have been brought.

1. **Generally enforceable:** Plea bargains are generally *enforceable*. For instance, if D pleads guilty to a charge, is sentenced, and then has a change of heart, he is almost always stuck with his bargain.

2. **Prosecutor may refuse to bargain:** The prosecutor has *no obligation* to bargain. Even if the prosecutor routinely offers a plea bargain in other, similar, circumstances, she has a right in a particular case to decide to go to trial without offering a plea bargain. [*Weatherford v. Bursey* ("There is no constitutional right to plea bargain…")]

B. Promises by prosecutor:

1. **Threats by prosecutor:** There are relatively few constraints on the prosecutor's right to use *threats* during the negotiation. For instance, the prosecutor may charge one crime, and then tell D, "If you don't plead guilty to this charge, I'll file more serious charges." So long as the threatened extra charges are reasonably supported by the evidence, D will not be able to plead guilty, then attack the plea on the grounds that he was coerced. This is true even if D shows that the prosecutor has treated him more harshly than the prosecutor treats others accused of the same crime.

   a. **Threats about third person:** But if the prosecutor tries to induce D to plead guilty by offering leniency to a ***third person*** (or, conversely, threatens to prosecute the third person if D does not plead guilty), D has a somewhat greater chance of getting the plea bargain overturned on the grounds of duress. This is especially true where the third person is D's ***spouse, sibling, or child*** — but even here, D usually cannot succeed in getting a plea bargain overturned on grounds of duress.

2. **Broken promises:** The plea bargain is essentially a contract, and the rules of contract law apply. Consequently, if the prosecution fails to ***honor its part of the bargain***, D may usually either "terminate the contract" (i.e., elect to go to trial) or seek "specific performance" (i.e., insist that the terms as originally agreed upon be carried out).

   a. **Judge disagrees:** But D only has the right to receive what the prosecution has promised, and no more. For instance, if the plea bargain is a "lesser sentence" arrangement, in which the prosecutor has promised to ***recommend*** a particular lighter sentence, D's constitutional rights are not violated where the prosecutor keeps this part of the bargain but the trial judge unexpectedly ***imposes a more serious sentence***. (But many states, and the federal system, although not constitutionally required to do so, would allow D to ***withdraw*** his guilty plea at that moment and go to trial.)

   b. **Breach by defendant:** If *D* fails to live up to the plea bargain, then the *prosecution* has the right to elect to terminate the agreement and try D on the originally-charged offense. This is true even if a judgment of conviction has already been entered as the result of the plea bargain.

      Example: D agrees to testify against his confederates in return for a lesser charge or lesser sentence. He receives the reduced charge or sentence, then refuses to testify. The prosecution has the right to withdraw the conviction and try D on the original charge. [*Ricketts v. Adamson*]

C. **Receipt of plea:** The trial judge will not "receive" (i.e., accept) the plea until she has assured herself that certain requirements, designed to protect D, have been complied with. Thus the judge must be satisfied that: (1) D is ***competent*** to enter into the plea, and the plea is truly voluntary; (2) D ***understands the charge***; and (3) D understands the ***consequences*** of the plea, such as the minimum and maximum possible sentences.

1. **Factual basis:** Some states, and the federal system, also require that the judge not take the guilty plea unless the judge is convinced that there is a ***factual basis*** for the plea. Thus if D continues to protest his innocence, and says that he is pleading guilty only to avoid the risk that the judge or jury may disbelieve his truthful professions of innocence, the judge will normally ***not accept*** the guilty plea. In this scenario, it is ***constitutional*** for the trial judge to refuse to take the guilty plea — there is no absolute constitutional right to have one's guilty plea accepted by the court. [*North Carolina v. Alford*]

D. **Withdrawal of plea by defendant:** Under some circumstances, D may have the right to ***withdraw*** his guilty plea.

1. **Before sentencing:** *Before sentencing* has taken place, most jurisdictions give D a broad right to withdraw the plea.

2. **After sentencing:** But *after sentencing*, it is far **harder** for D to withdraw the plea. Courts normally don't let D get two bites of the apple (i.e., they don't let D plead guilty, see what sentence will be imposed, and then rescind the arrangement if he is disappointed).

   a. **Trial judge ignores recommendation:** But in one situation courts usually *do* allow a post-sentencing withdrawal of the plea: where the prosecution agrees to recommend a certain sentence, and the trial judge ignores the recommendation and sentences more severely, most jurisdictions allow D to withdraw and go to trial (though it is probably **not** a violation of D's constitutional right for the court to refuse to allow withdrawal in this situation).

E. **Rights waived by plea:** Normally, a defendant who enters a guilty plea and undergoes sentencing is deemed to have **waived** any rights, including constitutional ones, that he could have asserted at trial. With rare exceptions, therefore, D may not **appeal** the pleaded-to conviction or the sentence under it. This is true even where D now asserts constitutional rights that were not recognized until **after** the plea was entered. [*McMann v. Richardson*]

IV. RIGHT TO SPEEDY TRIAL

A. **The right generally:** The Sixth Amendment provides that "In all criminal prosecutions, the accused shall enjoy the right to a *speedy . . . trial.*" This right applies to both federal and state prosecutions.

   1. **Factors:** There is no bright-line rule setting forth exactly how speedy a trial must be. Instead, the Supreme Court uses a "balancing test," in which both the prosecution's and the defendant's conduct are weighed. There are four factors which courts are to consider in deciding whether the trial has been unreasonably delayed: (1) the *length of the delay* (with most delays of eight months or longer found "presumptively prejudicial"); (2) the *reason* for the delay (the more culpable the government's conduct regarding the delay, the better D's speedy trial claim); (3) whether D *asserted* the speedy trial right *before* a trial began (as opposed to an assertion of the right after the trial was conducted and D lost); and (4) what *prejudice* D has suffered by the delay (with the most weight given to any impairment of D's ability to defend himself, such as by the death or unavailability of witnesses).

B. **Federal Speedy Trial Act:** In federal prosecutions, speedy trial problems are covered by the Speedy Trial Act, which as a very general rule provides that the time between indictment and commencement of trial must normally be no more than 70 days (but which allows various "periods of delay" that do not count in the 70-day limit).

V. PRE-TRIAL DISCOVERY

A. **Discovery for the defense:** The defense may be entitled to advance *disclosure* by the prosecution of evidence relevant to the case.

1. **Prosecutor's constitutional duty to disclose:**   There is no *general* constitutional duty on the part of the prosecutor to disclose material evidence to the defense. But there is one constitutional rule: the prosecution must disclose to the defense *exculpatory evidence within the prosecution's possession.* [*Brady v. Maryland*] (A defense request for exculpatory material is called a "*Brady* request.")

   a. **Good faith irrelevant:**   Even if the prosecution's failure to disclose exculpatory evidence is *not* motivated by a desire to hamper the defense, and is truly the result of *negligence* or even circumstances beyond the prosecution's control, this makes no difference. (But if the prosecution is *unable* to disclose exculpatory evidence because the evidence has been *lost* or *destroyed*, the *Brady* doctrine does *not apply* unless the defense shows *bad faith* on the part of the police. [*Arizona v. Youngblood*])

2. **Practice:**   Apart from constitutional requirements, most states, and the federal system, have enacted elaborate *statutory* pre-trial disclosure schemes. For instance, nearly all states and the federal system require the prosecution upon request to give the defense copies of *prior recorded statements* by the defendant. Similarly, many states also require the prosecution to disclose to D any recorded statements made by a *co-defendant*, as well as copies of scientific tests, physical examinations, and a list of witnesses whom the prosecution intends to call at trial. (But the defense usually may *not* get ahold of *police reports*.)

B. **Discovery for the prosecution:**   Most states and the federal system give the *prosecution* some discovery rights. These are usually less broad than those given to the defense. For instance, most states, and the federal system, require D to give advance notice of his intent to raise an *alibi* defense.

VI. THE RIGHT TO A JURY TRIAL

A. **The right generally:**   Criminal defendants have a right to a *jury trial*. This right is conferred by the Sixth Amendment, which says that "The accused shall enjoy the right to a ... public trial, by an *impartial jury* of the State and district wherein the crime shall have been committed[.]"

1. **Applicable to state trials:** This right applies to both *federal* and *state* trials.

2. **Serious criminal prosecutions only:** The Sixth Amendment right to jury trial applies only to *criminal prosecutions* for *serious* crimes. That is, the right does not apply where what is charged is a *petty* rather than serious crime.

   a. **Six months as dividing line:**   As a general rule, the dividing line between a "serious" crime and a "petty" one is a *potential sentence of greater than six months*. Thus there is automatically a right to jury trial for any crime punishable by more than six months in prison, regardless of whether a more-than-six-month sentence is *actually* imposed.

      i. **Multiple offenses:** Where D is charged with *multiple offenses* that are to be tried together, the Court will *not "aggregate"* these offenses together for purposes of the six-month test — each is evaluated on its own.

B. Waiver: The defendant may *waive* the right to jury trial, provided that the waiver is *voluntary*, *knowing* and *intelligent*.

1. **Prosecution's right to veto:** But most states, and the federal system, allow the judge or the prosecutor to *"veto"* the defendant's waiver of a jury. That is, the judge or the prosecution may *insist on a jury trial* even though the defendant does not want one. [*Singer v. U.S.*]

C. Issues to which the right applies: Once the right to jury trial applies to an offense, D has the right to have the jury, rather than the judge, decide *every element* of the offense. Furthermore, the jury must find each element to exist *"beyond a reasonable doubt."*

1. **No jury right as to sentencing:** On the other hand, the right to a jury trial does not extend to the area of *sentencing*. For instance, the determination of whether particular *"sentencing factors"* specified by the legislature (e.g., existence of a prior conviction) do or do not exist in the particular case can be made by the judge.

2. **Fact increases the maximum sentence:** But if the existence of a particular fact *increases the maximum punishment* to which D is subjected, the existence of that fact will be treated as an element of the offense, as to which the jury must make the decision.

   a. **New "elements" added to the crime:** So whenever a legislature says that the *maximum* statutorily-authorized sentence for *a given set of elements* is X, but that the maximum-authorized sentence becomes *higher* than X if a particular *extra fact* is found to exist, that extra fact must be found by the jury, not the judge. [*Apprendi v. N.J.*]

   Example: New Jersey defines the crime of possession of a firearm for an unlawful purpose as a "second degree" offense. The punishment for a second-degree offense is imprisonment for between *5 and 10 years.* A separate statute, however, says that if a second-degree offense is committed "with a purpose to *intimidate* an individual or group ... because of *race, color* [or] *gender[,]"* the crime is punishable by an *"enhanced sentence"* of between *10 and 20 years*. D is charged with possessing a firearm for an unlawful purpose, and pleads guilty. During the sentencing phase the trial judge (not a jury) conducts a hearing on the basis of which the judge concludes that D's unlawful purpose included racial bias. Therefore, the judge sentences D to an enhanced (more-than-10-year) sentence. D claims that his Sixth Amendment right to have a jury decide each "element of the offense" means that he had a right to have a jury, not the judge, decide whether D's use of the firearm was motivated by racial bias.

   Held, for D. "Other than the fact of a prior conviction, any *fact* that increases the *penalty* for a crime beyond the [otherwise-applicable] *prescribed statutory maximum* must be submitted to a jury, and proved beyond a reasonable doubt." Since D's possession of a race-based motive increased the penalty beyond the 5-10 year maximum that would otherwise apply, the existence of such a motive was required to be determined by a jury. [*Apprendi v. N.J.*]

      i.   **Death penalty cases:** This principle that any fact that increases the maximum statutory punishment must be found by a jury has important applications to *death-penalty* cases. If the legislature says that the maximum penalty for a crime is something *less than death* in the absence of some statutorily-specified *"aggravating factor,"* then the existence of that aggravating factor must be determined by the jury (beyond a reasonable doubt) rather than by a judge. [*Ring v. Arizona*]

  b.   **Sentence within range:** If, by contrast, the existence of a particular fact merely bears on *where within the range of possible sentences* the defendant's sentence should fall, the existence of that fact will merely be a *sentencing factor* (on which the judge may constitutionally make the decision). [*Apprendi v. N.J., supra*]

  c.   **Increase in mandatory minimum:** A fact whose existence increases the *mandatory minimum* sentence that the court is *required* to impose must be decided by the jury, just as a fact that increases the maximum allowable sentence must be.

      Example: D is charged with the federal crime of carrying a firearm in relation to a crime of violence (in this case, a robbery). The statute says that if the firearm is "use[d] or carrie[d,]" the mandatory minimum sentence is five years; but if the firearm is *"brandished"* during the crime, the mandatory minimum becomes seven years. The jury convicts D, and indicates on the verdict form that D "used or carried" a firearm during the crime. But the jury does not put on the form any finding about whether D "brandished" a firearm. The judge finds that D "brandished" that firearm, and therefore sentences D to a mandatory minimum of seven years. D argues that he had a right to have a jury decide (under a "reasonable doubt" standard) whether he did or did not "brandish" the firearm.

      Held, for D. The rule that every "element" of a crime must be found by the jury applies not only to facts that *increase the "ceiling"* of permissible sentences (i.e., facts that increase the statutory *maximum*) but also to facts that increase the *"floor"* (i.e., facts that increase the statutory *minimum*). Therefore, D was entitled to have the jury, rather than the judge, decide whether he "brandished" the weapon. [*Alleyne v. U.S.* (2013)]

  3.   **Sentencing guidelines:** The principle that punishment-increasing facts must be found by a jury also means that schemes involving mandatory *"sentencing guidelines"* will typically be *invalid*. In such schemes, the legislature establishes both a maximum sentence for a particular offense (say 10 years), and a standard sentence *range* for that offense (say 3-5 years). The legislature then orders trial judges to add to or subtract time from the standard range according to various aggravating or mitigating factors found to exist by the judge, with the result never exceeding the maximum.

      The Court has held that *any increase* in the sentence given to a defendant — beyond the standard range — by virtue of the judge's finding on a guideline-mandated factor *violates* the defendant's right to a jury trial. [*Blakely v. Washington*]

Example: D is convicted of kidnapping, a Class B felony. The maximum penalty for Class B penalties is 10 years. But state sentencing guidelines prescribe a standard range of 49 to 53 months for kidnapping. However, the guidelines instruct the judge to consider various aggravating (or mitigating) factors that if present can move the sentence out of the standard range. The judge finds that D acted with "deliberate cruelty," an aggravating factor that under the guidelines can add 37 months to the standard range; therefore, the judge sentences D to a term of 90 months (37 months more than the top of the standard range).

Held, for D: the application of the guidelines to increase D's sentence beyond the maximum that it could otherwise have been (i.e., beyond 53 months), based on a fact (deliberate cruelty) found by a judge, violated D's right to a jury trial on all punishment-increasing elements. *Blakely v. Washington, supra.*

a. **Federal Guidelines are invalid as written:** This principle means that the *Federal Sentencing Guidelines are unconstitutional as written.* The Guidelines *cannot require* (as they purport to do) a federal judge to impose a heavier sentence based solely on a fact found by the judge. Instead, the Guidelines are merely *"advisory,"* and it's essentially up to the judge whether to follow them or not. [*U.S. v. Booker*]

   Example: D is found by the jury to have possessed "500 or more grams" of cocaine. For this offense, the maximum sentence authorized by the Federal Sentencing Guidelines is 78 months. The judge finds, in a postconviction proceeding, that D actually possessed much more than 500 grams (and also that D was the leader of a drug-dealing enterprise). The Guidelines require the judge, if he finds these "aggravating facts," to sentence D to an "upward departure," namely a term of 188 to 235 months.

   Held, insofar as the Guidelines require this upward departure beyond the longest sentence that could have been based on the jury's 500-gram finding (i.e., beyond 78 months), the Guidelines violate D's Sixth Amendment rights. Because of this unconstitutionality, the Guidelines cannot be mandatory. Instead, it is left to the judge's reasonable discretion what sentence to impose (though the judge must "consult" the Guidelines). [*U.S. v. Booker, supra*]

   i. **Right to appeal judge's actual sentence:** Given that the Federal Sentencing Guidelines are merely advisory, what happens if the trial judge seems to *disregard* them by imposing a sentence *outside the Guidelines' range?* If that happens, the prosecution (or the defense) may *appeal* the sentence as being too low (or high), and point to the judge's departure from the Guidelines' range in support.

      (1) **Abuse-of-discretion standard:** But the federal appeals court may *reverse* the outside-of-Guidelines-range sentence (assuming the actual sentence fell within the *statutory* minimum and maximum) *only* for "*abuse of discretion.*" And the abuse-of-discretion standard is a very *deferential* one. So even where the trial judge imposes a sen-

tence well outside of the Guidelines' range, the appeals court will rarely find "abuse of discretion," and thus rarely reverse on that ground. [*Gall v. U.S.*]

D. Size and unanimity of the jury: The Sixth Amendment places limits on states' ability to restrict the *size* of juries, and forbids *less-than-unanimous* verdicts in federal and state felony trials.

1. **Size:** Historically, juries have of course been composed of 12 persons. However, the Court has held that *juries of six or more satisfy the Sixth Amendment.* [*Williams v. Florida*] On the other hand, juries of *five or fewer violate* the Sixth Amendment. [*Ballew v. Georgia*]

2. **Unanimity:** The Sixth Amendment is now interpreted to require that the jury's verdict in *both state and federal felony* trials be *unanimous.* [*Ramos v. Louisiana* (2020)]

E. Selection of jurors: There are constitutional limits on the procedures by which jurors are *selected*.

1. **The venire, and the requirement of a "cross-section of the community":** The Sixth Amendment guarantees the accused the right to a trial by "an *impartial jury.*" This requirement of has been interpreted to mean that the venire (jury pool) from which petit juries are selected must *represent a fair cross-section of the community*. [*Taylor v. Louisiana*] Thus if a state or federal venire systematically excludes or underrepresents, say, African-Americans or women, the Sixth and Fourteenth Amendments are violated.

2. **Peremptory challenges:** With respect to the selection of the "petit jury" (the jury that actually decides a case) the main area of constitutional concern involves *peremptory challenges.* In nearly all jurisdictions, both the prosecution and defense are given a certain number of peremptory challenges, i.e., the right to have prospective jurors *excused without cause*.

    a. **Race- or gender-based challenges:** The most important rule regarding peremptory challenges is that in both federal and state trials, it is a violation of equal protection for the prosecution to exercise its peremptory challenges for the purpose of excluding jurors *on account of their race or gender*. [*Batson v. Kentucky; J.E.B. v. Alabama ex rel. T.B.*] Such a claim that the prosecution has used its peremptory challenges in an illegal race- or gender-based way is known as a *"Batson claim."*

        i. **Procedure for *Batson* claim:** The procedure by which D may make a *Batson* claim is as follows:

            (1) Prima facie case: First, D must, while jury selection is still proceeding, establish a *prima facie* case of intentional racial (or gender) discrimination. He must do this by showing that: (a) at least some members of a *particular cognizable racial group* (or gender) have been *eliminated* from D's jury; and (b) the circumstances of the case raise an *inference* that this exclusion was *based on race* (or gender). In demonstrating (b), D can rely on any relevant circumstances, but especially probative are (i) a ***pattern*** of strikes (either as to this particular petit jury, or as to other juries drawn from the same venire) and (ii) ***questions asked by the prosecution*** during voir dire that tend to show race- (or gender-) consciousness.

(2) Rebuttal by prosecution: If D makes this *prima facie* showing, the ***burden then shifts*** to the prosecution to ***come forward with a "neutral explanation"*** for challenging jurors of a particular race (or gender). This requires more than a conclusory denial of a discriminatory motive. Nor does the prosecution's belief that jurors of that race would be partial to the defense suffice.

(3) Decision by court: If the prosecution comes up with a race-neutral explanation, it is up to the trial court to decide ***whether the defendant has borne his burden*** of establishing that the real reason for the strikes was racial (or gender) discrimination. For a successful *Batson* claim, the court must conclude, as a finding of fact, that the race-neutral explanation proffered by the prosecution was a ***pretext***, rather than the real reason, and that the real reason was some sort of intent to make strikes on race- or gender-conscious grounds. In that case, the trial court must order the struck juror to be ***reinstated*** absent a successful for-cause challenge. The trial court's ruling will be reversed on appeal only if it is clearly erroneous.

VII. THE TRIAL

A. The right to a "public" trial: The Sixth Amendment provides that "In all criminal prosecutions, the accused shall enjoy the right to a . . . *public* trial." This right means that there must be ***some access*** by members of the public. Thus it would be a violation of D's public trial right for the trial to be held against his wishes in a closed judge's chambers, or in a prison.

1. **D does not have right to closed trial:** D does ***not*** have the right to insist on a ***private*** trial — the court may, without violating D's constitutional rights, order that the trial be conducted publicly over D's objection.

2. **Partial closure:** Occasionally, D's right to a public trial may be ***outweighed*** by a competing interest, on the part of the public or a witness, in having ***part*** of the trial ***closed***. In general, the party (usually the prosecution) seeking to close part of a trial must show: (1) that there is a ***compelling state interest*** in favor of closure; (2) that the closure will be ***no broader than necessary*** to protect that state interest; and (3) that there are no ***reasonable alternatives*** to closing the proceeding. [*Waller v. Georgia*]

    Examples: If D is being tried for raping V, a minor, the court probably can order the trial closed during the testimony of V, to protect her interest in confidentiality; but it probably cannot close the entire trial — the judge should instead consider ordering the parties not to refer to V by name. Similarly, if the case involves testimony by W, an undercover informant, it would probably be constitutional to close just the portion of the trial involving W's testimony, but probably not to close the entire trial.

B. D's right to be present: The defendant has a constitutional right to be *present* at his trial. This right derives from the Sixth Amendment's right of the accused "to be confronted with the witnesses against him." (However, this right can be lost by D's disruptive behavior which persists after a warning.)

C. D's Confrontation Clause rights: The Sixth Amendment gives any criminal defendant "the right . . . to be *confronted with the witnesses against him*." This is the Confrontation Clause. It applies to the states as well as the federal government. The Confrontation Clause has two main components: (1) the right to compulsory *process*; and (2) the right to *cross-examine* hostile witnesses.

   1. Compulsory process: The compulsory-process branch of the Confrontation Clause means that D has the right to have the court *issue a subpoena* to compel the testimony of any witness who may have information that would be useful to the defense.

      a. Assistance by the prosecution: Sometimes, the compulsory-process right means that the prosecution must *assist* the defense in finding witnesses. Thus if the prosecution knows the whereabouts or identity of a witness who would be useful to the defense, the prosecution may be constitutionally compelled to disclose that information. [*Roviaro v. U.S.*] (But in the case of an undercover *informant*, D's Confrontation Clause right to learn the informer's identity may be outweighed by the interest of the state, or the informer, in confidentiality to protect ongoing investigations or the informer's safety.)

   2. Right of cross-examination: The Confrontation Clause puts limits on the government's ability to restrict D's right of *cross-examination*.

      Example: A rule preventing D from cross-examining juvenile witnesses based upon their juvenile court records violates the Confrontation Clause. [*Davis v. Alaska*]

      a. Limits on hearsay: Similarly, the Confrontation Clause places some limits on the state's right to use *hearsay* evidence against D. For instance, hearsay may not be admitted unless it was obtained under circumstances providing reasonable *"indicia of reliability."* [*Ohio v. Roberts*] (But hearsay admitted under long-standing *common law exceptions* to the hearsay rule, such as the dying declaration exception, will almost always be found to have sufficient "indicia of reliability.")

D. Defendant's right to remain silent: The Fifth Amendment provides that no person "shall be *compelled* in any criminal case to be a witness *against himself*."

   1. Right not to take the stand: The privilege does not mean merely that D may refuse to answer questions asked of him by the prosecution. Instead, it means that D has the right to *not even take the witness stand*. (Most criminal defendants take advantage of this right.)

a. **Waiver:** But the privilege may be *waived*. A defendant who *does* take the witness stand has waived his privilege as to *any matters* within the fair scope of cross-examination.

Example: Once D takes the stand at all, he may be cross-examined about any prior convictions that shed light on his propensity to tell the truth, such as convictions for any crime involving dishonesty or false statement. See FRE 609(a).

2. **Comment by prosecution:** The privilege against self-incrimination means that the prosecution may not *comment* on the fact that the defendant has declined to take the witness stand. [*Griffin v. California*]

VIII. DOUBLE JEOPARDY

A. **The guarantee generally:** The Fifth Amendment provides that no person shall "be subject for the same offence to be twice put in jeopardy of life or limb." This is the guarantee against "double jeopardy." The most classic application of the doctrine is to prevent D from being retried after he has been *acquitted* by a jury. But it occasionally applies in other contexts as well (e.g., if D's conviction is reversed on appeal on the grounds that the evidence at trial was insufficient to support a conviction, no reprosecution is allowed).

1. **Applicable to states:** The double jeopardy guarantee applies to *state* as well as federal trials. [*Benton v. Maryland*]

B. **When jeopardy attaches:** The protection against double jeopardy does not apply until jeopardy has *"attached."*

1. **Jury trial:** In a case to be tried by a jury, jeopardy is deemed to "attach" when the jury has been *impaneled and sworn*, i.e., when the whole jury has been selected and taken the oath. [*Crist v. Bretz*]

2. **Bench trial:** If the case is to be tried by a judge sitting without a jury, jeopardy attaches when the *first witness has been sworn*.

C. **Reprosecution after mistrial:** If the trial begins and is then terminated by a *mistrial*, the prosecution is usually *not barred* from retrying the defendant.

1. **With D's consent:** If the mistrial has been brought about by the request of, or the acquiescence of, the defendant, reprosecution is *always allowed*. This is true even though D's motion for a mistrial is required because of the prosecution's intentional misconduct.

2. **Without D's consent:** Even where the defendant has *not* consented, the mistrial will frequently not bar reprosecution. If the court finds that the mistrial is required by *"manifest necessity,"* reprosecution will be allowed.

a. **Hung jury:** Most commonly, the retrial issue arises in cases where there is a *hung jury*. As long as the court is reasonably satisfied that the jury is truly deadlocked, and that additional deliberations will be fruitless, the situation meets the manifest-necessity standard, and the court can declare a mistrial over the defendant's objection. The decision of the trial judge that the jury is hopelessly deadlocked is given *"great deference"* by the appellate courts. [*Arizona v. Washington*]

   i.   Time spent in deliberation: One factor to which trial courts give a lot of weight is whether the jury has *deliberated* for a *significant period of time* before reaching the apparent deadlock — the longer the deliberation, the more likely the court is to conclude that the disagreement cannot be overcome. Consequently, if the jury reports a deadlock after a relatively brief deliberation period, the trial court is likely to (and should) instruct the jury to *continue further deliberation*.

   (1) Deference to trial court: But because of the large deference given by appeals courts to trial court judgments on the issue of deadlock, a trial judge will typically *not be reversed* even if she orders a mistrial following a very brief period of deliberation by the jury, and even if she does not order the jury to make another attempt to break the deadlock.

D. Reprosecution after acquittal: The classic application of the Double Jeopardy Clause is to prevent reprosecution after the defendant has been *acquitted*.

   1. Acquittal by jury: Where the case has been tried to a *jury* and the jury has come in with a verdict of *not guilty*, the clause always prevents D from being retried. This is true even though the acquittal was brought about by the admission of what should have been inadmissible evidence, and even if it was brought about by what can later be proved to have been *perjured testimony* offered by the defense. For this reason, the prosecution is *never* permitted to *appeal* a jury acquittal.

   2. Acquittal by judge: Similarly, an acquittal by the judge sitting alone is final, and cannot be appealed.

E. Reprosecution after conviction: Occasionally, the fact that D has been *convicted* may bar a later prosecution.

   1. Verdict set aside on appeal: If D is convicted at trial, and then gets the verdict *set aside on appeal*, the double jeopardy rule usually does *not* bar a retrial.

   Example: D is convicted based on the fruits of a search and seizure which, D contends, violated the Fourth Amendment. The appellate court agrees. The Double Jeopardy Clause does not prevent the state from retrying D on the same charge.

   a. Insufficiency of evidence: But there is one big exception: if the appellate court reverses because the evidence at trial was *insufficient* to support a conviction (i.e., no reasonable jury could have found D guilty on the evidence presented), a reprosecution is *not* allowed.

   2. Resentencing: Where D is convicted, then appeals and receives a new trial, the Double Jeopardy Clause places some limits on the *length of imprisonment* that may be imposed on the new conviction.

   a. Credit for time served: The Constitution requires that D be given *credit* for the time he served under the first charge before it was overturned. [*North Carolina v. Pearce*]

b. Longer sentence: On the other hand, the judge hearing the second trial is *not* prevented from giving D a *longer sentence* than was imposed following the first conviction. [*North Carolina v. Pearce, supra.*] (But if D in a death penalty case is sentenced to something less than death in the first trial, he may not be sentenced to death upon retrial.)

F. Reprosecution by a different sovereign: A conviction or acquittal by *one jurisdiction* does *not* bar a reprosecution by *another jurisdiction*. This is the so-called *"dual sovereignty"* doctrine.

Example: D, a police officer, is charged in a state trial with aggravated assault upon X, a suspect in custody. D is acquitted. D is then charged with the federal crime of violating X's civil rights; all of the facts making up this offense are the same as they were in the earlier, state, trial. The federal prosecution does not violate D's double jeopardy rights, because it is being brought by a different jurisdiction than brought the first case. The same would be true if the federal case came before the state case.

1. Non-constitutional limits: But many states have state-constitutional or statutory provisions protecting D against reprosecution after conviction by some other jurisdiction. Similarly, federal guidelines bar a federal trial where a comparable state prosecution has already occurred, unless an Assistant Attorney General has approved the reprosecution.

G. Overlapping offenses: Occasionally, two different offenses involve the same set of facts to such an extent that the two offenses are deemed the "same" for double jeopardy purposes. You probably need to worry about this "overlapping offenses" problem only where one charge is a *lesser included offense* of the other.

1. Lesser included offense tried first: Suppose the lesser included offense is *tried first*. Here, whether the first trial results in an acquittal or conviction, the prosecution cannot bring a later prosecution for the greater offense. [*Brown v. Ohio*])

2. Lesser included offense tried second: Conversely, the Double Jeopardy Clause also bars prosecution for the lesser included crime *after* conviction of the greater one.

3. Unable to try both at once: But the rule barring serial prosecutions on the greater and lesser included offenses does *not apply* where the prosecution is *unable* to try both cases at once for reasons that are not the government's fault.

Example: If facts needed for proving the second crime had not yet been discovered at the time of the first trial, despite the prosecutor's due diligence, the second trial will not be barred.

EXAM TIPS

TABLE OF CONTENTS
of EXAM TIPS

EXAM TIPS

Exam Tips on
CRIMINAL PROCEDURE GENERALLY

Here are the most frequently tested areas on criminal procedure generally:

State vs. federal constitutions

☛ Always consider that a state criminal defendant with a constitutional challenge may be able to rely on *both* the U.S. Constitution and the constitution of the *state* prosecuting him. States are free to *give greater procedural protection* to criminal defendants than that conferred by the U.S. Constitution, but *may not give less.*

Example: Bob grows marijuana in a fenced-in area of land 50 feet from his home. Although he may not have an expectation of privacy in the area as interpreted under the U.S. Constitution, the state constitution may grant him a privacy interest in the area that would give him protection against warrantless searches and seizures.

Jury trial right

☛ Remember that the right to a *jury trial* is fundamental. Exam questions frequently require you to explain its parameters.

☞ The Sixth Amendment guarantees all defendants the right to a jury trial if they are charged with a *felony,* or with a misdemeanor punishable by more than six months in prison. This right has been incorporated, so it *applies to states* as well as the federal government.

☞ Most states give defendants the right to a jury trial in *lesser misdemeanors* as well, but they are not required to do so. Defendants in other proceedings do not necessarily have a right to trial by jury.

☞ Even when there is a right to a jury trial, be on the lookout for express or implied *waiver*. A knowing and intelligent plea agreement is an example of express waiver. Implied waiver is when the defendant fails to specifically invoke the right or attempts to do so too late in the process of the criminal prosecution.

Government vs. private conduct

☛ Exam questions frequently test your knowledge of the fact that the Bill of

Rights only protects against ***governmental*** conduct. It does ***not*** restrict the conduct of ***private entities,*** unless they are acting at the express direction of a government agent.

Example: Defendant goes to a bus terminal run by a private bus company. The gun in his pocket triggers the metal detector. Bus company officials require him to submit to a search, find the gun, then turn it over to the police. At Defendant's trial for carrying a gun without a license, the gun will be admissible no matter how unreasonable the search; Defendant has no basis in the Fourth Amendment to challenge the bus company's conduct, because that conduct was private, not governmental.

Exam Tips on
ARREST; PROBABLE CAUSE; SEARCH WARRANTS

Here are the things to remember about arrests, probable cause and search warrants:

Fourth Amendment generally

☛ **What is a search:** Remember that the Fourth Amendment prohibition against unreasonable searches and seizures can be triggered in ***only two types of situations***:

❑ Where the police ***physically intrude*** on D's property (in essence, a ***trespass***), in an attempt to find evidence or information; or

❑ Where the police infringe on D's ***"reasonable expectation of privacy,"*** in an attempt to find evidence or information.

☛ **Reasonable expectation of privacy:** Therefore, unless the police have intruded on D's property (e.g., by attaching a tracking device to D's car), there cannot be a Fourth Amendment "search" unless the defendant had a ***"reasonable expectation of privacy"*** in the area that was searched.

☞ **Aerial surveillance:** For instance, there is no reasonable expectation of privacy from ***aerial surveillance*** of an area over which there is an ***established aerial route.*** This is true regardless of the owner's clear intent and efforts to maintain his privacy in the area, because such attempts are unreasonable.

Example: Defendant owns a home with a yard, around which he puts a very tall privacy fence. The police fly over his yard and use binoculars to take aerial photographs of the marijuana growing in Defendant's yard. This does not violate the Fourth Amendment, because Defendant is deemed not have had a reasonable expectation of privacy with regard to those parts of his yard that can be seen from a legal overflight.

☞ **Public vantage point:** Similarly, visual *surveillance* of a person by the police from the ground will usually *not* constitute a search of him — assuming no physical intrusion on D's property, surveillance will only constitute a search where the conduct violates D's reasonable expectation of privacy. So if police watch D from a *public vantage point,* their conduct is not a search, and no warrant is required.

Example: Police suspect Defendant of drug activity. Detective maintains visual non-contact surveillance of Defendant by stationing himself in the lobby of Defendant's apartment building and watching Defendant's movements as he enters and leaves the building. This is not a search, because Defendant has no expectation of privacy in the lobby. Therefore, the Fourth Amendment is not implicated (and no search warrant is needed).

☞ **Curtilage:** Remember that a homeowner has a reasonable expectation of privacy not just in the inside of her house, but also in the *"curtilage,"* i.e., the area *immediately surrounding the house*, typically including things like *garages, porches* and *backyards*.

Example: The police, accompanied by a trained drug-sniffing dog, climb the stairs onto the front porch of D's house. The dog sniffs the outside of D's front door and signals that drugs are present. The front porch is a part of the curtilage of D's house. Therefore, D is deemed to have a reasonable expectation of privacy in that front porch. By bringing the dog onto the porch without D's consent to drug-sniffing activities, the police have carried out a Fourth Amendment search (which was probably illegal unless they had both probable cause and a search warrant). [Cite to *Florida v. Jardines.*]

☛ **Driveway:** Curtilage may also include *part of a driveway*. That is, the part of the driveway that immediately abuts the house is usually part of the curtilage. [Cite to *Collins v. Virginia.*]

Obtaining search warrants

☛ Remember that search warrants must be *based on probable cause* and must *specifically identify the premises or persons* to be searched.

☛ Probable cause for a search warrant exists if it is *reasonably likely* that *incriminating evidence will be found* at the time and place the search is made. (But the likelihood probably *doesn't* need to be *greater than 50%* — a 1/3 chance might well be enough. Cite to *Maryland v. Pringle* on this point.)

☞ Probable cause is a very *fact-intensive* determination, so your professor will have to give you lots of facts if probable cause is an issue. The conclusion you come to will probably be a judgment call; at least recognize that probable cause is an issue, and explain which facts are relevant to the determination of whether it is more likely than not that evidence of criminal activity will be found.

☞ Remember that an *illegal search cannot form the basis of probable cause* to obtain a search warrant. (*Example:* Police can't make an illegal warrantless search of D's apartment, find cocaine, then seek a search warrant for that apartment based on their knowledge of the cocaine.)

☞ Look out for scenarios in which D *turns over data to a third person*: that turnover may mean that D *no longer has an expectation of privacy* in the data, so the police can demand that the third party turn over a copy to it, even though the police *don't have a warrant or probable cause.*

> *Example:* D opens a checking account with Bank. As D knows, every time D writes a check, Bank keeps a digital copy of it in a database. Even without a warrant or probable cause, the police can demand that Bank supply copies of all checks written by D during, say, a particular time period. Because D "voluntarily" turned over the check copies to a third party (Bank), he is deemed to have surrendered any reasonable expectation of privacy with regard to those copies. [Cite to *U.S. v. Miller*.]

☞ But keep in mind that the third-party doctrine probably *won't* apply in the case of most *modern-era digital databases* kept by companies, if the database captures large numbers of details of individuals' electronically-recorded transactions. Government requests that a company supply significant chunks of data about a suspect from such a database will probably be *considered to be Fourth Amendment searches*, if

[1] the information is *"deeply revealing"* about the suspect;

[2] the information's *"reach"* is *"deep," "broad,"* and *"comprehensive"*; and

[3] the *process* by which the information has been collected is *"inescapable and automatic."*

> *Example:* Police arrest D in connection with 10 robberies of local Radio Shack stores over a 2-month period. Suspicion — not amounting to probable cause — focuses on D, who the police know owned a cell phone serviced by Sprint Wireless at the time of each of the robberies. The police — without a search warrant — send a subpoena to Sprint, asking the company to supply "CSLI" ("cell-site location infor-

mation") showing where D's phone was at the time of each of the robberies. Sprint does so, supplying CSLI that shows, on each of 10 days, where D's phone was at the time of each robbery. D moves to suppress the CSLI from his trial, arguing that when the police demanded the data from Sprint, this was a Fourth Amendment search, which should not have been performed except pursuant to a search warrant issued upon probable cause.

You should say that D's argument is correct, and that the CSLI should be suppressed. The CSLI data requested by the police is highly revealing of D's intimate details, and is "broad" and "comprehensive." Also, the collection of the data was "inescapable and automatic" (since anyone needing a cell phone, a virtually indispensable product for modern life, would have to allow such data to be automatically collected). Therefore, the police committed a Fourth Amendment search when they subpoenaed the data. That subpoena should have been issued only by a "neutral magistrate," after the police showed probable cause to believe that the CSLI would constitute evidence of crime. [Cite to *Carpenter v. U.S.*]

Plain view doctrine

☛ Keep your eyes peeled for applications of the *"plain view"* doctrine: if authorities view an item of evidence from a *vantage point where they have a right to be,* that item is *admissible* even though the police don't have a warrant.

☞ A variant of the "plain view" doctrine applies to *senses other than sight,* such as hearing and smell.

Example: Officer goes to Defendant's hotel room to execute what turns out to be an invalid search warrant. While standing in the hallway, he hears the sounds of a struggle taking place within the hotel room. At Defendant's murder trial, Officer can testify about the sounds he heard. This is so because Officer had the right to be in the hall at the time he heard the struggle (an Officer has the right to execute what turns out to be an invalid search warrant so long as the Officer is acting in good faith without reasonable grounds to suspect the invalidity.) Therefore, Officer's discovery of the sounds fell within the plain-view exception.

Informers

☛ *Confidential informers* are a rich source of exam questions. If the warrant is based on the hearsay of a police informer, the sufficiency of the information is determined based on the *"totality of the circumstances."* There must be corroboration of the facts, or other means of determining that the informer is credible.

Example: An arrest warrant is issued based on an affidavit that states merely that a confidential informant "knows" Defendant and knows that stolen merchandise is now in Defendant's apartment. This is probably insufficient, because there is no reason given for believing that the informant is reliable, and no way to tell what the basis of the information is (e.g., personal observation, versus mere hearsay from another party).

Executing search warrants

☞ A *misidentification* of the premises to be searched will invalidate the warrant unless officers executing it could not mistake the place to be searched.

☞ A search warrant gives the police executing it the right to *scan the entire premises* if they have reasonable suspicion that *other armed persons* may be present (based on a concern for officer safety.)

Example: Officer goes to a home to confiscate contraband. He knows that the contraband will be located in the bedroom, but he opens a door in the hall which he correctly assumes to be a closet and finds a different item of contraband. He also knows that the Homeowner/Defendant has a violence-prone boyfriend. The discovery of the second item is legal, because Officer reasonably feared that an armed person, the boyfriend, might be hiding in the closet.

☛ Police may not, however, search places where the item they are looking for *cannot possibly be concealed* and where no armed person could possibly be hiding. (*Example:* Officer executing a search warrant for a counterfeiting machine may not look inside a jewelry box, since neither the machine nor an armed person could possibly fit inside it.)

Arrest warrants

☛ The requirement of an *arrest warrant* is the perfect example of exceptions swallowing the rule. There are, however, some limited circumstances when a warrant is still required to make an arrest. Generally, arrest warrants are *not required* even when the police have time to obtain them — there is no exigent-circumstances requirement. However:

☞ If the offense is a *misdemeanor* and wasn't committed in the *officer's presence*, an arrest warrant is required.

☞ Police need a warrant to arrest a defendant *inside his own home,* if there's no emergency.

☞   Don't assume that because officers don't need a warrant to make an arrest that they also don't need probable cause. Even without a warrant, officers *still have to have probable cause* to make a legal arrest.

◎ *Exam Tips on*
 WARRANTLESS ARRESTS AND SEARCHES

Warrantless arrests and searches are a *very* big topic with examiners. Keep in mind the following:

Warrantless arrests and searches generally

☛ *Warrantless arrests* are more common than those with a warrant. No arrest warrant is needed so long as the defendant is not taken into custody in his home. (With or without warrant, police can't arrest D unless they have probable cause to believe that D has committed a felony.)

    ☞   Also, no arrest warrant is needed (even to go into a home) when the police are in *"hot pursuit"* or *exigent circumstances* exist (e.g., the defendant may flee the jurisdiction if not arrested immediately.)

☛ Warrantless *searches*, on the other hand, *must fit within one of the exceptions to the warrant requirement to be valid.* When you are faced with a warrantless search, consider each of these before deciding that the search was invalid. They are:

    ❏   search *incident to arrest*;

    ❏   *inventory* search;

    ❏   *exigent circumstances*;

    ❏   *plain view*;

    ❏   *automobile* searches;

    ❏   *consent* searches;

    ❏   *stop and frisk*; and

    ❏   *regulatory inspections* (which sometimes actually require a warrant, but the standards to obtain a warrant aren't stringent).

Search incident to arrest

☛ **Search incident to arrest:** Police may *search a suspect incident to a valid arrest* — regardless of whether the officers actually fear for their safety or believe that evidence of a crime will be found.

☞ Contrast this with a frisk in a *"stop-and-frisk"* situation. In stop-and-frisk, the police may pat down the suspect's outer garments to detect *weapons only* — they may *not* use a "frisk" as a basis to discover and seize anything other than a weapon, such as *contraband*.

☞ The police may also conduct a *full body search* prior to the defendant's incarceration, as long as they made a valid, full custodial arrest.

☞ Police may also search the *area within the suspect's immediate control* pursuant to a valid arrest.

Example: Drug dogs sniff the baggage unloaded from an airplane, and alert police to Defendant's bag. Police wait for Defendant to claim her bag, then arrest her as she walks through the airport carrying her bag. They then open her bag and find marijuana. At her trial, the evidence is admissible. Police had probable cause to arrest Defendant based on the dogs' reaction to her bag. Pursuant to this valid arrest, police had the power to search the area within Defendant's immediate control, including the bag that she was carrying.

☞ Remember that when a search is properly made incident to a lawful arrest, the police may examine *items of personal property found on the person of the arrestee* (e.g., a wallet or pocket diary).

☞ But also remember that even if the police properly make a custodial arrest of a person who happens to be carrying a *cell phone*, the incident-to-arrest doctrine does *not* permit the police to perform a *warrantless search of the digital contents of the phone.* Cite to the 2014 case of *Riley v. California* on this point. (This "no warrantless search" rule probably applies to *laptops* and *other digital devices* carried by the arrestee, not just cell phones.)

☞ When the arrest is of a driver of a *vehicle*, remember that the area deemed under the arrestee's control does *not* include the *passenger compartment,* so the police cannot use the search-incident-to-arrest exception to search the compartment. For more about this, see p. 178 *infra* (discussion of *Ariz. v. Gant*).

☞ If the police have "specific and articulable facts" suggesting that *another person may be present* at the location of the arrest, the police may do a *"protective sweep"* of the entire premises, incident to the arrest.

Example: The police properly get a warrant to search for certain criminal evidence (a brown suitcase with leather straps, thought to contain cocaine) in the master bedroom of David's house. (They have information that David also possesses many weapons and is perhaps dangerous.) They knock on David's door, shout "Police," and get no answer. They force open the door and enter. Hearing noises in the basement, they go there, where they find David holding a brown suitcase with leather straps. They seize the suitcase, discover it contains cocaine, handcuff David, then search his person. They find a .22 caliber revolver, which they seize. David is charged with possession of an unlicensed revolver (the .22). David argues that the weapon is the fruit of an unlawful search, and must be suppressed.

David loses — the revolver was lawfully seized. The police entered the house validly (because of the search warrant). Once inside, they were entitled to conduct a protective sweep, since they had "specific and articulable facts" leading them to believe that David might be present and dangerous (knowledge that he possessed weapons). Therefore, they were entitled to go to the basement once they heard noises from there, since that indicated that this was where David or someone else might be. Once they saw David with the suitcase (the apparent object of the search warrant), they were entitled to seize the suitcase and to open it. Once they saw it contained contraband, they were entitled to arrest David, and to search him incident to that arrest. Since the gun was properly found by that search incident to arrest, it is admissible.

☛ But remember that the protective sweep covers *only places where a person might be hiding*, not areas *too small* for a person (e.g., a small box or suitcase).

Example: Same facts as prior example. After the police arrest David in the basement, they search the entire house. They find a small box on a shelf in the attic. They open it, and find an illegal Uzi submachine gun inside.

This evidence must be suppressed. Neither the search warrant nor the search incident to arrest nor the right to do a protective sweep entitled the police to open small boxes throughout the house. (The warrant didn't cover the box; the attic wasn't within the area possibly under David's control and was therefore not searchable incident to the arrest; the protective sweep didn't cover a shelf with a box, since no person could have been hiding in the box.)

Exigent circumstances

☛ **Exigent circumstances:** Evidence that tends to *dissipate over time* creates exigent circumstances that justify a warrantless search. (*Example:* Fire marshals can make an immediate warrantless search of the premises in which a suspicious fire has taken place, because if they wait for a warrant the smell of gasoline, and other clues, may dissipate.)

☞   **Destruction of evidence:** Be on the lookout for situations in which the police reasonably suspect that if they don't enter the premises immediately, the people inside will *destroy evidence* (e.g., narcotics). This is a kind of exigency that justifies a warrantless search. (But if the police "manufacture" the emergency by violating or threatening to violate the Fourth Amendment, the destruction-of-evidence rationale doesn't apply.)

Plain view exception

☛ **Plain view:** If the police are in a *place where they have the right to be,* any item that they *observe* is "fair game" for seizure if it is evidence of criminal activity. This includes other contraband not named in the search warrant they see when properly executing a valid warrant.

Example: Police arrest D in front of his home for bank robbery. After he is handcuffed, he asks if he can go back into the house to telephone his wife. Officer accompanies him back into the kitchen, dials the number for him, and holds the receiver to his ear. While standing there, Officer notices the corners of three $20 bills protruding from a closed breadbox on the counter, and notices that the bills are all new with consecutive serial numbers. Officer, remembering that a number of $20 bills were taken in the robbery, opens the breadbox, discovers a total of 50 consecutively-numbered $20 bills, and seizes them. Later examination of the serial numbers proves that the bills were taken from the bank.

The bills are admissible under the plain view doctrine. D impliedly consented to Officer's entry into his home by requesting to make a phone call (presumably he did not expect to be allowed to go by himself), so Officer was standing where he had a legal right to be when he saw the bills in plain view. His plain view of the bills (including their newness and their consecutive serial numbers) was then enough to give him probable cause to believe they were connected to the robbery, and thus probable cause to open the breadbox to explore further.

Vehicle searches

☛ **Automobile searches:** In practical terms, all of the special constructions and exceptions carved out for searches of automobiles mean that police officers have considerable leeway to search them. When faced with a warrantless automobile search, consider each of the following:

☞ **General "automobile search" exception:** Under the separate, free-standing "automobile exception," a police officer may *search a motor vehicle without first getting a search warrant,* as long as she has *probable cause to believe that evidence or contraband is located in the vehicle.*

Example 1: Officer O has probable cause to believe that a car parked on the street in front of D's house is owned by D, and has heroin in it. Even if O would have plenty of time to get a search warrant, O may instead open the car's unlocked door to search the passenger compartment for the heroin. O may also open the trunk for the same purpose.

☞ **Closed containers:** When the automobile exception applies to allow a warrantless search of a vehicle, the exception also allows the police to *search any closed container inside the vehicle.* (This assumes that the container might plausibly hold evidence or contraband relating to whatever it was that gave the police probable cause to stop and search the vehicle.)

Example 2: Same basic facts as Example 1 above. O may open a closed, opaque plastic bag in the trunk, to see if it contains heroin. And if it contains some other type of contraband, or evidence of crime, O can seize the bag without first getting a warrant.

☞ **Passenger's belongings:** Also, if the automobile exception applies to allow a warrantless search of closed containers inside the vehicle, the police can search those containers *even if they belong to a passenger* (or to someone other than the vehicle's owner or driver), and even if there is no probable cause to believe that the container's owner has been involved in carrying the contraband or any other illegality.

Example 3: Same basic facts as Examples 1 and 2. Now, assume that (1) O knows that D (the vehicle's owner) is a man named "John Smith," and (2) O sees that a suitcase in the trunk has a luggage tag on it with the name "Mary Smith." O may open the suitcase to see if it, too contains heroin. And that's true even though O has reason to know that the suitcase does not belong to D, and even though O does not have probable cause to believe that Mary Smith has been involved in carrying heroin or any other illegality.

☞ **Search of vehicle parked on non-curtilage part of a home's driveway:** If the vehicle is located not on a public street, but on a portion of a homeowner's *residential property* that is *not* part of the property's "*curtilage*," then the automobile exception will *still apply*, assuming the police have probable cause to believe the vehicle contains contraband or evidence of crime.

Example 4: Same basic facts as Examples 1 through 3. Now, however, assume that the vehicle is parked on a part of D's driveway that's next to the front lawn, and not adjacent to the house. Since the place where the car is parked is not part of the house's curtilage, O may perform the searches in Examples 1 through 3 just as he could do if the car was parked on the street.

☛ **Search of vehicle parked on curtilage part of a home's driveway:** But where the vehicle *is* located within the curtilage of a person's dwelling, the automobile exception will *not apply* to allow the warrantless search of the vehicle, even if the police have probable cause for a search. That's because the automobile exception *does not "override"* the special Fourth Amendment protections given to the "home" (and a home's curtilage is deemed part of the home, just as, say, any room inside the home would be).

Example 5: Same basic facts as Example 4, except that the vehicle is parked on a part of D's driveway that's adjacent to the house, and within the house's curtilage. Now, the automobile exception will *not apply* to allow the warrantless search of the vehicle, even if the police have probable cause for a search. That's because the automobile exception *does not "override"* the special Fourth Amendment protections given to the "home" (and a home's curtilage is deemed part of the home, just as, say, any room inside the home would be). [Cite to *Collins v. Va.*]

☞ **Search incident to arrest:** Since 2009, the police may no longer *automatically* search the passenger compartment *incident to the arrest* of the driver. But they may search the compartment incident to the driver's arrest if *either*:

❏ they have *failed to secure* the driver (e.g., with handcuffs), so that at the time of the search he might plausibly *still gain access* to the passenger compartment; or

❏ they have *"reason to believe"* that the compartment (or any other part of the vehicle) *"may"* contain *evidence of the crime* for which the arrest occurred. (This is not likely in traffic-arrest cases, but might well work in drug-arrest cases, including arrests pursuant to an outstanding arrest warrant for drug trafficking.)

☞ Cite to *Ariz. v. Gant* on these incident-to-arrest possibilities.

☞ **Inventory search:** An *inventory search* is permissible without a warrant any time a vehicle is rightfully in police possession.

Example: D is validly arrested on a charge of drunken driving. Over his objection, police bring D's car to a police-owned lot and inventory the contents of the car. Under the front seat, the police find a plastic bag of heroin. In the back seat, police find a gun in a suitcase sealed by a zipper. The heroin and the gun are admissible. The search of the vehicle (including closed containers) was a valid inventory search, even though it was conducted long after D was arrested.

☞ **Plain view:** *Plain view* will provide a basis for validating a warrantless search, *so long as the stop of the vehicle was also valid.* (If the stop was invalid, though, the officer's plain view into the car will also be insufficient, since it was acquired illegally.)

Example 1: Defendant murders a passenger in his car and disposes of the body. He is unable, however, to remove blood stains on the front seat. Several days later, he unknowingly drives with his hazard lights on. Officer notices Defendant's lights and stops him, not for a violation, but only to make him aware of the danger of the hazard lights. As Officer approaches the car, he sees the blood stains on the front seat. Since the stop was legal, and Officer got the plain view by being where he was legally entitled to be, he may now seize the car (since the evidence is affixed to it) under the plain view doctrine.

Example 2: Police institute a plan of randomly stopping vehicles in a high crime area between midnight and dawn. Pursuant to this plan, they stop Defendant. When Officer approaches the vehicle, he observes marijuana in the vehicle in "plain view." Because the initial stop was illegal (police cannot conduct roving random stops), the officer was not viewing the car's interior from a lawful vantage point, and the marijuana is inadmissible.

Consent searches

☛ **Consent searches:** The three big issues for consent searches are the *scope* of the consent, whether *deception* nullifies the consent, and whether the person who consented had *authority* to do so.

☞ **Scope:** "Consent" is broadly construed. Even when suspects are *in custody*, you should find the consent to be voluntary and valid unless the police falsely assert or imply they have the right to make the search.

Example: Defendant is stopped for a traffic violation and taken into custody. He is patted down, and the police discover a vial of pills for which Defendant does not have a prescription. Officer then asks Defendant for permission to search the car, and Defendant replies, "Go ahead. Why not?" This consent is voluntary, thus valid.

☞ **Deception:** Deception on the part of the police may or may not nullify the consent.

☛ If the police say that they have a warrant when they don't, this will nullify the consent.

☛ If the police *misrepresent their identity,* and thus procure consent, it's *not clear* whether the consent is valid. You should say that the case could come out either way.

Example: Police want to gain entry into D's house. During surveillance, they see D leave. They knock on the door of D's home, and his teenage daughter Terry answers. The police say they are friends of her father and want to talk to him. Terry lets them in and asks them to wait in the living room for her father to return. It's not clear whether Terry's consent to the police's entry into the home was valid, voluntary consent; certainly D has a decent chance of having the consent ruled involuntary because based on deception.

☞ **Authority:** Be sure that police get consent from the right person, i.e., one who had *authority* to consent to a search of the particular premises. This is a common issue on exams.

☛ A *homeowner* can consent to the search of the home even where the home is also being occupied by a *social guest.* (However, the homeowner probably cannot consent to the search of a *suitcase* or other small personal item as to which the guest has a high expectation of privacy.)

Example: Owner lets Stranger stay in Owner's house overnight, because Stranger says his car has broken down. Early the next morning, Owner gets suspicious of Stranger, and calls the police. Owner then lets the police into Owner's house, including the kitchen. While in the kitchen, the police see Stranger, and recognize him as a suspect in a pending robbery; they arrest him.

The arrest of Stranger is legal. Although the police would not have had the right to be in the position from which they recognized Stranger had it not been for Owner's consent, Owner had the right to give that consent to the police's entry into his kitchen. Therefore, at the moment when the police spotted Stranger in the kitchen, they were not engaged in an illegal search.

☞ A *hotel keeper* or *landlord cannot* consent to the search of leased premises that are under the direct control of the guest/tenant.

☞ A *teenage or older child can* consent as to the *common areas* of his parents' home (but generally not as to the private areas, such as the parents' bedroom).

☞ An *employer can* consent to a search of the employee's work area.

☞ Any of two or more *joint occupants* (e.g., husband and wife, or roommates) *can* consent to a search of the *jointly occupied space* if the other is *not present*.

Example: Police suspect that Defendant is dealing marijuana from his home. They go to his home and his estranged wife W answers the door. (Defendant is not present.) The police ask for consent to search. W consents, saying "Search everywhere. That S.O.B. has ruined my life. I hate his guts." The police do so, including a detached garage, which has a lock that the police break to gain entry. They find marijuana in the garage. W's consent to the search of the house was valid, since she clearly had access and control over it. Whether her consent to the search of the garage was valid depends on whether the garage was used exclusively by Defendant. If it was, and he kept it locked even against W, W did not have authority to consent to the search. (And if Defendant had been *present* and objected to the house search, even W's consent to the house search would have been invalid as against Defendant.)

Stop and frisk

☞ **Stop and frisk:** Remember that the police may make a brief "investigatory stop" — colloquially called "stop and frisk" — if they have *reasonable suspicion*, based upon *objective, articulable facts,* that *criminal activity may be afoot. This is a lesser standard than probable cause.*

☞ If during questioning, the officer develops reason to believe that the suspect may be armed, he may *frisk* the suspect, but for weapons only (not for contraband or other objects).

☞ *Traffic stops* are a great source of exam questions. Here are some general guidelines about traffic stops:

☞ If the car has been stopped for a valid reason (e.g., a traffic infraction), the officer may request to see the driver's *license*, and run a check on that license — this is a valid form of administrative search. (But an officer can't arbitrarily stop a car just to check whether the driver has a valid license.)

☞ ***Stationary roadblocks*** are fine, so long as police use some ***objective, constant criteria*** to determine which cars they will stop. They can also stop every car to try to find ***witnesses*** to a recent crime. ***Random stops,*** on the other hand, are ***invalid.***

☞ Police have the right to ***order all passengers out of the vehicle*** pursuant to a ***valid stop for an infraction*** (including a traffic infraction). If they have a reasonable belief based on specific and articulable facts that a passenger (or the driver) may be ***armed and dangerous***, they may also ***pat down*** the person's ***outer clothing*** to find weapons (but not non-weapon evidence of crime).

☞ Be alert for situations in which, during the course of the traffic stop, the officer ***learns further information*** about some criminal activity. This further info must be taken into account in deciding whether the officer can take a further, more-intrusive, step.

Example: Officer stops D for not signalling. While writing D a ticket, Officer notices a plastic bag with white powder on the floor. At this point, Officer is entitled to search the bag, and the rest of the vehicle (even the trunk) — seeing the bag has given him probable cause to suspect drug offenses, so he can do a search that he wouldn't be authorized to do at the first moment of this non-custodial traffic stop.

Regulatory and administrative searches and inspections

☞ **Regulatory inspections:** Here are the most important types of "regulatory searches," which don't require either probable cause to search or a warrant focusing on the particular person being searched:

☞ Government inspectors may perform inspections of physical premises (***"building searches"***) to ensure that ***health, fire and other safety regulations*** are being complied with.

☞ The inspector needs a warrant, but does ***not*** have to show ***probable cause*** that the particular building to be inspected ***violates*** any health or safety regulation. Instead, the inspector merely has to show that government is proposing to conduct an ***"area inspection"*** that is ***reasonably tailored to making sure that the relevant health or safety codes are being observed.*** The warrant then covers the whole area, or certain types of structures within the area — it doesn't have to mention individual addresses.

☞ In the case of certain types of *closely-regulated businesses, not even an area warrant is required* for a premises search. This "closely-regulated business" exception applies only to businesses that "pose a clear and significant *risk to the public welfare.*" (*Examples:* Liquor stores, firearms dealers and auto junkyards are "closely regulated" and thus subject to warrantless, suspicionless searches. But *hotels* are *not.*)

☞ **Border searches:** An important type of regulatory search is a *"border search."* Remember that police need not have probable cause or even reasonable suspicion to conduct a search of a person or his belongings at a fixed border checkpoint.

☞ **Alimentary canal:** One topic that crops up with border searches for drugs is *alimentary canal smuggling.* Police can perform an *intrusive body cavity search* if they have a particularized and objective basis for suspecting a traveler of alimentary canal smuggling.

> *Example:* Inspector sees D speaking to Anon as the two walk across the international border into the United States. Inspector recognizes Anon as someone who has previously been convicted of smuggling narcotics. Inspector searches the pair's luggage and finds a large quantity of drugs in Anon's bag and drug paraphernalia in D's. Inspector orders a male physician to conduct a body cavity search of D. This search is permissible — the total of facts known to Inspector created a particularized and objective basis for believing that D might be smuggling drugs in his alimentary canal.

☞ **DNA sample:** If the police properly arrest someone for a *serious offense* (e.g., a violent felony), remember that they may take a *DNA sample* from the arrestee's cheek, as part of the routine booking process. [*Maryland v. King*]

☞ Other examples of regulatory searches:

❑ metal detection in *airports.*

❑ *school searches* (e.g., searches of student lockers). The test is generally that school officials must have a reasonable basis for suspecting criminal conduct or a violation of school rules. (*Example:* School officials can't randomly search lockers, but can search lockers of those students as to whom the officials have a particularized basis for suspecting possession of contraband.)

  ❑ But *drug tests* in schools may be required as a condition of participation in most *extracurricular activities,* as long as the results are not shared with the police. That's true even if school officials don't have any basis for suspecting that any particular student is using drugs.

❑ Searches of *parolees* and people on *probation* — parolees (and probably probationers) can be stopped at any time or place even without suspicion of wrongdoing, and searched without a warrant.

Exam Tips *on*
ELECTRONIC SURVEILLANCE & SECRET AGENTS

Here are some of the ways issues discussed in this chapter can appear on exams:

Electronic surveillance (bugging and wiretapping)

☛ *Electronic surveillance* questions are rare because the rules are based on statutes.

☞ The most important thing to remember is that electronic surveillance (e.g., bugging or wiretapping) *without a warrant* is *improper unless one of the parties to the conversations consents.*

Example: Suspecting that students are using illegal drugs, a college president arranges for local police to put concealed microphones in several dormitory suites. The police do not get a search warrant. With these microphones, officers record an offer by D (one of the students) to sell drugs to another student. The tapes are inadmissible against D at his trial for dealing in narcotics, because electronic surveillance requires a warrant.

Secret agents

☛ You are much more likely to get an exam question about *secret agents*, an area in which there have been a number of cases on point.

☞ Remember that *before there has been an indictment,* a defendant *assumes the risk of his own misplaced trust,* that is, the risk that the person in whom he confides will relay the information to police.

Example: Police recruit Brother (D's brother) in an attempt to catch D gambling. Brother wears a recording device and meets D to place a bet. D takes the bet and the conversation is recorded. The tape is used against D at his gambling trial. D's constitutional rights have not been violated; he assumed the risk that Brother would not keep his confidences.

☞ *After indictment,* the state is very *limited* in how it can use secret agents to gather evidence to use in the criminal prosecution. States can only use passive "listening post"-type secret agents; any ***active conduct*** to elicit information — even if it's not a direct question — will violate a defendant's ***Sixth Amendment right to assistance of counsel.***

Example: D and X are involved in a bomb plot. After D is arrested and charged, the government turns X against D, and sends X to visit D in jail. During the meeting, X says to D, "Gee, I was surprised to hear they nabbed you." D's response is inadmissible, because it was obtained in violation of D's Sixth Amendment right to counsel: the purpose of X's comment was to elicit a response, impermissibly transforming X's conduct from passive to active. Since D had already been indicted, he was entitled not to have the government try to elicit information from him in the absence of his lawyer.

Entrapment

☛ ***Entrapment*** is sometimes a hidden issue. To make a claim for entrapment, the defendant must show that the police ***planted the suggestion*** of the crime in D's mind. If D had a ***"predisposition"*** to commit this type of offense, his entrapment defense will ***fail.***

Example: Burglar, who has prior convictions for burglary, meets Undercover Agent, who is posing as a "fence." Undercover Agent suggests a plan of a staged burglary to Burglar, with the two of them splitting the profits. Burglar agrees, then is charged with conspiracy to burgle. Because of Burglar's prior prior convictions, he will probably not be able to argue that he was an innocent person not predisposed to commit this criminal act. Thus his entrapment defense will probably fail.

Exam Tips on
CONFESSIONS & POLICE INTERROGATION

Here's what to look for in questions about confessions and police interrogation:

Miranda generally

☛ Although *Miranda* requires four different warnings, even when some of these are ***omitted*** the warnings as will not be deemed inadequate, if the message as a whole was ***clear and unambiguous.***

Example: D is arrested and told that anything he says can be used against him in court; that he has the right to consult an attorney before questioning; and that counsel will be appointed for him if cannot afford to retain one. D initially makes no statements, then later changes his mind and confesses. At trial, D tries to have his statements suppressed, on the grounds that he was never told he had the right to remain silent. D will probably lose, since he was warned that what he said could be used against him, he did not in fact make any statements at that time, and the omission of the "right to remain silent" language probably didn't affect his conduct.

The "custody" requirement

☛ Remember the one clear, bright-line rule of law that applies to *Miranda* rights: ***once a defendant has invoked his right to counsel, police cannot question him further until they provide one.*** (Of course, the prosecution can always argue that the defendant did not clearly invoke the right, or that the defendant initiated subsequent questioning.)

Example: Officer arrests D for possession of stolen property. She knows D has other property concealed. She advises D of his *Miranda* rights, and he responds that he will not say anything until he speaks with an attorney. Officer then tells D that he will not be subject to further charges if he speaks up immediately and tells her the location of the remainder of the property. D speaks. D's *Miranda* rights have been violated by the attempt to elicit information from him after he invoked his right to counsel.

☞ However, police can still take a statement from D after D requests counsel if (1) D ***initiates*** the conversation and (2) D makes a ***knowing and intelligent waiver*** of her right to counsel.

The "interrogation" requirement

☛ Remember that *Miranda* only applies to ***custodial interrogation.*** Therefore, it's important for you to determine, as a preliminary matter, whether the defendant was in custody. The general test is ***whether a reasonable person in the suspect's position would believe he is in custody at that moment.*** Some examples of how this test has been applied on exams include:

❏ Being held by the police at ***gunpoint*** (in any situation) — probably custody.

❏ ***Roadside questioning*** of the operator of a motor vehicle who has been stopped for a ***traffic violation*** — probably not custody.

❏ ***Participation in a lineup*** before being charged with a crime — probably not custody.

Example: D voluntarily agrees to participate in a lineup. After being identified by the victim, he states, "This isn't my day. I might as well confess." This statement is admissible, in spite of the lack of *Miranda* warnings, because D was not in custody at the time.

❏ Conversations with ***undercover or secret agents*** — not custody.

❏ ***Voluntarily coming to police headquarters*** — not custody.

☞ Remember that if the suspect is a ***minor***, his age is considered as part of the "reasonable person's belief" test — so a reasonable young child taken from a classroom to be questioned might well think he is not free to leave (and thus be in custody) where a reasonable adult would have believed he was free to leave.

☛ The other part of the foundation for a *Miranda* challenge is that there must have been ***interrogation***. Interrogation need not be direct questioning — any comment by police that is ***reasonably likely to produce an incriminating response*** qualifies.

Example 1: D is arrested for theft and placed in a "holding cell." Meanwhile, the police search his car. Later, Officer comes to D's cell and holds up an envelope of stolen merchandise that was found in the car and says, "You're in big trouble now." D blurts out, "Donna was the one who did it." Officer's comment probably (though not certainly) constituted interrogation and thus triggered D's *Miranda* rights, because a defendant in this situation would be reasonable likely to make an incriminating response.

Example 2: D is arrested and brought in for booking. The booking officer is D's neighbor. On seeing D, Booking Officer says, "Hey, what are you doing here?" D makes an incriminating response. Booking Officer's question probably does not qualify as interrogation, because Booking Officer did not know any facts to suggest that his innocuous comment was reasonably likely to elicit an incriminating statement.

☞ The two most important situations that are ***not interrogation*** (and therefore do not require *Miranda* warnings for the defendant's statement to be admissible) are:

❏ ***General factual inquiries*** at a ***crime scene***;

Example: Officer, standing outside a bar, hears gunshots inside. She rushes in, gun drawn, and asks "What the devil happened here?" Defendant responds, "I shot them in self-defense." Although Defendant may argue that this was custodial interrogation because Officer had her gun drawn, her question was more in the nature of a general inquiry to those present, not directed at any particular person for any particular purpose. Therefore, it won't be considered "interrogation" that triggered the right to *Miranda* warnings.

❏ ***Volunteered statements.*** Questions on this issue often use the term "blurt out." If your question describes a defendant as "blurting out" something, you should discuss whether the statement was volunteered (and you should probably find that it was.)

Example: Police arrest D and give her *Miranda* warnings. D states that she wants to call her lawyer and is told that she can do so as soon as she is fingerprinted. While being fingerprinted, D blurts out "Paying a lawyer is a waste of money because I know you guys have me." Her statement was volunteered, not the product of interrogation. Therefore, even though it was obtained at a time when D had not yet consulted with the lawyer she asked for, the statement was not obtained in violation of *Miranda*.

Exceptions to the effect of *Miranda*

☛ Remember that there are various scenarios under which *Miranda* either doesn't apply, or doesn't block use of the non-*Mirandized* statement:

☞ Even if a statement is inadmissible because of a *Miranda* violation, it can still be used to **impeach** the defendant — it just can't be used in the prosecution's case in chief.

Example: Officer takes D into custody, and without giving her *Miranda* warnings asks her where she was at the time of the theft. D responds that she was present at the scene of the crime, but saw nothing. At trial, the prosecution cannot use this non-*Mirandized* statement for its case-in-chief. D then testifies at trial that she was not at the scene at the time of the crime. The prosecution may now offer D's non-*Mirandized* statement for impeachment purposes only.

☞ A **second**, *Mirandized* confession following a first non-*Mirandized* confession will be admissible. The first confession does not taint the second (even though D may have made the second only because he felt that "the cat was already out of the bag").

☞ *Miranda* does not require police to tell the defendant **what crime** he is being charged with. It also does not prohibit questioning about a **different crime** than the one the defendant thought he was being charged with at the time he received the warnings.

☞ And don't forget the (limited) **public safety exception** to *Miranda* — if the statements are voluntary and the questions are prompted by a concern for public safety, they will be admissible even though no *Miranda* warnings are given.

Example: Police chase Suspect, who they think has committed armed robbery. After they arrest him and don't find the gun that they believe he used, they ask him, "Where's the gun." D gives the location of the discarded gun. Assuming that this question was or might have been motivated by concern for public safety, D's response is admissible under the public-safety exception.

☛ Be careful to spot the issue of whether D *waived* his *Miranda* rights.

    ☞   A waiver of *Miranda* rights (especially the right to **remain silent**) can be **inferred** from D's actions. For instance, suppose D is given (and understands) his right to remain silent, but does not expressly agree to answer questions. The police ask him lots of questions, and after remaining silent for all of them, he finally **answers** one, with an incriminating response. This will be an implied waiver of D's right to remain silent.

    ☞   A waiver of *Miranda* rights is **valid** even if D suffers from a **mental illness** that interferes with his ability to understand his rights and make rational choices. The critical factor in these cases is the behavior of the police. As long as the statement was not made as a result of **police coercion**, the fact that D may have been subjected to **third-party force** (e.g., mental illness, or pressure from a relative) that overbore his free will **won't** be enough to vitiate the waiver.

☛ Evidence of an accused's **silence** after he has received *Miranda* warnings is generally **not admissible.**

    Example: D is arrested and charged with murder. While she is in custody, she is read her *Miranda* rights, and refuses to give a statement. At trial, she takes the stand and gives a lengthy alibi defense. On cross-examination, the prosecutor asks her why, if her story was true, she did not tell it to police at the time of her arrest. The prosecutor's question was impermissible: D's election to exercise her *Miranda* rights and remain silent cannot be used against her at trial. [Cite to *Doyle v. Ohio.*]

    ☞   On the other hand, if a suspect agrees to undergo **voluntary (i.e., non-custodial) interrogation**, and therefore does not receive the *Miranda* warnings, his general silence or refusal to answer a particular question **may** be put into evidence by the prosecution. Only in the unusual situation where D **formally mentions his privilege against self-incrimination** as the reason he's refusing to continue the voluntary interrogation will the prosecution be prevented from using the silence.

    Example: D is suspected of a murder that took place on the evening of April 5. The police ask him to come to the police station voluntarily to answer some questions. D agrees, and starts to answer questions. But when the police ask him, "Where were you on the evening of April 5?" D refuses to answer and cuts off the questioning without further comment. At trial, D offers an alibi defense for the evening of April 5. The prosecution *may* prove that D refused to answer when he was asked his whereabouts. Since D was not in custody at the time of the questioning, and did not formally invoke his privilege against self-incrimination when he cut off the questioning, he's not entitled to block this evidence that he remained silent. [Cite to *Salinas v. Texas.*]

Exam Tips *on* LINEUPS & OTHER PRE-TRIAL ID PROCEDURES

Lineups and pretrial-identification questions allow an examiner to test your knowledge of several constitutional rights of criminal defendants. In your answer, be sure to demonstrate that you know that many rights are implicated. In particular, look for the following:

Pre-trial identifications generally

☞ Every time you have a lineup or pretrial identification procedure in your facts, consider all *four* constitutional protections that a defendant can assert:

❑ *self-incrimination* (Fifth Amendment)

❑ *search and seizure* (Fourth Amendment)

❑ *right to counsel* (Sixth Amendment)

❑ *due process* (Fifth or Fourteenth Amendment)

☞ Remember that defendants have no Fifth Amendment protection against being required to provide exemplars of *physical attributes.* Thus they can be made to *speak certain words* at a lineup, or to provide *handwriting samples.* (The Fifth Amendment protects only *testimonial* communications.) There is also *no right to have counsel present* when these procedures are done (assuming that D hasn't been arrested or indicted yet), since the procedures are not deemed to be a "critical phase" of the prosecution.

> *Example:* Witness, who sees a murder, tells police that the murderer uttered, "Good Lord, what will the stock exchange think of me!" At the lineup, D (who hasn't been charged yet) and the others in the lineup can be required to repeat that phrase so that Witness can identify the perpetrator by voice. Also, D has no right to have counsel present during this procedure.

The right to counsel

☞ Exam questions often require you to figure out whether D has the *right to counsel* at a lineup or other pre-trial identification procedure. This generally turns on **whether "adversarial judicial proceedings" have already been initiated.** Look for whether the defendant has been indicted, arrested, or otherwise formally charged. If so, the defendant had the right to counsel. If not, he did not.

> *Example:* On the facts of the above example, if D had been arrested for the murder prior to the lineup, he'd have a right to have counsel present during the lineup, and the lineup results would not be admissible if this right were not honored.

☛ Two primary **exceptions** to the right to counsel are also frequently tested. These are:

❏ **scientific tests** to establish identity

> *Example:* Defendant is arrested for possession and use of heroin, and over his objection, is subjected to a blood test to determine if he is currently using heroin. Defendant has no right to have counsel present when blood is drawn.

❏ **photographic identification procedures**, in which a witness is asked to pick the perpetrator from among a group of photos. (There's no right to counsel here even after the suspect has been indicted.)

Due process

☛ A pretrial identification violates **due process** only if two requirements are met: (1) the procedure is **unduly suggestive**; and (2) there is substantial likelihood of **irreparable mistaken identification**.

☞ There is no *per se* test for when a lineup is unduly suggestive. Here are some of the factors that are likely to constitute undue suggestiveness plus risk of irreparable mistake in identification:

❏ there is a great disparity in **height** between the defendant and all others in the lineup;

❏ the police **address a specific question** to the witness about one of the lineup participants (e.g., "Look closely at suspect 3 — is he the one?");

❏ there is a disparity of **race, gender or age** between D and all others in the lineup;

❏ the police require only the suspect to **dress to match** a witness' description of the perpetrator.

☞ Identifications made by victims on their **deathbed** are a good source of issues on an exam. In these cases, defendants often have pretty good arguments that their Sixth Amendment right to counsel was violated and that the procedure violated due process because it was unduly suggestive.

☛ Of course, you should say that the prosecution can counter this with evidence that there was no time to arrange a more objective procedure (because the victim was about to die) and/or that the victim saw the attacker well enough that misidentification would be unlikely.

Exam Tips on
THE EXCLUSIONARY RULE

The concepts from this chapter go hand-in-hand with those in Chapters 2 and 3. Make sure you understand how all of these relate to one another. Here are some tips to help you with exclusionary rule questions:

The exclusionary rule generally

☛ The exclusionary rule is very basic: *if the evidence in question was seized in violation of the defendant's constitutional rights, it is inadmissible at the defendant's criminal trial.*

Example: The police are looking for a bank robber. Officer sees D sitting on his front porch, and on a mere hunch that D "looks like the type who might rob banks," arrests D. Officer then frisks D, feels a soft container in D's pocket, pulls out the container, and discovers cocaine. The cocaine will not be admissible against D, because it was seized in violation of D's Fourth Amendment rights: the arrest of D was made without probable cause, so the search of him incident to arrest was also invalid. (The drugs are "fruit of the poisonous tree," i.e., the illegal arrest.)

☞ A key point to remember on exams is that you must check for *standing*: a defendant does *not* have standing to object to the violation of a *third party's* constitutional rights. Thus a defendant may only exclude evidence that was obtained in violation of *that defendant's* own constitutional right.

☛ Questions on this issue frequently involve a party attempting to contest the search of *another person's car, person, or clothing.* The objecting party does not have standing to object to any of these searches.

Example: D sells Customer some bagged heroin. Customer is later stopped for a traffic violation and the heroin is found in the vehicle, in a bag whose markings indicate that it was supplied by D. Even if the traffic stop violated Customer's Fourth Amendment rights, this does not help D: D may not challenge the search of Customer's car, because he had no reasonable expectation of privacy in someone else's car and thus lacked standing to object to the stop and search.

☞ But if D *does* have a ***reasonable expectation of privacy*** in the place or property searched, he can get the evidence excluded if it was obtained pursuant to an unreasonable search or seizure,

Example: Store is having problems with shoplifting. It stations Officer at a vantage point from which she can see into the ladies' dressing rooms. D takes a dress into the dressing room and stuffs it into her purse. Officer apprehends D at the front of the store. The dress will be inadmissible at trial, because D was stopped only because Officer knew D had taken the dress, and Officer's knowledge came from a violation of D's reasonable expectation of privacy in the dressing room she was occupying.

☛ An often-tested area involves ***items held out to the public.*** Much personal information that we would not necessarily want people to know about us will still be determined to be "held out to the public" and thus ***not*** subject to a reasonable expectation of privacy. For instance, ***garbage put out for collection***, ***tax returns***, ***bank statements*** held in the bank's records, and registers of the ***telephone numbers*** called from a home telephone are all items as to which there is generally no expectation of privacy. Another is the ***view into our homes*** from a public area, obtained either with the naked eye or with binoculars.

☛ A gray area concerns matters that the public ***could conceivably view,*** but only with great difficulty. If this issue arises on an exam, you should weigh the factors and determine whether it would be reasonable for a defendant to expect privacy in the area.

Example: D's home has a window nine feet above the ground. Passers-by cannot see into the house through the window, but a neighbor could, if he climbed onto his roof. The police climb on to the neighbor's roof to have this view. Although people could theoretically see in the window, D probably has a reasonable expectation of privacy in this area of his home, because it would be very unlikely that his neighbor would attempt to look inside his home this way.

The "inevitable discovery" exception

☛ Keep in mind the possibility that the *"inevitable discovery"* theory may apply: Even if the evidence was illegally seized and there is no independent lawful basis for its discovery, if it would have inevitably been discovered it will be admissible.

Example: D shows Undercover Agent stolen guns that he has in the trunk of his car. Undercover Agent reports this to her superiors. Instead of getting a warrant, the superiors immediately order a search of the trunk of D's car, which is parked in D's driveway. The search reveals the stolen guns. D challenges the admissibility of the guns, on the theory that they were the fruit of the warrantless search. A court might well hold that the guns are admissible, because a search warrant would "inevitably" have been issued for the car based on Undercover Agent's information, and the guns would then inevitably have been discovered.

Other exceptions to the exclusionary rule

☛ **Good faith reliance on search warrant:** If a search warrant turns out to be invalid, keep in mind that this may not make the seized evidence inadmissible. Remember that the evidence will still be admissible if (1) there was a **substantial basis** for issuing the warrant, and (2) the officers executing it objectively and in good faith **believed** that the warrant was valid.

☛ **"Purging the taint of the illegality":** Even where you conclude that a stop, arrest or questioning violated the suspect's constitutional rights, don't presume that evidence derived from it necessarily will be excluded. Keep in mind the *"purged taint"* doctrine: if significant **additional events intervene** between the original illegality and the final discovery of evidence, that may be enough to *"purge the taint"* of the **original illegal police conduct.**

   ☞ **Three factors used:** Here are the *three factors* the Court takes into account in deciding whether the taint from the illegality has been "purged" by the time the evidence in question is discovered:

   [1] The *"temporal proximity"* of the illegality to the fruit (so the **longer the time** between the illegality and the discovery of the ultimate evidence, the more likely it is that the taint has been purged);

   [2] The nature of any *"intervening circumstances"* that occurred between the illegality and the fruit (so that events that are truly *independent* of the illegality are more likely to produce a purging of the taint);

   [3] The *"purpose and flagrancy* of the **official misconduct"** (so that

an illegal stop or arrest arising from a good-faith police mistake as to probable cause is more likely to lead to a purging of the taint than an arrest/stop that the officer *knows* is illegal).

Example of purging the taint: Officer genuinely (but unreasonably and inaccurately) believes that he has sufficient objective grounds to stop D to investigate whether D has just shoplifted. from a store. D is in fact completely innocent of shoplifting. As part of the stop, Officer demands photo ID from D, which D supplies. Officer radios to headquarters with D's name, and is told that there is a 6-year-old warrant outstanding for D's arrest for an unpaid traffic ticket. Officer arrests D on the warrant (pursuant to police department policy requiring arrest of anyone found to be the subject of an outstanding arrest warrant), and searches D's person incident to the arrest. That search discovers heroin in D's pocket.

In D's prosecution for heroin possession, the heroin (the fruit of the search incident to the arrest) will be admissible, even though Officer's discovery of it stemmed directly from the illegal stop. That is, the **taint** of the illegal stop will be found to have been **"purged"** by the discovery of the arrest warrant. Of the three factors mentioned above governing when the taint is deemed purged, two favor a purging. (The "intervening circumstance" was the discovery of the arrest warrant, and the warrant's existence was causally independent of the illegal stop, cutting in favor of a finding of purging. And the "official misconduct" inherent in the stop was at most a negligent but good-faith mistake by Officer, not an intentional act of wrongdoing by Officer or a product of systemic police wrongdoing, so that, too, cuts in favor of a finding of purging.) Cite to *Utah v. Strieff,* whose facts are similar.

☞ **Fruit of confession:** Evidence that's the *fruit of a confession* given in custody without required *Miranda* warnings generally **won't be inadmissible** as fruit of the poisonous tree. That is, any taint from the lack of warnings will likely be deemed purged. So **physical evidence** — or **leads to third-party witness testimony** — won't be inadmissible even if they stem directly from a *Miranda* violation (as long as the confession is "voluntary"). *U.S. v. Patane.*

Example: D is arrested for domestic violence. He's questioned without *Miranda* warnings, and reveals that he's in possession of an unregistered pistol, whose location he shows the police. The gun will be admissible against D — the fact that the police would never have found the gun had D not confessed to its location during unwarned custodial questioning is irrelevant, because an unwarned confession won't ever be a "poisonous tree" with respect to physical fruits (or third-party witness testimony) derived from that confession.

☞ **Fruit of illegal arrest:** Evidence that derives from an *illegal arrest* is not *per se* inadmissible. Even if the arrest was illegal, if there were *significant intervening factors* that broke the chain of causation between the illegal arrest and the evidence, this will be enough to trigger the doctrine of "purging the taint" of the illegality, in which case the evidence will be admissible. Look for *remoteness in time or place* from the illegality.

> *Example:* D is illegally arrested on Tuesday, and released on bail. On Wednesday, the police question D at his home after giving him *Miranda* warnings, and he confesses. The confession will be admissible: even though the confession derived from the initial illegal arrest, the passage of time, and D's freedom from custody, will be enough to purge the taint of the illegal arrest.

☛ **Impeachment use:** Illegally-seized evidence can always be used to *impeach* the defendant, even though it is inadmissible in the prosecution's case-in-chief.

Example: D is arrested and charged with distributing controlled substances. As part of its case, the prosecution wants to introduce a 20 kilos of cocaine that were seized at D's summer home. The drugs, however, are ruled inadmissible because they were discovered pursuant to a warrantless search. At trial, D takes the stand and testifies that, while his brother is heavily involved in the drug trade, he himself has never even been in possession of a small amount of cocaine. The prosecution asks on cross, "How come 20 kilos of cocaine were discovered by police at your summer home?" This question is proper, as impeachment, even though the drugs were illegally seized. If D denies that any drugs were found, the prosecution will be allowed to introduce the drugs themselves, again as impeachment rather than as substantive evidence.

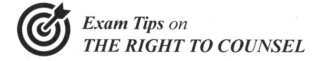

Exam Tips on
THE RIGHT TO COUNSEL

Here are the issues from this chapter that you are most likely to see on an exam:

The right generally

☛ **Indigent's right to appointed counsel:** The right to counsel includes the right of an *indigent* defendant to *appointed* counsel. Indigence is a vague concept, meaning "lacking funds to hire a lawyer."

☛ **Imprisonment actually imposed:** The right to counsel exists in any situation in which *imprisonment*, however short (even one day), is *actually imposed*.

☛ **Prior convictions:** One tricky issue about the right to counsel involves the use of *prior convictions.* A prior conviction in which the defendant did not have counsel (because no imprisonment was imposed) *can* be used under an *enhancement statute* to increase the sentence for a subsequent conviction.

Where the right attaches

☛ The right to counsel attaches at *every critical stage,* that is, any context in which the substantial rights of the accused may be affected. This includes initial appearance, preliminary hearing, trial, sentencing and plea acceptance.

☞ The filing of *charges or an indictment* signals the point at which the right to counsel attaches to all further proceedings. Therefore, questioning or police investigation before that point do *not* trigger the right to counsel.

Example 1: D is suspected in a bank robbery in which the robber handed the teller a written note demanding the money. Before any charges have been filed against D, police require her, over her objections, to furnish a handwriting exemplar. She asks to have a lawyer present, but the police refuse. There has been no violation of D's right to counsel, because no charges had been filed.

Example 2: D is arraigned on charges of burglary. He is then told that he will be appearing in a lineup. He asks to have his lawyer present, but is told that he has no right to have his lawyer present at the lineup. The lineup takes place, and a witness identifies D. This procedure violated D's right to counsel, because once charges are filed, the right to counsel attaches to all further proceedings. Therefore, the identification at the lineup will be excluded from D's trial.

☞ Remember that the right to counsel exists during *plea-bargaining*. That's true whether the defendant ends up *accepting* or *rejecting* a plea bargain offered by the prosecution.

Secret agents

☛ *Questioning by a secret agent* can violate the right to counsel, if that questioning occurs after indictment or the filing of charges. Keep in mind the "active/passive" distinction discussed in Chapter 4: "active" conduct by the secret agent (conduct reasonably likely to elicit an incriminating result) will violate the Sixth Amendment, but "passive" conduct won't.

Example: D has been charged with a crime, and imprisoned. Informer is placed in the same cell as D, with strict instructions not to ask any questions of D, but to listen if D wants to talk. Informer complies, and D confides that she feels guilty about what she has done. D's right to counsel has not been violated in this case. But if Informer had asked leading questions, or had made remarks for the purpose of causing D to incriminate herself, then D's right to counsel would be violated by this post-charge behavior.

Other exceptions

☛ **Self-representation:** A defendant normally has an absolute right to *represent himself,* even if the trial judge reasonably believes that the defendant will do an incompetent job. (But that's not true if the defendant has a *severe mental illness* that would prevent him from competently putting on a defense — here, the court may insist on appointing counsel over the defendant's objection.)

☛ **Waiver:** Anytime the right to counsel is at issue, you should also determine whether the defendant has *waived* the right. The right to counsel may be waived if done "knowingly and intelligently." Waiver is judged particularly strictly, though, when it is followed by entry of a guilty plea.

☛ **Effective assistance:** The right to counsel includes the right to *effective assistance* of counsel. To succeed with a claim for ineffective assistance, D must show 2 things (the *"two prongs"* of *Strickland v. Washington*):

   [1] **First prong:** that counsel's performance fell below an objective standard of "reasonable representation" (below-average representation is not enough to meet this standard); and

   [2] **Second prong:** that "but for" such unprofessional conduct there is a *reasonable probability* that the *result* of the proceedings would have been *different*. In practice, this standard is very difficult to meet, and you should probably conclude that D has no viable ineffective-assistance claim.

   Example: D's counsel fails to independently interview the only eyewitness, fails to formally request any exculpatory evidence, and fails to raise an available *Miranda* issue. If in fact any investigation or requests would clearly have been fruitless and the *Miranda* argument would not have been successful, D will lose on his ineffective-assistance claim no matter how far below a reasonable standard his counsel's performance fell. That's because D can't meet the second prong of Strickland, that "but for" the unprofessional conduct, there is a reasonable probability that the result of the proceedings would have been different.

☞ **Effective assistance during plea-bargaining:** The right to effective assistance can be violated during the course of *plea-bargaining.* But again, it's hard for D to get actual relief for claims of ineffective assistance during the plea-bargaining.

☛ **"Prejudice" standard for bad-plea-bargain cases:** Where D's claim is that he was not accurately advised about the potential *negative consequences* of a plea bargain, the requirement to show prejudice means that D has to show "a reasonable probability that, but for counsel's unprofessional errors, *the result of the proceeding would have been different"* (the second prong of the *Strickland* formulation).

☞ **The "I would have insisted on going to trial" standard:** This *doesn't* mean that D has to make the difficult showing that had he not taken the bad plea-bargain, he would probably have been *acquitted* at trial. Instead, he *merely* has to make a much easier showing: a *"reasonable probability that,* but for counsel's errors, he *would not have pleaded guilty and would have insisted on going to trial."* [Cite to *Hill v. Lockhart.*]

Example: D is a non-U.S. citizen who pleads guilty to a narcotics crime in order to get a somewhat shorter sentence (the difference between an 18-year sentence and one of 16 or 17 years) than he would get if convicted at trial. Before D takes the plea, his lawyer erroneously assures him that he will not be deported if he pleads guilty. After taking the plea, D discovers that deportation is not just possible but *mandatory* upon conviction.

The issue is whether D can show a "reasonable probability that, but for counsel's errors, he would not have pleaded guilty and would have insisted on going to trial." Even though D would have had no "viable defense" at trial, he can still meet this "reasonable probability" test if there is substantial evidence that because of his circumstances he would have found it attractive to pursue "even the smallest chance of success at trial." There *is* such evidence here. Therefore, D has shown the required "prejudice" — that without the incorrect advice he would probably have gone to trial. Consequently, D is entitled to a new trial. [Cite to *Lee v. U.S.*]

Exam Tips on
FORMAL PROCEEDINGS

Here are the most testable concepts from this chapter:

Grand juries

☛ Questions about *grand juries* occasionally crop up on exams. When they do, they usually focus on the following three points:

☞ Grand juries may *consider any evidence*, regardless of its admissibility in a criminal trial.

☛ There is *no right to have counsel present* at grand jury proceedings.

☛ A grant of *use immunity* with respect to grand jury testimony (the narrower and more common type of immunity) precludes the prosecution from using the testimony or any evidence directly or indirectly *derived from it* against the one who gave the testimony. This standard is applied very strictly against the government.

Example: The prosecutor has no information about a bank robbery, other than a rumor that Defendant was involved. The grand jury subpoenas Defendant, who refuses to testify. The prosecutor grants use immunity; Defendant testifies that she and Co-Defendant (who has not previously been under suspicion) robbed the bank. The grand jury indicts both of them. The prosecutor negotiates a plea agreement with Co-Defendant, and Co-Defendant testifies against Defendant at trial. The prosecution's use of Co-Defendant's testimony in its case against Defendant is improper, because Co-Defendant's identity was discovered only because of Defendant's grand jury testimony.

☛ Remember that the Bill of Rights guarantee against *excessive bail* (which has never been held to apply to the states anyway) does not amount to a "constitutional right to bail" — the Eighth Amendment guarantees only: (1) the right not to have bail set at an *excessively high amount* if and when it is set; and (2) the right to have the court make an *individualized consideration* of the defendant's *particular circumstances* in setting the amount.

Guilty pleas

☛ Before the court accepts a *defendant's guilty plea,* it must determine that the plea was *intelligent* and *voluntary,* and that the defendant understands: (1) the nature of the charge, (2) the maximum possible penalty and the minimum mandatory penalty for the offense, and (3) that he is waiving his right to a jury trial.

☞ Guilty pleas can be ***withdrawn*** for any fair and just reason, probably including mistakes about whether items of evidence will be admissible.

Example: D pleads guilty on the mistaken belief that his confession will be admissible at trial. After he learns that his confession is inadmissible, the court will probably let him withdraw his guilty plea and proceed to trial.

Jury trials

☛ Remember that the right to a ***jury trial*** is fundamental. Exam questions frequently require you to explain its parameters.

☞ The Sixth Amendment guarantees all defendants the right to a jury trial if they are charged with a ***felony,*** or with a misdemeanor punishable by more than six months in prison. This right has been incorporated, so it ***applies to states*** as well as the federal government.

☛ Most states give defendants the right to a jury trial in ***lesser misdemeanors*** as well, but they are not required to do so. Defendants in other proceedings do not necessarily have a right to trial by jury.

☛ ***Sentencing-guideline*** schemes pose a great risk of violating the Sixth Amendment. If guidelines result in D's being sentenced to a harsher sentence than the facts found by the jury would justify, based on some "aggravating" fact found by the judge, that's a Sixth Amendment violation. Cite to *Blakely* and *Booker* on this point.

Example: The jury finds that D possessed 100 grams of cocaine, for which the maximum sentence under guidelines is 2 years in prison. The judge can't find that D really possessed 300 grams and because of this sentence D to a longer time than 2 years.

☞ Even when there is a right to a jury trial, be on the lookout for express or implied ***waiver***. A knowing and intelligent plea agreement is an example of express waiver. Implied waiver is when the defendant fails to specifically invoke the right or attempts to do so too late in the process of the criminal prosecution.

Fifth Amendment right against self-incrimination

☛ Be clear that the **Fifth Amendment** does not allow defendants to "have their cake and eat it too." Although a defendant has an absolute right under the Fifth Amendment not to testify in his own defense, if he chooses to, he has waived that right. He may not take the stand to tell his version, then plead the Fifth Amendment in response to a prosecutor's cross-examination on matters within the scope of his testimony.

     ☞ However, if D *does* exercise his Fifth Amendment right by not taking the stand, the prosecution *may not comment* adversely on this fact to the jury (e.g., the prosecutor may not say, "If he's so innocent, why hasn't he taken the stand to tell you his story?")

Double jeopardy

☛ **Double jeopardy** is an important topic for exam questions. Remember that it involves two important ideas: (1) a defendant cannot be retried on the same charges; and (2) a defendant cannot be tried on two different charges if the defendant's acquittal on Charge A necessarily means the defendant could not be guilty of Charge B (collateral estoppel.)

Example: D kills V1 and V2 in the same incident. He is charged with both crimes. He is first tried for the murder of V1. D is acquitted because the jury finds that his intoxication prevented him from forming the necessary intent for murder. In D's trial for the murder of V2, the prosecution is bound by the findings in the first trial about D's intoxication, so he may not be found guilty of this murder either.

     ☞ In jury trials, jeopardy attaches *when the jury is sworn.*

     ☞ Two offenses are not the same for double jeopardy purposes if each requires proof of *one additional fact* which the other does not.

     ☞ If there is a *mistrial* (e.g., a *hung jury*), generally a retrial will *not* violate double jeopardy.

     ☞ Typically, a true double jeopardy issue will be obvious from the facts you're given in the question. The most important things to remember about double jeopardy are two situations that seem like double jeopardy, but are *not*:

         ❏ Reprosecution by a *different jurisdiction*. (*Example:* A state prosecutes D for murder and loses; the federal government then prosecutes D for civil rights violates for the same conduct. The "different sovereign" rule means that the federal prosecution does not violate the double jeopardy clause.)

         ❏ Reprosecution after a *hung jury.*

SHORT-ANSWER QUESTIONS

CHAPTER 1

CONSTITUTIONAL CRIMINAL PROCEDURE GENERALLY

1. Until 2012, there had been no definitive answer to the "second interrogation" problem. This issue arises in the following kind of situation: the suspect is in custody, is given his *Miranda* warnings, and states that he does not want to talk to the police unless he can speak to his lawyer first. He is allowed to speak to his lawyer. The police then want to conduct another interrogation; they start asking questions, and the suspect does not ask to speak to his lawyer at that time. The issue is whether this "second interrogation" — done without the presence of counsel — violates *Miranda*.

In 2012, the Supreme Court, deciding a case involving a federal prosecution and interrogation by FBI agents, held that this "second interrogation" violates *Miranda*, and that in federal prosecutions, the authorities may not initiate, without a lawyer present, a conversation with a suspect who has previously asked to have his lawyer present for questioning. *Smith v. U.S.* (not a real case). The Supreme Court, in *Smith*, referred to general *Miranda* principles and to cases decided under *Miranda*, but gave no indication of whether this principle would be binding on the states. In 2020, the Supreme Court of the State of Ames had to decide, on appeal, a case presenting precisely the same "second interrogation" issue, but this time one involving a state prosecution and state police officers. Assuming that the Supreme Court's 2012 *Smith* decision was based solely on the Fifth and Sixth Amendments, is the Ames Supreme Court constitutionally required to follow the decision in that case? _____

2. Until 2012, the State of Langdell instituted all felony prosecutions by having a prosecutor present his case to a grand jury, which then issued an indictment. In 2012, the Langdell legislature passed a statute setting out a new procedure, to be applicable to all crimes committed after the date of the statute. Under this new procedure, a prosecutor, when he wished to bring charges, would issue something called an "information," setting forth the charges. The information would serve as the basis for an arrest warrant. Immediately after the defendant was arrested, a "preliminary hearing" would be held before a judge, to determine whether there was probable cause to believe that the defendant had committed the crime charged. No involvement of the grand jury, and thus no indictment, would be needed.

Applicable U.S. Supreme Court decisions make it clear that as a constitutional matter, no federal prosecution for a felony (that is, no prosecution for a crime punishable by more than one year in prison) may commence except by a grand jury indictment. Smith, charged by Langdell with the crime of murder committed in 2013, has challenged the proceedings against him; he asserts that it violates his federal constitutional right to a grand jury indictment for him to be prosecuted for a felony based on a method other than a grand jury indictment. Should the Langdell Supreme Court order that the proceedings be dismissed until Smith is indicted by a grand jury? _____

CHAPTER 2
ARREST; PROBABLE CAUSE; SEARCH WARRANTS

3. The Empire Police Department received an anonymous and unsubstantiated "tip" that Dexter, an Empire resident, was buying and selling unlicensed handguns in violation of an Empire statute. This information did not, under applicable U.S. Supreme Court decisions, give the Empire Police probable cause to arrest Dexter for any crime. However, the police arrested Dexter anyway, and charged him with violating the state's handgun statute. Shortly after the arrest (before it had been at all publicized) Wendy, Dexter's ex-wife, came of her own volition to the Empire police station and furnished compelling evidence that Dexter had indeed been buying and selling unlicensed handguns. Wendy turned out to be the anonymous informant — she had not wanted to be deeply involved, but then had changed her mind.

Dexter is now being tried for the crime of buying and selling unlicensed handguns. He argues that because his arrest was made without probable cause and was thus a violation of his Fourth Amendment rights, he may not be tried for this crime. Assuming that Dexter is correct in asserting that his arrest was in violation of his federally-guaranteed Fourth Amendment rights, must the prosecution against him be dismissed? _____

4. Law enforcement officials working for the Jefferson State Organized Crime Task Force suspected Johnny ("The Cigar") Jordan of being the boss of a local organized-crime family. However, they had never been able to get any evidence of criminal activity conducted by Johnny. Johnny was known for never conducting business at his apartment, and for not maintaining any office. Instead, at nine o'clock every evening, under cover of darkness, Johnny would take a walk through Central Park, accompanied by two or three people who police thought were his henchmen. Johnny and his companions would walk through the park, and only when no one was nearby would they say anything.

However, unbeknownst to Johnny, a new invention just acquired by the Task Force was about to change the equation. The invention was an infrared telescope. From high up in an office building next to the park, the Task Force set up this device, which looked like an ordinary telescope. However, it was a telescope that worked on infrared light given out by human bodies. Therefore, even though it was dark, officials could spot Johnny in their telescope, focus in tightly on his face, and have an experienced lip reader interpret what Johnny and his companion were saying. By the use of this method, they were able to learn that Johnny's organization was processing raw cocaine into crack at a "still" in downtown Jefferson City. (The police did not have a search warrant or probable cause to search or eavesdrop on Johnny.) Using the telescopically-obtained information, they procured a search warrant, raided the still, and charged Johnny with various violations of state drug laws.

Johnny now argues that his initial words describing the drug operation were intended to be private, that the infrared operation was an illegal Fourth Amendment search of him, and that the search warrant thus obtained was illegal. Should the court accept Johnny's argument and rule that the search warrant was invalid? (For this question, assume that the answer is "yes" if by using the infrared device to read Johnny's lips the police were carrying out a Fourth Amendment search.) _____

5. The police heard rumors that Darwin had carried out a murder for hire of Victor at the behest of Victor's estranged wife Delia, and that Darwin would soon be picking up his payment from Delia's house. The police knew that because of the unsubstantiated nature of these rumors, they did not have probable cause to believe that Darwin was the hit-man in the Victor killing. Therefore, they did not try to procure a search or arrest warrant. Instead, the police followed Darwin from his home to a local fast-food restaurant. Darwin left his briefcase on the table while he went to the bathroom. The police quickly attached a small flat electronic device to the outside of the briefcase, hoping that Darwin wouldn't notice the device. The device was a GPS tracker that wirelessly broadcast, to a police-controlled Internet address, the tracker's location. The device remained undiscovered by Darwin for 60 days. On the 58th day, the website showed that Darwin had visited Delia's house. Darwin and Delia were charged with murdering Victor. At the start of the trial, the police sought to introduce the Internet record showing Darwin's visit to Delia's house. Darwin objected that the evidence had been obtained by a violation of his Fourth Amendment rights. The prosecution answered this objection solely on the grounds that no Fourth Amendment search had ever occurred, thereby relieving the police of either the requirement to have probable cause before tracking Darwin's movements or a search warrant to do so.

(a) Should the court conclude that a Fourth Amendment search occurred? _____

(b) Based on your answer to (a), what consequences will flow with respect to the admissibility of the record showing Darwin's visit, and why? _____

6. Elaine came to the police station to report that her car had been stolen from a mall parking lot one hour earlier. She described the vehicle as a cobalt-blue, 2019 Jaguar F-Type convertible with a vanity plate on the front with the words "sweet ride." The detective who took the information immediately transmitted it to all officers on patrol within a ten-mile radius of the mall. As he was driving down Magnolia Avenue, Officer Pete saw a cobalt-blue sports car that he thought was a Jaguar pull into the garage that was attached to the side of a private home, # 123 Magnolia. As Pete watched from the street, the driver exited through the garage door (leaving it open), then entered the house through its front door. Since the open garage door was only about 20 feet from the street, Pete entered the garage through that door and looked closely at the front of the car. He confirmed that it was a Jaguar F-Type with a front vanity plate saying "sweet ride." Pete used this information to secure an arrest warrant for the driver, Matt, who lived at # 123 Magnolia. Now, Matt has moved to quash the arrest warrant, claiming that Pete's conduct violated Matt's Fourth

Amendment rights. Should the motion be granted? _____

7. Police Officer Baker was walking her beat one day when she discovered a small cocker spaniel which appeared to be lost. The dog was wearing a collar saying, "My name is Rex. If I'm found, please return me to my home at 123 Maple Street." Baker decided to do just that. She took the dog to 123 Maple, and rang the doorbell. The door was answered by a white-haired grandmotherly-looking woman, who identified herself as Mrs. Jones, owner of Rex. While the door was open, Baker happened to look past Jones into the center hall of the house, where she spotted what she instantly recognized (from reading *Soldier of Fortune* magazine) to be an Uzi submachine gun. Since Uzi submachine guns are illegal in every state, Baker knew that somebody was committing a felony. She kept her cool, did not give any hint about what she had seen, got a search warrant, and seized the submachine gun. Jones was prosecuted for illegal possession of the gun, and defended on the grounds that Baker's act of spotting the gun, which began the whole episode, occurred without probable cause or a warrant, and that the gun must therefore be suppressed.

   (a) If you were the prosecutor, what doctrine or rule should you cite in opposition to Jones' suppression motion? _____

   (b) Should the judge grant Jones' suppression motion? _____

8. Same basic facts as the prior question. Now, however, assume that Officer Baker did not see any submachine gun, or anything unusual, while she stood in the hallway returning the dog. Mrs. Jones invited her in to her living room to give her a cup of tea. When she went out of the room to prepare the tea, Officer Baker noticed a long, narrow case in the living room, which she knew to be of a type that often contains a gun; she had never seen such a container used for anything but a gun. She flipped open the top (which was not secured in any way), and discovered an Uzi submachine gun inside. Since Uzis are not permitted in private dwellings in the state under any circumstances, Officer Baker immediately confiscated the box and the weapon. At Jones' trial, if Jones moves to suppress the Uzi and the box, should her motion be granted? _____

9. Same facts as prior two questions. Now, however, assume that at the start of the whole episode, Baker had had an unsubstantiated and anonymous tip that there might be some sort of illegal weapon stored at 123 Maple Street. Baker didn't know how she would get probable cause for a search warrant. She hung around the outskirts of Jones' house at 123 Maple for some time, hoping to catch some sort of break. Then, the dog (see Question 6) emerged from a small dog-sized door at the side of the house, and ran out to the sidewalk. Baker knew perfectly well that the dog was not lost. She seized upon this as a pretext, gathered up the dog, and rang the doorbell, hoping to get a glimpse into the house. Events later transpired as in Question 7. Should the judge grant Jones' suppression motion?

_____

10. Officer White was patrolling her beat one day. While she was standing on the sidewalk, she happened to look over into the big picture window on the first floor of a house owned by Desmond. White could see through the window what appeared to be two large marijuana plants. She went up to the window (standing on Desmond's property to do so), opened the window, which was not locked, and stepped inside. There, she confiscated the two plants, which turned out to indeed be marijuana. Desmond was charged with violating

state anti-drug laws. He has moved to suppress the plants as the fruits of an illegal search.

(a) If you were the prosecutor, what doctrine would you cite, as your best chance to defeat Desmond's motion? _____

(b) Would the argument you make in (a) succeed? _____

11. Police had probable cause to believe that evidence of a recent robbery might be found in the master bedroom of a house owned by Dubinski. They procured (using proper procedures) a warrant to search that room in the house. Officer Piston rang Dubinski's bell, showed him the warrant, and immediately went to the bedroom. While in the bedroom, Piston (who had an unusually strong sense of smell) detected an odor which he believed was that of rotting meat or flesh. Since the kitchen was in an entirely different part of the house, Piston believed (assume reasonably) that this smell must belong to some fairly large organism that was dead, either a large pet or, perhaps, a human being. Piston followed his nose into the basement, where he discovered the partially decomposed body of a woman who turned out to be Dubinski's wife. The officer immediately impounded the body as evidence, and Dubinski was ultimately charged with murdering his wife. Dubinski has moved to suppress the body as evidence, arguing that Piston only found the body by going into a part of the house (the basement) where his warrant did not authorize him to be.

(a) If you were the prosecutor, what argument or doctrine might you cite to help defeat Dubinski's motion? _____

(b) Should Dubinski's suppression motion be granted? _____

12. Oscar was a police officer who had for several months worked as the handler of a trained drug-sniffing dog, Rover. Oscar was standing at an intersection of public streets, while wearing his police uniform, and accompanied by Rover on a leash. Gina, wearing a backpack, approached Oscar and asked for directions to a nearby location. Oscar, who had no suspicion that Gina was engaged in any sort of wrongdoing, began to answer. During the ensuing brief conversation, Gina put her backpack on the pavement. Rover circled around the backpack, sniffed it several times, and gave a special signal (sitting and raising his paw). As Oscar knew, this signal meant "I smell narcotics here." Oscar therefore, without asking Gina's permission, picked up the backpack and opened it; when he did so, he immediately spotted a large packet of marijuana, and arrested Gina for marijuana possession. At a suppression hearing, Gina argued that unless the prosecution could show that, based on recent statistics about Rover's record of "hits" and "misses" in the field, a positive drug signal by Rover was generally reliable, the marijuana must be excluded as a Fourth Amendment search made without probable cause. The prosecution did not have any evidence available to show how frequently Rover's in-the-field positive drug signals had recently proved accurate or inaccurate. However, the prosecution produced evidence that Rover had, three years before, completed a standard canine-drug-sniffing training program, and that at least monthly, the police department put him through "workouts" to keep his drug-detection skills up-to-date. Should the court grant Gina's suppression motion?

_____

13. Federal Treasury officials believed, without probable cause, that George was counterfeiting U.S. currency in his basement. They realized that it is almost impossible to counterfeit

bills without producing some unsuccessful ones that must be burned or otherwise discarded. They therefore decided to stake out George's garbage. Twice a week, George put several sealed opaque large garbage bags out on the curb in front of his house, to be picked up by Urban Carting (UC), the private sanitation company that supplied garbage-pickup service to George's neighborhood. Each morning, shortly before the UC truck came, the Treasury agents (acting without a search warrant) would open George's trash bags and see whether there was any evidence of counterfeiting inside. Eventually, they discovered a sheet of uncut $20 bills, which turned out to be counterfeit. They arrested George and charged him with counterfeiting. He moved to suppress the evidence found in his trash as a violation of the Fourth Amendment. Should George's suppression motion be granted?

_____

14. Same facts as the prior question. Now, however, assume that George did not put his trash out at curbside every day. Instead, he put the trash out in his back yard inside two garbage cans. Twice a week, the UC workers would (with George's implied consent), go into George's back yard, bring the bags out to the street, and put them into the garbage truck. One day, the Treasury officials snuck into George's back yard shortly after he had put out the trash, took the bags out to the street, and viewed their contents. They then gave all the contents except the counterfeit bills to the UC collectors to put into the garbage truck. May the counterfeit bills be suppressed? _____

15. Joe had been staying for several days in an apartment owned by his brother Bob, while Bob was away. While in the apartment, Joe periodically smoked marijuana. Occupants of neighboring apartments had called the police to complain about the suspicious smells. The police could have obtained a search warrant, but they lazily declined to do so. Instead, they rang the doorbell of the apartment, ascertained that Joe was not the owner of the apartment, forced their way in, and looked over the apartment. They spotted marijuana in an open pouch on a coffee table, and arrested Joe for possessing it. At Joe's trial for drug possession, can he have the marijuana suppressed on the grounds that it is the fruit of an unlawful search and/or seizure? _____

16. After Mimi missed the final commuter-train-ride home, she asked her co-worker Eric for a ride home, since they lived down the street from one another. Eric was happy to help her out but told Mimi that they needed to drop co-worker Jerry at Jerry's home first. When they arrived at Jerry's house, Eric wanted to visit with Jerry, and asked Mimi if she would be willing to drive his, Eric's, car to her house and park it out front; he would then take an Uber to her place to retrieve the car after he finished his visit with Jerry. Mimi agreed. Mimi always carried an unlicensed firearm for protection, and she placed it in the glove compartment of Eric's car before she started driving home. Thirty minutes later, as Mimi neared her residence, Officer Zohra pulled her over for speeding. Zohra thought Mimi seemed nervous and ordered Mimi out of the car. Zohra then searched the vehicle, finding the firearm in the glove compartment and cocaine in the center console. Eric was charged with possession of cocaine and Mimi with possession of an unlicensed firearm. Eric now moves to suppress the cocaine, and Mimi moves to suppress the firearm. Which of them has a sufficient Fourth Amendment interest to challenge Officer Zohra's conduct? _____

17. On October 1, after neighbors complained about a persistent foul odor coming from an apartment in Capital City, Ohio, rented by Justin, the landlord contacted the police. Officer Luke found Justin dead in his bedroom from a gunshot wound, which appeared to have been inflicted in that room. The coroner estimated that the victim had been killed sometime in August. Police suspicion centered on Marcus, with whom Justin had been heard arguing during the summer about a failed business venture in which Marcus had invested at Justin's recommendation. Marcus claimed that during August he was never within 50 miles of Justin's apartment. Acting without a search warrant, the prosecutor subpoenaed Marcus' cell phone carrier, requesting that the company review their records of Marcus' "cell site location information" ("CSLI") to determine whether he was within 50 miles of Justin's apartment at any time during August. If he was, the subpoena required the carrier to provide those dates and locations to the prosecutor's office. The carrier complied with the subpoena, providing the prosecutor's office with data showing that Marcus was in the 50-mile radius of the apartment on two separate occasions during August, each for no more than two hours. The company also provided the corresponding location coordinates on those dates for those time periods. Did the subpoena and the carrier's response violate Marcus' Fourth Amendment rights? _____

18. Police were investigating a sexual assault. Surveillance footage of the small apartment building where the assault took place showed an individual wearing a ski mask entering the building with a key just prior to the attack. Detectives focused their attention on the occupants of one unit, Terence and his fiancée Sally. They interviewed Terence and Sally at the apartment, and Terence gave conflicting accounts of his whereabouts at the time of the crime. While the detectives found Terence's answers suspicious, they lacked probable cause to arrest him at that point. However, as the officers were leaving, Detective Yasmin noticed an envelope addressed to Terence from 23andme.com on the kitchen table. When Yasmin commented that she had sent a DNA sample to that company to learn more about her own heritage, Sally volunteered that Terence had done the same and that the envelope probably contained the results.

As soon as the prosecutor's office learned this, they sent (without obtaining a search warrant) a package to 23andme containing (1) a printout of the DNA made from semen taken from the sexual assault victim; and (2) a subpoena demanding the identity of anyone who ever submitted a sample to 23andme matching that DNA printout. The company complied, and notified the prosecutor that Terence was a match. Terence has now moved to suppress the identification on grounds that the demand for it constituted a Fourth Amendment search of his private information, and therefore required a search warrant. Terence points out (correctly) that he never authorized 23andme to share any information about him with any other entity. Moreover, Terence points out that 23andme's website promises confidentiality from all inquiries, including those from law enforcement. Should the court grant Terence's motion? _____

19. After the city of Setonia experienced increased power outages during inclement weather, the city decided to upgrade its energy grid. As part of that upgrade, Setonia replaced all

residential, analog energy meters in the city with digital "smart meters." Residents could not "opt out" of meter replacement; the smart meters were mandatory for all households to sync with the new grid. Unlike the old analog meters they replaced, the new smart meters record consumption very frequently, collecting thousands of readings from each home every month. Each reading reveals when and where energy has been used in the household, and in fact tracks each home-appliance's distinct energy-consumption pattern or "load signature." The Setonia Police Department came to believe (for reasons not connected with the metering) that Jerry was using the three-car garage behind his house to grow marijuana. To investigate further, the Department subpoenaed the electric company that services Jerry's home for digital data about Jerry's energy use for the last three months; the Department believed that the data would likely disclose the "load signature" of lamps used in indoor-grow operations taking place in the garage. The electric company complied, providing data that supported the police department's theory. Jerry now argues that the police department's failure to obtain a warrant to secure this information violated his Fourth Amendment rights. Is his claim correct? _____

20. The police in a small town are trying to solve a recent burglary. They know from local probation records that Robert, the most prominent and active burglar in the town over the last two years, was released from prison on parole just two days before the burglary they are now investigating. The police want to search Robert's apartment. They have presented themselves to a neutral and detached magistrate, and have asked for a warrant to search Robert's house, based on the information summarized above. Assume that the above information, taken in its entirety, would justify a reasonable magistrate in concluding that proceeds of the recent burglary probably would be found at Robert's apartment. Assume furthermore that if Robert were to be charged with and tried for the burglary, evidence of his prior burglaries, and his recent release from prison (i.e., the items on which the request for the warrant is based), could not be admitted against Robert under the local rules of evidence. May the magistrate properly issue a search warrant? _____

21. Officer Brady submitted to a neutral and detached magistrate a request to search the home of Kaplan for evidence of drug possession. In support of the request, Brady submitted an affidavit written by him, stating that according to one Longo, a confidential informant who had previously been reliable, Kaplan was a drug user who kept large quantities of cocaine at his home. It was true that Longo did in fact give this information to Brady, and Brady honestly believed the information. However, in reality, the information was false — Kaplan was not a drug user, and (unbeknownst to Brady) Longo was Kaplan's archenemy and was merely trying to harass Kaplan. Brady was negligent in not quizzing Longo further about his information, but Brady did not behave recklessly in believing Longo's story or in submitting the affidavit.

The magistrate issued the warrant. Brady executed the warrant. He did not find any drugs, but he did find an illegal gun. At Kaplan's trial for unlawful possession of the gun, he has moved to suppress all the fruits of the search on the grounds that the warrant was improperly procured. Assuming that he demonstrates all of the above facts (including particularly that had the true facts been as stated in Brady's affidavit, there would not have been probable cause to search his premises for drugs), should the judge order the fruits of the search suppressed? _____

22. Authorities suspected that Desmond, an insurance broker, was defrauding his clients by taking premiums from them and then not paying the money to the insurance companies. An affidavit from a police officer described with adequate particularity why the police believed that Desmond was doing this. The principal reason for suspicion of Desmond was a complaint by Edward, a client of Desmond's, that Edward's coverage had been cancelled by the insurer for non-receipt of premiums. The police officer requested, and the magistrate issued, a warrant authorizing a search of Desmond's office and the seizure of "all business books and records relating to Desmond's insurance business." Authorities raided Desmond's office and seized virtually every piece of paper in it, including a diary in which he wrote statements making Desmond seem to be guilty of tax fraud in a transaction unrelated to Desmond's dealings with Edward. In Desmond's tax fraud trial, may he have the diary suppressed on the grounds that the warrant was issued in violation of the Fourth Amendment? _____

23. The police had probable cause to believe that a particular small convenience store was also used as a numbers betting operation. The police obtained a warrant entitling them to search the premises, and to seize any evidence of illegal betting. The officers went to the store to execute the warrant. First, however, they frisked all persons present, including the owner of the store and Doug, a customer who was standing with a dollar bill and a quart of milk at the counter. When they frisked Doug, they found drugs. May Doug have the drugs suppressed on the grounds that they are the fruits of an unlawful search?

_____

24. Armand Chisel, noted tycoon and art collector, suffered a terrible burglary in his collection. Chisel explained to the police that two valuable Van Gogh paintings had been stolen from him, one entitled "Irises" and the other entitled "Lilies." He showed them colored photographs of each. Later, the police developed probable cause to believe that both of these paintings might be found in the home of a notorious local fence, Frank. Due to their desire to do the least possible work, the police prepared an affidavit that listed these facts, but that requested a warrant to search for and seize only "Irises," without mentioning that "Lilies" might also be found at Frank's premises. The warrant was issued. The officers went into Frank's one-room studio apartment, saw (and seized) "Irises" right away, and then noticed "Lilies" on the wall right near where "Irises" had been. They seized "Lilies" as well. At Frank's trial for receiving stolen goods, may he have "Lilies" suppressed as the fruits of an unlawful seizure? _____

25. Same basic fact pattern as the prior question. Now, assume that the police found "Irises" as soon as they walked into Frank's studio. They nonetheless continued looking in other areas of the apartment to see if there was anything else they might find that was incriminating. In a closet, they found "Lilies." May Frank have "Lilies" suppressed from his trial for receiving stolen goods? _____

CHAPTER 3

WARRANTLESS ARRESTS AND SEARCHES

26. The police had probable cause to believe that a particular recent burglary had been carried out by Wilson, who lived at a known address in the community. There was no reason to believe that Wilson would flee the jurisdiction. The police considered getting a warrant for Wilson's arrest. But before they got around to doing so, one officer saw Wilson walking down the street. The officer went up to Wilson and arrested him for the robbery. The officer then searched Wilson incident to the arrest, and found in Wilson's pocket proceeds from the robbery (namely, a ring). At Wilson's trial for the robbery, he seeks to suppress the ring, on the grounds that it was the unlawful fruit of an arrest that was made without a warrant where a warrant could have been obtained. Should Wilson's suppression motion be granted? _____

27. Same basic fact pattern as the prior question. Now, however, assume that the police decided that, without getting a warrant, they would go to Wilson's house and arrest him. They rang his doorbell, but he did not answer the door. The police knocked down the door after Wilson didn't answer, and arrested him right inside the hallway. They informed him that he was under arrest, and he did not resist. During a search of Wilson's person they made incident to this arrest, they found the ring in his pocket, as in the above question. May the ring be suppressed on the grounds referred to in the prior question? _____

28. Same facts as the prior question. Now, assume that the police learned that Wilson knew that they were on to him, and the police were reasonably worried that Wilson might flee. It was a small town, and after hours, so no magistrate was available. The police rang Wilson's bell, saw that there was no answer, knocked down his door and went into his bedroom, where they found him. They then searched the area around his immediate control, and found underneath his pillow a gun which turned out to have been used in the robbery. May the gun be suppressed as the fruit of an unlawful arrest? _____

29. The police procured a validly-issued warrant for the arrest of Fred on an armed robbery charge. Two officers went to his house to execute the warrant. When Fred did not answer the doorbell, they broke down the door. (Assume that the police acted properly so far). They found Fred asleep in bed in one of the two bedrooms. The two officers handcuffed Fred to the wrought-iron bed. They then searched the rest of the premises, including the other bedroom. In the other bedroom, in a box the size of a package of cigarettes, they found five vials of crack. The robbery charge against Fred was ultimately dismissed, but he was tried for crack possession. At this trial, may he have the crack vials suppressed as being the fruits of an unlawful search? _____

30. The police had probable cause to believe that a particularly vicious murder had been committed by Gerald. They therefore obtained a warrant to arrest Gerald. They knew that Gerald lived with his brother, Harold, who was also thought to be a pretty nasty character (but who was not directly implicated in the murder for which they were about to arrest Gerald). The three arresting officers rang Gerald's doorbell and received no answer. They broke

into the house. In the basement, one of the officers found Gerald waiting with a knife in his hand; that officer disarmed Gerald and handcuffed him.

After this, another officer inspected the second floor of the house, calling out, "Harold, or anybody else who's there, come out with your hands over your head." He then looked in every room, and every closet large enough to hold a human being. In the closet of one of the bedrooms, he found a cache of weapons, which included what was eventually shown to be the murder weapon. It turned out that no one else was home, since Harold was away on vacation. At his murder trial, Gerald has sought to suppress the murder weapon found in the closet, on the grounds that it was the fruit of an unlawful search. Should Gerald's suppression motion be granted? _____

31. Davies, a state trooper, had long suspected Johnson of illegally possessing and selling handguns without the proper license; Davies knew that Johnson didn't have either a hand-gun dealer's license or a license to possess a handgun, but Davies didn't have probable cause (just inchoate suspicion, based on local rumors) to believe that Johnson possessed and dealt in these items. While on routine patrol one day, Davies spotted Johnson driving his car with a blown headlight, a minor traffic violation. Davies did not have any reason to believe that Johnson had any handguns in his car at that particular moment. Nonetheless, hoping that he might be able to catch Johnson red-handed with some unlicensed guns in the car, Davies decided to stop him, using the blown headlight as a pretext. He pulled Johnson over and wrote out a ticket for the headlight. While writing the ticket, Davies looked through the car's window and saw a handgun partially hidden under the front pas-senger seat. Davies then searched the entire car and found a cache of handguns, for which Johnson didn't have the required licenses. Davies seized the handguns. At his trial for ille-gal possession and sale of handguns, Johnson has moved to suppress the handguns as the fruit of an unlawful search. Should this motion be granted? _____

32. Two state troopers, Ginn and Cannon, who were sharing a single patrol car, spotted a car traveling 80 mph on a road where the speed limit was 55 mph. The officers pulled the car over, and ordered the driver, John, to get out. State law allowed officers to make a full cus-todial arrest of any driver driving more than 15 mph over the speed limit. Officer Ginn for-mally arrested John, put handcuffs on him, searched his body (found nothing incriminating) and placed him in the squad car, where Ginn remained with him. Officer Cannon then searched the entire passenger compartment of John's car. At the time of the search, Cannon did not have any cause to believe that any contraband or evidence of crime would be found. In the back seat of the car, Cannon found John's windbreaker. In the zip-pered pocket of the windbreaker, Cannon found a vial of crack. At his trial for crack pos-session, John has moved to suppress the vial of crack as the fruit of an unlawful search. Should his motion be granted? _____

33. Two police officers, Genson and Hingham, received word that a warrant had just been issued for the arrest of Jim, a local resident, on charges of selling from his car vials of her-oin, disguised in prescription-drug vials. The warrant mentioned that Jim customarily drove a late-model white Mercedes-Benz E350. Genson and Hingham happened to be passing Jim's house, and noticed a white Mercedes E350 pull into the driveway. While the driver was still inside, Genson and Hingham approached the vehicle, saw that the driver was Jim (whom they knew personally), told him he was under arrest pursuant to the war-

rant, asked him to exit the vehicle, handcuffed him, and placed him in the patrol car. Genson then asked Jim, "Do you have any drugs in the car — legal or illegal — or any prescription-drug bottles?" Jim responded, "I don't having any drugs, but in the trunk I've got a couple of empty vials that used to contain Valium." Genson asked for permission to search the trunk, and Jim said, "No way — go get a warrant if you want to do that." While Genson stayed with Jim in the patrol car, Hingham opened the trunk, and saw inside it two apparently-empty vials whose labels said that they contained Valium. (Assume that before Hingham opened the trunk, a reasonable officer in Hingham's position would have had a reasonable suspicion — not amounting to probable cause — that he might find prescription-drug vials there, and that the vials might contain trace evidence of heroin.) Hingham opened the vials, and saw tiny amounts of white powder inside. He submitted the vials for testing; they proved to contain trace amounts not of heroin, but of methamphetamine, a substance of whose sale or possession Jim had never previously been suspected. Jim was prosecuted both on the heroin charge covered by the warrant and an additional possession-of-methamphetamine charge. Jim moved to suppress the vials as evidence on the meth charge. Should the court grant the motion? _____

34. Officer Glower, an undercover narcotics officer, observed Denton making a series of apparent drug sales on a street corner. Then, in response to Glower's offer to buy heroin from Denton, Denton took off his backpack, removed a plastic baggie containing a white substance, and handed the baggie to Glower in return for a $20 bill. Glower then announced that he was arresting Denton for drug trafficking, and handcuffed him. Glower seized the backpack, opened it, and saw that it contained a laptop computer. While still on the street corner where the transaction and arrest had taken place, Glower opened the laptop's cover, saw a listing for a file named "My Current Inventory," and used the laptop's word processing program to open the file. When opened, the file contained a numbered list of various types of illegal narcotics. While Glower's partner took Denton to the station house for post-arrest processing, Glower printed out a copy of the Current Inventory file and handed the printout to the prosecutor on duty. At Denton's drug trafficking trial, the prosecution has offered the printout as evidence. Denton, after citing the above facts and no other material ones, has moved to suppress the printout as having been obtained in violation of his Fourth Amendment rights. Should the trial judge grant the motion?

_____

35. The state of Calizonia has made it a crime, punishable by up to three years in prison, for a driver who has been properly arrested on drunk driving charges to refuse to submit to a breathalyzer test (which tests a person's Blood Alcohol Concentration or "BAC"). Della, while driving in Calizonia, was pulled over by Officer Graham after Graham saw her driving erratically. As Graham asked Della for her license and registration, Graham smelled liquor on Della's breath, and heard her slur her words. Graham told Della that he was arresting her for drunk driving.

(a) For this sub-question only, assume the following additional facts: Graham, after placing Della under arrest for drunk driving, told her that under state law she was required to submit to a roadside breathalyzer test using a portable machine that Graham had in his patrol car. Della refused to blow into the breathalyzer tube. Graham took Della into custody, and no other attempts were made to test her BAC levels. Della was then prosecuted for violating the compulsory-breathalyzer statute. (The prosecutor decided to drop the underlying drunk-driving charge because no BAC test was ever administered.) Della has now moved to have the breathalyzer charge dismissed, on the grounds that (1) it would have been a violation of her Fourth Amendment rights for the police, acting without a search warrant, to compel her to submit to the breathalyzer test; and (2) it would therefore be a violation of her Fourth Amendment rights to convict her for refusing to take the test. Should the judge grant Della's motion? _____

(b) For this sub-question only, assume the following additional facts instead of the ones recited in sub-question (a): Graham normally carried a breathalyzer machine in his patrol car, but did not have it with him at that moment. He therefore handcuffed Della to the back of the patrol car, took her to a nearby hospital, and asked her to consent to have blood drawn so that her BAC could be measured. Della refused to consent. Graham and a colleague restrained Della while a nurse forcibly took a blood sample from her veins. (Graham made no attempt to get a warrant authorizing this test. There was in fact sufficient time available to seek and obtain a warrant, because BAC levels decline post-consumption at known rates, so the results of a sample taken even several hours after an arrest can be calibrated to show what the BAC was at the time of the arrest.) The compulsorily-drawn sample showed a BAC well in excess of permitted levels, and high enough to support a charge of drunk driving. When Della was prosecuted for drunk driving, she moved to suppress the blood test results on the grounds that the Fourth Amendment prohibited the police from performing the test without a warrant. Should the judge grant Della's motion?

---

36. While Officer Griswold was cruising in his patrol car one day, he spotted a car that had apparently just crashed into a tree at the side of the road. He found the occupant, Denker, seriously injured but alive. There were several empty liquor bottles in the car, and Griswold thought he smelled liquor on Denker's breath. (Assume that this was enough to give Griswold probable cause to arrest Denker and test his blood for alcohol level.) Because of the serious injuries, Griswold immediately called an ambulance, and didn't immediately arrest Denker. Griswold thought that the ambulance would be taking Denker to Adams Hospital, so he (Griswold) drove to Adams to find and arrest Denker on drunk-driving charges. But it turned out that Denker had been taken to Bates Hospital instead. By the time Griswold could get to Bates, over two hours had elapsed since the accident.

At Bates Hospital, Griswold immediately placed Denker under arrest for drunk driving. Griswold also wanted to do a blood alcohol concentration (BAC) test on Denker, which requires the drawing of blood. Griswold realized that Denker's BAC had already receded a lot, and would continue to recede, so that as the taking of blood was further delayed it would become harder and harder to make a case for drunk driving. Therefore, without Denker's consent, and without procuring a search warrant (which in this rural area would have taken several hours at that time of night), Griswold instructed hospital officials to take a blood sample from Denker's finger. A BAC test on this blood sample showed that Denker was still past the point of intoxication. Denker was charged with drunk driving. He seeks to have the blood sample excluded from evidence as the fruit of an illegal warrantless search and seizure. Should his suppression motion be granted? _____

37. Officer Henkle was an undercover "decoy" agent; it was her job to appear prosperous and relatively helpless, so as to induce muggers to attack her. Eugene, a mugger, tried to steal Henkle's purse and necklace. Henkle announced that she was a police officer, and Eugene immediately fled. Henkle followed him on foot until she saw him disappear into a private house. She went up to the front door of the house and, without knocking or ringing the bell, opened the door and went looking for Eugene. Before she found him, she noticed an open cardboard box filled with miscellaneous jewelry and purses, apparently the result of prior (more successful) muggings. She arrested Eugene in his bedroom, then seized the cardboard box. Eugene was charged with one of the prior muggings, and a purse found in the cardboard box was introduced as evidence. If Eugene tries to have the purse suppressed as the fruit of an unlawful search, should his motion be granted?

_____

38. Officer Johnson, while in his police cruiser, received a radio report that a robbery of a 7-Eleven store had just occurred, and that the robber was believed to now be escaping in a blue Ford two-door sedan. Near the scene of the crime, Johnson saw a car meeting that description traveling at a high rate of speed. He stopped the driver, Fred, on suspicion of being a robber, and arrested Fred for the robbery. (Assume that he had probable cause to do so.) Johnson did not search the car at that time for evidence of the crime. (Assume that he had probable cause to do so.) Johnson had the police department tow truck tow the car to the police station, where it was impounded. There, the next day, Johnson (without first having gotten a search warrant) searched the car's passenger compartment and trunk. In the trunk, he found a stocking mask and hold-up note, both of which turned out to have been used in the robbery. Fred has now moved to have these two items suppressed from his robbery trial. Should this motion be granted? _____

39. For some time, the Ames police department had believed that the recent murder of George's wife, Karen, had been carried out by George. An informant notified the police that he believed Karen's dead body had been transported by George in the trunk of his 1996 maroon Pontiac. The police could have gotten a search warrant; they had probable cause to seize and search the car in connection with the murder investigation. However, they had not gotten around to procuring a warrant, when Officer Karloff spotted George driving the car one day. Karloff had probable cause to arrest George for the murder. Karloff stopped George, arrested him for the murder, and took him and the car to the police station. At the station, Karloff opened the trunk, and searched its contents for blood stains, which he found. These blood stains turned out to be the same type as Karen's blood, and they were introduced against George at his murder trial. May George have the blood stains suppressed as the fruit of an illegal search? _____

40. Officer Jackson learned from a trusted informant that a white 1998 Buick driven by Harold, license number JRZ970, would be passing by a particular location at a particular time, and that it would contain heroin which Harold was planning to sell at retail. Jackson stationed himself at the appointed place and, sure enough, a 1998 white Buick with the correct license number drove by at the expected time. Jackson stopped the car (assume that he had probable cause to do so), but discovered that it was driven by Leonard, not Harold. Jackson did not arrest Leonard, because he had no probable cause for an arrest. He did, however, search the car, and found a zipped pouch in the trunk. He opened this pouch, and found heroin. The police eventually became convinced that Harold, not Leonard, was the owner of the drugs in the trunk, and Harold was charged with possession of illegal drugs. At his trial, he moved to suppress the zippered pouch as the fruits of a search that was unlawful because it was warrantless. Should Harold's suppression motion be granted?

_____

41. A car belonging to Marvin was towed by the police because Marvin had put insufficient coins in the parking meter, and time had expired. No search warrant was obtained, and the police did not have probable cause to perform a search. Once the car was in the police lot, the police unlocked and searched the car pursuant to a standard police procedure, by which all towed cars are searched, and a list made of all valuables in the car. The purpose of this procedure was to guard against theft by police employees, and also to prevent the owner of the car from making a false claim of theft by a police employee. When the police searched Marvin's car, they looked in the unlocked glove compartment, and found illegal drugs there. At his drug trial, may Marvin get the drugs suppressed as the fruits of an unlawful search? _____

42. Officer Baines was the head of the Empire City Art Fraud Detection Bureau, a division of the Empire Police Department. Baines had heard rumors that a citizen of Empire, Norma, was forging and selling fake lithographs purporting to be by Salvador Dali. Baines knew that he did not have probable cause either to arrest Norma or to search her premises. Therefore, Baines decided to see if a more consensual approach would work. He rang Norma's doorbell, and when she answered, said to her, "Ma'am, we've heard that some fake Salvador Dali prints may be being made in your apartment. May I have a look around?" Baines did not tell Norma that forging art prints was a crime, and Norma believed that this was not a crime. Norma responded, "Sure, officer."

Baines at no time gave Norma *Miranda* warnings, or otherwise suggested to her that anything he might find could be used against her. Also, Baines did not tell Norma that she had a right to refuse consent, and that if she refused he would not conduct a search at that time because he had no warrant. After Norma approved, Baines took a look around the apartment, and immediately spotted a fake Dali print being manufactured; he left to get an arrest and search warrant, then came back and seized the fake print. At Norma's trial for art forgery, she moved to suppress all fruits of Baines' initial search, on the grounds that it violated the Fourth Amendment. Should her motion be granted? _____

43. Same facts as the prior question. Now, however, assume that when Baines came to Norma's door, he was not wearing his police uniform. He said, "Ma'am, I'm a local art dealer, and I've heard that you've got a supply of fake Salvador Dalis that I could sell at a nice profit to tourists who don't know the difference between fake and real ones. Mind if I come in and take a look at your inventory?" Norma said, "Why, of course." At this time, she never dreamed that Baines was really a police officer working undercover. Baines spotted a fake print, then used this as the basis to get a search and arrest warrant. May the print be suppressed from Norma's ultimate trial? _____

44. Same basic facts as the prior two questions. Now, however, assume that wearing his uniform, Baines went to Norma's door, rang the bell, and stated, "I have a search warrant. Will you consent to let me search your premises for fake Dali prints?" Norma responded, "O.K." In fact, Baines did not have, and had never applied for, a search warrant. Baines

searched the apartment, found the fake print, and seized it. May Norma get it suppressed as the fruit of an unlawful search? _____

45. Henry and Wanda were a married couple living together reasonably happily. Officer Lemon had a vague suspicion (but not probable cause to believe) that a rifle owned by Henry had been used to fire the fatal shot in an unsolved murder. Acting without a warrant, Lemon came to Henry and Wanda's house. Henry was not home, but Wanda was. Lemon asked whether Wanda or her husband had a rifle. Wanda replied that there was a rifle that she and her husband both owned and used from time to time. Lemon asked whether he could inspect the rifle and remove it for testing. Wanda, knowing that she herself was innocent of wrongdoing and believing that her husband was also, consented. Lemon looked at the rifle, took it away for testing, and discovered that it had indeed been used to fire the fatal shot. At his murder trial, may Henry get the rifle suppressed as the fruit of an unlawful search? _____

46. Troy rented one room (a bedroom) in a house owned by Larry. Their arrangement permitted Larry to keep a key to Troy's room, and to enter that room in order to clean it once a week. The police suspected (without probable cause) that Troy possessed drugs. They came to the house, and found Larry (but not Troy) present. They asked Larry for permission to search Troy's room. Larry agreed, and let them use his key. In Troy's room, the police found illegal drugs. At his drug possession trial, may Troy get the drugs found in his room suppressed? _____

47. While Officer Noonan was patrolling his beat on foot one night, he saw a car with a broken window and the alarm blaring. When he looked inside the car's window, using his flashlight, he thought he could see that there was no radio in the spot where the radio would normally be. At about the same time, he noticed a young woman (who turned out to be Marla) walking away from the car at a rapid clip, carrying a shopping bag. Noonan did not have probable cause to believe that Marla had broken into the car, taken the radio, or committed any other offense. However, based on Noonan's 20 years on the police force, on the very fast rate that Marla was walking, on the fact that the alarm had only recently gone off, and on the bag Marla was carrying, Noonan had what could best be described as a "solid hunch" that Marla might have done the break-in and taken the radio.

Therefore, Noonan accosted Marla, asked her to stop for a moment, and asked her whether she had anything to do with the sounding of the car alarm. Noonan blocked Marla's way, in such a manner that it was clear to her that she would either have to answer his question or try to escape from him. Marla dropped the bag, apparently in a panic, and began to run. Noonan quickly looked in the bag, saw that it contained a car radio, and chased after Marla. He arrested her, and she was charged with burglary. At her trial, Marla has moved to suppress the radio, on the grounds that it is the fruit of a violation of her Fourth Amendment rights.

(a) What doctrine should the prosecutor cite in attempting to rebut Marla's suppression motion? _____

(b) Should Marla's suppression motion be granted, in light of the rebuttal you listed as your answer to (a)? _____

48. Officer Nelson, dressed in plain clothes, walked a foot beat around the neighborhood to try to spot criminal activity. His beat was a high crime area, in which there was an especially large amount of automobile theft. Nelson spotted a red Ferrari pull up and stop at a traffic light. Nelson could tell that the driver was a young black male. Nelson was quite prejudiced against blacks in general, and believed (in this case, quite irrationally) that few young blacks could afford Ferraris, and that this Ferrari was likely to have been stolen. (Not only did Nelson not have probable cause for this belief, but his belief would not even qualify as a "reasonable belief based upon objective criteria.")

Nelson went over to the car, asked the driver to roll down the window, and said, "Do you know where the nearest used-car dealer is?" Nelson was not in fact interested in getting an accurate answer to this question; he merely wanted to see whether the driver was nervous, whether there were lock-picking tools in the car, or whether there was any other sign of criminal wrongdoing. Nelson was prepared to let the car drive on if the driver didn't want to answer his question.

The driver had no idea that Nelson was a police officer. The driver (whose name was Vern) seemed extremely nervous; he tried to drive away, but the car stalled. Nelson saw through the rolled-up window that there did not seem to be a key in the ignition, but rather a series of loose wires hanging out. At that point, Nelson arrested Vern on charges of car theft. (Assume that by that time, Nelson had probable cause to believe that Vern had committed this crime.) At his trial, Vern has moved to suppress Nelson's testimony about what he saw, and any fruit of the subsequent search of the car, on the theory that all of this stemmed from an initial Fourth Amendment violation by Nelson in stopping Vern's car in the first place. Should Vern's motion be granted? _____

49. Same basic facts as the prior question. Now, however, assume that: (1) Officer Nelson was in his police uniform, rather than in plain clothes; and (2) Nelson, instead of asking for directions, asked Vern for his driver's license and registration. If the rest of the episode transpired as described above, may Vern obtain suppression of evidence stemming from this encounter (including Nelson's testimony about the loose wires sticking out of the ignition)? _____

50. Officer Mulroney was walking the night beat in a downtown area where there were a lot of office buildings and few nighttime pedestrians. At 1:00 a.m., she spotted a teenager, Evan, who was carrying a heavy desktop computer. Mulroney thought it was strange that someone, especially a teenager, would be carrying a heavy and expensive desktop computer through an office district late at night. Therefore, Mulroney stopped Evan and asked what he was doing. He said that he was borrowing the computer from a friend, and taking it to his apartment. Mulroney said, "Please come with me to the police station. I want to check the serial number of the computer, to make sure it's not stolen." (Assume that at this moment, Mulroney did not have probable cause to arrest Evan.)

Mulroney then escorted Evan to the police station; he made no attempt to resist. Evan was required to wait for 45 minutes while the police checked the serial number against a statewide stolen property listing. It turned out that the computer was indeed stolen, and Mulroney so informed Evan. At that point, Evan confessed to being the thief. At his trial for burglary, Evan has moved to suppress his confession as the fruit of a Fourth Amendment violation. Should his motion be granted? _____

51. Officer Pasternak was an experienced cop who had followed the same inner-city neighborhood beat for many years, and who knew almost everybody on that beat. In particular, he knew that Fiona sometimes used drugs (and even occasionally sold them), but he also knew that Fiona was as meek as a church mouse, and would never hurt anybody. One day, he spotted Fiona standing on a street corner, appearing to hand money to a stranger and to receive a package in return. Pasternak reasonably suspected (though he did not have probable cause to believe) that Fiona had just received drugs. He went up to Fiona, briefly detained her, patted the pocket of her coat, felt a soft parcel, and then reached inside. At no time did he suspect that Fiona was carrying a weapon; he did, however, suspect that the soft parcel he felt inside her coat pocket might well be drugs. The parcel did indeed turn out to contain cocaine, for which he arrested Fiona. At her drug-possession trial, Fiona has moved to suppress the parcel as being the fruit of a Fourth Amendment violation. Should her motion be granted? _____

52. Same basic facts as the prior question. Now, however, assume that Pasternak did not know Fiona, and reasonably believed that Fiona might be carrying either a knife or a gun. After stopping her, he patted her coat pocket, and felt the soft parcel, which he deduced might be cocaine. He reached inside her coat and retrieved the parcel, confirming his suspicions. May Fiona get the parcel suppressed at her trial for drug possession?

_____

53. Every member of the Langdell Police Department had been told to be on the lookout for a blue car (make unspecified) with a license plate beginning with the letters "JQ." This was based on a description from a witness to a bank robbery, who had reported that a car having those characteristics was driven away by the sole robber. Since the robber had fired a shot (which did not hit anybody) during the bank robbery, the advisory said that the robber might be armed and presumed dangerous.

The day after the robbery, Officers Quarles and Ramon spotted a blue Ford whose license plate began with JQ. The officers waved the car over to the side of the street, and saw that it contained a driver (Gerard) and a front-seat passenger (Howard).

(a) Officer Quarles asked the driver, Gerard, to get out of the car. He then asked Gerard whether Gerard had had anything to do with the bank robbery the other day. Gerard denied this, but did so in a manner that did not allay Quarles' suspicion that this might indeed be the bank robber and the getaway car. Quarles then did a pat-down of Gerard, and did not find any weapons. He asked Gerard to put his hands on the front hood of the car, and looked inside the passenger compartment. Quarles' motive in doing so was to find any weapon that might be in the passenger compartment, to which Gerard might get access during their encounter. Underneath the rear seat, Quarles found a bag of marijuana. It later turned out that Gerard was not the bank robber, but he was charged with marijuana possession. At his trial, Gerard has moved to suppress the marijuana as the fruit of an unlawful search. Should his motion be granted? _____

(b) Simultaneously with Quarles' encounter with Gerard, Ramon asked the passenger, Howard, to exit the car on the passenger side. After Howard exited, Ramon noticed that he had a distinctive tatoo marking him as a member of the Tweets, a gang whose members were well-known for (1) usually carrying electronic devices from which they could use Twitter to arrange street crimes and (2) nearly always carrying switchblades. Although at the moment Howard exited the car Ramon had no probable cause to suspect Howard of wrongdoing, he patted down Howard's pockets to see if he was carrying a weapon. Ramon found something hard that he reasonably thought might be a switchblade; he removed it from Howard's pocket, and discovered it was a box cutter the possession of which by Howard was illegal due to Howard's status (unknown to Ramon at the time of the encounter) as a convicted felon. At Howard's trial for illegal possession of the box cutter, he has moved to suppressed the cutter. Should his motion be granted? _____

54. Police in the town of Langdell were concerned that a substantial number of drivers were driving without being properly licensed, and were driving unregistered vehicles. The Department embarked on a program of occasional, random "spot checks" to discover and deter this conduct. Each officer was told that approximately twice per day, he or she should pick a car at random, stop it, and ask to see the driver's license and registration. All officers were scrupulously careful to perform this task quite randomly, and thus did not discriminate against blacks, teenage males, or any other recognizable sub-group. Officer Turner randomly selected Donald for a stop; Turner had no objective basis for believing that Donald was especially likely to be driving without a license, driving an unregistered car, or otherwise committing any traffic violation. After Turner asked Donald for his license and registration, he observed that Donald's speech was somewhat slurred, and smelled liquor on Donald's breath. Donald indeed turned out to be driving while drunk, and was prosecuted for this offense. May Donald suppress all evidence resulting from the stop (and thus the entire case), on the grounds that it stemmed from a violation of his Fourth Amendment rights? _____

55. A statute of the state of Erewon provides that whenever a person is arrested for any of certain specified crimes — including rape, murder, aggravated assault and burglary — a sample of that person's DNA may be taken as part of police booking procedures. The statute specifies that the sample is to be taken by requiring the arrestee to open his mouth, and then swabbing the inside of his cheek to gather some cells. Acting with probable cause but without a search or arrest warrant, the police arrested Devon for having burglarized a private premises the night before. The arrest took place while Devon was walking through a park. At the police station, the police took a DNA swab in accordance with the statutory procedure. Devin was then released on bail. Meanwhile, the DNA sample was sent to an out-of-state laboratory. Three months later, the FBI reported that Devon's DNA matched a sample from the scene of a never-solved murder that had been committed in Erewon in 2008. At Devin's trial on the 2008 murder, the prosecution relied heavily on the DNA match, and conceded that without that match, the police would never have had occasion to suspect Devon of that murder. Devon now objects to the introduction of the DNA evidence, claiming that his Fourth Amendment rights were violated when the DNA sample was taken without a search warrant, under circumstances in which there were no exigencies preventing the police from getting such a warrant. Putting aside the issue of the proper remedy for any illegality, is Devon correct in asserting that the taking of the swab was a violation of his Fourth Amendment rights? _____

CHAPTER 4

ELECTRONIC SURVEILLANCE AND SECRET AGENTS

56. The FBI had been trying to put organized-crime kingpin Lewis "Fat Louie" Lenkowitz away for a number of years, without success. Finally, the federal agents decided that the right kind of electronic "bug" might be just the thing. The agents knew that Louie often transacted business at a neighborhood social club. With the help of local police officials, a phony fire scare was arranged at the club, and all patrons were temporarily evicted. Federal agents disguised as firefighters went into the club, and clipped a bug on the wall of the room where Louie was known to transact business. This bug transmitted sounds in the room out to the local FBI office one block away. No permission of any judge or magistrate was sought or received for this operation.

Shortly thereafter, Louie mentioned in passing, while at the club, "You remember when we put the cement shoes on old Jimmy Boffa?" Federal agents immediately charged Louie with the murder of Boffa, which had occurred some years earlier. They then sought to introduce Louie's statement against him at his trial. Louie has moved to have the statement suppressed on the grounds that it was obtained in violation of his Fourth Amendment rights. Should his motion be granted? _____

57. Langdell police were convinced that Melvin had murdered his wife Wanda, who had disappeared one night after the two had been overheard arguing. However, the police had no direct evidence that Melvin did it. Harriet, an attractive young member of the Langdell force, volunteered for an undercover assignment to try to get evidence against Melvin. She arranged to "run into" Melvin at a local singles bar, and to become romantically involved with him. Soon, he invited her to move in with him. She did, but only after placing a "bug" under his bed, which transmitted to the police station everything spoken in the bedroom. Several nights later, after a particularly passionate interlude, Melvin mentioned to Harriet that he had murdered Wanda. The police's tape of this statement, recorded at the police station via the bug, was introduced against Melvin at his subsequent murder trial. Can Melvin have this tape suppressed on the grounds that it was obtained in violation of his rights? _____

CHAPTER 5

CONFESSIONS AND POLICE INTERROGATION

58. One night in Central Park, police officers in a roving patrol car suddenly heard muted cries that sounded like they were coming from an animal. They discovered a young woman lying beaten by the side of the path, her head terribly bloody. The officers immediately scouted around the area. They found a young man who was carrying a baseball bat, which appeared to have some dark, sticky substance on it. The officers arrested the young man, whose name was Claude, and took him to the police station. The officers did not say anything to Claude, either at the time of the arrest or during the trip, except, "Come on, guy, we're gonna have to take you into the police station."

At the station, Claude was booked on charges of committing the beating, and put in a temporary holding cell until he could be arraigned. Shortly after Claude was put in the cell, a police detective walked in, and without any preamble said, "We know you beat that girl in the park. Did you rape her too?" Claude responded, "No, I only hit her on the head once with the bat, to try to stun her." Claude was tried on aggravated assault charges, and the prosecution sought to introduce his confession as the main part of their case against him. May the confession be admitted, and why or why not? _____

59. The police had long believed that Dennis had murdered his wife, but they had no proof. One day, an officer happened to catch Dennis driving through a red light. Local law permitted a prison term for that offense. Dennis was arrested, taken to the station house, arraigned, and held in a cell pending trial, because he couldn't make the $200 bail. The police wanted to take advantage of this happy situation, so they put an undercover police officer, Alan, into Dennis' cell — Alan was dressed in regular prison garb, and was coached to tell Dennis that he, Alan, was in for car theft.

Alan hoped that Dennis would incriminate himself in his wife's murder without any prompting, but this did not happen. Therefore, during their second day as cellmates, Alan said to Dennis, "You know, once I get out again — and I'm sure I'm gonna beat this rap — I'd love to have a partner to do bank robbery jobs with, which are what I'm really good at. But I can't have a wimp as a partner; I could only use somebody who would kill if the need arose. Did you ever kill anybody?" Dennis had always dreamed of getting a chance to commit a lucrative crime or two with an expert as mentor. So he replied, "Well, as a matter of fact, about two years ago, I murdered my wife, and they never pinned anything on me."

Dennis was then charged with murdering his wife, and Alan was called to testify about what Dennis had told him in the cell. Dennis asserts that admission of this testimony would violate his rights, since he never got any *Miranda* warnings before he made his incriminating statement to Alan. Should Alan's testimony be suppressed on this ground?

_____

60. The police suspected (reasonably and accurately, as it turned out) that Elvira had committed a recent burglary of a valuable diamond-and-pearl necklace. The police decided to take a direct approach. Bess, one of the better detectives on the local force, was sent to Elvira's house. When Elvira answered the door, Bess inquired whether she could ask Elvira some questions about "a burglary that took place the other night, involving a necklace." Elvira invited Bess in. Bess questioned Elvira for nearly an hour and a half, about the burglary and about Elvira's movements on the night of the burglary. At no time did Bess give Elvira any *Miranda* warnings.

About 45 minutes into the interview, Elvira said, "I've really got to get to the grocery store before it closes in another 10 minutes." Bess replied, "No, I think we really have to get to the bottom of this." Elvira reluctantly agreed to stay, in part because she wasn't sure she had any choice. Near the end of the interview, Elvira said, "Anyway, I'd never bother to steal a necklace where the largest diamond was only one-quarter carat and the total weight was only two carats." Since the police had never released these details about the necklace, and Elvira had claimed that she did not know the owner and had never seen the necklace, this remark was incriminating. At Elvira's trial for burglary, the prosecution tried to introduce the statement against her. Elvira has objected, on the grounds that the statement was obtained from her in violation of her *Miranda* rights. Should the statement be allowed into evidence? _____

61. While the *USS Nebraska* was docked in San Diego, her officers discovered one of the sailors dead in his bunk, cause unknown. The police were immediately called, and sealed off the gangway, so that no one could leave or enter the ship. At the time, there were 15 men aboard. The police then said, "We're not sure whether this death was murder, accident, or natural causes, but nobody leaves the ship until you've answered our questions." Each seaman was then taken privately to a cabin where one of the police officers questioned him about what, if anything, he knew concerning the death. No seaman was given *Miranda* warnings.

One of the seamen, Frank, when asked, "Did you have anything to do with the sailor's death?" answered, "Well, he was being mean to me all the time, so I put a pillow over his face while he was asleep, till he stopped breathing." At Frank's trial for murder, this confession is sought to be introduced into evidence against him. The prosecution argues that since at the time of Frank's questioning it was not known whether there even had been a crime, and the investigation certainly had not focused on Frank, *Miranda* warnings should not be applicable. Should Frank's confession be excluded from evidence against him?

_____

62. Officer Nelson was on traffic patrol. He spotted a car driving with one tail light missing. (It was part of Nelson's job to stop and warn motorists of even minor infractions — he usually just warned them, and let them go on their way.) Nelson flashed his lights and pulled the car over. The car was being driven by Jermaine. He asked Jermaine for her driver's license and for the car's registration. Jermaine produced both. Nelson noticed that the owner of the car, according to the registration, was John Jones, not Jermaine. He asked Jermaine, "How do you come to be driving a car registered to John Jones?" Jermaine, suddenly very nervous, replied, "Well, I borrowed it from him. I was going to bring it back pretty soon." Nelson asked, "Does he know you have the car?" Jermaine said, "No, but I'm sure he wouldn't mind." This was enough to make Nelson quite suspicious. He radioed headquarters, where he found that the car had been reported stolen by Jones 12 hours before. Jermaine was charged with car theft, and her earlier statement to Nelson was admitted against her to show that she knew that she did not have authority to take the car. Jermaine has moved to have her statement excluded from evidence as rendered in violation of *Miranda*. Should the statement be excluded? _____

63. Ike was getting into a parked car, when Officer Quentin, of the Arbortown police, noticed that the registration on the car's front windshield had expired. As Ike drove away, Quentin stopped him, and arrested him for driving with an expired registration sticker. (Driving with an expired registration sticker is, under local law, punishable by at most a $200 fine, and a jail term may not be imposed for it. Normally, a driver would not be arrested for this offense, but merely given a citation; however, local law did permit an arrest in this situation.) Quentin was known as an especially tough "law and order" type. Therefore, he took

Ike back to the police station, where he was booked and then held for several hours pending arraignment. During this time, the police ran a routine ID check on Ike, and discovered that he was wanted by the police of another town (Elmont), for a burglary at 123 North Avenue in Elmont.

Officer Quentin went up to Ike and said, "Did you commit a burglary at 123 North Avenue in Elmont two weeks ago?" Ike responded, "Hey, officer, I didn't go in the house, I just drove the getaway car on that one." At no time during this exchange (or prior to it) did anyone give Ike any *Miranda* warnings. Ike was charged by the Elmont police with being an accomplice to the North Avenue burglary. His statement to Quentin was introduced against him. Ike protested that the statement was made in violation of the *Miranda* rules. The prosecutor argued in rebuttal that *Miranda* warnings need not be given where a person is in custody for a misdemeanor or other non-felony crime. Must Ike's confession be excluded from evidence against him? _____

64. Police were investigating a murder in which the victim, Molly, was found dead of stab wounds in her apartment. It turned out that Molly had been having an affair with a married man, Herb. Herb's wife, Jill, was known to the police to be a jealous sort who had become enraged in the past when Herb had carried on affairs with other women, though the police did not know whether Jill had been aware of the Herb-Molly affair. Finally, the police got a break — they found a couple of red hairs embedded in the carpet near Molly's body; since Molly was a brunette and Jill was a redhead, they were able to persuade a judge that this constituted probable cause for issuing a warrant for Jill's arrest. (Assume that the arrest warrant was properly issued.) They then arrested Jill for Molly's murder, and brought her to the police station.

The detective in charge of the case, Detective Reynolds, came into Jill's holding cell. Reynolds did not give Jill any *Miranda* warnings. Reynolds said, without preamble (and without Jill's saying anything to him first), "Look, we know you did it. We know all about the affair between Herb and Molly, and we've got evidence that you knew about that affair too. Furthermore, we've got several red hairs found at the crime scene, embedded in the carpet right near where the body was found. It would make life a lot easier for everybody if you would just confess." Jill responded, "Well, I went to Molly's apartment that night, and had a drink with her while I tried to talk her into stopping the affair. But I didn't kill her."

At Jill's murder trial, the prosecution, as part of its case in chief, introduced this statement to show that Jill was present at the murder scene. By then, Jill had changed her story, and claimed that she was never at the apartment. Therefore, Jill's lawyer objected to the introduction of the statement, on the grounds that it was obtained in violation of Jill's *Miranda* rights.

(a) What argument should the prosecutor make for holding that *Miranda* is inapplicable to Jill's station-house statement? _____

(b) Will this argument be successful? _____

65. Nell, a wealthy businesswoman, disappeared suddenly one day. Shortly thereafter, her family received a ransom demand for $1 million, together with instructions about where

and when the money should be delivered. Nell's husband, Lee, decided to pay the money, but to bring the police in on the ransom payment. Lee showed up at the ransom "drop" at the appointed time with the money. Police staked out the area.

Soon thereafter, Ken picked up the ransom, and began to drive away. The police, led by Officer Stone, stopped him, handcuffed him and put him in the back of the police cruiser. There, Stone, said to him, "If anything happens to Nell, you'll get the chair under the Lindberg law. Tell us where she is, and save your life. Where is she?" Ken replied, "I've got her tied up in an apartment I've rented," and took the police there. At Ken's later kidnapping trial, the prosecution anticipated that Ken might claim that his only involvement was to pick up the ransom, not to participate in capturing or holding Nell. Therefore, the prosecution sought to introduce Ken's statement to Stone, to show that Ken was the main or sole criminal. Ken has objected on the grounds that his statement to Officer Stone was taken in violation of his *Miranda* rights.

(a) What doctrine should the prosecution assert, in opposition to Ken's objection?
_____

(b) Will this doctrine apply to render *Miranda* inapplicable and the confession thus admissible? _____

66. Nestor was arrested on armed robbery charges, and taken to the station house. He was read a complete set of *Miranda* warnings. Nestor made no statement or even gesture indicating that he understood the warnings and was waiving his rights. The police immediately began questioning him. Nestor answered their questions, thus incriminating himself. May his statements be introduced against him at trial as part of the prosecution's case in chief?
_____

67. Same basic facts as prior question. Now, however, assume that after Nestor was read his *Miranda* warnings, the police officer said, "Do you understand these rights?" and Nestor replied, "Yes," but did not elaborate further. The police asked him questions without any response for half an hour, and then asked the question to which he gave an incriminating response. May his response be introduced against him at trial as part of the prosecution's case in chief? _____

68. Omar was a 21-year-old man who lived at home with his parents. A well-documented facet of his personality was that he was very much influenced by any older man in whose company he happened to be at the time. Omar was arrested by the police on charges of participating in a burglary, in that he drove the getaway car for the principal burglar, Bob, an older man. The police arrested Omar at his house, in front of his mother. Omar was taken to the station, and given his *Miranda* warnings. Simultaneously, Omar's mother (unbeknownst to Omar) arranged to have the family lawyer, Ralph, go to the station house.

Ralph arrived at the station house while Omar was being read his *Miranda* warnings. The officers at the front desk did not let Ralph see his client. Nor did they inform Omar that Ralph had been retained for him by his family, or that Ralph was there waiting to see him. Omar was read the *Miranda* warnings and said, "I don't want to hide anything"; he proceeded to answer questions concerning his role in the burglary. At Omar's burglary trial, his lawyer seeks to suppress statements made at the station house. The defense demonstrates that because of Omar's impressionable nature, there is a very high probability that had Ralph been permitted to see Omar, Omar would have taken Ralph's advice to remain silent. Must Omar's statement be excluded from the case against him?

_____

69. Same basic fact pattern as the prior question. Now, however, assume that: (1) no lawyer had been retained for Omar and thus none was waiting at the station; and (2) the officer interrogating Omar said to Omar (after giving him his *Miranda* warnings), "The guy you pulled the burglary with, Bob, has already confessed that you were in it with him. So you have nothing to lose by confessing, and it may even shorten your sentence for having cooperated with us." The officer knew that this was a complete lie (Bob had not even talked to the police about anything), and the sole purpose of the officer's statement was to induce Omar to waive his *Miranda* rights. Omar agreed to answer questions, and confessed. Must Omar's confession be excluded from evidence as a violation of his *Miranda* rights? _____

70. The police arrested Quentin on a murder charge, booked him, and put him in jail because he could not make bail. Shortly after he was first jailed, Detective Angstrom read Quentin his full *Miranda* rights, and asked if he would answer some questions regarding the murder with which he was charged. Quentin responded, "I want a lawyer, and I might talk to you after I talk to the lawyer." Over the weekend, while Quentin was still in jail, a court-appointed lawyer visited him, and discussed the charges. (The lawyer did not anticipate that Quentin would be questioned again, so he did not tell Quentin that he should remain silent if questioning resumed.) On Monday morning, Detective Butts came into Quentin's cell, ascertained that Quentin had met with the lawyer, gave Quentin his *Miranda* warnings again, and asked him if he would now discuss the case. Quentin agreed to do so. In response to questions by Butts, Quentin implicated himself. May these incriminating statements be introduced against Quentin at trial? _____

71. On October 1, the police arrested Quincy on a robbery charge, and brought him to police headquarters. There, they read him his *Miranda* warnings; Quincy responded that he wanted to deal with them only through an attorney that he asked the police to arrange to have appointed for him. The police decided that it was too much of a bother to get an attorney appointed right away, so they released him. On November 1, after the police got more evidence implicating Quincy on the robbery charge, they brought him back into custody, and once again read him his *Miranda* rights. Quincy orally agreed to waive those rights, made no reference to his prior request for a lawyer, and gave an incriminating response. May this response be introduced against Quincy at trial? _____

72. Raymond was arrested on suspicion of having committed a burglary in New York City on March 10. At the station house, the detective stupidly forgot to give Raymond his *Miranda* warnings, then interrogated him. In response to the detective's questions, Raymond confessed that he had indeed done the burglary. (This questioning did not take place in a particularly coercive manner, and under all the circumstance, a court would conclude that Raymond gave the confession "voluntarily.")

At Raymond's trial on the burglary charges, he took the stand in his own defense. Under questioning by his lawyer, Raymond asserted an alibi defense — he claimed that he had been in Chicago on the day and time when the burglary took place. On cross-examination, the prosecutor showed Raymond a transcript of his confession, and asked him, "If your alibi defense is true, how come you confessed to the crime, instead of either remaining silent, or telling the police about your alibi defense?" Over an objection by Raymond's lawyer, the judge let the question stand, and Raymond replied, "The confession is phony — I just gave it to get the police off my back. In fact, I was in Chicago that day, as I've just said."

The trial judge instructed the jury that they should consider this material only for purposes of evaluating Raymond's credibility as a witness, and not as bearing directly on the substantive issue of whether Raymond committed the crime. The jury found Raymond guilty. On appeal, should the appeals court order a new trial on the grounds that the material was admitted in violation of Raymond's *Miranda* rights? _____

73. On August 25, Stan was arrested on suspicion of being the masked rapist who had assaulted a woman in Boston on the evening of August 10. He was driven to the police station, booked, and then taken into a room used for interrogations. There, he was given his *Miranda* warnings. After reading him the warnings, Dave, the lead detective, said to him, "If you have any evidence that will help us exclude you as a suspect, you might want to help us out by answering a few simple questions, like where you were on the night of the 10th." Dave said, "No, I don't want to talk to you." The case went to trial. At the trial, Stan took the stand and testified that he could not have committed the rape because he was in New York the entire evening on which the rape occurred. On cross-examination, the prosecutor asked him, "If your story about being in New York was true, why didn't you tell that story to the police when they had you in custody, instead of refusing to answer any of their questions?" Stan's lawyer has objected to the question as an infringement of Stan's rights under *Miranda*. Should the court sustain the objection?

_____

74. Same basic facts as the prior question. Now, however, assume that after the police came to suspect Stan of being the masked rapist, Dave visited Stan at his house and asked him if he would voluntarily come to the police station to answer some questions, "so that we can clear you as a suspect." Stan agreed, and accompanied Dave to the police station. At an interrogation room at the station, Dave did not read Stan any *Miranda* warnings. Instead, he said to Stan (in front of what Stan knew was a video recorder), "Stan, you've agreed to this voluntary interview, which you may terminate at any time. Is that correct?" Stan answered, "yes." Stan then answered various questions asked by Dave. At one point, Dave asked him, "Were you in Boston throughout the evening of August 10, when we know the rape occurred?" Stan replied, "I'm tired of answering your questions, and I'm terminating this interview." Stan gave no other indication of why he was cutting off the questioning. Dave let Stan leave the police station, then immediately arrested him for the rape. At trial, Stan took the stand to offer the same "I was in New York" alibi as in the prior question. The prosecution attempted to rebut this testimony by offering testimony by Dave that Stan had suddenly terminated the voluntary interview when Dave asked about Stan's whereabouts on the evening in question. Stan's lawyer has objected on the grounds that this impeachment use of Stan's silence would violate Stan's privilege against self-incrimination. Should the court sustain this objection? _____

CHAPTER 6

LINEUPS & PRE-TRIAL IDENTIFICATION PROCEDURES

75. One day, the Ames Police Department received a call from an unidentified male caller, who stated, "You'd better evacuate the courthouse building. It will be blown up at 2:00 p.m." This call was automatically recorded, as are all incoming calls to the Department. The police evacuated the courthouse as urged, and tried (but failed) to find a concealed bomb. There was one, and it went off at 2:00 p.m., destroying the court house. Based on an informant's tip, the police focused their investigation on Stan. They arrested Stan for the bombing, and asked Stan to give them a "voice print" — they wanted him to speak into a telephone the same words that the unidentified caller had spoken, so they could have an expert produce a print-out of the sound waves from the two recordings and determine whether they were made by the same person. Stan refused, and the police got the court to order that he give the voice print or else be held in contempt. Stan reluctantly complied. At Stan's trial, the prosecution seeks to introduce the voice prints from the two recordings, together with the expert's testimony that the same voice appears on both recordings. Stan objects on the grounds that use of this information would violate his Fifth Amendment privilege against self-incrimination. Should the court exclude the evidence on the basis urged by Stan? _____

76. Based on the testimony of an accomplice, Tom was indicted for carrying out a particular burglary. He was then arrested, and brought to the police station. Because the owner of the burglarized house, Sheila, had gotten a brief look at Tom as he ran out of the house, the police decided to perform a lineup. They put Tom together with five other people (non-uniformed police officers) who approximately resembled Tom in terms of age, race, height, etc. Sheila was asked to look at the six men through a one-way mirror, and to state whether she could identify the burglar. She quickly picked Tom out of the lineup. At no time prior to or during this transaction did any police officer or other government officer say anything to Tom. At Tom's burglary trial, the prosecution offered into evidence the fact that Sheila had picked Tom out of the lineup. What, if any, constitutional right of Tom's would be violated by the admission of this evidence? _____

77. Same basic fact pattern as the prior question. Now, assume that the results of the lineup were ruled by the court to be inadmissible. Assume further that at the trial, Sheila took the stand, and was asked, "Can you identify the burglar as being somebody in this courtroom?" Over the defense's objection, the court permitted Sheila to answer, and she said, "Yes, it's the defendant." Sheila did not refer to the fact that she had made an earlier identification of Tom in the lineup. Neither side presented any evidence showing the reliability (or unreliability) of Sheila's in-court identification of Tom as being the burglar. Has the trial judge erred in permitting Sheila in court to identify Tom as the burglar? _____

78. The First National Bank of Ames was robbed at gunpoint by a dark-haired woman wearing sunglasses. One of the tellers stepped on the "panic button," sending an alarm to police headquarters, so the police got an early jump on the case. One officer who rushed to the scene saw a car travelling away from the bank at a suspiciously high speed, so he stopped the car. The car was driven by Ursula, who had sunglasses and was dark-haired. The officer made a warrantless arrest of Ursula. (Assume that the officer did not violate Ursula's Fourth Amendment rights in doing so.) The officer then took Ursula to the police station. It was now too late in the day to have Ursula brought before a magistrate, so she would have to stay in jail for the night. The police decided, however, that they should conduct a lineup while witnesses' memories were fresh.

Therefore, the police put Ursula in a lineup with five other women of approximately similar appearance, and asked two of the bank tellers to see if they could pick the robber out. Ursula protested prior to and during this lineup that she wanted to have her lawyer present during the lineup, but the police refused, telling Ursula that her lawyer would only delay the proceedings and make trouble. One of the tellers, Arlene, picked Ursula out of the lineup. At Ursula's bank robbery trial, she seeks to have this lineup identification excluded from evidence against her, on the grounds that the police's refusal to allow her attorney to be present violated her right to counsel. Should the lineup identification be excluded on this ground? _____

79. Same basic fact pattern as the prior question. Now, however, assume that Ursula was formally charged with the bank robbery, given a preliminary hearing, and then arraigned (at which time she pled not guilty). Shortly thereafter, detectives working on the case interviewed Bruce, another teller who had been present during the robbery. The detectives showed Bruce six photographs, each of a different woman, and asked him whether he recognized any of them as being the robber. Bruce picked out Ursula's photograph immediately. (Neither Ursula nor her lawyer knew that this photographic identification session was going to take place, and the lawyer was not present during it.) At Ursula's trial, the prosecution has offered into evidence the fact that Bruce picked Ursula's picture out of the bunch. Ursula objects, on the grounds that the photo ID session was carried out in the absence of her lawyer and thus violated her right to counsel. Should the fact that Bruce identified Ursula from the photos be excluded on this ground? _____

80. Tina was brutally raped one night in a poorly lit parking lot. She told police, shortly after the crime, that the rapist was not someone she recognized, that he was an Asian about six feet tall, and that he wore a "New York Mets" jacket. Because Vincent was found wandering near the scene of the crime several hours later, and had a previous conviction for rape under similar circumstances, he was arrested, charged and arraigned.

Two days after the crime, the police asked Tina to come to a lineup. There were six men in the lineup; Vincent was the only Asian, and he was taller than any of the others by at least five inches. The police made Vincent wear a New York Mets jacket, and none of the other men in the lineup had any kind of sports jacket. Vincent was given a court-appointed lawyer who was present at the lineup. Tina stated that she could not be sure whether her assailant was one of those in the lineup.

Three days later, the police asked Tina to come to another lineup. This time, there were six men, including two Asians; Vincent was the only person who was in both lineups. Vincent's lawyer was again present, and protested several ways in which the lineup was unduly suggestive (e.g., that Vincent was the only one who was in both lineups, that there were only two Asians, that Vincent was taller than everyone else, etc.). The police disregarded his complaints. This time, Tina picked Vincent out as her assailant. At Vincent's rape trial, the prosecution sought to introduce into evidence the fact that Tina picked Vincent out of the second lineup.

(a) What argument should Vincent's lawyer make about why this lineup identification should be excluded from evidence? _____

(b) Will the argument you recommend in part (a) succeed? _____

81. While jogging one night, Upton was struck and seriously injured by a car, whose driver drove away rather than render assistance. Upton told the police that in the split second before the impact, he had gotten a very brief glimpse at the driver, who was a young blond-haired woman. Based on an informant's tip, the police came to believe that Wendy was the hit-and-run driver. They procured Wendy's photo from her license application at the Department of Motor Vehicles. They then went to Upton's hospital room, and showed him the picture of Wendy. They did not show him any pictures of other possible suspects (i.e., they did not conduct any photo array). As the detective handed Upton Wendy's picture, he said to Upton, "We think this is the woman. Can you identify her from this photo?" Upton replied, "Yes." At Wendy's trial for leaving the scene of an accident and vehicular negligence, the prosecution has sought to introduce into evidence the fact that Upton recognized Wendy from her photo in his hospital room. Wendy seeks to exclude this evidence. Should the court find that the evidence would violate Wendy's constitutional rights, and therefore exclude it? _____

CHAPTER 7
THE EXCLUSIONARY RULE

82. The First National Bank of Pound was robbed by two masked gunmen, and for two months the police had no useful clues. Then, in an episode unrelated to the bank investigation, Officer Jackson of the Police Department learned from an informant that Albert possessed some illegal weapons in his apartment. The informant had proved unreliable in the past, so this tip did not give Jackson probable cause to obtain a warrant to search Albert's apartment, or to arrest Albert. Jackson decided to set forth without a warrant, since he knew he couldn't get one. At a time when he knew Albert was not home, he broke into Albert's apartment, and began ransacking the place. In a closed box underneath Albert's bed, Jackson found a batch of letters, which he started reading more from voyeuristic curiosity than for any other reason. The first letter, written by Bertha to Albert, contained one sentence which read, "When Carter and I robbed the First National Bank of Pound last month, we got away with $89,000 in loot, so I'd like to spend some of this money on one of the weapons you're selling."

Jackson immediately realized that this was probably the key to the bank job, so he took the letter and left Albert's apartment. Solely because of the letter, Bertha was charged with doing the bank job. At her trial, the prosecution sought to introduce the letter into evidence. Bertha objected, on the grounds that the letter was seized in violation of the Fourth Amendment. Must the judge exclude the letter from evidence? _____

83. Bart was a master drug smuggler, who specialized in importing cocaine from Colombia. Bart was smart enough never to smuggle the cocaine in himself. Instead, he used various

"mules." On one occasion, Bart recruited Karen to serve as a mule — Bart attached a kilogram of cocaine owned by Bart to the inside of Karen's thigh. Bart and Karen traveled on the same plane from Colombia to Miami. (They took the same flight so that Bart could immediately retrieve the cocaine after the flight and market it at retail.) At Miami Airport, Drug Enforcement Administration (DEA) agents focused their attentions on Karen not because of any objective grounds for suspicion, but merely because one of them thought that Karen "looked shifty and nervous." In violation of the Fourth Amendment, the DEA agent stopped Karen, took her into a private room, and performed a strip search on her. There, the agent found the cocaine. Bart was implicated because he showed up on the airline's computer reservation system as having been Karen's travelling companion.

At Bart's trial for cocaine smuggling, the prosecution plans to offer the cocaine into evidence against him. At a suppression hearing, Bart has moved to exclude the evidence on the grounds that it is the fruit of the detention and searching of Karen, in violation of the Fourth Amendment; Bart also points out that the cocaine belongs to him. Should Bart's suppression motion be granted? _____

84. Officer Katz had many prejudices, especially ones concerning blacks and women. One day, he spotted an expensive late-model Porsche being driven by Danielle, a black woman. Katz believed that no black woman could possibly have come to drive such a car except by stealing it, earning it through prostitution, or otherwise behaving unlawfully. Because of this belief and not because of any other objective clues, Katz pulled Danielle over and asked to see her license and registration. Both seemed in order, but Katz nonetheless believed that Danielle must be lying when she said she owned the car and had paid for it with honestly-earned money. Therefore, Katz arrested her on charges of prostitution (thinking that she had paid for the car through this means), even though there was not a shred of evidence to support this.

At the station house, Katz questioned Danielle, after first reading her her *Miranda* warnings. Under questioning, Danielle suddenly admitted that a large part of the money to buy the car had come from cocaine smuggling done by her and her boyfriend. Danielle was then charged with drug smuggling. At her trial, the prosecution sought to introduce her confession against her. Danielle has moved to suppress the confession on the ground that it is the fruit of a violation of her Fourth Amendment rights. Should Danielle's suppression motion be granted? _____

85. Federal prosecutors were trying to make an insider trading case against Gordon and Ivan, both wealthy and famous arbitrageurs. They began by breaking into Ivan's office at night, and seizing all of the records in his office, which they then carted to a warehouse. They did this without probable cause and without a warrant. Buried among these documents (and not seen by authorities until much later) was a copy of a July 1 letter from Ivan to Gordon concerning trading in the stock of ABC Corp.; the letter made it clear that Ivan and Gordon were both guilty of insider trading in that transaction. The federal authorities were so busy building their case that they did not go through the documents seized from Ivan's office, and merely kept them boxed in a government warehouse.

Shortly thereafter, federal agents arrested Gordon without a warrant and without probable cause, and then questioned him without first giving him his *Miranda* warnings. Under the questioning, Gordon broke down, confessed to the ABC transaction, and gave police a copy of the July 1 Ivan-to-Gordon letter. The agents realized that they had gotten the letter from Gordon by violating his Fourth and Fifth Amendment rights, and that they might have a hard time introducing the letter into evidence against him. However, since they now knew about the letter, and saw that it was from Ivan to Gordon, they went back into the warehouse, and discovered Ivan's copy of it in one of the boxes.

At Gordon's trial for insider trading, prosecutors offered into evidence against Gordon the copy Gordon had given them of the Ivan-to-Gordon July 1 letter. Gordon has moved to suppress this document on the grounds that it was obtained as the fruit of an unlawful search and interrogation of him.

(a) What doctrine should the prosecution cite in opposing Gordon's suppression motion? _____

(b) If the prosecution uses the doctrine you recommend in (a), should Gordon's motion be granted? _____

86. The police received a tip from a reliable informant that cocaine was being processed at a warehouse at 481 Main Street. The informant explained that he knew this because he had been a member of the operation, until he quarrelled with the other principals. The police went to the 481 Main address, and discovered a locked warehouse that could plausibly have been a cocaine processing factory. At this point, they knew they had probable cause to get a search warrant, and would normally have done so. Normally, they would have staked out the building while they got the warrant (so that no one could remove or destroy evidence). But to save time and to eliminate the need for a stakeout, they decided to see if they could break in first. They successfully broke into the building, and saw that it was indeed a cocaine-processing factory.

At that point, without touching anything, they re-locked the premises, applied for a warrant (using only the information that they had had prior to the break-in), received the warrant, went back to the building, broke in again, and seized the cocaine and other evidence. This evidence was introduced against Jerry, one of the principals, in his trial for drug-related offenses. Jerry has moved to suppress the evidence, on the grounds that it was obtained in violation of his Fourth Amendment rights (since he was the owner of the building, as well as one of the owners of the processing operation). Should Jerry's motion be granted? _____

87. Harry, a wealthy industrialist, was on his way to work in his chauffeured limousine one day, when two masked gunmen suddenly attacked the vehicle, spewing bullets into its tires. The gunmen then opened the door and forcibly abducted Harry. Shortly thereafter, Harry's family received a ransom demand, which the family complied with. Harry was released unharmed; however, since his captors had blindfolded him while they transported him to their hideaway, and kept masks on at all times, Harry was not able to help the police determine who had committed the crime. Starting shortly after the kidnapping, the police ballistics lab analyzed the bullets found in the car, and discovered that these had come from a Smith & Wesson .38 revolver, of a type manufactured between 1980 and 1988.

The police immediately began examining the records of every gun dealer and pawn shop in the metropolitan area, figuring that there was a good chance that the owner (or at least original purchaser) of the gun used in the abduction would be listed in these records. The police then began to interview each Smith & Wesson .38 gun owner shown in the records, and to test each of his or her guns. After the police had checked about 10% of the listed guns, they happened to get a call from an anonymous informant, who said, "You'll find evidence of a serious crime at 1025 South Avenue."

The police realized that this did not furnish them with probable cause to obtain a search warrant for that address. Therefore, they decided to wing it. They went to 1025 South Avenue, rang the bell, and broke in when there was no answer. They ransacked the house, and in so doing, found a Smith & Wesson .38 revolver. Just on a hunch that this might have been the gun used in the Harry kidnapping case, they seized the gun and took it back to the police station. (They did not find any other evidence of criminality.) The department ran a ballistics test on the revolver and, lo and behold, it turned out to be the gun that had fired the bullets into Harry's car. The police went back to 1025 South Avenue, staked it out, and eventually arrested the owner, Kent, when he entered one day. Meanwhile, it turned out that Kent was the registered owner of the gun, and that his name appeared on the records of a local pawn shop as being the owner of that gun. The 1025 South Avenue address was listed as Kent's address in the pawn shop records.

At Kent's trial for kidnapping, the prosecution seeks to enter the gun into evidence, and to tie it to the kidnapping by showing that it fired the bullets found in the car. Kent moves to suppress, on the theory that the police's possession of the gun stems directly from their illegal break-in of 1025 South Avenue at a time when they did not have probable cause or a warrant.

(a) What doctrine should the prosecution cite in support of its opposition to Kent's suppression motion? _____

(b) If the prosecution cites the doctrine you referred to in part (a), should the court grant Kent's suppression motion? _____

88. Leslie reported to the Ames police that her apartment had been burglarized. Officer Kaplan was sent to investigate the complaint. Leslie showed Kaplan into her home office, and had him sit in front of her desk. At one point during the interview, Leslie excused herself to go to the bathroom. Kaplan, with no evil purpose in mind, just curiosity, picked up a stack of letters from Leslie's desk. In the middle of the stack was a letter to Leslie stating, "Sis, I know you poisoned our mother to get her insurance money, but I so far can't bring myself to turn you in. I want you to know that I know, though. [signed] Morton." Kaplan deduced that this might be a clue to a murder case.

After leaving Leslie's apartment, Kaplan ascertained that Leslie indeed had a brother named Morton, and that their mother had died the month before; no one outside the family suspected foul play. Kaplan contacted Morton, who said, "Well, now that you're here, yes, I'd be happy to talk about why I think Leslie murdered our mother." Morton then described facts that made the police believe that Leslie had indeed killed her mother. Leslie was tried for this murder. At the trial, the prosecution relied heavily on Morton's testimony as to incriminating actions by Leslie. Leslie has moved to suppress Morton's testimony, on the grounds that the prosecution learned of Morton's existence only through

Kaplan's illegal ransacking of Leslie's mail. Should Leslie's motion be granted?

_____

89. Nelson's wife, Marie, disappeared without ever being heard from again. The police were convinced that Marie had been murdered, and that Nelson had done it. However, they did not have a shred of hard evidence to prove this. They therefore decided that they would have to play "hardball" to get anywhere with the case. Without probable cause and without a warrant, they arrested Nelson at his home, and took him down to the police station. They dutifully read him his *Miranda* warnings. He agreed to listen to their questions, though not necessarily to talk. After two hours of grilling, Nelson finally confessed that he had done it, and described the method used. A videotape was made of this interrogation session, and it is clear that Nelson's confession was "voluntary." Nelson was tried for murder, and the prosecution sought to introduce the videotape of Nelson's confession. Nelson has moved to suppress this confession, on the grounds that it was the fruit of the police's prior illegal arrest of him. Assuming that the arrest was indeed a violation of Nelson's Fourth Amendment rights, should Nelson's suppression motion be granted?

_____

90. Officer Quell, while walking a downtown beat in City, saw Diego, a young male in his early twenties, look repeatedly into the window of a jewelry store. Based solely on Quell's hunch that young males walking alone who look into the windows of jewelry stores are often up to no good, Quell approached Diego and demanded to see some ID. Diego (who was in fact considering buying an engagement ring displayed in the window and was thus completely innocent) complied by handing his driver's license to Quell. Quell radioed back to headquarters Diego's name and date of birth as shown on the license; after a brief pause, the dispatcher informed Quell (accurately) that a warrant had been issued six years previously for Diego's arrest, on the grounds that he had not paid a $100 fine for a minor traffic violation. Quell, acting pursuant to a City police department directive that any person discovered to have an outstanding arrest warrant should be immediately arrested regardless of the age or seriousness of the offense, told Diego that Diego was under arrest on the warrant. Quell then searched Diego's person incident to that arrest. As part of the search, Quell reached into Diego's pocket, pulled out a plastic bag, and saw that the bag contained a white powdered substance that reasonably appeared to Quell as though it might be heroin. The contents of the bag indeed turned out to be heroin, and Diego was prosecuted on a charge of heroin possession with intent to distribute. Diego moved to suppress the heroin from evidence on the grounds that the substance was discovered only as the direct result of an illegal stop of Diego by Quell. The prosecution con cedes that the stop was illegal based on the facts known to Quell at the time of the stop.

(a) If you are the prosecutor, what argument would you make about why the heroin should be admissible notwithstanding the illegal stop? _____

(b) Assuming you make the argument you mention in your answer to (a), should the court nonetheless grant Diego's suppression motion? _____

91. Officer O'Brien was irrationally prejudiced against young males with long hair, and against anyone who looked like a "hippie." O'Brien spotted Peter and Rachel walking down the street hand in hand, and developed a hunch, based solely on their long hair and style of clothing, that the two were probably in possession of drugs. He arrested them both on drug charges, and escorted them to the station house. There, each was subjected to a "clothing search," which was done to every arrestee in order to inventory their possessions and to protect against concealed weapons. The two were searched simultaneously. In Rachel's purse, five marijuana cigarettes were found. Rachel looked imploringly at Peter when this occurred. Peter then said, "I can't let Rachel take the rap for this — those cigarettes are mine." Peter was charged with marijuana possession, and the prosecution sought to use his station-house confession against him. Peter objected on the grounds that this statement was a direct fruit of his unlawful arrest. Should the court grant Peter's suppression motion? _____

92. The police had probable cause to believe that Veronica was the masked gunman who had recently robbed the local branch of the First National Bank. They properly procured a warrant for her arrest, and arrested her at her house. They handcuffed her, and brought her to the police department. There, Detective Usher questioned her about the robbery, without first giving her *Miranda* warnings. (He had learned from his personal experience that suspects often clam up when read their *Miranda* warnings, and are somewhat more likely to speak if not given the warnings. Therefore, he developed a standard practice of conducting his interrogations in two steps: question without warnings, obtain an admission, warn, then get the suspect to repeat the earlier admission.) In response to Usher's questions — but not in response to any overt coercion or trickery — Veronica confessed that she was the robber. Usher left the room briefly to get a police stenographer, then returned. At this point, he read Veronica her *Miranda* warnings, and did not mention to her that her earlier confession would be inadmissible because unwarned. He then reviewed her earlier answers to his questions, and asked her to confirm those answers.

Veronica, reasoning that she had already "let the cat out of the bag" by confessing, decided that there was no point in refusing to answer the same questions again, this time before the stenographer. Therefore, she confirmed her earlier answers, again confessing to being the robber. The stenographer recorded these answers, and Veronica then signed the confession. At Veronica's bank robbery trial, the prosecution seeks to enter the signed transcript of the second confession into evidence against Veronica. (The prosecution concedes that the first confession is inadmissible.) Veronica has moved to suppress that second confession as the fruit of the earlier, non-*Mirandized* confession. Should Veronica's suppression motion be granted? _____

93. Over the course of a year, three co-eds at Ames State University were found, each in her own off-campus apartment, each stabbed to death. The police believed that a single killer was at work. Detective Johnson of the Ames police force received an anonymous tip that Bernard, who the caller said lived at 141 West Street in Ames, was the killer. This information did not amount to probable cause to arrest Bernard or search his house. Nonetheless, Johnson felt that he had to act. After telephoning Bernard and ascertaining that he was out, Johnson broke into Bernard's house, and carefully searched it from corner to corner. He happened upon three separate snapshots, which he recognized instantly as being of the three dead girls. He immediately seized these photos, and left the house. Based in part on other evidence not illegally obtained, the police were eventually able to charge Bernard with the murder of one of the girls, Kelly.

At Bernard's murder trial, the prosecution did not use the snapshot of Kelly (or anything else derived from Johnson's illegal search of Bernard's house) as part of its direct case. The defense then put on its case. Its only witness was Bernard. On direct, Bernard denied committing the murder of Kelly and said nothing more. On cross-examination, the prosecutor asked, "Did you ever meet Kelly?" Bernard responded, "No." The prosecution asked, "Did you ever obtain a photograph of Kelly?" Again, Bernard answered, "No." Then, the prosecutor showed Bernard the snapshot and asked, "Isn't it true that this photo of Kelly was found in your house?" Bernard's lawyer objected to the prosecution's use of this photo, on the grounds that the photo was the direct fruit of an illegal search, and must thus be barred by the exclusionary rule. Should the trial judge sustain this objection?

_____

94. The police suspected that Egon was the person who had killed Gerald, a business associate of Egon's. However, they did not have probable cause to arrest Egon or to search his premises. Instead, they simply broke into Egon's house one day while he and his wife were away, and seized the most interesting item they found, a Remington .33 revolver. This gun was of interest to the police because they had already determined, from ballistics tests, that Gerald had been shot with a Remington .33. Ballistics tests later showed that the seized pistol was indeed the murder weapon. The police knew that their seizure of the gun was illegal, and they had no other way to prove that Egon had owned the murder weapon. However, they had enough other circumstantial evidence of Egon's guilt that Egon was prosecuted for the murder anyway.

In the prosecution's direct case, only this circumstantial evidence, not the fact that Egon owned the murder weapon, was introduced. During the defense case, Egon did not take the stand. However, Fran, Egon's wife, did take the stand. She stated on direct examination, "So far as I know, Egon never kept a gun at our house." The prosecution, on cross-examination, then showed Fran the Remington seized from the house, and asked, "Don't you recognize this gun as one that was in your house up until several months ago?" Egon's lawyer immediately objected to this evidence on the grounds that it was the fruit of the unlawful entry into Egon's house. Must the court sustain Egon's objection?

_____

95. Detective Lawrence of the Langdell police force received an anonymous call, in which the caller stated, "The occupant of apartment 3B in my building is selling drugs from that apartment. I live at 1865 Center Street." The caller did not say how he came by this information. Lawrence believed that this information was enough to establish probable cause to search apartment 3B at the 1865 Center Street address. He went before a neutral and detached magistrate, and presented the above facts to her in an affidavit. Lawrence did not conceal any relevant facts. The magistrate agreed with Lawrence that the facts here established probable cause, and the magistrate therefore issued a warrant to search apartment 3B of 1865 Center Street "for drugs or any paraphernalia associated with drugs." Lawrence executed the warrant by its terms (breaking into the apartment when there was no answer), and strictly confined his search to the scope of the warrant. He found cocaine that seemed to be held for resale, and seized it.

The occupant of the apartment turned out to be Herb. Herb was tried for a variety of drug charges. The prosecution offered the seized drugs as part of its case-in-chief. Herb moved to suppress the seized drugs, on the grounds that they were the fruits of an illegal search, since there was in fact no probable cause to support issuance of the search warrant. The trial judge has agreed with Herb that the warrant was issued without probable cause, because there was no indication that the informant was either generally reliable or reliable in this case, so that by the "totality of the circumstance" test (*Illinois v. Gates*), probable cause for the warrant did not exist. However, the trial judge has also concluded that Lawrence reasonably believed, on the facts known to him, that probable cause existed; the judge also believes that the magistrate similarly made a reasonable mistake as to the existence of probable cause. Must the trial judge order the drugs suppressed from Herb's trial?

_____

96. As of 2010, Supreme Court precedents left it unclear whether police use of a GPS device to track all the movements of a suspect's vehicle over an extended period constituted a search requiring a warrant. At that time, the binding precedent on this issue in states of the federal First Circuit was a 2009 First Circuit decision, *Adams v. U.S.* (not a real case), holding that even extended use of a GPS tracking device attached to a suspect's car was not a "search" and therefore did not require a warrant. In mid-2010, federal DEA agents in Massachusetts (part of the First Circuit) attached a GPS to the vehicle of Devin, who was suspected of being part of a drug-smuggling ring. They did not request a warrant, but they had probable cause to believe that tracking Devin's vehicle would lead to proof that Devin was involved in the ring. The agents were not aware of the *Adams* ruling, but believed no warrant was needed because no search would occur. After 15 days of surveillance, data gathered via the GPS revealed multiple trips by Devin to the home of another known member of the ring. At Devin's federal criminal trial in late 2010, this GPS data was allowed into evidence by the judge, who relied on the *Adams* decision. Devin was convicted. In 2012, while Devin was about to appeal his conviction, the Supreme Court decided in *U.S. v. Jones* (a real case) that use of a GPS tracking device attached to a suspect's property (such as a vehicle) automatically constitutes a search, and thus requires a warrant. Devin then argued, during a timely appeal to the First Circuit, that he should get the benefit of the *Jones* ruling, in which case the DEA use of the GPS search was illegal without a warrant, justifying a new trial. Should the First Circuit grant Devin's new-trial motion? _____

CHAPTER 8

THE RIGHT TO COUNSEL

97. Kathy was charged with shoplifting. Under state law, shoplifting, where the amount involved is less than $100, is classified as a misdemeanor. A jail sentence of up to six months is authorized. Kathy was indigent, and requested a lawyer for her trial. However, due to a shortage of funds, the county declined to provide one. Kathy was convicted, and sentenced to one night in jail. She has appealed her conviction (and has not done the one night in jail, pending the outcome of the appeal). She argues on appeal that the county's refusal to provide her with a lawyer for the trial, in these circumstances, violated her Sixth Amendment rights. Is Kathy's contention correct? _____

98. Same basic fact pattern as the prior question. Now, however, assume that because of the relatively large ($250) amount involved, Kathy was charged with petit larceny, a felony. The maximum sentence authorized for petit larceny is two years in prison. Because she was indigent, Kathy requested a court-appointed lawyer. The county declined to provide one due to budget constraints. Kathy was tried and convicted. The judge decided not to sentence her to jail, but sentenced her to pay a $100 fine. Have Kathy's Sixth Amendment rights been violated? _____

99. Lester was arrested for burglary, a felony, late one Friday afternoon. He was taken to the station house, booked, and then held in a cell at the county jail because no magistrate was available. Lester's confinement lasted from Friday afternoon until Monday morning. The police did not give Lester his *Miranda* warnings, or make any attempt to question him. On Friday evening, Lester stated that he was indigent (which was true), and demanded that the authorities furnish counsel for him. They refused to do so. (Lester wanted a lawyer over the weekend because he believed that a lawyer might be able to get him released. In fact, there were some special emergency procedures available, under which a knowledgeable lawyer might indeed have gotten Lester released over the weekend.) On Monday morning, Lester was taken to an initial appearance before a magistrate, at which time the charges were read to him, he entered a non-binding plea of not guilty, and counsel was appointed for him. Did Lester's confinement without counsel over the weekend violate his Sixth Amendment rights? _____

100. Norman was charged with murdering his second wife. While he was under arrest and kept at the police station, he was given his *Miranda* warnings, and made an extensive confession that was videotaped. In the confession, Norman disclosed facts that only the killer could have known. Since Norman was indigent, he requested and was given a court-appointed lawyer, Larry. The prosecution's case at trial rested mainly on the video-taped confession, which was shown to the jury. Larry presented a defense for Norman that fell far below the usual standards of competence. For instance, he put Norman on the stand without warning Norman that Norman's past criminal record could be used to impeach his testimony; as a result, Norman's prior conviction for murdering his first wife was brought out on cross-examination to impeach Norman. Nor did Larry object to the use by the prosecution of the videotaped confession; a more competent lawyer would probably have objected (though it is unlikely that the court would have excluded the confession from evidence even had the best available arguments been presented for exclusion). Needless to say, Norman was convicted on the murder charge. On appeal, he has argued that his lawyer's performance was so bad as to deny him the effective assistance of counsel, as guaranteed by the Sixth Amendment. Should the appellate court agree with Norman, and grant a new trial? _____

101. Otto was arrested on state-law charges of robbing two different Getty gas stations, one on July 4 and the other on July 5. In plea negotiations with Otto's court-appointed lawyer, Loretta, the state prosecutor, Pamela, disclosed that the principal piece of evidence that the prosecution intended to introduce at trial was a statement that Otto had made to a friend, Fred, who unbeknownst to Otto was a police undercover agent. As Pamela told Loretta, if the case went to trial Fred would testify that on July 10, Otto told Fred, "I'm the one who did both the Getty robberies last week." Pamela offered the following plea bargain: she would drop one of the two robbery charges, and would recommend a sentence of 25-to-30 months on the other. (Under state law, the trial judge would have discretion about whether to accept or reject this or any other plea bargain.) If Otto did not take the plea bargain, Pamela said, the prosecution would go to trial on both charges; if Otto was convicted of both, the prosecution would attempt to obtain two sentences of 35-to-40 months each, to be served consecutively. Loretta passed the offer on to Otto, but advised him not to take the offer because "It's very likely that we can keep Fred's testimony out of evidence because your Fifth Amendment privilege against self-incrimination protected you against having a government agent secretly elicit a confession from you." This was in fact blatantly legally-incorrect advice, because the Fifth Amendment privilege does not apply where the suspect does not know he is speaking to a government agent, and any competent criminal defense lawyer would have known this.

Otto unwisely took Loretta's advice, rejected the plea agreement, and soon thereafter went to trial. The trial judge correctly admitted Fred's testimony, and the jury convicted Otto on both counts. The judge sentenced him to two 40-month sentences (in the middle of the appropriate range for robbery under the state's advisory sentencing guidelines), to be served consecutively. In federal *habeas corpus* proceedings, Otto now argues that he was deprived of the effective assistance of counsel by Loretta's bad legal advice, and that the appropriate remedy is an order by the federal court that the state court reinstate the original single-count plea-bargain and under it, sentence Otto to no more than 30 months' imprisonment.

(a) Did Otto have a Sixth Amendment right to the effective assistance of counsel while he was deciding whether to accept the proffered plea bargain? _____

(b) Assuming for this sub-part (b) only that Otto had a right to the effective assistance of counsel, what fact(s) must he prove to show that he is entitled to relief? And what are the chances that he can prove whatever he is required to prove? _____

(c) Assuming for this sub-part (c) only that Otto has made whatever showing you mentioned in your answer to part (b), is Otto entitled to the remedy he has asked for (an order that the state-court judge reinstate the original plea-bargain)? If not, what remedy is Otto entitled to? (Assume that whatever relief the federal judge orders, the case will be remanded for enforcement to the same state court judge who set the original sentence.)

---

102. Oliver was charged in state court with the first-degree murder of his ex-wife, Vivian, by stabbing her to death in her apartment. Oliver and his court-appointed lawyer Les agreed that the best way to defend the case would be to raise the alibi defense that Oliver was out of state when the killing took place. As it happened, 12 years prior to the trial, in 2008, Oliver was convicted of stabbing his girlfriend Jane to death. Under the relevant state evidence rules in force at the present trial: (1) if Oliver took the stand to testify in his own defense, the prosecution would be permitted to ask him, "Isn't it true that you were convicted in 2008 of stabbing your girlfriend Jane?"; but (2) if Oliver did not take the stand, the prosecution would not be permitted to ask him about this conviction or to introduce any evidence of it. Oliver wanted to take the stand, because he thought that doing so would improve the odds that the jury would buy his alibi defense. Les, however, told Oliver that if he took the stand, the prosecution would be sure to bring up the Jane stabbing, and in Les's view the results would be disastrous. Over Oliver's vociferous objection, Les tried the case without calling Oliver to the stand, and Oliver was convicted. On appeal, Oliver now seeks a new trial, claiming that Les's refusal to call him to testify violated his Sixth Amendment right to the effective assistance of counsel.

(a) Did Les's refusal to put Oliver on the stand violate Oliver's Sixth Amendment right to effective assistance of counsel? _____

(b) For this sub-part (b), assume (whether the assumption is accurate or not) that the answer to sub-part (a) is yes. What else, if anything, will Oliver need to establish on appeal, beyond the above facts, in order to be entitled to a new trial?

_____

103. Osmond and Paula were co-indicted for bank robbery by a state grand jury, and arrested by local police. Since Osmond claimed to be indigent, counsel was appointed for him by the court. Osmond and Paula were then released from jail on their own recognizance. While both were out of jail, Osmond asked Paula if the two of them could meet to discuss their defense, without any lawyers present. Unbeknownst to Osmond, Paula had in fact already turned state's evidence. At the request of prosecutors, Paula wore a concealed transmitter to the meeting with Osmond. At that meeting, Paula said, "Don't you think we might be better off pleading guilty — you and I both know that we pulled this heist, and a jury's gonna believe we did too." Osmond replied, "You and I may know we did it, but a jury doesn't have to know. I want to plead not guilty and defend this thing all the way." Shortly thereafter, Paula pled guilty. At Osmond's trial, the tape of his statement to Paula was played before the jury. Osmond argues that the use of this tape violated his Sixth Amendment rights, since his lawyer was not present at the meeting where Paula elicited the statement from Osmond. Should the court exclude the tape on this ground? _____

104. Same facts as the prior question. Now, however, assume that Osmond had not been arrested or charged on the bank robbery charges, but he knew that the police regarded him as the principal suspect. The police knew that Osmond had consulted his long-time attorney about the charges that seemed likely to be filed against him. The police sent Paula to Osmond's house, so that they could discuss what to do if charges were in fact filed. Unbeknownst to Osmond, Paula had already turned state's evidence, and was wired for sound. The conversation described in the prior question then occurred. Would it be a violation of Osmond's Sixth Amendment rights for his incriminating statement on the tape to be played before his jury? _____

105. Same basic fact pattern as the prior two questions. Now, however, assume that Osmond was already indicted, and had retained a lawyer. Both Osmond and his lawyer, Loretta, believed that Paula was a true co-defendant; that is, neither realized that Paula had secretly turned state's evidence and was planning to plead guilty and testify against

Osmond in return for a lighter sentence. Loretta asked Paula to come to a strategy meeting with herself and Osmond. Paula came to the meeting. At the meeting, Osmond volunteered several self-incriminating statements. Paula did not report these statements to the prosecution. At Osmond's trial, Paula testified against Osmond, but did not report any statements made at the strategy session. Osmond was convicted. On appeal, he argues that Paula's presence at the meeting between Osmond and Loretta constituted a violation of Osmond's Sixth Amendment rights, thus requiring a new trial. Should Osmond's new trial motion be granted on this ground? _____

106. Rafael was arrested for robbing First Bank, a crime that the police believed was committed by at least two perpetrators. No one other than Rafael was initially charged. Rafael was arraigned, and because he was indigent, the arraignment judge appointed Lawt, a legal aid lawyer, to represent him. Rafael was then released on his own recognizance. The day after the arraignment, the police visited Rafael at his house. They asked him whether he had had a chance to consult with Lawt yet, and he said that he had not. They then said to him, "We know you weren't the only robber. If you tell us who helped you, we'll ask the prosecution to go easy on you." Rafael thought about this proposition for a while, and agreed to talk to the police. They asked him to sign a waiver of his right to consult counsel, a document that he understood and signed. They then emphasized to him that he was not in custody, that he was free to discontinue the questioning at any time, and that if he did so the police would immediately leave. Rafael answered the police's questions about the robbery, explaining how he and his friend Justin had carried it out. Later at his trial, the prosecution offered these statements as evidence against him. Rafael sought to have the statements excluded as fruits of a violation of his Sixth Amendment right to counsel. Should the court grant his suppression motion?

_____

ANSWERS TO SHORT-ANSWER QUESTIONS

1.   Yes. The Fifth Amendment privilege against self-incrimination and the Sixth Amendment right to counsel have both been held binding on the states (via the Fourteenth Amendment's Due Process Clause) just as they are applicable to the federal government. The prosecution here might try to argue that merely because these guarantees are in a general sense binding on the states, this does not mean that the precise *contours* of each are binding on the states in the same way as on the federal government. But the Supreme Court has consistently rejected this argument — the Court has always held that once a particular Bill of Rights guarantee is binding on the states, it is binding in *precisely the same way* as on the federal government. See, e.g., *Malloy v. Hogan*. Since the 2012 *Smith v. U.S.* decision held that the interrogation there violates the suspect's Fifth and Sixth Amendment rights, and since the facts here are virtually indistinguishable, the Ames Supreme Court is constitutionally bound to find in favor of the defense.

2.   No. It is true that in the vast majority of situations where the Supreme Court has found that a particular Bill of Rights guarantee exists as against the federal government, the Court has also found that guarantee binding on the states via the Fourteenth Amendment's Due Process Clause (the *"selective incorporation"* doctrine). But there is one notable exception to this general rule: The right to a grand jury indictment has never been held by the Supreme Court to be binding upon the states. Therefore, any state may (and indeed most states do) commence a felony prosecution against the defendant based on some method other than a grand jury indictment, even though a defendant would have the right not to have a *federal* felony prosecution commenced against him without a grand jury indictment.

3.   No. In all but the most unusual and shocking cases of violent police misconduct, the unconstitutionality of an arrest does not itself serve as a defense to charges. That is, a defendant may be tried and convicted regardless of the fact that his arrest was made in violation of the Fourth Amendment. (The legality of the arrest is, however, important in determining whether evidence obtained pursuant to a search that was incident to the arrest must be suppressed, an issue not present on these facts.) So the fact that Dexter was illegally arrested is of absolutely no value to him here — the prosecutor may proceed anyway, without even having to re-arrest Dexter or re-charge him.

4.   Yes, probably. *Katz v. U.S.* establishes that even communications which in some sense occur in "public" may be protected under the Fourth Amendment. Basically, if (1) the defendant had an actual (subjective) expectation of privacy about the communication, and (2) that expectation was one which society recognizes as reasonable, then the communication will be protected by the Fourth Amendment, even if it occurred outside of a private home or office. Here, Johnny's communication probably satisfied this test — (1) he certainly showed an actual or subjective expectation that his words were not being overheard, and (2) in private everyday life one's words are not overheard by such specialized devices, so that society ought to regard an expectation of privacy in these circumstances as being "reasonable."

Therefore, even though the communication occurred in a public place, it was probably protected by the Fourth Amendment. Since the police did not have a warrant or probable cause to monitor the conversation, Johnny will probably be entitled to have the conversation suppressed, and the search warrant therefore thrown out. (The facts are roughly analogous to those of *Katz* itself, where eavesdropping done from the outside of a public phone booth was found to violate the Fourth Amendment rights of the defendant who used the booth to make calls.)

If the police had merely been using a conventional device, such as an ordinary telescope, to get the information, then there would not have been a Fourth Amendment violation, because the *"plain view"* doctrine would have been applicable. But because the information here was attainable only by use of equipment that was not generally available, plain view probably does not apply, and Johnny's Fourth Amendment rights are probably violated. (See, e.g., *Dow Chemical Co. v. U.S.*, stating that "an electronic device to penetrate walls or windows so as to hear and record confidential discussions...would raise very different and far more serious questions" than would the ordinary generally-available aerial camera used in *Dow*.)

By the way, *U.S. v. Leon* might save the prosecution here — that case holds that if a search warrant is issued by a detached and neutral magistrate but is ultimately found to be unsupported by probable cause, the search and its fruits are nonetheless valid and admissible; so even if the Task Force relied on improperly-obtained materials (the conversation) to get their search warrant, they might be able to get the fruits of the warrant admitted under *Leon*. That is why the facts tell you to ignore all issues except whether the conversation in the park was protected by the Fourth Amendment.

5. **(a) Yes.** There are two different scenarios in which a Fourth Amendment search may be deemed to have occurred: (1) where the police infringe on a person's *"reasonable expectation of privacy"* in an attempt to find information; and (2) where the police *physically intrude* on (to use the Fourth Amendment's language) someone's "person, house, papers [or] effects" Here, whether or not the placement and use of the GPS qualifies under (1), it clearly qualifies under (2). We know this because, in *U.S. v. Jones*, the Court held that the attachment of a GPS tracking device to the underside of D's car while the car was parked in a public place constituted a Fourth Amendment search, without regard to whether the attachment or use violated D's reasonable expectation of privacy. *Jones* is indistinguishable from the situation here — the briefcase was an "effect" belonging to Darwin (just as the car belonged to the defendant in *Jones*), and attaching the tracker was a physical intrusion on that effect. So whether or not tracking Darwin's movements over the public roads for 60 days violated Darwin's reasonable expectation of privacy (which it probably did), the physical intrusion was enough to give rise to a Fourth Amendment search.

(b) The record must be excluded. Since there was a search, the police needed probable cause to believe that the search would likely lead to evidence of Darwin's involvement in the murder. But the facts tell us that the police did not have such probable cause at the time they attached the device. Furthermore, the police ordinarily need a *search warrant* before conducting a search; there are numerous exceptions to the search warrant requirement, but none of those exceptions applies here.

6. **Yes**. Under the *"automobile exception"* to the requirement of a search warrant, a vehicle may be searched without a warrant where there is probable cause to believe it contains contraband or evidence of a crime. *However*, absent exigent circumstances, an officer cannot enter a *home or its curtilage* to access the vehicle without a search warrant, even if the conditions for the automobile exception otherwise apply. *Collins v. Virginia*. Here, it's true that Officer Pete had probable cause for a search of the vehicle, since the vehicle matched the description provided by Elaine, and was spotted relatively close to the mall from where it was stolen. However, the garage was part of the curtilage of the home at # 123 Magnolia (since the garage was an enclosure attached to the home, and was part of "the area immediately surrounding and associated with the home," the definition of "curtilage"). Given that the garage was part of the curtilage, the automobile exception was irrelevant — Pete was required to get a search warrant before entering the garage and/or inspecting the car inside the garage, unless some other exception to the usual requirement of a search warrant applied. (But if Matt had parked the car on the *street*, Pete *would* have been entitled to do a warrantless search of the car (even its insides) there, in reliance on the automobile exception.)

It's conceivable that the "exigent circumstances" exception might apply. But since Pete could have just remained in front of the house to ensure that no one drove the Jaguar away (while radioing for someone else to obtain the search warrant), it's unlikely that a court would find that these facts qualified for this exemption. There are no other exceptions to the search warrant requirement that might plausibly apply here, so a warrant was required before the search began.

7. **(a) The "plain view" doctrine.** Under this doctrine, "objects falling in the plain view of an officer who has a right to be in the position to have that view are subject to seizure and may be introduced in evidence." *Harris v. U.S.* More precisely, where an officer standing where she has a right to be spots something in plain view, no "search" is deemed to have taken place. Therefore, even if the officer got to that spot without having probable cause, there has been no Fourth Amendment violation. (The view does not necessarily entitle the officer to go in and seize the item, it merely assures that the view will not be deemed an unreasonable and thus illegal search.)

(b) No. The plain view doctrine is applicable on these facts. Baker obviously did not violate any law by gathering up the dog and returning it home. Baker was certainly standing where she had a right to be when she stood at the door and looked in after it was opened. Therefore, her spotting of the weapon was not a Fourth Amendment search at all, so her lack of probable cause before the moment where she spotted it is irrelevant. The view itself then supplied probable cause to obtain the warrant, thus making the seizure legal as well.

8. **Yes.** It is true that Officer Baker was lawfully in the living room, which was where the gun was located. But the "plain view" doctrine does not apply here. Jones did not consent to Officer Baker's opening of the closed container, so the contents of that container will not be deemed to have been in plain view — the question is whether one in Jones' position would reasonably have expected a casual social guest to open closed containers, and the answer is almost certainly "no." Since Jones will thus not be found to have consented to Officer Baker's opening of the container, Baker will be deemed to have overstepped her invitation, and the plain view doctrine will not apply. See, e.g., *Walter v. U.S.* (the fact that police were legitimately in possession of a closed package did not mean that they were entitled to open it to see that it contained obscene films).

9.   No. As long as the officer did not violate any laws or engage in shocking conduct, the fact that she was standing in a place where she had a right to be at the time she got the view is dispositive. So the fact that Baker used a ***pretext*** to ring the bell and get her glimpse will not prevent the plain view doctrine from applying.

10.   (a) The "plain view" doctrine. According to the plain view doctrine, a defendant has no reasonable expectation of privacy, and thus no Fourth Amendment interest, in anything that is seen by a police officer "in plain view" while the officer is standing in a place where he has a right to be. When Officer White, standing on the public sidewalk where she had a right to be, saw the marijuana plant, no search occurred.

(b) No. As noted above, White did not commit a Fourth Amendment search by standing on the sidewalk and spotting the marijuana plant, since at the time she did so she was standing in a place where she had the right to be. But spotting the plant did ***not*** automatically give her the right to ***seize*** the plant without a warrant. Once she went onto Desmond's property, entered his house without a warrant, and confiscated the plant, she was then committing a seizure. This seizure, because it was warrantless and did not occur under exigent circumstances, was a violation of the Fourth Amendment's ban on unreasonable seizures. Therefore, Desmond is entitled to get the plants excluded from evidence against him. (Obviously, White should have gone to get a search warrant once she spotted the plants from the sidewalk. If she was worried about the plants being destroyed, she should have had a colleague stand on the sidewalk looking in the window while she went to get the warrant.)

11.   (a) The "plain odor" doctrine. The Supreme Court has at least implied that just as viewing objects that are in "plain view" does not constitute a search, so perceiving the nature of an object by the smell it emits does not constitute a search. See, e.g., *U.S. v. Place* (use of dogs to perform a canine "sniff test" on luggage in an airport does not constitute a Fourth Amendment search of the luggage).

(b) No, probably. The "plain odor" analogy to the "plain view" doctrine, which is pretty clearly valid, probably applies here. If "plain view" were being relied upon, the fact that the officer followed his line of sight into a place where he was not previously authorized to be would probably not be fatal — thus an officer who is entitled to stand in the foyer (perhaps because the owner of the house has consented to his being there), and who then sees an item in plain view in the living room, almost certainly has the right to go into the living room to inspect it more closely. By analogy, one who smells an odor while standing in a place where he has the right to be (the bedroom), probably has the right to "follow his nose" to get to the source. (The right to smell and thus find the body does not by itself automatically give the officer the right to seize the body; but since Officer Piston was already on the premises with a validly-issued warrant, he probably had the right to impound the body as yet another piece of evidence of crime.)

12.   No. The facts here are very similar to those in *Florida v. Harris*. There, the Supreme Court held that a positive signal from a police dog trained in narcotics-sniffing creates probable cause for a drug search, as long as there is evidence that the dog has been properly trained. According to *Harris*, the defendant is entitled to try to show that the dog's in-the-field performance is so inaccurate that a positive signal does not constitute probable cause; but the prosecution does not have the burden to come forward with in-the-field performance statistics (proof of adequate training suffices). So here, the prosecution's evidence that Rover was properly trained, and his skills were kept up-to-date, was enough to establish that his signal gave Oscar probable cause to search the backpack for narcotics. Now, if the episode had begun by Oscar's making an illegal stop of Gina (e.g., stopping her on the street on a random suspicionless hunch that she might be involved in illegality), then the fruit of the search would be excludable no matter how reliable Rover's post-stop signal was, since the police opportunity to get the signal would have derived directly from the illegal stop. But here, it's clear that the encounter was initiated by Gina, not Oscar, so there is no issue about whether police illegality proceeded Rover's sniff and positive signal. Therefore, the marijuana is admissible.

13. No. In *California v. Greenwood*, the Court held that trash (as well as other abandoned property) will normally not be material as to which the owner has an objectively reasonable expectation of privacy. Therefore, when a person puts trash out on the curb to be picked up by the garbage collector, the police may search that trash without a warrant.

14. Yes, probably. The Court in *California v. Greenwood* (see prior answer) seemed to be limiting its holding to trash left at curb-side, or picked up by the actual garbage collector and brought to curb-side. Probably the Court would hold that George, by consenting to have the UC workers come into his back yard, was not thereby consenting to have government agents come onto his property to inspect his (admittedly abandoned) trash. After all, suppose that George's arrangement for trash disposal was that his day maid would come inside the house each morning, and take the trash out to the street — this would almost certainly not constitute consent by George to have government agents come into his house and take the trash away. The area right outside George's house in his back yard is within the "curtilage," and thus has a legitimate expectation of privacy associated with it, so the agents were presumably unlawfully infringing George's privacy by going there even if the ultimate result of their actions was to look at trash which they could have legally looked at had it been in the street.

15. Yes. The Supreme Court has held that an overnight guest normally has a legitimate expectation of privacy in the home where he is staying. *Minnesota v. Olson*. Therefore, the police were required to get a search warrant, just as if the apartment had been owned by Joe. When they did not do so, they violated the warrant requirement, and the marijuana will be deemed the fruits of an illegal search.

16. Both Eric *and* Mimi. As the owner of the car, Eric has the authority to challenge a search of it; the fact that he was not present in the vehicle at the time of the search does not diminish his privacy interest in it. Mimi, too, can challenge the search of the car. Although she was not the owner, she was alone in the vehicle under circumstances in which she had dominion and control over it, including the right to exclude others. This dominion was enough to give her a legitimate expectation of privacy in the vehicle at the time of the search. *Byrd v. U.S.* (By contrast, if Eric had been present in, and driving, the vehicle at the time of the search, Mimi would have been considered a "mere passenger" and, as such, would likely have been found to lack a privacy expectation sufficient to allow her to challenge a search of glove compartment.)

17. Probably not, though it's a very close question. In *Carpenter v. U.S.* (2018), the Supreme Court held that a warrant was necessary to secure from cell phone carriers the CSLI at issue there. In that case, the government received data spanning 127 days, and showing every move of Carpenter's phone during that period. The Court held that this cell site location information ("CSLI") was deep enough, broad enough, and revealing enough that just seven days of it triggered the need for a warrant, because that much CSLI provided such "an intimate window into [Carpenter's] life" as to make the third-party doctrine inapplicable; this data was therefore distinguishable from the data from the far less-revealing data collections in *Smith* and *Miller* (bank records and telephone numbers dialed), where the Court had applied the third-party doctrine. Here, the government requested CSLI data covering one month, a far longer period than the seven days found sufficient to trigger the need for a warrant in *Carpenter* itself. So based solely on this fact, the subpoena here would be so invasive of Marcus' reasonable expectation of privacy that Carpenter suggests that the third-party doctrine would not apply, and that a warrant was required.

However, the above analysis is not sufficient. The *Carpenter* majority emphasized that the privacy interest being infringed by the CSLI demand there was the defendant's privacy interest "in the whole of his physical movements" throughout the full 127-day period. In this problem, by contrast, the subpoena only required the cell phone carrier to give a yes/no answer to whether CSLI indicated that Marcus was within 50 miles of the crime scene at any time during the one-month period and, if the answer was yes, to tell the police where he was, within that radius, and during exactly what time periods. Thus the subpoena did not request a detailed report of the totality of Marcus' movements during this period; in fact, if the CSLI had failed to disclose any presence within the 50-mile radius, the carrier would have reported nothing at all about Marcus' whereabouts. Furthermore, no more than four hours of total CSLI was furnished here. Based on the foregoing, the government would argue that its subpoena did not constitute the sort of pervasive privacy infringement that caused the Court in *Carpenter* to refuse to apply the third-party doctrine. In response, Marcus could claim that responding to the subpoena required the cell phone carrier to conduct an invasive review of the totality of his movements for one month, even though the carrier ended up disclosing to law enforcement only a few locations, over two two-hour time periods.

All in all, this is a close question, on which the Supreme Court would be likely to be split, just as it was in *Carpenter* itself. But the much smaller volume of data furnished to the government here, compared with that in *Carpenter,* would likely be decisive. That is, the volume would probably be just small enough to convince a majority of the Court that the privacy invasion here was enough smaller than in *Carpenter* as to justify treating the situation as being more like the scenario in *Smith/Miller* (third-party doctrine applied) than like that in *Carpenter* (third-party doctrine not applied).

18. Probably not. Terence probably has a reasonable expectation of privacy in the contents of his DNA. So the real question is whether the fact that he surrendered a sample of that DNA to a third party — 23andme — makes a constitutional difference. Until the 2018 decision in *Carpenter v. U.S.*, the answer would have been a clear "no" — the Court had held in a pair of cases from the 1970s (*Smith v. Maryland* and *U.S. v. Miller*) that when a person voluntarily discloses data to a third party, the person is deemed to surrender any reasonable expectation of privacy as to that data. But in *Carpenter*, the Court refused to extend the third-party doctrine to cell site location information ("CSLI"), so the issue is whether the DNA here is similar enough to the CSLI in *Carpenter* as to justify a similar treatment.

In *Carpenter*, the Court expressly noted that its decision was narrow and did not apply in a number of other contexts, such as "tower dumps" or "conventional surveillance techniques and tools, such as security cameras." In refusing to apply the third-party doctrine to the CSLI in *Carpenter*, the majority emphasized that the CSLI there provided "a detailed and comprehensive record" of the defendant's movements for 127 days and profoundly invaded the "privacies of life," including the cell phone user's "familial, political, professional, religious and sexual associations." Here, the genetic profile generated by 23andme arguably has less wide-ranging implications, in that the profile identifies nothing about an individual's political, professional or religious affiliations. However, by providing a blueprint of Terence's genetic make-up, the profile undoubtedly intrudes upon his deeply private and personal information. So based on privacy concerns alone, it's hard to say whether *Carpenter* dictates treating the DNA identification here in the same (protected) way as the CSLI in *Carpenter*.

Here is an additional consideration: in the two pre-*Carpenter* third-party doctrine cases mentioned above, the Court noted that information an individual **voluntarily discloses** to a third party loses privacy protection even if, as with the bank records at issue in *Miller*, the disclosing party assumes the information will be "used only for a limited purpose." Here, Terence voluntarily decided to disclose his DNA to 23andme, and the fact that the website promised confidentiality would not by itself prevent the third-party doctrine from operating. So this factor cuts in favor of applying the third-party doctrine even after *Carpenter*.

One further consideration: the *Carpenter* majority underscored that CSLI is not "voluntarily disclosed" in the conventional sense, since the carrying and use of cell phones is a "pervasive and insistent part of daily life" and thus "indispensable to participation in modern society." By contrast, providing a DNA sample to learn more about one's racial and ethnic heritage *is* truly voluntary in the conventional sense. (Nor is obtaining this knowledge "indispensable to participation in modern society"). In fact, providing such a sample is *more* voluntary than creating the bank records at issue in *U.S. v. Miller* or the phone-numbers-dialed at issue in *Smith v. Maryland*, since those items were linked to core services integral to daily life.

So, all in all, a court is likely to conclude that notwithstanding *Carpenter*, the third-party doctrine should *apply* here so as to free the police from the need to procure a search warrant prior to issuing their subpoena.

19. Yes, probably. This fact pattern is loosely based on a post-*Carpenter* lower-court decision, *Naperville Smart Meter Awareness v. City of Naperville*, 900 F.3d 521 (7th Cir. 2018). In that case, an association of homeowners argued that the collection of similar smart-meter data by a city's publicly-owned utility violated the owners' Fourth Amendment rights. The court held that the third-party doctrine should not apply to the smart-meter data collected by the utility, in part because, like the phone customer whose CSLI was collected in *Carpenter*, the homeowners here had no choice but to share their data with the city. The court also found that smart-meter data was the kind of modern technology that implicates the Fourth Amendment under *Kyllo*: (1) smart meters are not in general public use, since they have been adopted only by a small portion of utilities; and (2) they provide detailed information about what is going on inside individuals' residences. However, the court in *Naperville* concluded that although the collection of smart-meter data constituted a "search" for Fourth Amendment purposes, the fact that the search was warrantless was not enough to make it an "unreasonable" search, since the data was viewed only by workers at the city-owned public utility, not by law enforcement. But if the utility workers in *Naperville* had had "prosecutorial intent" (i.e., an intent to investigate a suspected crime) when the utility collected and viewed the data, then presumably a warrant *would* have been required, since no exception to the warrant requirement would have applied.

Here, by contrast, the data was subpoenaed by law enforcement for the purpose of investigating Jerry for a suspected crime. In other words, the police *were* acting here with "prosecutorial intent." That fact, coupled with the fact that *Naperville* court treated the collection of similar data as a Fourth Amendment search, suggests that here, the police *were* required to get a search warrant.

20. Yes. Any trustworthy information may be considered in determining whether probable cause to search or arrest exists, even if the information would ***not be admissible*** at trial. Thus the police may use hearsay information, or even a prior criminal record of the suspect, as part of their showing of probable cause.

21. No. In general, the issue is whether the *magistrate* acted properly — that is, whether detailed assertions making out probable cause are presented to the magistrate — not whether the officer acted properly. So it will normally not matter that false information is supplied to the magistrate. This is true even where the officer acted negligently in not catching the error. (But if the officer intentionally perjured himself in the affidavit, or acted recklessly in not catching the error, the result will probably be different.)

22. Yes, probably. The Fourth Amendment provides that no warrant shall issue except one "***particularly describing*** the…things to be seized." Probably the warrant here was so broad as to violate this requirement. Clearly the warrant could have been limited to records relating to Desmond's dealings with Edward, or in the worst case, records dealing with payments remitted to insurance companies on behalf of customers. The warrant here was utterly unparticular — it asked for all books and records, yet there is very little in an insurance office except books and records. Also, where the items seized have First Amendment value (like the diary here), the requirement of specificity is usually enforced somewhat more strictly.

23. Yes, probably. The police may protect themselves while performing a search, in the sense that they may check any person in control of the premises who is likely to be dangerous. But where a person simply happens to be on the premises to be searched, and appears not to have any connection with the criminal activity that gave rise to the warrant, that person may not be searched or frisked. Since Doug, here, seemed to be an ordinary patron unconnected to any illegal betting that may have been going on on the premises, the police probably did not have the right to stop him and frisk him. See *Ybarra v. Illinois* (warrant to search a bar and its bartender did not allow the police to frisk each patron).

24. No. Even though "Lilies" was not mentioned in the warrant, the police were entitled to seize it because it was in plain view while they were carrying out their lawfully-issued warrant for "Irises." It is not required, for application of the plain view doctrine, that the police's discovery of an item in plain view be "inadvertent," so the fact that the police knew in advance that they were just as likely to find "Lilies," which was not named in the warrant, does not matter. See *Horton v. California*.

25. Yes. The police are not permitted to go beyond the scope of the warrant. They may seize items that they find in plain view while they are properly executing the warrant (as happened in the prior question). But once they have found what they came for, they must stop. Similarly, if they are looking for something large, like a human body, they may not look in places that could not possibly hold the item they are looking for (e.g., small closed containers).

26. No. Arrest warrants are as a general rule not constitutionally required. This is true even where the police have sufficient advance notice that procurement of a warrant would not jeopardize the arrest. See *U.S. v. Watson.*

27. Yes. The only situation in which an arrest warrant may be constitutionally required is where the police wish to ***enter private premises*** to arrest a suspect. If there are no exigent circumstances (e.g., a serious threat that the suspect will flee or will destroy evidence), the police may not enter a private home to make a warrantless arrest.

28. No, probably. The police may enter even private premises to make a warrantless arrest, if there are ***exigent circumstances*** that make it impractical for the police to delay the entry and arrest until they can obtain a warrant. Since the crime was a serious one here, and there was reason to believe that Wilson might flee at any moment, the requisite exigent circumstances seem present. If the police were entitled to enter Wilson's premises at all for this purpose, they were entitled to go throughout the house until they found him, so the fact that they intruded further than in the prior question is irrelevant. Once they arrested him, they were entitled to search the area around his control as a search incident to arrest (at least for purposes of protecting themselves), and were entitled to seize any weapon they found as a result of that limited search.

29. Yes, probably. The police will, of course, argue that the search took place incident to a valid arrest, and that the fact that there was no search warrant is therefore irrelevant. But the search-incident-to-arrest exception to the normal requirement of a search warrant (an exception that stems from *Chimel v. California*) covers only the area within the arrestee's ***possible control***. Since there were two officers, and since Fred was already handcuffed to the bed, it was very unlikely that Fred could get into the other bedroom to seize any weapon that might have been present there. Also, it was quite unlikely that any weapon would be in something as small as the container here. Therefore, it seems very unlikely that the search of that container aided the police's interest in protecting their safety or protecting against the destruction of evidence, the two reasons for the search-incident-to-arrest exception.

30. No, probably. The search of the closets here cannot be justified as a search incident to the arrest of Gerald, since the area of the search went far beyond any area to which Gerald could possibly have had ready access once he was handcuffed. But the Supreme Court has held that once an arrest takes place in the suspect's home, the officers may conduct a ***protective sweep*** of all or part of the premises, if they have a "reasonable belief" based on "specific and articulable facts" that ***another person*** who might be dangerous to the officer may be present in the areas to be swept. *Maryland v. Buie.*

While doing such a protective sweep, the police may not make a detailed search of the premises, merely a cursory look to make sure that there is no one else around who may be dangerous. This seems to be what the officer was doing, since Harold was known to live at that address and thought to be possibly dangerous; also, the degree of risk was magnified by the fact that Gerald was found in the basement holding a knife, indicating that he had somehow learned of the possibility of the arrest (so that he could have tipped off Harold as well). Since weapons were found in a closet large enough to hold a man, and thus large enough to be a proper subject of the protective sweep, the officer probably acted legally in opening that closet. Once he rightfully opened the closet, he had the right to seize anything that was in plain view, including the murder weapon.

31.   No. A stop of a driver is not made "unreasonable" (and thus does not violate the Fourth Amendment) merely because the stop was based upon a minor traffic violation that served as a pretext for a stop made for some other purpose. *Whren v. U.S.* In other words, the real reason for the stop is ***irrelevant*** — once a police officer has probable cause to believe that even a minor traffic violation has occurred, he may stop the vehicle even though the stop is being used for the purpose of seeking evidence of some other crime for which the police officer has no probable cause or even reasonable suspicion. If the stop and its consequences then give the officer probable cause to believe that contraband or evidence of crime may be found in the car, the officer may go on to make a warrantless search.

In this "pretext stop" situation, you must look for ***two elements***: (a) a ***valid reason for the original stop*** (i.e., probable cause to believe some sort of offense has been committed, or at least an objective reason for suspecting criminality [see "stop and frisk"]); and (b) something (perhaps something that only occurs as a result of the stop) that then gives the stopping officer ***probable cause*** to conduct a ***warrantless search***. For instance, suppose Davies had stopped Johnson, written the ticket, and then searched the entire car *without* first seeing the handgun under the front passenger seat. Under these facts, (b) would not be satisfied, and Davies would *not* have had probable cause to conduct a warrantless search of the car; therefore, the seizure of the handguns *would* be suppressed at trial. See *Knowles v. Iowa* (where officer makes stop for traffic ticket and does not make arrest, officer may not without more conduct search of car's interior).

32.   Yes. The arrest of John was clearly proper — since the police directly observed the speeding, they had probable cause to arrest John for it. But the legal consequences of that arrest — in terms of what search of the car the police were entitled to perform — changed dramatically in 2009. Prior to 2009, the law (under *N.Y. v. Belton* (1981)) was that if the stop of a car and the arrest of the driver were valid, the police could automatically, incident to the arrest, make a search of the car's entire passenger compartment, and of the contents of any containers found in that compartment. But in *Arizona v. Gant* (2009), the Court effectively overruled *Belton*. *Gant* holds that even where the police make a custodial arrest of the driver, if they are able to secure the driver so that he cannot gain access to the passenger compartment, the police may not then use the search-incident-to-arrest rationale to search the compartment.

So here, where the arresting officers had handcuffed John to the patrol car, they did not have to worry that he could get access to the passenger compartment. Consequently, the officers could not search the passenger compartment incident to John's arrest, even though the arrest was proper. Nor was there any other exception justifying a warrantless and without-probable-cause search of the compartment; for instance, at the moment the police started that search they had no probable cause to suspect that drugs or contraband would be found. (On the other hand, if the police had found drugs on John's person when they properly searched his person pursuant to the arrest, then this discovery *would* have supplied probable cause to search the passenger compartment for drugs; there would still be an issue about whether a warrant was required, but the mobility of the car, and the easy destructibility of any evidence or contraband in it, meant that the circumstances qualified for the exigent-circumstances exception to the requirement of a warrant, in which event the follow-on search of the compartment would have been valid.)

33. No. The 2009 decision in *Arizona v. Gant* says that it is no longer the case that when the police make a valid custodial arrest of a driver and ensure he has no further access to the passenger compartment, they have the automatic right to search the entire compartment incident to that arrest. (By the way, even pre-*Gant*, the search-incident-to-arrest rule would have only extended to the passenger compartment, not to the trunk.) However, *Gant* also says that if the police who are making the arrest "reasonabl[y] believe that evidence *relevant to the crime of arrest* might be found in the vehicle," they may use the search-incident-to-arrest rationale as authority for searching any part of the vehicle (and any containers found in the vehicle) where such evidence might be found, even though the vehicle is no longer within the immediate control of the arrested driver. This "reasonable belief that evidence might be found" standard is clearly less-demanding than "probable cause."

The police here qualify under this rule. The facts tell us that Officer Hingham had a "reasonable suspicion" that the trunk might contain prescription-drug vials, and that those vials, if they were found, might contain trace evidence of heroin. Since Jim was being arrested for selling heroin from prescription-drug vials, Hingham's suspicions related to the "crime of arrest." Therefore, even though Hingham did not have full probable cause to believe the vials would contain contraband or evidence of crime, he was entitled to make a search incident to arrest of the trunk (the place to which the "reasonable suspicion" pointed), and then to make a search of any containers in the trunk if such suspected evidence of the crime of arrest (heroin sales) might be found in those containers. Once he found the vials, any contraband they turned out to contain could be the basis for criminal charges as to a crime (meth distribution) different from the crime of arrest (heroin trafficking), to which the reasonable-suspicion pertained.

34. Yes. The Supreme Court has recognized an exception to the general search-incident-to-arrest doctrine for ***digital cell phone data***, and this exception would almost certainly be extended to cover digital data on laptops.

Under the general search-incident-to-arrest exception to the requirement of a search warrant, the Supreme Court has long allowed the arresting officer to seize and search any ***physical item*** found on the person of the arrestee, or within the arrestee's reasonable area of control. A backpack carried by the arrestee would almost certainly qualify, so Glower would have been justified in opening and examining, say, a letter or photo found in hard-copy form inside the backpack. But in a major 2014 decision, *Riley v. California*, the Court decided that the incident-to-arrest doctrine does **not** authorize the police to make a warrantless search of digital data on a cell phone, even incident to a perfectly legal arrest — the Court's rationale was that people carry such huge amounts of personal data on their cell phones that the interference with privacy that would result from warrantless searches of that data would be unreasonably large. Although *Riley* applies expressly only to data on cell phones, the Court's reasoning would almost certainly apply to the potentially even larger amounts of data on a laptop computer. Therefore, the Supreme Court would almost certainly hold that even though the arrest here was proper and made with probable cause, the police were required to obtain a search warrant before opening the laptop and examining its digital contents. If there were particular *exigent circumstances* present — e.g., if Glower had had reason to believe that the laptop was set up to erase its contents within a short period of time — those circumstances might have justified Glower's immediate examination of the data without first seeking a warrant; but the fact pattern, by telling you that Denton did not allege any "other material facts" in his suppression motion, indicates that no such exigent circumstances existed.

35. **(a) No.** The Supreme Court has held that when the police have made a proper arrest for drunk driving (i.e., one supported by probable cause), they do not violate the arrestee's Fourth Amendment rights by requiring her to submit to a breathalyzer test as a form of search incident to arrest. *Birchfield v. North Dakota* (2016). That's because a breathalyzer test — which requires the suspect to blow into a tube for a few seconds — is relatively non-intrusive, and the governmental need to deter drunk driving is very great. Since it would not be a violation of Della's Fourth Amendment rights for the police, after lawfully arresting her on drunk-driving charges, to make a warrantless demand that she undergo the breathalyzer test, it also was not a violation of her rights for the state to make her refusal to take such a test a crime. *Id.*

(b) Yes. In the same case referred to in part (a) above (*Birchfield v. No. Dakota*), the Supreme Court held that in contrast to a breathalyzer test, a *blood test* is so intrusive — and the information it supplies is so unlikely to be materially more useful than information from a breathalyzer test — that it *does* violate the Fourth Amendment rights of a drunk-driving arrestee to be forced to undergo such a test if the police have not procured a search warrant. In other words, in the case of drunk-driving arrests, the search-incident-to-arrest doctrine does *not* cover a search that takes the form of a blood test. Therefore, Graham either should have administered a warrantless breathalyzer test, or kept Della in custody until Graham was able to get a magistrate to issue a search warrant. (Had there been *exigent circumstances*, such as reasonable grounds to test for other substances of abuse that wouldn't be revealed by breathalyzer test, coupled with too little time to procure a search warrant before these other substances would likely have disappeared from Della's bloodstream, the exigent-circumstances exception to the warrant requirement might have applied; but there is no indication on our facts that any such exigent circumstances existed, and *Birchfield* makes it clear that the ordinary incident-to-arrest exception to the warrant requirement does not apply to blood tests.)

36. **No, probably.** The taking of the blood sample here clearly constituted a Fourth Amendment "seizure." Since it was done without a warrant, it violated Denker's Fourth Amendment rights unless some exception to the usual requirement of a search warrant applies. The search-incident-to-arrest exception does not apply, because there was no formal arrest (even though there was probable cause for one).

However, the Supreme Court has recognized that where probable cause to search exists, and where *exigent circumstances* make it impractical to take the time to procure a search warrant, an exception to the warrant requirement will be recognized. In the case of a Blood Alcohol Concentration (BAC) test to support a drunk-driving charge, the Court has held that the police do not have a *"per se"* or automatic right to carry out a warrantless taking of blood. *Missouri v. McNeely* (2013). Rather, each BAC-testing case is to be decided on its own facts — the trial court is to decide whether the facts of that particular situation indicated that a delay for getting a warrant would have substantially prejudiced the usefulness of the BAC test. *Id.*

Here, given Griswold's honest error about where Denker was being taken, the substantial loss of time before Griswold even got to the right hospital to make the arrest, and the unavailability of a quick warrant in this rural area, a court would probably hold that the likelihood of a further lowering of Denker's BAC constituted exigent circumstances, thus excusing the failure to take the time to get a warrant.

37. No. Normally, a police officer may not enter a private home to make a search, even with probable cause, unless a warrant has been procured. One of the common exceptions to this rule is for a search incident to arrest, but the police may ordinarily not enter a private dwelling to make an arrest without an arrest warrant. However, there is an exception to both the search warrant and arrest warrant requirements where the police enter a private dwelling in ***"hot pursuit"*** of a suspect. Since Henkle was in hot pursuit of Eugene at the time she entered the house, the exception applies. Since she was entitled to be in the house while looking for him, anything she saw there could be seized without a search warrant under the "plain view" doctrine. See *Warden v. Hayden*, allowing the seizure of evidence under similar "hot pursuit" circumstances.

38. No. This was a warrantless search, so Fred's motion must be granted unless some exception to the search warrant requirement applies. The search-incident-to-arrest rationale cannot apply, since the search took place a significant time after the arrest. Nor does the "routine inventory search" exception apply (see *Illinois v. Lafayette*), since there is nothing in the facts to suggest that the car's contents were being subjected to a routine inventory itemization.

But in a series of cases, the Supreme Court has recognized a ***"vehicle impoundment"*** or "station house search" exception to the warrant requirement: where the police have probable cause to both search and seize the car, and they exercise the right to seize it by taking it to the police station, they need not get a warrant before later searching the car's contents. See, e.g., *Chambers v. Maroney*, allowing a warrantless station-house search of the impounded car under similar circumstances. This exception to the warrant requirement for an impounded vehicle seems to stem from the Supreme Court's perception that "one has a lesser expectation of privacy in a motor vehicle because its function is transportation and it seldom serves as one's residence or the repository of personal effects...." *U.S. v. Chadwick.*

39. No, probably. As set forth in the prior answer, the Supreme Court has generally recognized an exception (stemming from *Chambers v. Maroney*) to the search warrant requirement where an automobile is seized at the time of its owner's arrest, then taken to the police station and searched there. The question is whether the fact that the police had lots of time to get a warrant and didn't bother to do so makes a difference. *Florida v. White* strongly suggests that the answer is no, i.e., that the failure to get a warrant when there is time to do so does not make the eventual warrantless seizure unlawful. (In *Fla. v. White*, the police failed to get a warrant to seize a car that they knew was used for drug dealing; this failure did not make the police's later seizure of the car under state forfeiture laws a violation of the owner's Fourth Amendment rights.)

40. No, probably. For the police conduct here to be valid, two different rules must be combined. First, the doctrine of *Carroll v. U.S.* holds that where the police stop a car and need to perform a search in order to preserve evidence (because the car can quickly be driven out of the jurisdiction), they may search the car without a warrant even though no arrest has been made. (They must have probable cause to make the search, however.) Second, the Court held in *U.S. v. Ross* that where a warrantless search (with probable cause) of a lawfully-stopped vehicle is allowed (i.e., the *Carroll* doctrine applies), the police may also open any ***closed container*** which they find during the search, on the theory that the intrusion is not materially greater. Since Jackson had probable cause to stop the vehicle, and then probable cause to search it, he was also entitled to open containers that he found in it. This was true even though he had not arrested Leonard, so that the search-incident-to-arrest rationale does not apply.

41. **No.** If a car is impounded because it has been towed for some kind of traffic or parking violation, the car may be subjected to a warrantless *"inventory search."* This is true even though the police do not have probable cause at the time they make the search. *South Dakota v. Opperman.* (In fact, the police may even open closed containers found in the vehicle, if they do so as part of standardized procedures that apply to every towed or impounded car. *Colorado v. Bertine.*)

42. **No.** This is a classic situation demonstrating that where a person *voluntarily consents* to a search, any Fourth Amendment objections she might have are waived. Nothing in the facts suggests that Norma's consent was other than voluntary — there is no sign, for instance, of coercion or deception by Baines. The fact that Baines did not give Norma her *Miranda* warnings or otherwise advise her of the possible consequences of the search is irrelevant — there was no arrest, so *Miranda* warnings were not required, and the Supreme Court has never held that anything like the *Miranda* warnings must be given before permission to search is requested. Nor does it make any difference that Norma thought she had not committed a crime.

43. **No.** "When an individual gives consent to another to intrude into an area or activity otherwise protected by the Fourth Amendment, aware that he will thereby reveal to this other person either criminal conduct or evidence of such conduct, that consent is not vitiated merely because it would not have been given but for the non-disclosure or affirmative misrepresentation which made the consenting party unaware of the other person's identity as a police officer or police agent." L&I, p. 207. Here, Norma knew, at the time she let Baines into the house, that she would thereby expose her art fraud to him. The fact that she didn't know he was a police officer should make no difference. Her consent will be deemed "voluntary," and thus effective.

44. **Yes.** Where the consent to search was procured after the officer falsely stated that he had a search warrant, the consent will be deemed to be invalid. *Bumper v. North Carolina.* In this case, it is easy to see that the person's consent is not really "voluntary" — the person is or may be responding to the fact that a refusal to consent will be meaningless because the officer has a warrant.

45. **No.** If the third person and the defendant have joint authority over the premises or over an object, the third party's consent to a search (given while the defendant is absent) will normally be binding on the defendant. Where a husband and wife live together, they will almost always be presumed to have joint control over the premises, and the facts here tell us that Henry and Wanda both had ownership and control over the rifle. Therefore, Wanda had authority to consent to the search of the premises and the search and seizure of the rifle, so her consent will be binding on Henry. The fact that Wanda was mistaken about her husband's guilt or the danger from consenting to a search is irrelevant.

46. **Yes.** This is not a case in which the two parties, Troy and Larry, had "joint authority" over the premises. Instead, Troy had a vastly greater right of access to, and expectation of privacy in, his bedroom. Therefore, Larry did not have joint authority over the room, or even "apparent" authority (since it should have been clear to the police that Larry was merely a landlord, not a joint occupant, of the bedroom). Therefore, Larry's consent was not effective vis-a-vis Troy. See *Stoner v. California* (the management of a hotel may not consent to a search of a guest's room).

47. **(a) The "stop and frisk" doctrine.** By this doctrine, an officer may stop and briefly detain a person, even without probable cause for an arrest, if the officer has an ***articulable reason, based on objective facts,*** for suspecting that the person may have committed a crime. (The officer may also do a superficial frisk of the suspect if he has reason to believe the suspect dangerous, an aspect not at issue on these facts.)

(b) No. The "stop and frisk" doctrine applies here. The stop of Marla was certainly a Fourth Amendment "seizure," since it was reasonably apparent to Marla that she was not free to leave without answering Noonan's questions. However, this is a situation in which the "stop and frisk" doctrine makes the Fourth Amendment seizure a "reasonable" one even though there was not full probable cause for an arrest. Noonan certainly had a number of objective reasons for suspecting that Marla might have something to do with the break-in. The fact that the break-in had just occurred, that the alarm had just started, that Marla was walking more rapidly than a person usually would, and that she was walking away from the car holding a bag that might easily contain a radio — all of these factors were, when taken together, enough to raise the kind of "reasonable hunch" that would justify at least a brief stop. (For instance, *Ill. v. Wardlow* establishes that the fact that a person appears to be fleeing from the police is a factor that will usually significantly raise an officer's level of suspicion.)

And, by the way, the fact that each individual factor that Noonan relied on (e.g., fast walking away from a car) was "innocent" or "consistent with lawful behavior" doesn't change this — the reasonableness of the suspicion is evaluated under the ***"totality of the circumstances"*** standard (see *U.S. v. Arvizu*), and under the totality of circumstances here Noonan's suspicion was reasonable.

Then, once Marla refused to answer the questions, ran away, and left a bag holding a radio, Noonan of course now had probable cause to arrest her.

48. No. This question, at first glance, seems to involve the issue of whether Nelson had enough suspicion to make a "stop" of the *Terry* "stop and frisk" variety. However, in reality, no stop (or other Fourth Amendment seizure) occurred at all. In deciding whether a Fourth Amendment seizure has occurred, the Supreme Court uses a "reasonable person" test, by which a seizure has occurred only "if, in view of all of the circumstances surrounding the incident, a reasonable person would have believed that he was not free to leave." *U.S. v. Mendenhall*.

Vern did not know, initially, that Nelson was a police officer, or that he was anything other than what he purported to be, which was a civilian who wanted directions. Therefore, a reasonable person in Vern's position would have believed that he was free to disregard the request for information and to drive on. Since Vern's freedom of motion was not circumscribed, there was no Fourth Amendment "seizure" of his person or of his vehicle, up till the moment where Nelson saw the hot-wiring and made the arrest. Therefore, it didn't matter that Nelson had absolutely no rational grounds for suspicion at the time he walked up to the car and requested the information.

49. Yes, probably. Here, there was a true "seizure" within the meaning of the Fourth Amendment — Vern knew he was dealing with a police officer, and a reasonable person in his position would have understood that he was not free to disregard Nelson's request and drive away. Therefore, the "stop" violated the Fourth Amendment unless Nelson had a "reasonable suspicion, based on objective facts, that the [suspect] is involved in criminal activity." *Brown v.*

Texas. The facts tell us that he did not — for instance, the fact that Vern "looked suspicious" and was seen driving in a high crime area will not suffice to justify a stop. Since Nelson would not have gotten his "plain view" through the window if he had not made the stop, and since the stop was an unreasonable seizure (even though it did not amount to a full arrest), presumably the fruits of that plain view will be suppressed.

50. Yes, probably. The initial stop probably did not violate the Fourth Amendment — the facts here suggest that Mulroney had "reasonable suspicion, based on objective facts" that the computer may have been stolen and that Evan either stole it or knew that it was stolen. She was therefore entitled to detain him briefly, and to question him briefly. But she was almost certainly not entitled to require him to come to the station house to answer additional questions — this was such a more intrusive procedure, and of such greater duration, that it probably raised the episode from a "stop" to a full-fledged arrest, for which probable cause was required. See *Hayes v. Florida*, holding that a station-house detention, even though brief and unaccompanied by interrogation, is "sufficiently like [an] arrest to invoke the traditional rule that arrests may constitutionally be made only on probable cause."

There is some chance that the prosecutor can succeed with the argument that the police worked as rapidly and unintrusively as possible, consistent with their need to discover whether a particular computer with a particular serial number was indeed stolen. But this argument will probably be rejected on the grounds that the time and distance were simply too great to constitute a stop. Since Evan confessed only after the police learned that the computer was stolen, he has a very good chance of having his confession ruled the fruit of the illegal pseudo-arrest.

51. Yes, probably. Pasternak was acting properly when he detained Fiona, since his suspicions were sufficiently reasonable and objective that they justified a "stop," even though not a full-fledged arrest. An officer, once he has made a lawful stop, is entitled to do a protective two-part frisk (first a pat-down, then a reaching under the surface if the pat-down discloses something), provided that the pat-down is for a ***weapon***. Even where an officer has made a legitimate stop, he may not perform a frisk whose sole purpose is to find contraband or evidence. *Ybarra v. Illinois.* Since Pasternak did not suspect that Fiona was armed or dangerous, and he was merely frisking her to find the contraband, this frisk was unlawful since he did not have probable cause to arrest her or probable cause to believe that he might find contraband. Because the frisk went beyond the bounds of the Fourth Amendment, the fruits from that frisk (the packet) must be suppressed.

52. Yes, probably. On these facts, as opposed to those of the prior question, Pasternak was at least justified in conducting the initial pat-down to discover whether Fiona carried a weapon. But since Pasternak was looking for a knife or a gun (and certainly knew that virtually any dangerous weapon would have to be hard), he could not have believed that the soft object he was feeling could be a weapon. The second stage of a frisk (the reaching in to take out the item that was located through the pat-down) may only be accomplished to take out something that might reasonably be a weapon. So Pasternak was not entitled to reach into Fiona's pocket to retrieve the soft parcel.

53. (a) No. First, the officers were justified in performing a "stop" of Gerard's car — relatively few cars are both blue and have a license plate starting with "JQ," so this combination of factors was enough to justify a stop, even though it did not amount to probable cause for a search or arrest. Quarles was also within his rights in asking Gerard to leave the car, since that was a reasonable safety measure; the description of the bank robber as "armed and presumed dangerous" was enough to justify Quarles in performing the pat-down of Gerard.

The Supreme Court has also held that in circumstances where the officer makes a *Terry*-like stop of a vehicle and believes that the driver may be dangerous, the officer can not only perform the pat-down but also check the inside of the passenger compartment (even if the driver has been asked to exit); see *Michigan v. Long*, to this effect. (And nothing in *Arizona v. Gant*, eliminating the police's automatic right to search the passenger compartment incident to a driver's arrest, changes this fact, since the search here was a *Terry/Long* officer-safety check, not a search incident to arrest.) Since Quarles had the right to look for weapons (although not to look for the purpose of finding contraband or evidence), he was entitled to seize any contraband that he found in plain view while performing this weapons scan. Therefore, the marijuana should be admissible.

(b) No. As discussed in part (a), the officers were justified in performing a "stop" of the car. Once a proper *Terry/Adams*-style stop of a vehicle occurs, the police are entitled to do a pat-down of any passenger — even one as to whom they have no suspicion of wrongdoing — as long as the police have a reasonable suspicion that the passenger may be armed and dangerous. *Arizona v. Johnson* (2009). Once Officer Ramon saw Howard's tattoo and understood that it marked Howard as a member of the Tweets, Ramon's knowledge that Tweets members typically carry switchblades gave him a reasonable suspicion that Howard might be armed and dangerous. (In *Johnson* itself, for instance, the officer's discovery that the passenger was a member of the often-violent Crips gang and had been in prison was enough to create a reasonable suspicion that the passenger might be armed and dangerous.) Therefore, Ramon was permitted to pat Howard down for weapons. Since he reasonably thought the hard object he felt was a weapon, he was entitled to pull it (a Fourth Amendment seizure) from Howard's pocket. At that point, even though the item turned out to be a different sort of weapon than he had suspected, it was admissible since it had been obtained by proper stop-and-frisk procedures.

54. Yes. The Supreme Court has held that the police may not follow a practice of randomly stopping cars in order to check such things as licensing and registration. *Delaware v. Prouse*. Only if the officer has some objective suspicion that the particular driver has committed an offense, may he stop the car. (A check-point scheme where *every* car was stopped would pass muster; the problem comes where each officer is given discretion about which cars to stop randomly.)

55. No. The Supreme Court has held that when the police make an arrest on probable cause for a serious offense, they may collect a DNA sample from the inside of the arrestee's cheek as part of their routine booking procedure. *Maryland v. King* (2013). The taking of such a sample constitutes a Fourth Amendment search, but that search is deemed to be a ***"reasonable"*** one even though warrantless, because of the search's limited intrusiveness, its high value to law enforcement for identification of the person who has been arrested, and the reduced reasonable expectation of privacy on the part of one arrested for a serious crime. Once the police have properly collected the sample, *King* says that they may use it to match samples from unsolved crimes, apparently without there being any incremental Fourth Amendment implications. So nothing that happened here violated Devon's Fourth Amendment rights.

56. Yes. Bugging and wiretapping are "searches," as the term is used in the Fourth Amendment. Therefore, absent exigent circumstances, bugging and wiretapping may not occur except on probable cause, and with a warrant. In fact, a federal statute, so-called "Title III," (18 U.S.C. §§ 2510-20) prohibits all eavesdropping and wiretapping without a court order. So the bugging here clearly violates both Title III and the Fourth Amendment, and Louie can keep his bugged statement out of evidence.

57. No. The Supreme Court has held that *"secret agents"* — that is, people who engage in conversations with a suspect, without the suspect's knowing that the other party is a police officer or informant — are not conducting "searches," and thus cannot violate the Fourth Amendment. This is true whether the agent is "bugged" or "unbugged." See, e.g., *U.S. v. White.* Furthermore, the prohibitions against bugging and wiretapping contained in Title III expressly exclude (and thus permit) interceptions made by or with the *consent of a party to the conversation.* So even though Harriet was a police officer, and Melvin did not know this, the recording of Melvin's statement does not violate either the Fourth Amendment or Title III. (However, if the bug had been used to record a conversation between Melvin and someone else, at which Harriet was not present, then Title III would apply and the statement could not be used — what makes the difference here is that Harriet was a party to the communication being intercepted.)

58. No, because Claude was not given his *Miranda* warnings. This is a classic illustration of when *Miranda* warnings must be given: The suspect was in custody, and he was questioned by the police; therefore, the police were required to tell him: (1) that he had the right to remain silent, (2) that anything he said could be used against him in a court of law, (3) that he had the right to have an attorney present before any questioning, and (4) that if he could not afford an attorney, one would be appointed for him before questioning, if he wished. Since Claude was not given these warnings, nothing he said may be used against him. It doesn't matter that Claude's confession was in a sense "voluntary," rather than "coerced" — *Miranda* is a "bright line," i.e., automatic, rule.

59. No. It is true that Dennis was in "custody" at the time he made his statement, and that his statement was in response to a question asked by someone who was in fact a police officer. Thus the formal requirements for *Miranda* (custody and police interrogation) seem to be met. However, the Supreme Court has held that where the defendant talks to an undercover agent or a government informant, and the defendant does not *know* that he is talking to a law enforcement officer, no "custodial interrogation" will be deemed to have taken place, even if the exchange occurs while the defendant is in jail. Therefore, *Miranda* warnings do not have to be given in this situation. See *Illinois v. Perkins*, involving facts similar to those in this question.

60. No, probably. The issue, of course, is whether Elvira was "in custody" at the time she made the statement. The Supreme Court follows an "objective" standard for determining whether somebody is in custody for *Miranda* purposes: the suspect will be deemed to have been in custody if a *reasonable person* in the suspect's position would have *understood that he or she was not free to go.* See *Berkemer v. McCarty*, establishing this test.

Here, the situation probably amounted to custody by this standard — a reasonable person in Elvira's positions, after being told that she could not (or at least should not) go to the grocery store, would probably have felt that she was not free to leave or to evict Bess whenever she wanted. Since Elvira was in custody, and since Bess was a police officer interrogating her (and Elvira knew that Bess was a police officer), the requirements for *Miranda* warnings were satisfied. Since those warnings were not given, her statement may not be introduced against her as part of the prosecution's case in chief.

61. Yes. The requirement of *Miranda* warnings is triggered wherever the police conduct a custodial interrogation of someone who they think *may* have something to do with or know something about a possible crime. The fact that the police are not certain that a crime has been committed, or the fact that the investigation has not "focused" on the person being interrogated, does not make a difference. See *Stansbury v. California*. Since Frank was clearly in custody here (in the sense that a reasonable person in his position would have known that he was not free to leave without answering the questions), and since he was clearly being interrogated by a police officer, *Miranda* warnings needed to be given.

62. No, probably. Again, the issue is whether this interrogation was "custodial." The Supreme Court has held that ordinary stops of a driver for minor traffic violations normally will not constitute a taking into custody, for *Miranda* purposes. See *Berkemer v. McCarty*, holding that since such stops are generally temporary and brief, and the motorist knows that he will probably be allowed to go on his way, *Miranda* warnings do not have to be given. Here, Jermaine had no reason to believe (at least, no reason apart from her own knowledge that she had committed a crime) that this was anything other than a routine traffic stop that would allow her to go on her way when she promised to get the tail light fixed. She had no reason to believe that she had been arrested or would be arrested. Therefore, the coercive element usually associated with custodial interrogation was not present here, and it is unlikely that the court would find that *Miranda* warnings had to be given.

63. Yes. There is no **"minor crimes"** exception to the *Miranda* requirement — if an interrogation meets all of the standard requirements for *Miranda* warnings (especially the requirement that the suspect be "in custody"), these warnings must be given no matter how minor the crime, and regardless of the fact that no jail sentence may be imposed for it. *Berkemer v. McCarty*.

64. (a) That Jill's statement was not in response to any "interrogation." It is not enough that the suspect makes an incriminating statement while in custody — *Miranda* only applies where there is "interrogation" during the custody. The prosecutor should argue that Detective Reynolds may have made statements, but he did not ask questions, so that there was no interrogation.

(b) No, probably. The Supreme Court has held that there can be "interrogation" even though there is no direct questioning. The Court has held that "the term 'interrogation'...refers not only to express questioning, but also to any words or actions on the part of the police (other than those normally attendant to arrest and custody) that the police ***should know are reasonably likely to elicit*** an ***incriminating response*** from a suspect." *Rhode Island v. Innis*. Here, Reynolds, by going into such detail about the evidence the police had against Jill, and by mentioning how desirable it would be if Jill were to confess, should probably have known that some incriminating response was likely to be made by Jill in response. The fact that Reynolds volunteered the information on his own, without stating it in response to a question by Jill, further reinforces the argument that Jill must have understood Reynolds' statements as an attempt to get her to talk.

65. (a) The "public safety" exception to *Miranda*. The Supreme Court has recognized a "public safety" exception to the *Miranda* rule — *Miranda* warnings are simply unnecessary prior to questioning that is "reasonably prompted by a concern for the public safety." *New York v. Quarles*.

(b) Yes. Ken was certainly in custody at the time he made the statement, and he certainly made the statement in response to interrogation. But since it was quite possible that other accomplices were holding Nell, and that time might be of the essence in saving her from further harm, the court would almost certainly find that the "public safety" exception applied here.

66. No. The defendant's silence and his subsequent answering of questions, without anything more, will never be held to be a valid waiver of the right to remain silent or of the right to have a lawyer present.

67. Yes. Waivers of *Miranda* rights may be implied, not just express. In particular, there are situations in which the suspect's actions and words justify the inference that he waived his right to silence. As the prior question shows, a suspect's mere silence, followed by the answering of a question, is not enough to demonstrate a waiver. But the conduct of answering, when coupled with proof that the suspect *understood* his *Miranda* right to remain silent, *does* qualify as an implied waiver, as long as nothing indicates that there was police coercion. Furthermore, an *invocation* of a *Miranda* right must be unambiguous; Nestor's initial silence after being read his warnings was not sufficiently clear to be an invocation of his right to silence. Therefore, in contrast to the prior question, the fact that Nestor said that he understood his rights after they were read to him, when added to the fact that he eventually answered a question, gave rise to an implied waiver of the right to remain silent.

68. No. In a case involving similar facts, the Supreme Court held that the defendant's waiver was "knowing and voluntary," and thus effective. *Moran v. Burbine*. Even though the defendant might have reached a different decision about whether to waive his rights if he had known that a lawyer had been retained and was trying to reach him, the *Moran* Court felt that this was irrelevant — the defendant knew his rights and made a conscious decision to waive them; this was all that mattered. So Omar will be held to have knowingly waived his rights, and the confession will be admitted against him.

69. No. The Supreme Court has never dealt with whether police trickery regarding the strength of their case voids a *Miranda* waiver. However, almost certainly the decision in *Moran v. Burbine* (see prior answer) would be binding in this situation as well, since the fact that the police have a strong or weak case has no bearing on whether the defendant understands his rights and has consciously chosen to waive them. Lower courts that have considered this "trickery regarding the strength of the police case" issue have generally held that the waiver is nonetheless effective.

70. No. On almost precisely these facts, the Supreme Court has held that the resumption of questioning without the suspect's lawyer present violates *Miranda* and the post-*Miranda* case of *Edwards v. Arizona*. See *Minnick v. Mississippi*: "When counsel is requested, interrogation must cease, and officials may not re-initiate interrogation without counsel present, regardless of whether the accused has consulted with his attorney." So observe that Quentin does better by asking for a lawyer than he does by merely asserting that he wants to remain silent — he scores a clear "win" (whereas if he had remained silent, and was later re-questioned, the admissibility of his statements would turn on the length of time between the two sessions, whether the second interrogation concerned the same crime, and other factors. See *Michigan v.*

Mosley).

71. Yes. The normal rule laid down by *Edwards v. Arizona* is that once a suspect asserts his right to counsel, all questioning must cease until the requested lawyer is made available, and the police may not reinitiate questioning before then. However, in the post-*Edwards* case of *Maryland v. Shatzer*, the Court set out a bright-line exception to *Edwards*: once the suspect has been out of custody for at least 14 days following his invocation of the right to counsel, *Edwards* no longer applies, and the police *may* re-initiate questioning even though they never furnished counsel in response to the initial request. The facts here qualify for this *Shatzer* exception. Therefore, since the police reinitiated their questioning of Quincy more than 14 days after he had been released from custody, they were entitled to re-arrest him, give him a new set of *Miranda* warnings, procure a waiver, and start the entire process of interrogation anew even though they had never furnished a lawyer following Quincy's original request for one.

72. No. The Supreme Court has held that where the defendant takes the stand and makes a statement, the prosecution may use a confession obtained in violation of *Miranda* to **impeach the defendant's credibility** as a witness. *Harris v. New York*. (But if the statement was not only obtained in violation of *Miranda*, but also was coerced or was involuntary, then it cannot be used even for impeachment purposes. See *Mincey v. Arizona*. However, there is no evidence of coercion or involuntariness on the facts here.)

73. Yes. Once a suspect has been taken into custody and given his *Miranda* warnings, if the suspect declines to answer questions the prosecution may not comment on that silence at trial. *Doyle v. Ohio*. That's true even if the defendant takes the stand and affirmatively gives testimony whose truthfulness would be impeached by a showing that the defendant elected not to answer police questions while in custody. In *Doyle*, the Supreme Court said that even though the *Miranda* warnings contain no express assurance that silence will carry no penalty, such an assurance is "**implicit** to any person who receives the warnings" and that allowing the silence to be used later to impeach the defendant's testimony would be "fundamentally unfair."

74. No. The fact pattern here is very similar to that in *Salinas v. Texas* (2013). In *Salinas*, a 5-justice majority held that the defendant's invocation of his right to silence during a voluntary (non-custodial) interrogation *may* be commented upon by the prosecution, at least if the defendant never **expressly invoked** his Fifth Amendment privileges. (A three-justice plurality in *Salinas* said that in this voluntary-interrogation scenario, a defendant who does not expressly invoke his Fifth Amendment rights, but remains silent, won't be inferred to have relied on those rights; therefore, the prosecution may comment on the silence. Another two members said that whether the defendant does or doesn't expressly invoke the Fifth Amendment, as long as the questioning is voluntary the prosecution may comment about the silence. So a majority of the *Salinas* Court believed that a defendant who simply cuts off voluntary questioning can't prevent the prosecution from commenting on that fact.) Thus here, given that Stan agreed to the voluntary questioning but then suddenly ended the interview, and given that he did this without expressly invoking his privilege against self-incrimination, under *Salinas* the prosecution may (1) present evidence at trial showing that Stan refused to answer a particular question, and (2) encourage the jury to infer that a person with a true alibi in that situation would not have refused to answer.

75. No. The privilege of self-incrimination applies only to responses by the suspect that are essentially *"testimonial."* A wide variety of physical identification procedures have been held not to be testimonial, and thus not subject to the privilege against self-incrimination. For example, the suspect may be ordered, against his will, to furnish a blood sample. *Schmerber v. California.* Similarly, a person arrested for a serious crime may be required to furnish a DNA sample. *Maryland v. King.*

76.   The Sixth Amendment right to counsel. The Supreme Court has held that a suspect has an absolute right to have *counsel present* at any pre-trial confrontation procedure (e.g., lineup or show-up), if "adversary judicial criminal proceedings" have commenced against him (e.g., an indictment). *U.S. v. Wade*; *Kirby v. Illinois*. Since Tom had already been indicted, and thus "adversarial judicial criminal proceedings" had commenced against him, he had an absolute right to have a lawyer (a court-appointed lawyer if necessary) present to advise him and to make sure that the proceedings were not unduly suggestive. Because the police did not honor this right, the fruits of the lineup will be excluded, even though nothing in these facts suggests that the lineup was in fact unduly suggestive or otherwise unfair to Tom.

77.   Yes. Where a lineup is held without the presence of counsel, and thus violates the rule of *U.S. v. Wade*, not only may the prosecution not introduce at trial the fact that the defendant was picked out of a lineup, but the prosecution will even have to make a special showing before the witness who made the lineup identification will be allowed to testify in court that the person sitting in the dock is the person observed by the witness at the crime scene. The prosecution must show by "clear and convincing evidence" that the in-court identification is not the "fruit of the poisonous tree," i.e., not the product of the improper lineup identification. Here, the prosecution has made no showing that Sheila's in-court identification does not stem from her lineup identification. (That is, the prosecution has not shown that Sheila had a long time to identify Tom during the burglary, that she correctly described Tom before the lineup, or anything else to dispel the possibility that Sheila may be remembering Tom's face from the lineup, not from the earlier burglary). The prosecution therefore loses.

78.   No. As noted above, the right to have counsel present in lineup proceedings only attaches when "adversary judicial criminal proceedings" have commenced against the defendant. An indictment, a formal charge, a preliminary hearing, an arraignment — any of these would constitute the initiation of adversary judicial criminal proceedings. But the mere making of a warrantless arrest, even when coupled with taking the defendant to the police station and holding her in custody, does *not* amount to adversary judicial criminal proceedings, according to nearly all lower courts that have considered the issue (although the Supreme Court has never decided this point). So even though Ursula actually requested her lawyer, and even though the risk to her of unfairness from the lineup was arguably just as great as if she had already been, say, arraigned, she is deemed to have no right to counsel. Therefore, the lineup results may be admitted against her (at least if the way the lineup was carried out was not grossly unfair judged by the "totality of the circumstances").

79.   No. Even after adversary judicial criminal proceedings have begun against the defendant, the defendant has no right to have counsel present where witnesses view still or moving pictures of the suspect for ID purposes. In other words, picking Ursula's photo out of a "photo array" is deemed to be something quite different from picking Ursula herself out of a lineup — in the former situation, there is no right to have counsel present, whereas in the latter there is. See *U.S. v. Ash*.

80. (a) That the identification violated Vincent's right to due process. If a lineup identification (or other confrontation) is so *"unnecessarily suggestive* and conducive to irreparable mistaken identification" that it denies the suspect *due process of law*, that identification will not be admitted into evidence. Whether the identification procedure was so unfair as to amount to such a due process violation is determined by looking at the "totality of the circumstances" surrounding it. *Stovall v. Denno.*

(b) Yes, probably. It is very hard for the defendant to show that the lineup procedure was so suggestive and unfair that it amounted to a violation of his due process rights. But one of the very rare cases in which the Supreme Court so held involved facts quite similar to these (and in fact, the lineup here was probably even more suggestive, since Vincent was the only Asian the first time). See *Foster v. California.* In *Foster*, the Court concluded that the procedures were so suggestive that an identification of the defendant as the perpetrator was "all but inevitable" — this seems to be an accurate description of the procedures here as well. (Also, courts take into account the likely *reliability* of the identification, not just the degree of suggestiveness. Here, since the place where the crime took place was very poorly lit, Tina's ability to clearly perceive the rapist and thus later correctly identify him was somewhat impaired, making it more likely that the court would find a due process violation.)

81. Yes, probably. Just as a lineup or showup may be excluded on the grounds that it is so suggestive that it violates the defendant's due process rights, so a photographic identification may be that suggestive. Here, the photo ID was equivalent to a one-person show-up — the police did not see whether Upton could pick out Wendy's picture from among a group of photos, but rather, handed him just one photo and also said, "We think this is the woman." In that situation, it was almost certain that Upton would identify Wendy. Also, given the short period of time that Upton had to glimpse the driver, there is additional reason to doubt the reliability of his identification.

But such due process issues are determined by the "totality of the circumstances," and there are no hard-and-fast rules. So a court might conclude that the photo ID, although suggestive, was not so unfair as to be a due process violation. See, e.g., *Simmons v. U.S.*, finding that a photo ID did not violate the defendant's due process rights, even though he appeared, together with others, in all six of the photographs shown to the victim.

82. No. It is true that the exclusionary rule allows evidence seized in violation of the Fourth Amendment to be suppressed ("excluded") from criminal trials. However, the defendant may only obtain suppression of materials that were seized in violation of *her own* expectation of privacy. This is the rule of *"standing."* See *Alderman v. U.S.* The break-in by Officer Jackson, made without probable cause and without a warrant, was clearly illegal and a violation of Albert's Fourth Amendment rights. But that break-in did not violate *Bertha's* rights, since she had no possessory interest in Albert's apartment, was not present there, and did not "own" the letter once she had sent it. Since no reasonable expectation of privacy on Bertha's part was violated by the search, the illegality cannot serve as the basis for suppression of the letter in her trial.

83. No. As in the prior question, Bart's problem is that he lacks standing to object to the unlawful seizure and search of Karen. The fact that Bart had a possessory interest in the cocaine seized is not by itself enough to allow him to challenge the constitutionality of the seizure. Only if Bart's possession of the cocaine gave him a legitimate expectation of privacy with respect to that item will Bart be allowed to protest. *Rawlings v. Kentucky*. Here, once Bart put the cocaine on Karen's person, where any customs agent might look at it, and where Karen might have shown it to third persons (e.g., her friends), Bart almost certainly lost any expectation of privacy he had regarding that cocaine. The facts here are similar to those in *Rawlings* (D put his drugs in X's handbag, which was then illegally searched; D was held to have no right to object to the search and seizure of the drugs).

84.   Yes. Where evidence is indirectly derived from a violation of the defendant's constitutional rights, that evidence will often be suppressed — this is the ***"fruit of the poisonous tree"*** doctrine, by which an initial constitutional violation (the "tree") will be deemed to "taint" the evidence that is indirectly found because of it (the "fruit"). Here, Danielle's confession would almost certainly be found to be tainted fruit from the "tree" of the stop made without probable cause, and the arrest made without probable cause. If Katz had never made his illegal stop of Danielle's car, and his illegal arrest, she never would have been in a position to confess at the station house.

In cases where the confession derives from an illegal arrest or stop, the prosecution can sometimes show that the taint was ***"purged"*** by intervening events. But the mere giving of *Miranda* warnings, and the suspect's "voluntary" decision to confess, are generally held not to be the kind of intervening events that will purge the taint. So here, the relation between the confession and the prior illegal stop/arrest is so strong, and the police wrongdoing so great, that the "fruits of the poisonous tree" doctrine will almost certainly be applied. See, e.g., *Wong Sun v. U.S.* (illegal arrest of D was followed by his confession; the confession must be suppressed because it was the fruit of the illegal arrest).

85.   (a) The "independent source" doctrine. If a particular piece of evidence comes from two sources, only one of which derives from the illegality that the defendant complains of, the exclusionary rule does not apply.

(b) No. Since the government has an "independent source" for the contested evidence, the illegality is not the "but for" cause of the evidence's availability, and the illegality is thus ignored. Here, the prosecution already had the July 1 letter in its possession, so this constituted an "independent source" for that letter. The fact that the government did not focus on the document, and learned of the document's significance only due to the illegal questioning of Gordon, will probably not prevent the independent source doctrine from applying here. Also, although the government acted illegally in getting Ivan's copy of the letter, Gordon does not have standing to object to the violation of Ivan's rights. So even though every step taken by the federal agents was grossly illegal, they end up with evidence they can use to convict Gordon.

86.   No. Here, as in the prior question, the "independent source" exception saves the prosecution. On very similar facts, the Supreme Court held that since the police ultimately seized the evidence based on a properly issued warrant, the fact that they first viewed the evidence by an illegal break-in was irrelevant — the subsequent with-warrant seizure was an "independent source." See *Murray v. U.S.*

If the court believed that the police would not have bothered to get a warrant had they not first broken in and seen the evidence, the result might be otherwise. But here, the facts tell us that if the police had been unable to break in, they would have taken the extra trouble to get a warrant anyway. That being the case, the second entry is viewed as an independent source. The fact that the first break-in made life easier for the police (in the sense that had they not discovered anything wrong once they broke in, they would not have bothered to get the warrant) is viewed as irrelevant.

87. **(a) The "inevitable discovery" doctrine.** Under this exception, evidence may be admitted if it would "inevitably" have been discovered by other police techniques had it not first been obtained through the illegal discovery. The prosecution bears the burden of showing, by a preponderance of the evidence, that the information would inevitably have been discovered by lawful means. *Nix v. Williams.*

(b) No. This is a situation in which the "inevitable discovery" rule should apply. The police were in the process of examining the records of every local pawn shop and gun shop, to check on anyone who had bought a Smith & Wesson .38. Although they had not yet found Kent's name, the police would inevitably have gotten to that particular pawn shop, and would then have found Kent's name and address. Therefore, they would have looked for Kent until they found him, and would have then either discovered the gun or become increasingly suspicious of Kent if he couldn't produce it. So a court would probably be satisfied that the police really would have inevitably discovered the gun even had no illegality taken place.

88. **No, probably.** It is true that the police's lead to Morton as a witness (and, indeed, the entire police knowledge that a crime was committed) stemmed directly from Kaplan's illegal look at Leslie's mail. (Kaplan may have had the right to sit at Leslie's desk, since he was there to investigate a burglary reported by her. But this consent clearly did not extend to Kaplan's ransacking through a stack of letters on Leslie's desk, so what he did went beyond the scope of the consent and constituted an illegal search.) However, the courts are extremely reluctant to find that a *"witness lead"* is the tainted fruit of a poisonous tree. As the Supreme Court has put it, "The exclusionary rule should be invoked with much greater reluctance where the claim is based on a causal relationship between a constitutional violation and the discovery of a live witness than where a similar claim is advanced to support suppression of an inanimate object." *U.S. v. Ceccolini.*

Since Kaplan was not actively looking for evidence against Leslie when he stumbled upon it, and since Morton was in fact anxious to testify (and thus was a most "voluntary" witness), it is unlikely that the court will view Morton's testimony as the tainted fruit of the admitted poisonous tree (the illegal search). (The facts here are somewhat similar to those of *Ceccolini*, where the witness' testimony was admitted.)

89. **Yes.** This is a classic illustration of the "fruit of the poisonous tree" doctrine. The confession derived directly from the arrest — without the arrest, Nelson would not have been subject to station house questioning by the police, and would therefore not have confessed. Furthermore, there was a quality of "purposefulness" in the police's conduct — they knew they were violating Nelson's right to be free of unreasonable seizures, yet they violated that right precisely in order to have the chance to question him and thus the chance to get a confession. In this situation, a court is very unlikely to hold that the taint of the illegal arrest was "purged" by any subsequent event. The giving of the *Miranda* warnings, and the fact that the confession was "voluntary" rather than "coerced," will almost never by themselves be enough to purge the taint of an illegal arrest. See *Brown v. Illinois*, excluding a confession derived from a similar illegal arrest.

90. (a) That Quell's discovery of the outstanding warrant, and his arrest of Diego on that warrant, were sufficient to "purge the taint" of the illegal stop.

(b) No. Even if a search that discloses a piece of evidence comes about as the result of a stop conducted in violation of a person's Fourth Amendment rights, events occurring after the illegal stop may be sufficient to *"purge the taint"* of the illegality. The Supreme Court considers three factors in deciding whether the taint of illegality has been purged by the time the search occurs: (1) the "temporal proximity" between the illegal stop and the search (so that the longer the passage of time, the more likely the taint is to be found purged); (2) the "presence of intervening circumstances" (so that if events truly independent of the illegal stop bring about the search, that factor cuts in favor of a finding that the taint was purged); and (3) the "purpose and flagrancy of the official misconduct" (so that if the illegality was the result of a good faith mistake and not the product of "systemic police misconduct," that factor cuts in favor of a finding that the taint was purged). *Brown v. Illinois*.

In an arrest-on-an-old-warrant case with facts fairly similar to the ones here, the Supreme Court applied the three-factor test and concluded that the taint of the illegal stop was purged by the discovery of the arrest warrant, making the evidence found incident to the warrant arrest there admissible. See *Utah v. Strieff* (2016). Applying the three factors to our present facts, here's how a court would likely analyze the situation in light of *Strieff*: (1) the "temporal proximity" cuts in favor of Diego, since the Supreme Court's case law suggests that a gap of less than two hours between illegality and search will normally be too brief for purging the taint, and the gap here (as in *Strieff*) was just a couple of minutes. (2) The "intervening events" factor cuts strongly in favor of the government, because the outstanding warrant long pre-dated the illegal stop, and was thus logically completely independent of that stop (as was the warrant in *Strieff*). (3) The "purpose and flagrancy of the official misconduct" also cuts in favor of the government; Quell's mistaken belief that he had enough objective indicia of suspicion to justify an investigative stop seems to have been at most negligent (i.e., nothing in the facts suggest that Quell *knew* the stop was unlawful), and there's no indication of systemic official misconduct by the City police department (as there would be if, for instance, the heads of the department instructed officers to make many stops that they knew were invalid in the hopes of finding outstanding warrants that could serve as pretexts for searches). (Again, the type of police misconduct here is comparable to that in *Strieff*.) Therefore, two of the three *Brown v. Illinois* factors favor the government, and a lower court here would probably thus conclude (as the Supreme Court did in *Strieff*) that any taint from the illegal stop had been purged by the time the search incident to the arrest on the warrant occurred.

91. No. Clearly there was some connection between the illegal arrest, and Peter's self-incriminating statement. But this does not automatically mean that the statement is the tainted fruit of the illegal arrest. The issue is always whether there have been intervening events sufficient to "purge" the taint. Here, the fact that Peter's statement was somewhat voluntary, and was not in response to any questioning, is a factor strongly tending to purge the taint. On very similar facts, in *Rawlings v. Kentucky*, the Supreme Court concluded that the spontaneous outburst was not the tainted fruit of the admittedly illegal arrest.

92. Yes, probably. In this "two confession" scenario, the second confession will not *normally* be deemed to be the tainted fruit of the earlier poisoned confession. *Oregon v. Elstad* says that if the second confession was "knowingly and voluntarily made," it will not be invalidated merely because there was a prior, illegally-obtained confession having the same substance. And that's true even if the suspect reasons that the "cat's out of the bag" — the fact that the suspect may be at a psychological disadvantage from having already confessed is ordinarily irrelevant, so long as the second confession was "knowingly and voluntarily made." But the post-*Elstad* case of *Missouri v. Seibert* says that where the police make a conscious decision to *follow a two-step process whose purpose is to undermine Miranda* — doing unwarned questioning until they get a confession, then giving the *Miranda* warnings, then asking the suspect to repeat the confession — there will be a presumption that the warnings were not effective as to the second confession. That's what happened here, so *Seibert* means that the warnings will probably be found to be ineffective, in which case the second confession will be found inadmissible.

93. No. The Supreme Court has held that evidence obtained in violation of the Fourth Amendment may always be used to *impeach* statements made by the defendant. This is true even if the illegal evidence is used to impeach statements elicited by the prosecution from the defendant on cross-examination. See *U.S. v. Havens*. This is what happened here. So even though it was only in response to the prosecution's questions on cross-examination that Bernard denied having the photo, the prosecution is able to impeach Bernard's testimony by presenting that illegally-seized photo. (Of course, Bernard is entitled to a jury instruction stating that the snapshot should only be considered as evidence of Bernard's trustworthiness as a witness, not as direct evidence of whether he committed the crime. But it is questionable whether the jury will truly disregard the snapshot when deciding Bernard's guilt.)

94. Yes. The prosecution may use evidence obtained in violation of the Fourth Amendment to impeach the defendant on cross-examination. But illegally-obtained evidence may *not* be used to impeach the testimony of *defense witnesses* other than the defendant himself. *James v. Illinois*. Since the testimony being impeached here was that of Fran, not the defendant, *James* means that Egon may successfully object to use of the gun to impeach the testimony. (If the prosecution can convince the judge that the "inevitable discovery" exception, or some other exception to the exclusionary rule, is applicable, then the result would be different. But there is nothing on these facts to suggest that the prosecution can make such a showing.)

95. No. The Supreme Court has held that the exclusionary rule does not bar the use, even in the prosecution's case-in-chief, of evidence obtained by officers who acted in *reasonable reliance* on a search warrant that was issued by a detached and neutral magistrate but that was ultimately found to be unsupported by probable cause. *U.S. v. Leon*. Since the facts tell us that Lawrence reasonably believed that he had probable cause, furnished an affidavit stating everything he knew, and got the affidavit approved and the warrant issued by a neutral and detached magistrate, the requirements for the special "good faith" exception of *Leon* are satisfied. The net result is that the prosecution gets to use evidence in its case-in-chief that was seized in direct violation of the Fourth Amendment's prohibitions on warrants issued without probable cause.

96. No. *U.S. v. Leon* says that in some circumstances, if the police have a good faith belief that the search they are doing is lawful, the fact that it turns out not to be lawful does not trigger the exclusionary rule. This principle has been extended to the situation in which the police rely on a particular binding (and applicable) precedent that makes the search legal, but where that precedent gets overruled before the present case has been finally decided. *Davis v. U.S.*

(2011). This principle applies here: for a search done in 2010 in Massachusetts, the applicable constitutional rule on the issue of whether GPS tracking for an extended period requires a warrant was the rule set forth in *Adams*, that no warrant was required. The fact that this rule was overturned by the Supreme Court while D's case was still pending does not prevent the evidence from being admissible despite the exclusionary rule. So Devin ends up not getting the benefit of the law as it exists at the time of his appeal.

97. Yes. An indigent person must be given court-appointed counsel for her trial, if she is to be sentenced to prison for any length of time upon conviction. It does not matter that the offense is classified as a "misdemeanor" under state law, or that the jail term actually imposed is very brief. *Argersinger v. Hamlin.*

98. No. As long as an indigent defendant is not sentenced to imprisonment, the state is not required to appoint counsel for her, even if the offense is one which is punishable by imprisonment. This rule seems to apply even where the offense charged is a felony under state law, so long as the judge does not in fact impose a jail sentence. *Scott v. Illinois.*

99. No. The Sixth Amendment right to appointed counsel applies only at "critical stages" in the prosecution. The fact that Lester was confined over the weekend, due to the unavailability of a magistrate, did not make this confinement a "critical stage," so he was not entitled to counsel during that time. Typically, the earliest "critical stage" in the prosecution will be the arraignment, at which the defendant enters a plea. So usually, counsel does not have to be appointed for a defendant prior to the arraignment. The fact that a lawyer might have been of some use to Lester — for instance, by getting him released over the weekend — is irrelevant to whether Lester had a Sixth Amendment right to counsel at that time.

100. No. It is true that the Sixth Amendment does not merely entitle the defendant to have a lawyer, but rather, entitles him to the "effective assistance of counsel." However, a defendant whose lawyer has actually participated in the trial must make two showings in order to sustain his "effective assistance" claim: (1) that the counsel's performance was "deficient," in the sense that it was not a "reasonably competent" performance; and (2) that these deficiencies were *prejudicial* to the defense, in the sense that there was a "reasonable probability that, but for [the] unprofessional errors, the *result of the proceeding would have been different*." *Strickland v. Washington.*

Norman can make the first of these showings easily. But he cannot make the second — the proof of his guilt here is so overwhelming that he cannot show a reasonable probability that had he had a competent lawyer, he would have been found not guilty. (All Norman has to do is to show that with competent counsel, there was a reasonable probability that the fact finder would have had a "reasonable doubt" as to Norman's guilt. But Norman almost certainly cannot make even this limited showing.)

101. (a) Yes. In twin 2012 cases, *Missouri v. Frye* and *Lafler v. Cooper*, the Supreme Court held that a defendant has a Sixth Amendment right to the effective assistance of counsel during the plea-bargaining process, even in the situation in which the defendant ends up *not taking the plea bargain,* then gets convicted at trial and sentenced to a longer sentence than was available under the plea bargain. So while Otto was deciding whether to accept the 25-to-30-month deal, he was entitled to receive effective advice from Loretta.

(b) Two things: (1) incompetent advice, and (2) resulting prejudice; he has a decent

chance of showing these two things. It's pretty clear that Otto can establish point (1), since the facts tell you that any competent criminal defense lawyer would have known that the evidence would be admissible notwithstanding any Fifth Amendment issue. To prove (2) — "resulting prejudice" — however, Otto will have to prove, under the "second prong" of *Strickland v. Washington*, that absent the incompetent advice, there is a reasonable probability that the **result of the proceeding would have been different.** In the case of rejection of a plea bargain, the Court held in *Missouri v. Frye* that the defendant must prove **three different things** in order to prove the requisite prejudice:

[1]   "a **reasonable probability** [the defendant] **would have accepted** the earlier plea offer had [he] been afforded effective assistance of counsel";

[2]   "a reasonable probability the plea would have been **entered without the prosecution canceling it**" (assuming the prosecution had the power under state law to make such a cancellation); and

[3]   "a reasonable probability the plea would have been entered **without ... the trial court refusing to accept it**" (again assuming the prosecution had the power under state law to refuse to accept the plea).

The odds are pretty good that Otto can establish [1] and [2]. As to [1], if Otto had known that Fred's testimony would be admissible, common sense would have suggested to him that conviction at trial would be likely, and that a 30-month sentence (less than half the 80-month sentence actually imposed, which you are told was in the midpoint of the advisory guidelines range) was a good deal. As to [2], there is no indication that the prosecution would have revoked the deal once accepted, even if she had power under state law to do so (since there is no indication that, for instance, Otto committed any further crimes prior to his trial on robbery charges). [3] poses the biggest hurdle for Otto: you're told that the trial judge has **discretion** to **reject** any plea bargain that the prosecutor has agreed to. But as long as Otto can show (which he probably can) that the trial judge has tended to rarely exercise his discretion to reject plea bargains, and that there was nothing about the present plea bargain that would likely have struck the judge as being unduly favorable to the defendant, Otto can probably establish [3]. So he's got a decent chance of being entitled to some "relief" (but see (c) below about the likely nature of that relief).

(c) No. The fact pattern here involves "charge bargaining" (i.e., one or more charges are proposed to be dropped under the plea bargain), and *Lafler* sets forth special rules for determining the proper relief in charge-bargaining cases. In fact, *Lafler* expressly indicates that the *"order of specific performance"* relief requested by Otto is *not* the appropriate remedy. Since the trial judge would have had *discretion to reject* the plea bargain, *Lafler* says that the proper remedy for an effective-assistance violation is to (1) require the prosecution to re-offer the original plea deal, *but* then (2) allow the trial judge to exercise his *original discretion*, i.e., to decide whether the correct remedy now is to accept the plea bargain, or reject it (thereby leaving the original conviction in place). So at best, Otto will be entitled to be put back in the position he would have been in had he accepted the plea proposal and was in front of the judge asking him to accept that bargain. Since the judge has already concluded that the two 40-month sentences should run consecutively (not concurrently), Otto's odds of convincing that same judge not to reject a plea bargain calling for less than half as much trial time are not so high — but he'll just have to wait and see what the trial judge does.

102. (a) Yes. Under the Supreme Court's Sixth Amendment case law, some types of decisions in connection with trial are deemed to be matters of "trial strategy," and as to these, the lawyer has the authority to make the decision even if the client objects. (An example would be whether to move to suppress evidence on constitutional grounds.) But there is a category of decisions that are so "***fundamental***" that the Court confers the decision-making power on the *client*, not the lawyer. *McCoy v. Louisiana* (2018). A decision falls into this "fundamental" category if it concerns not how to achieve the client's objectives, but rather, "what the client's objectives in fact <u>are</u>." *McCoy*. In *McCoy*, the Court gave a list of decisions falling into this "fundamental" category, and that list included "whether to testify in one's own behalf." So no matter how stupid Oliver's choice to testify might have been, he had a right to insist on that choice, and Les's refusal to call him so he could exercise that right violated Oliver's Sixth Amendment right to effective assistance of counsel.

(b) Nothing. Normally, even when a defendant shows he has been denied the effective assistance of counsel, he will not be entitled to a new trial unless he also shows that the denial was "***prejudicial***" to him. (That is, the defendant must rebut the presumption that the error was harmless.) This requirement to show prejudice means that the defendant must show that there was "a ***reasonable probability*** that, but for counsel's unprofessional errors, the ***result of the proceeding would have been different***." But when the error consists of depriving the defendant of the right to make one of the "fundamental" decisions referred to in sub-part (a), the error is deemed to be "***structural***." When an error is structural, the usual harmless-error analysis does not apply. Instead, the defendant has an ***automatic right to a new trial***, without the need to show anything other than that the structural error occurred. *McCoy*.

103. Yes. An indicted defendant who already has a lawyer has a Sixth Amendment right not to have the police elicit statements from him in the absence of that lawyer. Since Paula was acting as a government agent, and deliberately elicited the incriminating statement from Osmond, Osmond's Sixth Amendment rights were violated. See *Maine v. Moulton*, finding a Sixth Amendment violation on similar facts. The fact that it was Osmond, not Paula, who requested the meeting, will be irrelevant so long as Paula went out of her way to elicit the incriminating statement. (But if Paula had merely listened passively to remarks volunteered by Osmond, there would be no Sixth Amendment violation even though Paula was acting as a government agent and went to the meeting wired, in the hopes of hearing such a statement. See *Kuhlmann v. Wilson*.)

Observe that Osmond wins with his Sixth Amendment argument even though he loses with both a Fourth Amendment argument and a *Miranda* argument. There is no Fourth Amendment violation, because the bugging was done with the consent of one of the participants, and the fact that the participant was a "secret agent" makes no difference. The *Miranda* "self-incrimination" argument loses because Osmond was not in custody. So the Sixth Amendment argument is the difference for Osmond between keeping the damaging evidence out and having it come in.

104. No. The Sixth Amendment right to counsel does not attach until formal judicial proceedings have been commenced against the defendant (e.g., by indictment, arraignment, formal charge, etc.). The mere fact that the police have already focused their investigation on the defendant, and expect to bring charges against him, is not enough. *Hoffa v. U.S.* This is true even though the police know that the suspect has a lawyer with whom he is consulting on the matter. So the fact that Paula was in effect a police agent, and deliberately elicited incriminating material from Osmond, still does not violate Osmond's Sixth Amendment right to counsel.

105. No. The presence of an undercover agent at a conference between a suspect and his lawyer will be a violation of the suspect's Sixth Amendment right to counsel, but only if material from the conference is somehow used by the prosecution. Since no use of the material was made by the prosecution here, Osmond has no Sixth Amendment claim. See *Weatherford v. Bursey*, finding no Sixth Amendment violation on similar facts.

106. No. Rafael's argument for suppression would be based on the idea that since the police knew that he had counsel, the questioning that they initiated, outside the presence of counsel, should be deemed a violation of his Sixth Amendment rights, and that his uncounselled decision to talk to them should not be viewed as a valid waiver of those rights. But Rafael will lose with this argument. As long as the court finds that his decision to speak to the police without first consulting his counsel was a "knowing and intelligent" waiver of the right to have counsel present, the confession will be admissible. And the court *will*, under the circumstances, almost certainly conclude that Rafael's waiver of his Sixth Amendment rights was indeed knowing and intelligent.

Prior to 2009, the Court imposed a bright-line rule that once an arraigned suspect asked for counsel, any police-initiated questioning of the suspect outside the presence of counsel would be deemed involuntary and thus a violation of the Sixth Amendment. See *Michigan v. Jackson* (a case that analogized to the still-valid *Miranda*-derived decision in *Edwards v. Arizona*, under which once a suspect in custody has asked for a lawyer, no results from police-initiated questioning may be used against him until counsel has been furnished). And under *Jackson*, Rafael would have won. But the 2009 decision in *Montejo v. Louisana* overruled *Jackson*, and held that no automatic Sixth Amendment violation occurs when a suspect who is represented by counsel voluntarily submits to non-custodial police-initiated interrogation outside the presence of that counsel. So Rafael's decision to speak to the police will be treated as a valid waiver of his Sixth Amendment right to counsel. (Furthermore, since the questioning was not done in custody, Rafael does not have a valid *Miranda/Edwards* claim either.)

ESSAY EXAM
QUESTIONS & ANSWERS

The following questions were asked on various Harvard Law School First-Year Criminal Law examinations. The questions are reproduced as they actually appeared, with only slight modifications. The sample answers are not "official" and represent merely one approach to handling the questions.

QUESTION 1

Arn, Bur and Coy were members of PFF (Peace and Freedom Forever), a radical political group. Learning that Shaw, the ruler of an oil producing country, was to make a ceremonial visit to Aubon, oil capital of the United States, they developed the following plan. They would kidnap Shaw when he was at city hall at noon on December 15 to receive the key to the city; and they would hold him in PFF headquarters, which were in the back room of Arn's residence, until he publicly announced a reduction in oil prices. They planned to make good their escape by threatening to detonate, by radio transmitter, thirteen powerful bombs which they would have previously placed in mail boxes on street corners throughout the downtown area.

On December 12, before the explosives were placed, Coy lost his nerve and told Police Inspector Kopp of the plan. Kopp was at first skeptical and asked Coy for evidence of the plan. Coy sent the police detailed charts of City Hall Plaza which he had surreptitiously photographed in the PFF's headquarters. He also sent the original of a letter from Bur to Arn discussing Shaw's visit, which Coy found rummaging through Arn's bed table.

Kopp persuaded Coy to continue working with the group while keeping the police fully informed. Kopp planned to have Coy substitute harmless talcum powder for the explosives sometime before Shaw's arrival.

On December 14, Coy still had not been told where the explosives were kept. When Arn and Bur were absent, Coy asked Kopp to come to the PFF meeting place in Arn's house and help him locate the explosives. Kopp brought with him the police's best bomb-detection device, a dog specially trained to smell dynamite. The dog detected nothing in the headquarters in the back room, but barked insistently at the dresser in the entrance hall. A check revealed a large cache of dynamite which Kopp removed, substituting talcum for it.

As he left Arn's house, Kopp saw on a table near the door a postcard addressed to Arn. Turning it over he read the message: "Let me know if you ever need more dynamite or other building supplies. The deal is good for both of us since I get them wholesale." The card was signed "Dan."

Early the next day, December 15, Arn and Bur planted dynamite charges, which they kept elsewhere, in 13 downtown mail boxes. Arn retained the detonator. Coy was told of their activities without being informed of the specific mail boxes.

Inspector Kopp made his move immediately after hearing of this development from Coy. Kopp took steps at once to locate the bombs. Coy informed Kopp that "Dan" was probably the first name of a building demolition contractor, a cousin of Bur who had sold them the explosives when they had told him about their plan. Coy recalled a tattoo of the word "Mother" high on this contractor's left arm. Hoping that Dan might have been told of the proposed location of the bombs, Kopp went to the offices of all seven demolition contractors in Aubon. Kopp ordered each to roll up his left sleeve. The last had the tattoo. Kopp took the contractor outside to the street where Coy was waiting. Coy took one look at the contractor's face and said, "that's the guy." Instantly Kopp demanded of Dan: "Did you sell dynamite to Arn and Bur?" Dan replied, "yes."

Furious, Kopp shouted at him, "Damn you! Either you help me find those bombs or you're never going to see daylight again." Dan said he had at his house a postal map of the city on which Arn and Bur had made some marks and maybe that would help. Kopp said, "Can we get it right away?" and Dan, after some hesitation, said, "O.K."

At Dan's house, Dan turned over the map to Kopp. The bomb squad was called, but needed an hour to disarm all of the bombs. Kopp's men, heavily armed, had occupied city hall plaza. When Arn and Bur arrived, they were at once surrounded, but, on Kopp's arrival, he directed that his men stand back with guns drawn in response to Bur's threat to detonate the bombs. Kopp asked Arn and Bur, "Why are you doing this?" Arn replied, "To force a reduction in oil prices." The stand-off remained for several more minutes until Kopp got word that all of the bombs were disarmed. Arn and Bur surrendered when they realized that this was so.

Discuss all issues relating to the admissibility of evidence.

ANSWER TO QUESTION 1

Coy's initial statement to Kopp: Coy's initial statement to Kopp is clearly admissible. It was completely voluntary, and Coy was not in custody at the time it was made. Nor did the police exploit the station-house setting to induce Coy to tell them more than he had originally wished to say. Therefore, the *Miranda* warnings did not have to be given, even though the statement was self-incriminating.

Charts of City Hall: The charts of City Hall provided by Coy are probably admissible. There would be no doubt at all of their admissibility if Coy was found not to have been acting as a police agent at the time he procured them, since the Fourth Amendment (as applied to the states through the Fourteenth Amendment) restricts only the actions of state officials, and of persons acting on behalf of state officials.

However, it seems likely that Coy will be deemed to have been acting as a police agent at the time he surreptitiously photographed the plans, at least if he did not do so until after Kopp had asked him for evidence. If Coy was indeed acting as a police agent, a Fourth Amendment search and seizure may have taken place. The prosecution could argue that Arn and Bur had no justifiable expectation of privacy in the charts, since they shared the charts with Coy; this situation might be analogized to the drugs in the handbag in *Rawlings v. Kentucky* (where D was found to have lost his expectation of privacy in the drugs by putting them in someone else's handbag).

If Arn and Bur had no legitimate expectation of privacy in the charts, Arn, as the owner of the residence where the charts were kept, might argue that he had a legitimate expectation of privacy in his residence which was violated by Coy's search-and-photography-expedition. However, under *Rakas v. Illinois*, mere possession of the premises is probably not sufficient to establish a legitimate expectation of privacy, and Arn might be found to have lost his expectation by giving Coy access to the premises.

Even if Arn and Bur were found to have had a legitimate expectation of privacy in the charts, they might be held to have impliedly consented that Coy use them. If so, Coy's mere examination of the charts did not by itself violate the Fourth Amendment rights of Arn and Bur — the "unbugged agent" cases (*Lewis* and *Hoffa*) make it clear that Arn's and Bur's misplaced trust in Coy as a co-conspirator did not vitiate their implied consent to Coy's access to the charts.

Letter from Bur to Arn: Much the same analysis applies to the letter as to the charts. The chief difference, of course, is that the letter was seized in the private portion of Arn's house. Even assuming that Coy was legitimately in the office part of the house, he almost certainly exceeded his authority by entering Arn's bedroom and rummaging through Arn's personal effects. *Gouled v. U.S.*, holding a similar rummaging to be an unlawful search, seems on point.

Arn certainly seems to have a legitimate privacy expectation in the letter, since it was kept in a private part of the house and as far as we know was not shown to anyone else. Therefore, he should be able to have it kept out of evidence against him. Bur, however, will have difficulty doing the same. He may not keep out the evidence merely on the grounds that its seizure violated the rights of another (Arn). Bur himself seems to have no legitimate expectation of privacy in either the letter or in Arn's bed table (where the letter was found).

Bur might try, as a last-ditch argument, the contention that the introduction of the letter violates his Fifth Amendment right against compulsory self-incrimination. The letter is clearly testimonial, but it is unlikely that Bur can convince the court that the testimony is compulsory, since: (1) the letter was written and mailed in the complete absence of any law-enforcement influence whatsoever; and (2) Bur was not compelled to produce the letter (since it was taken by Coy). This situation seems indistinguishable from the seizure of business records in *Andresen v. Maryland.*

Search of PFF Headquarters by Kopp and Coy: Although Coy's information probably gave Kopp probable cause to believe that evidence (explosives) would be found in the house, there do not appear to have been any exigent circumstances justifying a warrantless entry, particularly since Kopp had ample opportunity to obtain a warrant. Therefore, the search is valid only if Coy had authority to consent to it.

Although the house was not his, Coy might nonetheless have had authority to consent to the search, depending on the extent of his own privileges in the house. Coy himself clearly had authority to be present in the back-room headquarters, but it does not necessarily follow from this that he had the right to invite others (e.g., the police) to search it. The test should probably be whether Arn assumed the risk that by allowing Coy access to the premises, he would invite someone else in. Alternatively, if Kopp reasonably but mistakenly believed that Coy had joint authority over the back room, the search will be upheld. See *Illinois v. Rodriguez*. Most courts would probably hold that Coy had authority to consent at least to the search of the back room.

If Coy did have authority to consent to Kopp's search of the back-room headquarters, the question remains whether Kopp exceeded the scope of the consent, or of Coy's authority to consent, when the dog entered the front entrance. Even if Coy did not have the authority to consent to search of the front hall because he himself did not have the privilege of being there, a variant of the "plain view" doctrine may apply to validate the dog's (and Kopp's) entry into the front hall. That is, if the dog smelled the bomb when he was still in the back room, the government could argue that the bomb was in "plain smell." This situation seems somewhat similar to the police's use of a dog to sniff for drugs in luggage in *U.S. v. Place*, or to sniff for drugs from outside a stopped car in *Ill. v. Caballes*; in both of those cases, the Court held that no search occurred at all. However, the present situation might be distinguished from the ones in *Place* and *Caballes* — in both of those cases, the Court emphasized that the dog was sniffing for *contraband*, which no one has the right to possess, so the sniffing could not have revealed anything as to which the owner had a legitimate expectation of privacy. Here, by contrast, the dog was sniffing for explosives, which may be legitimately possessed. Therefore, the dog's sniffing might be found to have violated Arn's legitimate expectation of privacy in the dresser's contents, in which case the *Place* and *Caballes* precedents may not help the government, possibly making the use of the dog an invalid warrantless search. (The Supreme Court has left open the possiblity that there is a *general* "plain smell" doctrine even outside of the canine-sniffing-for-contraband context, but has never expressly so held. If there were such a general plain-smell doctrine, the dog's use would presumably be valid.)

Even if the entry by Kopp and the dog into the front hall *was* justified on a "plain smell" theory, Kopp might nonetheless have exceeded the scope of that theory by *opening* the dresser. If it could be proved that the dog's barking was a very clear indication of the presence of dynamite, a court might be convinced that the opening of the drawer and the seizure of the dynamite were justified by newly-encountered exigent circumstances, namely, the possibility that the dynamite might be used before a warrant could be obtained. Alternatively, the court might hold that the evidence was fully discovered by the dog, and that the opening of the drawer did not constitute a further investigation, but merely a seizure, following naturally from the dog's discovery, and therefore within the scope of the plain view doctrine.

If the "plain smell" doctrine does *not* apply, it seems almost certain that Arn's right of privacy was violated by the opening of the drawer and the seizure of the dynamite. Although the dresser itself may have been in plain view, the dynamite was not, and Arn almost certainly had a justifiable expectation that it would not be opened.

Reading of the post card: The validity of Kopp's reading of the post card found on Arn's table raises similar issues. If Kopp had a right to be near the door by virtue of Coy's consent, the card falls within the plain view exception. However, it is not clear that Kopp had the right to turn the card over and read the reverse side; the situation seems analogous to that in *U.S. v. Catanzaro* (inspector takes rifle off the wall to examine serial number), which was found to fall within the plain view exception. Also, the government might argue that Arn, since he left the card lying on the table, had no justifiable expectation of privacy concerning it, but this argument is unlikely to succeed, since Arn probably had a justifiable expectation that people would not read mail addressed to him in his own house.

It is doubtful whether Dan, the card's sender, can keep the card from being admitted against him, for the same reasons cited previously in connection with Bur's letter to Arn. Bur has no expectation of privacy in the card at all.

Search of Dan for identification purposes: Kopp's order to Dan to roll up his sleeve to determine whether he was the "Dan" who signed the postcard was probably valid in itself, although it may have been the fruit of a previous illegality (the reading of the postcard).

The order to Dan to roll up his sleeve probably constituted a "search" within the meaning of the Fourth Amendment, since it is unlikely that Kopp would have allowed Dan to refuse, and Dan can fairly be said to have been detained. However, the search can probably be justified under either of two theories. First, this confrontation may fall within the *Terry* and *Adams* "stop and frisk" rationale. Since the detainment of Dan was only long enough to establish whether he had the tattoo, the stop fell within the principle that such brief detainments must not be longer than necessary to accomplish their purpose. Also, Kopp had at least the less-than-probable-cause degree of suspicion necessary to support a *Terry-Adams* stop, based on Coy's information — the officer's information in *Adams* was probably less impressive than Kopp's information. Under the "totality of the circumstances" test used for evaluating informants' tips, Coy's information probably provided the "reasonable suspicion" necessary for a stop. See *Alabama v. White*. And although *Terry* involved only questioning, and not an order to the suspect to expose part of his body, dictum in *Davis v. Miss.* indicates that certain reliable identification procedures (e.g., fingerprinting) may sometimes be imposed on a suspect even without probable cause. And whether or not a search warrant would normally be necessary for such fingerprinting, the exigent circumstances of the impending bomb blasts and kidnapping here would excuse the lack of a warrant even if it were ordinarily required.

Secondly, even if the limited intrusions were not justified under the *Terry* rationale, Kopp probably had probable cause for a full-scale arrest by the time he reached Dan, since every other local demolition contractor had been eliminated by prior search. Since Dan could have been arrested and then searched incident to arrest, a search immediately prior to the arrest would also be permitted. (The Court held that warrantless searches made immediately pre-arrest fall under the incident-to-arrest doctrine, in *Rawlings v. Kentucky.*) Therefore, the examination of Dan's arm appears "reasonable" under the Fourth Amendment.

It is true that Kopp's probable cause to believe the last suspect to be Dan was derived in part from earlier searches, probably made without probable cause, and perhaps without even the degree of suspicion necessary for a *Terry* stop. But Dan has no right to complain of these earlier illegal searches, since it was not his own constitutional rights that were violated by them. Nor could he object that the examination of his arm violated his Fifth Amendment right against self-incrimination, since *Schmerber* makes it clear that such physical examinations are not "testimonial" and are therefore not covered by the privilege against self-incrimination.

Show-up of Dan by Coy: The confrontation in which Coy identified Dan as the contractor who sold them the dynamite was a show-up, rather than a lineup, since only the suspect was brought before the witness. While show-ups are considerably more suggestive than lineups, they may be justified where they are not "unnecessarily suggestive." (See *Stovall v. Denno*). The case for the government here is easily as strong as in *Stovall*. The necessity for acting immediately, rather than taking time to form a lineup, is apparent from the threat of the bombs. Furthermore, Coy's prior exposure to Dan was sufficiently detailed and lengthy to provide him with an "independent basis" for the identification, avoiding intolerable suggestiveness, and also removing the taint of any suggestiveness for purposes of an in-court identification of Dan by Coy.

Dan was not entitled to counsel at this show-up because it preceded formal charges. See *Kirby v. Ill.*

Dan's admission to having sold the dynamite: Dan's admission, at the scene of his arrest, that he sold the dynamite to Arn and Bur, may have been obtained in violation of Dan's *Miranda* rights. Although Dan was not in the station house, he may have been in custody from the moment he was identified by Coy, since Kopp would never have let him leave. (A court would phrase the issue in terms of **whether a "reasonable suspect" in Dan's position would have known** that he was not free to leave; if the hypothetical "reasonable suspect" wouldn't have known this, Dan would not have been in custody under this view. See *Berkemer v. McCarty*.)

If *Miranda* warnings were required, his admission to having sold the dynamite, and any direct "fruits" from that admission, would not be usable against him. Dan should argue that the postal map is a "poisonous fruit" of the (possibly) illegal confession, since it is unlikely that he would have given it to the police had he not first implicated himself by confessing to having made the sale. The government will counter with the argument that the giving up of the map was a voluntary, free, act by Dan, which "purged the taint" of the illegal questioning. Many lower courts have been sympathetic to the prosecution's attempt in such cases to introduce physical evidence obtained through illegally-obtained confessions. Similarly, *Oregon v. Elstad* suggests that the Supreme Court may be reluctant to exclude evidence merely because its acquisition by the police is somehow related to an illegally-obtained confession. Thus it's not at all clear that Dan can keep the map out of evidence by use of the "poisonous fruit" argument.

The government can also plausibly argue that at the time Kopp questioned Dan, there was an emergency, and that the ***"public safety"*** exception to *Miranda* (see *New York v. Quarles*) should apply. Dan could retort that there was no reason for Kopp to believe that use of the bombs was imminent. However, since Kopp knew that the bombs had already been put in the mailboxes, the "public safety" exception will probably be applied.

If, despite the government's public-safety argument, a court found that *Miranda* warnings were required, Dan's admission to having sold the dynamite would not be usable against him. The more interesting question is whether the postal map would also be inadmissible. Dan could argue that the postal map is a "poisonous fruit" of the (possibly) illegal confession, since it is unlikely that he would have given it to the police had he not first implicated himself by confessing to having made the sale. However, this type of argument was expressly rejected by the Supreme Court in *U.S. v. Patane*: even where an unmirandized (but non-coerced) confession leads directly to physical evidence, the physical evidence will not be inadmissible fruit of the poisonous tree. So Dan will not be able to keep the map out of evidence by use of the poisonous-fruit argument.

Arn, like Dan, will try to exclude the map as being the fruit of a poisonous tree. From Arn's point of view, the poisonous tree is the reading of the postcard from Dan to Arn, which was probably an illegal search. Since that card led Kopp to Dan, Arn may be able to argue that Dan's arrest, and his production of the map, were both fruits of the original illegal search and hence not usable against Arn. This is particularly convincing in view of the fact that it is unlikely that Kopp would ever have been put on to Dan had he not read the postcard; even courts applying the "inevitable discovery" extension to the "independent source" rule would be reluctant to apply the extension to a discovery as speculative as the one in the present case.

The government will argue that Dan's production of the map was an independent act of free will, and thus "purged the taint" of the original illegal means by which Kopp was led to Dan. Some support for this position is given by *U.S. v. Ceccolini*'s readiness to find witness' testimony to be untainted. However, Dan produced the map only after insistent questioning by Kopp, and his act does not therefore appear very much more voluntary than Toy's confession in *Wong Sun*. Arn should also try to get Dan's admission of having supplied dynamite excluded; although Arn cannot have this statement excluded from use against himself even if Dan's *Miranda* rights were violated (these rights may only be asserted by Dan himself), Arn can claim, as with the map, that the confession was the "fruit" of the original unlawful reading of the postcard; this contention is likely to be treated the same as is the attempt to exclude the map, whatever that treatment is.

Arn's admission: Arn's admission in the plaza that he was carrying out the scheme in order to force a reduction in oil prices, may have been obtained in violation of *Miranda*. It is hard to say whether Arn was in custody at the time, since he might have been able to use the threat of the bombs to bargain for his escape; as with Dan's initial statement, the existence of custody depends on whether a reasonable person in Arn's position would, at the time he made the statement, have believed that he was free to go. (*Berkemer v. McCarty*.)

QUESTION 2

A report by a private detective, Breuer, confirmed Walter Jacke's suspicions that his wife, Molly, was having an affair with Walter's old friend, Frank Moreweather. Frank had married a very emotional, extremely jealous woman, Irma. On discovering Frank's infidelities in the past, Irma had reacted almost violently; but she seemed to know nothing about this latest interlude in Frank's life.

Walter loved his wife and wanted her back. He was deeply embittered by Frank's actions, but he was also a careful man. A homicide arrest was the last thing he needed. There is always more than one way to skin a cat, however. For Christmas, Walter insisted that he and Molly give the Moreweathers a pearl-handled pistol.

Soon after Christmas, Irma began receiving a series of phone calls, always when her husband was out. Each involved a lady's voice referring obliquely to Frank's "real reason" for being out and suggesting that it would be wrong, deeply wrong, not to put a stop to this offense. Of course, Irma had no way of knowing that Walter's mistress, Ethel Hogarth, was making the calls at his request.

Suspecting a violation of the harassment and adultery statutes, the Acton police department agreed to Irma's request that they put a tap on the Moreweather phone without Frank's knowledge. The tap picked up conversations between Frank and Molly which would have confirmed Irma's worst suspicions. A trace on the calls to Irma, moreover, showed that they were made from a particular apartment rented to Ethel Hogarth, a woman Irma did not know.

The question, was, of course, who was putting Ethel up to this. The answer required finding first the overlap between her associates and Irma's, and then a motive for one of them to harass Irma. The management of Ethel's apartment building agreed to an arrangement between the police and the maid responsible for Ethel's floor. The maid would, in the course of her regular duties, try to observe anyone coming to and going from Ethel's apartment. If she noted photographs or names when cleaning up in the apartment, she would refer them to the police. Any letters found in the trash would be turned over to the officer in charge of the case.

Meanwhile the calls continued, with Irma becoming increasingly distraught. On January 15 the matter came to a dramatic head. Irma had confronted Frank with her suspicions at dinner. His response had been to slap her and walk out. Another call from Ethel followed his departure. This time Ethel also relayed the information, uncovered by Breuer, as to where Frank and Molly could be found.

Irma had reached the point where she could take no more. She drove to the address of Frank's and Molly's secret rendezvous and waited with gun in hand. An hour later, when she saw them leaving, she fired into their car, wounding Frank and killing Molly. She then called the police who, after arresting her and hospitalizing Frank, set about tying up the loose ends of the case.

The maid had delivered to the police a letter from Walter found in Ethel's trash. The letter included a proposed schedule of telephone calls, and Ethel had put a check mark next to each as she made the call. The maid had also observed other letters apparently from Walter and a picture in the room that looked like a man she had once seen in the corridor. The detective in charge of the case telephoned Walter and asked him to come to the police station, where the maid at once identified him during his fingerprinting as the man seen in the corridor whose picture was on Ethel's dresser.

Next, the police obtained a warrant on the basis of an affidavit alleging that "a reliable informant with no criminal background who has been working with the police in the investigation of the case for several days has advised that she had personally observed in the location to be searched letters from Miss Hogarth's paramour, Walter Jacke, and other incriminating evidence with respect to the crimes of Harassment and Adultery." While she was out, Ethel's apartment was searched for the incriminating picture and letters, which were seized.

Shortly thereafter, she was arrested, informed of Irma's shooting of her husband and Molly, and advised of her rights. Ethel refused to discuss the matter further in the absence of her lawyer.

At the police station Walter was ushered into a seemingly private but secretly bugged room with her where, before he could hush her up, she exclaimed: "Oh Walter, you should have told me who this woman was and what could happen!" Walter's response, "Shut up, you dumb bitch," was elicited before he was advised of his *Miranda* rights. Thereafter, he gave a full account of his involvement and the circumstances that led to his actions. On the basis of Walter's statement, Breuer was arrested.

Evaluate all issues relating to the admissibility of evidence.

ANSWER TO QUESTION 2

Wiretapping of Moreweather phone: The wiretap on the Moreweather phone was conducted without a search warrant and so is in violation of *Katz v. U.S.* and of Title III of the Omnibus Crime Control Act of 1968, at least with respect to the conversation between Frank and Molly. Frank has the right to object to the introduction against him on an adultery charge of this conversation, since he had a legitimate expectation of privacy concerning it. The conversation between Ethel and Irma, however, was probably not illegally intercepted, since the tap was placed with Irma's consent. The tap was not in violation of Title III, which specifically exempts taps to which one party consents; nor was it in violation of the Fourth Amendment, in all probability, since Ethel would most likely be held to have assumed the risk that the other party to her conversation would betray it. See *U.S. v. White*, in which the Supreme Court held that *Katz* did not render illegal the use of a "bugged agent" to transmit the defendant's voluntary conversations; *White* seems applicable here, even though it involved a transmitter and not a tap.

Maid's search of room and seizure of papers: Despite the apartment manager's agreement to have the maid "keep her eyes open" while in Ethel's room, the maid was working for the police in a sufficiently direct way so that she should be considered a police agent or informer, and her actions must be judged as if they were the actions of the police. The manager's consent to the maid's actions does not by itself prevent them from being a violation of the Fourth Amendment, since by the principle of *Stoner*, such a manager does not have authority to consent to a search of a guest's (or here, a tenant's) room.

The maid may not have conducted a Fourth Amendment search merely by keeping her "eyes open," as long as she performed only the chores which she was supposed to perform, and did not go rummaging; anything she came across while doing her job could probably be turned over to the police under the plain view doctrine. But her rummaging through the wastebasket presents a closer issue. *Cal. v. Greenwood* establishes that a person who puts trash on the sidewalk has no reasonable expectation of privacy in it. But this rule does not necessarily apply to trash within one's residence — a person arguably has a reasonable expectation that her trash will not be scrutinized (at least until it has been carried out of the premises); people often retrieve things that they have inadvertently thrown into the trash, and most of us would feel much more intruded upon by scrutiny of our trash while it was still in our premises than once we had placed it out on the street knowing that scavengers could look through it. In any event, a person almost certainly has a reasonable expectation that the police will not recruit "agents" to scour his residence looking for clues in the trash.

If Ethel did have a justifiable expectation of privacy with respect to the trash, then the maid's action constituted a Fourth Amendment search and seizure. Since there were no circumstances justifying a warrantless search or seizure, Ethel's Fourth Amendment rights were violated, and she has the right to exclude the letter found in the trash.

The maid's scrutiny of the picture of Walter, and the letters from Walter that were not in the wastebasket, might also fall within the plain view exception. Since it is hard to say that Ethel had a justified expectation of privacy as to items which were more or less on display (as the photo probably was), there was probably no Fourth Amendment search as long as the maid discovered these items while she was performing her job. But again, if she found them while rummaging rather than while cleaning, the plain view doctrine does not apply, and her examination of them constitutes a Fourth Amendment search, which in the absence of either a warrant or of circumstances justifying a warrantless search and seizure, is in violation of the Amendment.

If the maid's actions did violate the Fourth Amendment, the items cannot be introduced, since although seized pursuant to a valid warrant they are the fruit of a poisonous tree; the police were able to obtain the warrant only through the maid's illegally-obtained knowledge. Other aspects of the warrant will be discussed below.

If any of the items are found to have been illegally searched for or seized, Ethel will definitely have the right to object, since she had a justifiable expectation of privacy in the premises searched. Walter, however, probably does not have the right to exclude any of the items, since he probably would be held to have abandoned any expectation of privacy in the items by giving them to Ethel. If he pays for the apartment for Ethel, however, and uses it frequently he may be able to assert a sufficient justifiable expectation of privacy in the apartment to allow him to object to the search and seizure occurring there.

The show-up of Walter by the maid: Walter was not entitled to a lawyer when he was identified by the maid because, though the investigation had focused upon him, formal judicial proceedings had not yet been commenced against him. See *Kirby v. Ill.* He was, however, as a matter of due process entitled to an identification free from unnecessary suggestion. *Stovall v. Denno.* Using a show-up rather than a lineup here seems to have been unnecessary, since there was plenty of time to arrange a lineup. On the other hand, the show-up might be found not to have been unduly suggestive, even though unnecessary. In *Neil v. Biggers*, the Court concluded that the inherent suggestiveness of the show-up in question was countered by the good opportunity that the identifier had had on a previous occasion to observe the person now being identified. It is unclear from the facts of the instant case how closely the maid observed the man she later identified as Walter, but it is clear from *Neil* that the Court does not require much. The government can argue that the maid made the connection between the photograph, the man in the corridor, and the suspect being fingerprinted, without being specifically asked if there was any connection. The government can also point out that there were two things, not one, in the maid's mind enabling her to identify Walter — the picture *and* the view she had in the corridor.

An additional difficulty with the show-up is that it occurred while the suspect was being fingerprinted; fingerprinting is such an indication of police suspicion that the show-up might be held intolerably suggestive, to a degree violative of due process, on that ground alone. However, if the government were able to show by "clear and convincing evidence" that the maid had had ample opportunity to examine the photograph and to scrutinize the man in the corridor, she might be permitted to make an in-court identification of the defendant, since that identification would have been shown to be sufficiently independent of the illegal show-up identification to purge the taint of it. See *U.S. v. Wade.*

Even if the show-up was itself valid and not violative of due process, the maid's identification might be excluded on the grounds that it was the fruit of a poisonous tree, the maid's illegal search of the room. The government could argue that the independent source exception applies, since there were two distinct sources for the identification, the picture and the view of Walter in the corridor; only the first could possibly have been illegally obtained. But the government, if it prevailed in this argument, could presumably introduce only the fact that the defendant was identified as having been in the corridor, and not that he was seen to be the man in the photo.

Search warrant: The affidavit submitted by the police to obtain the warrant to search Ethel's apartment was based upon information from a confidential informant. Nonetheless, it provided sufficient information to establish probable cause under the "totality of the circumstances" test of *Illinois v. Gates* — the affidavit contained both information about the reliability of the informant, as well as some information about how the informant obtained the knowledge (personal observation). Taken together, these facts would justify a neutral magistrate in concluding that evidence of crime would probably be found.

The warrant is thus good as to the letters, which were particularly described by reference to their sender and addressee. It is unclear whether it is good as to the picture, which was not particularly described, but which would fall within the catch-all phrase "other incriminating evidence." In *Andresen v. Maryland*, the Supreme Court approved the phrase " . . . other fruits, instrumentalities and evidence of crime . . . ," so the phrase used here may avoid impermissible vagueness. If the phrase is held too vague, the photograph might still be admitted — if the police had probable cause to have listed the photograph and the photograph was in plain view the search will be upheld. See *Horton v. California.*

Even though the warrant may be formally valid, the introduction of the items seized under it might still be excluded by the "fruits of the poisonous tree" doctrine, if Ethel can show that the probable cause for the issuance of the warrant was based on information obtained through violation of her constitutional rights (i.e., the maid's search of her room.) Even if Ethel made such a showing, however, the police may well be able to successfully argue that their reliance on the warrant was ***"objectively reasonable,"*** so that the exclusionary rule should not apply. (See *U.S. v. Leon.*)

"Bug" in the station: Two possibly valid objections may be raised against the bugging of the remarks exchanged between Walter and Ethel in the police station.

(1) *Katz:* The conversation, though within the confines of the police station, was probably initiated with the expectation that it would not be overheard. While this expectation is not as clearly reasonable as the expectation maintained by Katz while in his phone booth, it may be reasonable for a prisoner to expect that electronic devices will not be used to overhear his conversations. The fact that the building is used for police purposes should not automatically mean that no privacy may exist anywhere within it. Furthermore, the police placed the suspects in a room which was designed to convey a false sense of privacy, so the police should not be able to claim now that the expectation was not reasonably maintained. However, *Kuhlmann v. Wilson* indicates that if the police (or their informants) merely listen "passively" to in-custody conversations, no constitutional violation takes place; this rationale may apply to bugging as well as to the informant-based listening used in *Kuhlmann*.

Assuming that reasonable expectations of privacy were violated, the police would be required to seek a warrant under Title III of the Omnibus Crime Control Act, since this was the electronic interception of an "oral communication." Both Ethel and Walter, as parties to the conversation, have standing to object to its interception under Title III.

(2) *Miranda:* Ethel, having refused to speak in the absence of an attorney, could not have been formally interrogated further or even encouraged to change her mind, according to *Miranda*. She may be able to argue that the arranged meeting with Walter in the confines of the police station was a deliberate attempt to bypass the protections of *Miranda*, and that that decision should apply to exclude any incriminating statements made by her. While the encounter with Walter was not "interrogation" in the strict sense, it did utilize the inherent, subtle, coercive pressures of the police station and the anxiety of the two suspects in meeting each other to induce speech by one who did not want to speak with the police while under restraint by them. However, the police conduct in setting up and monitoring a meeting between two spouses here is similar to that in *Arizona v. Mauro*, where the Court held that no interrogation occurred and that no *Miranda* warnings needed to be given.

Even if each suspect can, by one or both of the arguments set out above, object to the admissibility of his own statements, it is less clear that Walter can also suppress Ethel's remark from use against him, and vice versa. Since the police were counting on the confrontation of the two suspects and then the interactions of their remarks to cause admissions by both, Walter and Ethel might successfully argue that the statements of each are the product of both, and hence that each may object to all statements made. But the court may hold that each statement violated the rights of only the person who made it.

Walter's Confession: Assuming that Walter was given his *Miranda* warnings before making his confession, his only chance to have the confession excluded is to show that it was tainted by earlier illegality. His best bet for this is to show that it was the direct product of the trickery used by the police to induce his incriminating remark to Ethel; he can point out that when he realized how he had incriminated himself, he no longer saw any point in denying the crime, and that he therefore made a confession which he otherwise would have had no reason to make. But *Oregon v. Elstad* establishes that where a confession is preceded by *Miranda* warnings, it will be presumed voluntary (and admissible) even though the suspect may have been influenced by his belief that the "cat's out of the bag." But *Elstad* also holds that the presumption of voluntariness will not apply if the confession derives from "deliberately coercive or improper tactics in obtaining the initial statement," and Walter may be able to persuade the court that the police tactics here were coercive or improper.

Even if Walter is able to exclude his confession, by showing that it was the product of trickery and thus not voluntary under all the circumstances, Ethel will have difficulty in similarly excluding it from use against her. Although she can try to show that it was the direct product of the illegal bugging of her own incriminating remark to Walter, it is unlikely that this argument will be persuasive; two important factors, Walter's own incriminating statement and the *Miranda* warnings, intervened between her remark and Walter's confession.

Breuer's arrest: Breuer will not be able to exclude from the case against him Walter's remarks in the confession incriminating him. Even if the confession was illegally obtained from Walter, Breuer's rights were not thereby violated, and he cannot assert Walter's rights to bar the confession.

TABLE OF CASES

This table includes references to cases cited in all sections
of this book except the Flow Charts.

SUBJECT MATTER INDEX

This index includes references to the Capsule Summary
and Exam Tips, but not to the Flow Charts or the Short-Answer
and Essay Questions and Answers